LATIN AMERICAN
PHILOSOPHY

FOR THE 21ST CENTURY

LATIN AMERICAN PHILOSOPHY

FOR THE 21ST CENTURY

The Human Condition,

Values, and the

Search for Identity

edited by

JORGE J. E. GRACIA

and

ELIZABETH MILLÁN-ZAIBERT

Prometheus Books

59 John Glenn Drive
Amherst, New York 14228-2197

Published 2004 by Prometheus Books

Inquiries should be addressed to
Prometheus Books
4501 Forbes Blvd, Suite 200
Lanham, MD 20706 • www.rowman.com

Distributed by NATIONAL BOOK NETWORK
800-462-6420

08 07 06 05 04   5 4 3 2 1

Library of Congress Cataloging-in-Publication Data

Latin American Philosophy for the 21st century : the human condition, values, and the search for identity / edited by Jorge J. E. Gracia and Elizabeth Millán-Zaibert.
    p. cm.—
Rev. ed. of Latin American philosophy in the twentieth century. c1986.
Includes bibliographical references
ISBN 1–57392–978–6 (alk. paper)
    1. Philosophy, Latin American. I. Gracia, Jorge J. E. II. Millán-Zaibert, Elizabeth. III. Latin American philosophy in the twentieth century.

B1001.L39 2003
199'.8—dc21
[B]   2003043184

CONTENTS

PART IV: The Search for Identity

A. *THE NATION AND THE PEOPLE*

Preface

A collection of philosophical readings is justified if it responds to a need. It is clear that the English-speaking world needs a representative collection of readings from Latin American philosophers. Recently, as universities strive to diversify the canons used to provide students with a liberal arts education, more attention is drawn to traditionally marginalized areas of philosophy, such as African and Latin American philosophy. Yet, access to the latter is difficult because of a language barrier. There are few English-language anthologies of Latin American philosophy. An early one was Aníbal Sánchez Reulet's *Contemporary Latin American Philosophy* (1954). Another, put together by Jorge Gracia, Eduardo Rabossi, Enrique Villanueva, and Marcelo Dascal, joined its company thirty years later, *Philosophical Analysis in Latin America* (1984). Yet, as its title suggests, this anthology had the narrow focus of tracing and divulging contributions from Latin American *analytic* philosophers, and analytic philosophy is but one (and not the most widespread at that) philosophical current in Latin American philosophy.

Recently, there has been a steady increase in the number of books and articles published on Latin American philosophy. In 1989 the *Philosophical Forum* dedicated a double issue to Latin American philosophy, with articles from the leading scholars in the field. Ofelia Schutte's study, *Cultural Identity and Social Liberation in Latin American Thought*, appeared in 1993. And other philosophers, such as Linda Martín Alcoff, have begun to turn their attention to issues within the Latin American philosophical tradition. Alcoff's recent work on mixed-race identity shows that much fertile ground remains to be explored in Latin American thought, especially as North American intellectuals become more interested in race. Eduardo Mendieta and Mario Sáenz have edited collections of articles on

Latin American philosophy with a primarily continental bent. Iván Jaksic, through his translation and scholarly work on the Venezuelan philosopher Andrés Bello and other key figures of the period, is drawing attention to South American philosophical and political traditions. And Susana Nuccetelli has recently published a textbook, *Latin American Thought*, and a collection of texts, *Latin American Philosophy*. Clearly, scholars in the English-speaking world are turning to Latin America as a place of more than just magical realism and political turmoil, and discovering a rich and variegated philosophical tradition.

The present volume seeks to provide some insight into the tradition of philosophical thought in Latin America. However, the preparation of a truly representative collection of readings from Latin American philosophers encounters serious difficulties. Generally, Latin American thinkers have an extensive list of publications. In several cases, their collected works extend to more than twenty volumes. Other difficulties are the heterogeneity of the themes in their works. Indeed, the very expression *Latin American philosophy* poses problems, for Latin America is a diverse region comprised of many countries with philosophical traditions that differ in focus and quality. Furthermore, philosophy did not become institutionalized in Latin America as early as it was in Europe and the United States, and so the writings of philosophers are often scattered in short-lived journals that are difficult to locate. These factors, among others, account for the limited number of anthologies of Latin American philosophical texts in English. The initial edition of the current volume was the first such attempt since Reulet's 1954 collection, and we are bringing out this revised edition in order to provide an even more representative set of readings.

The first edition was limited to twentieth-century authors, but the present volume provides a broader historical dimension by including contributions from two of the earliest phases of Latin American philosophy. The texts we have included from the colonial and independentist periods shaped the development of Latin American thought and represent a concern for social justice that came to characterize the work of many Latin American thinkers in the centuries to follow. The previous edition focused on three fundamental and concrete problems: man, values, and the search for philosophical identity. The present edition has replaced the focus on man with a focus on the human condition, or what we call philosophical anthropology. The section on values remains the same as the section from the first edition. The section on the search for identity has been substantially expanded and broken down into two parts: one on the nation and the people and another on the thought and philosophy.

Whereas the first edition did not include selections by Domingo Faustino Sarmiento, José Martí, José Carlos Mariátegui, Jorge Gracia,

Linda Martín Alcoff, Ofelia Schutte, or Enrique Dussel, their work is represented here. The selections from José Vasconcelos and Samuel Ramos that appear in this edition are different from those that appeared in the first. And the selection from Augusto Salazar Bondy now appears in complete form, whereas it was abbreviated in the first edition.

Although the publisher has indulged us with more pages for the present volume, because we have added more texts, we were forced to drop others. One victim of such cuts was the selection from Antonio Caso. Caso is an important figure in the history of Latin American thought and it is with regret that we exclude his work, but the new focus of the volume did not leave room for his text. There are, of course, many important philosophers whose work was not included in the previous edition and is not included in the present volume.

The goal of this collection is twofold: (1) to provide the English-speaking reader with a historical lens through which to begin a study of Latin American philosophy; and (2) to illustrate in some depth several contemporary trends that we believe will shape Latin American philosophy throughout the twenty-first century. In a volume of this size, it is impossible to offer a comprehensive sample of Latin American philosophy, but we hope to have provided a kind of textual map for readers who wish to explore further the rich tradition of Latin American philosophy.

The volume begins with an essay on contemporary Latin American philosophy. Each of the four parts into which the book is divided is also introduced by an essay, the first on the colonial beginnings and independentist period, the second on philosophical anthropology, the third on value, and the fourth on the search for identity. The essays introduce the thought of the thinkers represented in the various sections and their themes. A brief biographical sketch precedes each author's text. A select bibliography at the end is intended as a source of authors and works not included here (but important in the field) and of information on other texts by authors who are included in the volume.

The selections for Parts II and III have been taken from the first edition. Those selections were made in collaboration with Risieri Frondizi, who was the senior editor of a more extensive collection, published in Spanish and Portugese, entitled *El hombre y los valores en la filosofía latinoamericana del siglo XX* (1975; reprint, México: Fondo de Cultura Económica, 1980). The introductory essays to those parts as well as the biographical sketches of the various authors contained therein have also been translated from that edition, although modifications were introduced to adapt them to the present context. The textual selections follow the order of the discussion in the introductory essays. Square brackets indicate additions made by the editors or the translators.

The institutions and persons who have provided assistance in the preparation of this work are numerous. To each of them we would like to express our profound appreciation, but limitations of space prevent us from doing so explicitly in every case. We remain grateful to the late Mrs. Josefina Barbat de Frondizi for her permission to print Frondizi's introductory essays and for allowing us to edit them to fit the present context. We are also grateful to the translators who spent long hours at their difficult task. The individual translators are indicated at the end of their respective selections. Melanie Jopek Shaker, who was Elizabeth Millán-Zaibert's undergraduate research assistant at DePaul University for the 2000–2001 academic year (through the support of the College of Liberal Arts and Sciences Dean's Office), helped collect the new materials and wrote the biographical sketch for the Dussel entry. She also assisted in the process of updating the bibliography. Many thanks are owed to her. We also consulted several scholars who work in the field. Oscar Martí, Ofelia Schutte, and Leo Zaibert were most generous with their advice and we are indebted to them for their suggestions. We would also like to thank the authors and publishers who generously granted permission for the publication of the texts included here.

General Introduction

The encounter between Iberia and pre-Columbian America posed new challenges to European thought and initiated new developments in both places. In Iberia, new issues, primarily concerned with the rights of conquered peoples, took center stage, and the greatest Iberian philosophers of the times, such as Bartolomé de Las Casas (1474–1566), Francisco Suárez (1548–1617), and Francisco Vitoria (1492/3–1560), grappled with them. In the colonies, pre-Columbian worldviews receded into the background, making way for the concerns, first of the Iberians living in the colonies, and then for native-born authors.

Given the colonial roots of Latin American philosophy, a strong concern for sociopolitical issues, such as human rights and social justice, have guided philosophical development in the region. In addition to answering standard philosophical questions, such as What is goodness? What is beauty? What is truth? Latin American philosophers have demonstrated a firm commitment to more concrete problems involving educational policy, political organization, and social reform. Many of these philosophers (see especially those included in Part IV) developed their ideas not in technical articles and systematic treatises intended for specialized audiences, but in newspaper essays meant to be read by a broad public. This is consonant with the view that philosophy should be a tool for social change.

Four major periods in the history of Latin American philosophy stand out and are represented in this collection: colonial, independentist, positivist, and contemporary. During the colonial period (ca. 1550–1750) scholasticism prevailed, partly as a result of its importance in Iberia at the time. However, growing and pressing social concerns forced the scholastic focus on technical metaphysical issues to make room for humanism and a concern with more

13

concrete problems, such as the just way to treat "the Indians" and how to determine their rights. Las Casas was the leading humanist of the time.

A more complete break with scholasticism took place during the independentist period (1750–1850), which takes its name from the goals of the intellectuals in the New World who wished to gain independence from Portugal and Spain. Its leading figures include Simón Bolívar (Venezuela, 1783–1830), who is featured in Part I; José Joaquín Fernández de Lizardi (Mexico, 1776–1827); Mariano Moreno (Argentina, 1778–1811); José Cecilio del Valle (Honduras, 1780–1834); José de San Martín (Argentina, 1778–1850); Miguel Hidalgo (Mexico, 1753–1811); and José Antonio Páez (Venezuela, 1790–1873), among others. These were men of action, committed to the cause of independence from Spain, and they were responsible for redrawing the map of colonial Latin America. Their actions, more than their body of writings, influenced later thinkers such as José Martí, Samuel Ramos, and Leopoldo Zea whose work is featured in Part IV.

Once political independence had been achieved, a somewhat more stable period began. This, known as positivism (1850–1910), shaped a great part of philosophy in the twentieth century. With the exception of scholasticism, positivism has been the most widespread and deeply rooted philosophical current in Latin America. The depth of its impact was due to historical factors: it arrived at the proper time and it addressed the need for nation building in the region.

Positivism was initiated by French philosopher Auguste Comte (1793–1857), who attempted to develop a rigorous and systematic understanding of human beings, in both their individual and their social dimensions. He emphasized experience over theoretical speculation and empirical science over metaphysics. The value of knowledge rested, according to Comte, on its practical applications. He was not moved by a mere desire to know: Knowledge was a servant of action and should lead to the solution of concrete problems. This practical aspect was one of the most captivating aspects of positivism for Latin Americans, who wished to overcome anarchy, eradicate poverty and disease, and place their own countries on the path of progress.

This, however, was not the only reason for the wide acceptance that positivism experienced. There were also reasons of a strictly cultural and theoretical nature. Since the colonial period, Latin American philosophy had been nurtured by scholasticism and, consequently, important practical issues had been neglected. Conceptual and terminological vagueness, expansive speculation, as well as unfounded and archaic dogmatism were predominant characteristics of much of the philosophy done in the region. Positivism, by contrast, emphasized principles based on experience and logical rigor, and offered the assurance of progress, insisting that its claims rested on solid empirical evidence. There would be no more fruitless theories, idle speculations, and vain attempts. The newly liberated republics of Latin America would finally leave not only the political legacy of colonization behind, but the philosophical one as well.

Positivism benefited greatly from the increasing prestige of science, because it proposed to limit its methods to those used by natural scientists. It was widely believed by the thinkers who favored this perspective that a new era had begun in which scientific study would make it possible to identify the causes of social evils and to eliminate them, just as medicine had begun to eradicate endemic diseases.

Comte's law of the three stages captured the attention of many Latin American intellectuals. According to this law, humanity passes through three stages, the theological, the metaphysical, and the scientific or positive. In the theological stage, the interpretation of reality is founded on prejudice and superstition. The metaphysical stage is dominated by speculation in which facts are either ignored or are not given adequate attention. Finally, in the positive stage, speculation is replaced by the establishment of facts, and knowledge is founded on experience.

Latin American thinkers applied this law to the history of their own countries and believed it was confirmed by experience. An example of this application is found in the *Civic Oration* that was delivered by the Mexican positivist Gabino Barreda in Guanajuato (1867), in which he refers to, and uses, Comte's ideas. With this oration in mind, President Benito Juárez named Barreda member of a committee to draft a law, approved on December 2, 1867, that gave birth to public education in Mexico. The fact that another renowned teacher, Justo Sierra, succeeded to Barreda's position and continued to apply positivist principles to educational policy explains the strength that this perspective acquired and its predominance in Mexico until the fall of the dictator Porfirio Díaz in 1911. Positivism was the official philosophy in Mexico during the twenty-seven years of the dictatorship, and the government was guided by Comte's slogan "Order and Progress."

The chaos and backwardness that prevailed in some Latin American countries as the power vacuums left in the wake of the colonial rule were filled by *caudillos* and other nondemocratic political figures and structures helps to explain in part why positivist teachings captivated the minds of so many intellectuals and politicians. The influence of positivism can be observed in the work of Argentine thinker and statesman Domingo Faustino Sarmiento. In the passages from his *Civilization and Barbarism*, included in Part IV below, one can see that his notion of civilization is shaped by positivist principles.

Positivism exercised strong influence on Argentine education, especially in the "School of Paraná," where Scalabrini, Ferreira, Herrera, and others provided leadership. This influence was further enhanced by the work of José Ingenieros, the *Revista de Filosofía*, and the Cultura Argentina publishing house. Positivism was especially strong in Brazil, where the positivist slogan, "Order and Progress," was incorporated into the Brazilian flag and reflected in the attitude of its political leaders.

Most countries of Latin America had their own particular way of receiving positivism. One should also keep in mind that Latin American positivism was shaped not only by the influence of Comte, but also by that of the English philosopher Herbert Spencer (1820–1903). Comte had a stronger impact in Brazil, Mexico, and Chile, whereas Spencer's thought was more influential in Argentina, Uruguay, and Cuba. In some cases preference was given to one thinker over the other for purely political reasons. In Cuba, for example, Enrique José Varona (1849–1933) rejected Comte's ideas because they did not favor the emancipation of Cuba from Spanish rule, and he adopted instead Spencer's idea of liberty. In spite of these and many other national differences, one can speak of Latin American positivism as a unified, yet evolving movement in which the influence of Comte was greater toward the beginning of the period and that of Spencer predominated toward the end.

The general decline of positivism stems from several factors. National distinctions, of course, must be taken into consideration insofar as the predominance of any particular cause varies from country to country. Although there were causes common to all Latin America, the reaction against positivism in each country emerged from complex national situations, rooted in cultural, political, and philosophical conditions that make it difficult to isolate specific factors. Thus it is best to speak of predominant influences.

The first general cause is the disappointment that Latin American intellectuals experienced when reality did not measure up to positivism's promises and aspirations. Immediate and assured results were envisioned and anxiously awaited, but progress was slow and uncertain. To uphold general principles and criteria for the study of social problems is one thing, but it is quite a different matter to develop effective, scientifically based procedures that can be applied in order to solve concrete problems.

Stark reality shattered many illusions. It soon became evident that divesture of traditional prejudices was not sufficient. The ideal of a scientific knowledge of social reality began to crumble in the face of difficulties, and the initial, naïve optimism gave way to corroding pessimism.

The application of Comte's views did not satisfy the expectations they had awakened and, to make matters worse, no thinkers who measured up to his standards emerged in Latin America. The majority of his followers were content to repeat the ideas of the master without applying them to the reality in which they lived. Philosophical theory should not be converted into dogma; rather, it needs a continuing creative direction since its application to reality is not a routine, mechanical task.

Moreover, many thinkers began to discover fundamental theoretical shortcomings in positivism. The indiscriminate application of the principle of causality to everything led positivism to deny freedom to human beings. Theoretical objections to determinism acquired great momentum in the moral realm. No one can be responsible for an act if it is determined, the critics of positivism claimed. If an act is a physically determined bodily movement, there is no room left for human will; human actions become mere mechanical occurrences, and the human firing of a gun and killing of another human being is no different than a tornado destroying a house. Positivism seemed to lead to an ethical dead end. Hence, when Henri Bergson's vitalism, with its rejection of determinism and its defense of liberty, crossed the ocean from France, it is not surprising that it met with a warm reception in Latin America.

One feature of positivism that led to frustration and its ultimate rejection in Latin America had to do with the devastating effects that its proposed determinism was perceived to have for aesthetic creation. If humans are not free, how can they be aesthetic agents? A mechanical explanation of the creative process factored out the very meaning of artistic creation, something that many Latin American thinkers found unacceptable, including the Peruvian philosopher Alejandro Octavio Deústua (1849–1945).

Another important reason for the rejection of positivism had to do with politics. In some countries, as in Mexico, positivism was associated with a dictatorship that had been overthrown; in others, such as Cuba, it was believed to support the colonial status quo against the possibility of independence to which many Cubans aspired. For countries which had suffered first under Spanish oppression and then under a succession of dictators, setting freedom aside seemed too high a price to pay for the promise of progress. Indeed, freedom had become the battle flag, so if positivism could not make room for freedom, then positivism must be abandoned.

In each country, the reaction against positivism took on a characteristic expression, although the dissatisfaction was fairly uniform throughout Latin America. Mexico, however, was the first outlet for this dissatisfaction and shaped it into a unique series of events. With the fall of the dictatorship of Porfirio Díaz in 1911, positivism also fell, for its foundations had already been undermined.

In 1909 a group of young intellectuals, who later acquired well-deserved renown in the field of philosophy and literature, founded the "Ateneo de la Juventud" (Atheneum of Youth). They studied the classics, especially Plato and Kant, and contemporary philosophers who had rejected positivism in Europe, such as Bergson and Croce. The influence of Nietzsche and Schopenhauer, who had thrown their weight against the narrow and scientific emphasis of positivism, was also felt. Following these studies, lectures were given in which positivist doctrine was roundly criticized and new ideas were proposed. Two figures from the Ateneo led the drive to find philosophical alternatives to positivism: Antonio Caso and José Vasconcelos.

In Argentina, the struggle against positivism was quite different. In the first place, positivism was not involved in any political movement. Furthermore, positivism had an effective role in the development of educational institutions and, through José Ingenieros, had acquired renown in scientific and philosophical circles. This explains why Argentina has remained a strong center of analytic philosophy, for positivism and analytic philosophy share a method connected to logic and science.

Nonetheless, although positivism was not completely rejected in Argentina, as it had been in Mexico, important criticisms of it were voiced. The two most distinguished figures in the opposition to positivism in Argentina were Alejandro Korn and Coriolano Alberini. The latter, although less gifted in creative ability, had more influence than the former in casting positivism out of official teaching programs. A caustic spirit, Alberini allowed no truce with positivism at the University of Buenos Aires, an institution in which he was dean of the Faculty of Philosophy and Letters on several occasions. Korn was less aggressive and fought positivism through his own, original position. In addition to his writings, his major contribution was to encourage the formation of a group of students whose philosophical orientation was not at all linked to positivism. Francisco Romero, who was introduced to philosophy through reading Spencer, felt the influence of the group that surrounded Korn. Thus in Argentina, positivism was overcome through the development of a philosophical alternative to it, rather than through the kind of sharp polemics that had characterized its demise in Mexico.

Similar reactions developed in other Latin American countries. Metaphysics, vehemently attacked by Comte and his followers, returned to philosophy. In some cases, this was due to the renewal of the classical concerns of scholastic philosophy, and in others to the rise of philosophical speculation in contemporary German thought which had come to hold sway in many intellectual circles throughout Latin America.

The contemporary period, which is how we refer to the period that follows positivism, can be broken down into three phases: foundational stage (1910–1940), period of normalcy (1940–1960), and period of maturity (1960–present). The first is usually referred to as the stage of the founders, a description introduced by Francisco Romero. The philosophers who are included in this group were the first to reject positivism even though some of them had been among the first to embrace it. They include: Alejandro Deústua, Antonio Caso (Mexico, 1883–1946), José Vasconcelos (Mexico, 1882–1959), Alejandro Korn (Argentina, 1860–1936), Carlos Vaz Ferreira (Uruguay, 1872–1958), and Raimundo Farias Brito (Brazil, 1862–1917), among others. These authors were influenced by French vitalist philosophers such as Boutroux and Bergson.

The generation that followed the "founders" continued in their thrust, further developing the vitalism and intuitionism that had been picked up in the wake of positivism's demise but adding a dimension inspired by German thought. A major figure in this development was the Spanish philosopher José Ortega y Gasset (1883–1955). He introduced the thought of such philosophers as Max Scheler and Nicolai Hartmann to a generation of Latin American thinkers, thereby expanding the philosophical horizons of the entire region. This generation, free of the polemic with positivism that had fueled the generation of founders, has been characterized by Francisco Miró Quesada (Peru, b. 1918) as the "generation of forgers." Major thrusts of this group include historicism, existentialism, and philosophical anthropology. Samuel Ramos (Mexico, 1897–1959), Carlos Astrada (Argentina, 1894–1970), and Francisco Romero (Argentina, 1891–1962) are the key philosophers of this period.

Throughout the history of Latin American thought there is a tension between those philosophers who focus on the universal human condition and those who focus on the particular conditions of specific cultural circumstances. In Mexico, for example, many philosophers have discussed the impact of colonization on the development of culture. This particularist tendency grew out of a historical event that brought two traditions into close contact with one another and heralded yet another stage in the development of Latin American philosophy.

During the late 1930s and 1940s, owing to the upheavals created by the Spanish civil war, a significant group of thinkers from Spain arrived in Latin America. These philosophers became known as the *transterrados* (translanded), those who had crossed over from their land to settle in various Latin American countries. Among these were Joaquín Xirau (1895–1946), Eduardo Nicol (1907–1986), José Ferrater Mora (1912–1991), José Gaos (1900–1969), Luis Recaséns Siches (1903–1977), and Juan D. García Bacca (1901–1992). Their presence helped to break some of the national barriers that had existed in Latin America before their arrival. The conception of *hispanidad* that they inherited from the Spanish philosopher Miguel de Unamuno, and the need to establish themselves in their adopted land, helped the process; they went from country to country, spreading ideas and contributing to an ever-broadening philosophical dialogue. Their influence showed itself most strongly when the generation born around 1910 reached maturity.

José Gaos was one of the most influential *transterrados*. He was a student of Ortega and became the teacher of one of Mexico's most important philosophers, Leopoldo Zea (b. 1912). Gaos encouraged Zea to study the history of Mexican thought, and this resulted in one of Zea's most significant books, *El positivismo en México* (1943). Through Gaos, Ortega had a strong influence on Zea. One of Ortega's most important insights was that in order to understand ourselves, we must understand our circumstance. In Zea's work, a central topic of discussion is the meaning of the Latin American circumstance for the development of the philosophy of the region.

Zea's unique philosophical approach was also influenced by the Mexican Samuel Ramos. The latter's existential, psychoanalytic approach to the problem of cultural identity was transformed by Zea into a critique of philosophy and the articulation of a *mestizo* (mixed) consciousness. The term *mestizo* points to an interest in issues associated with race and culture, and opens a philosophical discussion concerning the meaning of the being of a person who is of both Spanish and indigenous heritage. The source of this line of questioning can be traced back to the events following colonization, when the Spaniards mixed with indigenous people to create what became known in the cultures of Latin America as a new, *mestizo* race. Zea's notion of *mestizaje* had a strong influence on the Argentine philosopher Arturo Andrés Roig (b. 1922) and the Peruvian Francisco Miró Quesada. The relation between these thinkers constitutes an example of a growing philosophical Pan-Americanism. During this period, philosophers from different countries in Latin America began to respond to each other and to interact critically with one another.

This Pan-American trend continues and is further supported by the activities of several philosophical societies founded to facilitate meetings and publications. During the last fifty years, the level of philosophical activity in several Latin American countries has improved significantly. This is due, in part, to the institutionalization of philosophy. The number of national philosophical societies and of centers, institutes, faculties, and departments that have as their exclusive end the teaching and investigation of philosophy has increased substantially as has the number of philosophy journals. All of this activity has begun to awaken interest outside of Latin America.

One recent philosophical current that deserves mention is the philosophy of liberation. It grew out of liberation theology, which in turn began in Peru and Brazil. The immediate origins of this perspective can be traced to the 1970s in Argentina, with a group of thinkers that included Arturo Andrés Roig (b. 1922), Horacio Cerutti Guldberg (b. 1950), and Enrique Dussel (b. 1934). Because of the political turmoil at the time, many of these philosophers were forced into exile, thus disrupting the continuity of the movement and leading to the creation of two distinct strands in the philosophy of liberation, a historicist strand and an essentialist one. In spite of differences, both share a common concern with what it means to do philosophy from the periphery, that is, from the condition of dependence that these thinkers claim characterizes Latin American culture. The philosophy of liberation has been shaped by Marxist and Catholic ideas to a great extent.

Latin American philosophy has a rich and variegated history. Latin American philosophers continue to address specific social and political problems that plague the population of the Americas, while remaining engaged with the universal concerns that have characterized philosophy since its inception. These have to do with problems related to truth, goodness, and justice, among others—problems that are not the product of any political structure or geographical location, but part of the human condition itself.

PART I
Colonial Beginnings
and Independence

Introduction

Latin American philosophy begins with the process of colonization. There are no surviving records of Mayan, Toltec, Aztec, or any indigenous contributions to philosophy considered strictly. Colonial Mexican philosophy may very well have taken up elements of the indigenous thought already developed in that region of the continent, but as most of what happened in the wake of the colonization, the colonizers took control over the development of philosophy.[1] This meant that scholastic philosophy became the most influential trend in the New World.

The colonial period (ca. 1550–1750) begins within the scholastic fold provided by the Iberian clergy sent by the Spanish and Portuguese Crowns to convert indigenous people. The main philosophical centers during the early part of the period were Mexico and Peru, the two places where there had been substantial indigenous empires and rich natural resources such as gold and silver, coveted by Europeans. The texts studied were those of medieval scholastics and of their Iberian commentators. The major issues addressed were similar to those prevalent in Spain and Portugal; thus, logical and metaphysical questions dominated philosophical discussion. Antonio Rubio's (1548–1615) *Logica mexicana* was one of the most important scholastic texts written in the New World.

Yet, although scholasticism was central and many thinkers continued to write within this tradition, others were guided by humanism. These thinkers were more concerned with the political and legal questions raised by the colonization of the Americas. Arguably, the most important of these thinkers is Bartolomé de Las Casas (1474–1566), a Dominican friar who became the leading champion of the rights of the "Indians." His long life was devoted to arguing before the Spanish Crown that Indians, although different, were just as human as the Spaniards and therefore just as deserving of the same basic human rights.

It was Las Casas who first brought up what became known in Spain as the "Indian Question." As early as 1515, he began to petition the Crown to enact laws that would eliminate the whole system of slavery. In 1550 an important debate took place in Valladolid, Spain, between Juan Ginés de Sepúlveda, a leading ideologue of the *Conquista*, and Las Casas. Las Casas argued that it was unjust to wage war against the indigenous peoples and to enslave them.

Las Casas also claimed that one of the first steps in the devastation of these people was the system of forced labor known as the *encomienda*, and he fought to have it abolished. In this system, a random number of Indians was assigned by the local Spanish commanders to individual landowners and "recommended" to them for the reason that they required this protection for their prompt conversion. In effect, they became serfs, for they were totally at the mercy of their new masters, and received no wages or upkeep for the work that their protector or *encomendero* asked them to do. Las Casas brought this unjust system to the attention of Holy Roman Emperor Charles V (Charles I of Spain), and in 1542 new laws were written for the colonies that prohibited the Spaniards from taking Indians into service by way of the *encomienda* system. Sadly, these new laws were revoked just three years later.

The colonization was fraught with social injustice. Yet, as the selection from the famous debate that Las Casas had with Sepúlveda in Valladolid shows, the Spaniards did not unequivocally support the oppression of the Indians. At the same time, while Las Casas has been heralded as the "Defender of the Indians," one must be careful not to paint too rosy a picture of him. For a brief period in 1516, Las Casas endorsed the practice of importing Africans to the New World to do the work Indians had been doing, in order to spare the Indians the hard labor that was leading to their death.

Throughout his writings and deeds, it is clear that Las Casas was a humanist who did not want to participate in unjust actions resulting from colonization, but more than anything, he was a Christian who wanted more souls for the Catholic Church. Before the Indians could be converted to Christianity, first it had to be shown that they were human and therefore capable of understanding and voluntarily embracing the Christian faith. Las Casas spent much time during his debate with Sepúlveda arguing that the Indians were not barbarians by nature. In the debate, he refutes Sepúlveda's thesis that a war is justified against the Indians because they are barbarians who must yield to the civilized Spaniards and must be punished for the human sacrifices they have committed.

Las Casas's defense of the Indians reflects the influence of several sources. The thought of Aristotle (384–322 BCE), known as "the Philosopher" among scholastics, is behind several distinctions upon which Las Casas based his arguments. Other sources include Canon and Roman Law, and such Christian thinkers as Augustine (354–430) and Thomas Aquinas (1225–74). Las Casas was scholastically trained and the scholastic method informs the structure and content of his rebuttal of Sepúlveda.

In particular his case is based upon the distinction between essence and accident, and a division of barbarians into those who are so "in the strict sense," or essentially, and those who are barbarians "in the restricted sense," or merely by circumstance or accident. This kind of distinction can be traced to Aristotle. According to Aristotle, every substance has characteristics that are essential as well as others that are accidental. Take for example, a cat: an essential characteristic or attribute of a cat is that it has a head, for having a head is a necessary condition for something to be a cat. On the other hand, cats may be large or small, black or white, so size and color are merely accidental attributes and play no role in the definition of cat. Of human beings, Aristotle claimed that the essential attributes were rationality and other physiological attributes pertaining to their animal nature, such as being a mammal and having lungs. Among accidental attributes, on Aristotle's scheme, are skin tone and height.

As part of his argument, Las Casas seeks to explicate the correct meaning of the term *barbarian*. He points to the four types of barbarians that Aristotle had discussed in the *Politics*, and proceeds to demonstrate that the category of "barbarian in the strict sense" does not apply to the Indians. He therewith refutes Sepúlveda's claim that "Indians are by nature barbarians."

Sepúlveda and Las Casas represent two radically different responses to the questions posed by the existence of people who appear unfamiliar. Their debate in Valladolid raised questions concerning the definition of humanity and the nature of justice, issues that continue to be pertinent in the twenty-first century.

Social injustice did not have only one face in Latin America. Women also suffered oppression, although for most of the thinkers of the colonial period, this went unnoticed. Aristotle had claimed that women were inferior to men, and most of his scholastic followers did not question this view. But there were isolated voices in Latin America that cried out against the claim that women were fit only for the kitchen. One of the most eloquent and powerful of these voices was that of the seventeenth-century nun Sor Juana Inés de la Cruz (Mexico, 1651–1695). The two selections from her work presented here reflect her intelligence and wit, but most of all, her awareness of the unjust position of women in colonial Latin American society.

A recurring theme in Sor Juana's writings is the image of the human being as a microcosm. This theme reflects the influence of Neoplatonic philosophy upon her thought. In a time during which women were not supposed to be educated, the philosophical formation that Sor Juana was able to achieve was most impressive. She is known to have written a work on logic which unfortunately has been lost. This text was composed in Latin, the language of learning at the time. This is particularly noteworthy when one considers the stereotype of women from this period, according to which they could not learn Latin and studying it could even hurt them. As a proverb of the time goes, *Mujer que sabe latín, tiene mal fin* (A woman who knows Latin will come to a bad end).

It was not easy for Sor Juana to pursue her philosophical studies, for even her superiors at the convent forbade it. As is evident in the selection from *Respuesta* included here, Sor Juana took full advantage of any opportunity to learn; she even used her time in the kitchen (a place in which she was encouraged to stay) to reflect upon philosophical issues. With her characteristic wit, she observed that: "If Aristotle had cooked, he would have written more." *Respuesta* is largely biographical and provides us with details concerning the difficulties that Sor Juana faced as a woman with a desire for knowledge in a society that viewed the pursuit of learning as an exclusively male enterprise. This work was written in response to a letter from Sor Filotea de la Cruz, a pseudonym used by the bishop of Puebla, Manuel Fernández de Santa Cruz, who wrote to Sor Juana to remind her of her position as a nun, that is, a woman of modesty for whom it would be best to remain silent on issues where a woman's voice was not welcome. Sor Juana's *Respuesta* was a protest against any such a call to silence her, even though she had in fact to hide some of her thoughts behind a veil of humility and self-effacement. For example, in speaking of one of her most important poems, *Primer sueño*, widely recognized for its philosophical content, she says: "I recall having written nothing at my own pleasure save a trifling thing that they call the *Dream*." Sor Juana had to present her ideas in this belittling way in order to escape the censure of the authorities.

The final two selections of Part I in this collection are from Simón Bolívar (Venezuela, 1783–1830), more commonly known as "the Liberator." His writings belong to the independentist period (1750–1850). The leading intellectuals from this time were men of action who used ideas for practical ends. The strong influence of Utilitarianism is reflected in their emphasis on progress and the use of ideas as tools for social change. Another source of their thought was the liberal views of the French *philosophes*, who made reason a measure of legitimacy in social and political matters.

Not all of the leading figures from this period were philosophers in the strict sense. Bolívar, José Joaquín Fernández de Lizardi (Mexico,

1776–1827), Mariano Moreno (Argentina, 1778–1811), and José Cecilio del Valle (Honduras, 1780–1834) can be most accurately characterized as political leaders rather than strictly as philosophers. Instead of devoting their lives to philosophical speculation, they were more interested in concrete actions that would lead to the political independence for the Iberian colonies. Bolívar successfully led northern South America to independence from Spain and was the founding father of five republics (Colombia, Venezuela, Ecuador, Peru, and Bolivia). The two selections from his works express some of the ideas that were used to change the political structures in America.

The first selection is an excerpt from the "Letter from Jamaica" (1815). This letter is addressed to the governor of Jamaica and responds to the latter's request for Bolívar's views on prospects for Latin American liberation and the establishment of one unified nation. It is a call to independence from Spain.

Bolívar complains of both a state of permanent infancy experienced by the nations of Spanish America and their dependency upon Europe. (The problem of dependence is an enduring one, and it has shaped one of the most important recent strands of Latin American thought, the philosophy of liberation, as is evident in the selections from Arturo Andrés Roig and Enrique Dussel.) A major theme of Bolívar's letter is the problem of identity, of what it means to be American. He points to the following tension: "In short, though Americans by birth we derive our rights from Europe, and we have to assert these rights against the rights of the natives, and at the same time we must defend ourselves against the invaders." The problem of identity is one that continues to hold the attention of philosophers in Latin America, as the selections from Leopoldo Zea and Augusto Salazar Bondy in this volume illustrate.

The second selection from Bolívar is from the speech he delivered to the Congress of Angostura in 1819. Here it is Bolívar "the good citizen" speaking, and not Bolívar "the Liberator." He argues that Venezuela has been liberated, and now the long task of nation building must begin. He discusses the particular problems that the newly born nation faces in light of its colonial past. He draws attention to what he calls the "racial mixture" of the people of the region, while emphasizing the unity that must prevail if the country is to prosper, claiming that political equality must trump the physical and moral inequalities present among the people of Venezuela.

Each of the three thinkers included in this section is not a philosopher in the strict sense. Nonetheless, in order to understand Latin American philosophy, some familiarity with the thought of Las Casas, Sor Juana Inés de la Cruz, and Simón Bolívar is necessary because these authors initiated the discussion of topics that were later to be treated more systematically by philosophers. These three thinkers laid the groundwork for a tradition of thought rooted in pressing social and political problems.

NOTE

1. Consider the claim of Alexander von Humboldt (1769–1859), one of the first non-Spanish Europeans to be granted permission to explore the colonies of Spain (in 1799 he undertook a voyage that was to last until 1804). In his *Political Essay on the Kingdom of New Spain*, trans. J. Black and ed. Mary Maples Dunn (Norman: University of Oklahoma Press, 1988), Humboldt challenged the widespread European view that there had been no serious scientific or cultural achievements made by the indigenous civilizations that preceded the Spanish Conquest: "How shall we judge, from these miserable remains of a powerful people, of the degree of cultivation to which it had risen from the twelfth to the sixteenth century, and of the intellectual development of which it is susceptible? If all that remained of the French or German nation were a few poor agriculturists, could we read in their features that they belonged to nations which had produced a Descartes and Clairaut, a Kepler and a Leibnitz?" (pp. 53–54).

Bartolomé de Las Casas (1474–1566)

Las Casas was born in Sevilla in 1474, the son of a Spanish aristocrat. He studied theology and law in Salamanca. In 1502 he set sail for the New World and arrived in Santo Domingo (then known as La Española). In 1507 Las Casas traveled back to Europe, but in 1511 he returned to Santo Domingo and on November 30 of that year, he heard the famous sermon of Friar Antonio de Montesinos, in which the conduct of the colonizers toward the Indians was sharply criticized. Las Casas's debate with Juan Ginés de Sepúlveda came at the end of a long life that had been devoted to defending the cause of the Indians. He debated Sepúlveda in 1550, when he was seventy-six years old. The path that led him there was fraught with difficulties and not devoid of some poor judgments.

The source of many of his difficulties came from the publication in 1552 of a text entitled *The Devastation of the Indies: A Brief Account*. In this work, he documented the savageries that the Spaniards had committed against the Indians. This text was immediately translated, appearing in Paris in 1579, in London in 1583, in Amsterdam in 1607, and in Venice in 1630. It was used by the enemies of the Spanish Empire to show how cruel the Spaniards were and how unjust the treatment of their new subjects was. Between 1810 and 1830 in Latin America, the book had a direct influence on the leaders of the wars of independence against the Spanish colonial power. In the Spanish-American War, Spain's opponents used the book to defame Spain.

This work offered startling figures on the number of Indians who had been killed during the conquest, victims of malaria, famine, forced labor, smallpox, and even of murder. In fact, however, his figures are more modest than those of some researchers who speak of genocide and claim that in Central Mexico alone the population dwindled from twenty-five million to six million.

After the rapid depopulation of the region, the colonizers began to run out of labor power, and they then initiated the slave trade with Africa. Las Casas's tragic mistake was that for a brief period, in 1516, he defended the practice of importing Africans to be slaves in the New World, if only to try to spare the lives of the overworked indigenous population. He quickly realized that the importation of African slaves was no solution to the problem of the exploitation of the natives of New Spain, but rather a broadening of this exploitation and therefore withdrew his support.

Although Las Casas's mistake needs to be acknowledged and its gravity should not be overlooked, this should not overshadow his genuine concern for the rights of the indigenous people of New Spain. It is important to remember that it was Las Casas who first opened what became known in the Spanish courts as the "Indian Question." As early as 1515 he began to petition the Spanish courts to enact laws that would eliminate the whole system of slavery. In 1520, owing to the reports of Las Casas, King Charles I of Spain (Holy Roman Emperor Charles V) recognized that the procedures of the *conquistadores* in the Indian lands had been illegal, and in 1542 new laws were written for the Indies. These laws prohibited taking Indians into service by way of the *encomienda* system. Pearl fishing, which had led to the death of many Indians, was also prohibited. The new laws end with the following sentence, which offered much promise to the defenders of the Indians: "The inhabitants of the Indian Lands are to be treated in every respect as free subjects of the Crown of Castile: for there exists no difference between the latter and the former." Sadly, the laws were revoked only three years later, on November 20, 1545.

Las Casas's efforts to improve the lives of the native inhabitants of the New World met with much opposition from the Spaniards who had immigrated to the Spanish colonies. He was charged with treason and accused of being disloyal to the Crown, and had to make the long trip back to Spain on several occasions to defend himself.

Las Casas died in Madrid, Spain, in 1566, and his remains were later moved to Valladolid. He was neither a revolutionary nor a radical. He was loyal both to the Catholic Church and to the Spanish Crown, he fought for the equal rights of the Indians, yet for him the notion of a radical transformation of the social order, which would allow Indians to choose a religion other than Catholicism, was unthinkable.

In Defense of the Indians

They who teach, either in word or in writing, that the natives of the New World, whom we commonly call Indians, ought to be conquered and subjugated by war before the gospel is proclaimed and preached to them so that, after they have finally been subjugated, they may be instructed and hear the word of God, make two disgraceful mistakes. First, in connection with divine and human law they abuse God's words and do violence to the Scriptures, to papal decrees, and to the teaching handed down from the holy fathers. And they go wrong again by quoting histories that are nothing but sheer fables and shameless nonsense. By means of these, men who are totally hostile to the poor Indians and who are their utterly deceitful enemies betray them. Second, they mistake the meaning of the decree of bull of the Supreme Pontiff Alexander VI, whose words they corrupt and twist in support of their opinions, as will be clear from all that follows.

Their error and ignorance are also convincingly substantiated by the fact that they draw conclusions on matters which concern a countless number of men and vast areas of extensive provinces. Since they do not fully understand all these things, it is the height of effrontery and rashness for them to attribute publicly to the Indians the gravest failings both of nature and conduct, condemning en masse so many thousands of people, while, as a matter of fact, the greater number of them are free from these faults. All this drags innumerable souls to ruin and blocks the service of spreading the Christian religion by closing the eyes of those who, crazed by blind ambition, bend all their energies of mind and body to the one

From *In Defense of the Indians*, trans. Stafford Poole; foreword by Martin L. Marty (DeKalb: Northern Illinois University Press, 1992), pp. 25–36, 41–53. Copyright © 1992 by Northern Illinois University Press. Used by permission of the publisher.

purpose of gaining wealth, power, honor, and dignities. For the sake of these things they kill and destroy with inhuman cruelty people who are completely innocent, meek, harmless, temperate, and quite ready and willing to receive and embrace the word of God.

Who is there possessed of only a sound mind, not to say a little knowledge of theology, who has dared to pronounce a judgment and opinion so un-Christian that it spawns so many cruel wars, so many massacres, so many bereavements, and so many deplorable evils? Do we not have Christ's words: "See that you never despise any of these little ones," "Alas for the man who provides obstacles," "He who is not with me is against me; and he who does not gather with me scatters," and "Each day has trouble enough of its own"? Who is so godless that he would want to incite men who are savage, ambitious, proud, greedy, uncontrolled, and everlastingly lazy to pillage their brothers and destroy their souls as well as their possessions, even though war is never lawful except when it is waged because of unavoidable necessity?

And so what man of sound mind will approve a war against men who are harmless, ignorant, gentle, temperate, unarmed, and destitute of every human defense? For the results of such a war are very surely the loss of the souls of that people who perish without knowing God and without the support of the sacraments, and, for the survivors, hatred and loathing of the Christian religion. Hence the purpose God intends, and for the attainment of which he suffered so much, may be frustrated by the evil and cruelty that our men wreak on them with inhuman barbarity. What will these people think of Christ, the true God of the Christians, when they see Christians venting their rage against them with so many massacres, so much bloodshed without any just cause, at any rate without any just cause that they know of (nor can one even be imagined), and without any fault committed on their [the Indians] part against the Christians?

What good can come from these military campaigns that would, in the eyes of God, who evaluates all things with unutterable love, compensate for so many evils, so many injuries, and so many unaccustomed misfortunes? Furthermore, how will that nation love us, how will they become our friends (which is necessary if they are to accept our religion), when children see themselves deprived of parents, wives of husbands, and fathers of children and friends? When they see those they love wounded, imprisoned, plundered, and reduced from an immense number to a few? When they see their rulers stripped of their authority, crushed, and afflicted with a wretched slavery? All these things flow necessarily from war. Who is there who would want the gospel preached to himself in such a fashion? Does not this negative precept apply to all men in general: "See that you do not do to another what you would not have done to you by another"? And the same for the affirmative command: "So always treat others as you would like them to treat you." This is something that every man knows, grasps, and understands by the natural light that has been imparted to our minds.

It is obvious from all this that they who teach that these gentlest of sheep must be tamed by ravening wolves in a savage war before they are to be fed with the word of God are wrong about matters that are totally clear and are opposed to the natural law. Moreover, they commit an ungodly error when they say that these wars are just if they are waged as they should be. They mean, I suppose, if they are waged with restraint, by killing only those who have to be killed in order to subjugate the rest. It is as if they held all the peoples of the New World shut up in cages or slave pens and would want to cut off as many human heads as are usually sold each day in the markets for the feeding and nourishment of the populace. (I suggest this as a comparison.) But if they would consider that war and the massacre of this timid race has lasted, not for one day or a hundred days, but for ten or twenty years, to the incredible harm of the natives; that, as they wander about, hidden and scattered through woods and forests, unarmed, naked, deprived of every human help, they are slaughtered by the Spaniards; that, stripped of their wealth and wretched, they are driven from their homes, stunned and frightened by the unbelievable terror with which their oppressors have filled them through the monstrous crimes they have committed. If those who say such things would only consider that the hearts of this unfortunate people are so shattered with fear that they want to hurl themselves headlong into the deepest caverns of the earth to escape the clutches of these plunderers, I have no doubt that they would say things that are more temperate and more wise.

To come to the point, then, this *Defense* will contain two main topics. First, I shall show that the Reverend Doctor Sepúlveda, together with his followers, is wrong in law in everything he alleges against the Indians. While doing this, I shall provide an answer to all his arguments and to the authorities he violently distorts. Second, I shall show how wrong they are in fact, with great harm to their own souls. For the Creator of every being has not so despised these people of the New World that he willed them to lack reason and made them like brute animals, so that they should be called barbarians, savages, wild men, and brutes, as they [Sepúlveda et al.] think or imagine. On the contrary, they [the Indians] are of such gentleness and decency that they are, more than the other nations of the entire world, supremely fitted and prepared to abandon the worship of idols and to accept, province by province and people by people, the word of God and the preaching of the truth.

As to the first point, which we have discussed elsewhere at greater length and in general against all those infected with errors of this kind about the question of unbelievers; for now, as a sort of assault on the first argument for Sepúlveda's position, we should recognize that there are four kinds of barbarians, according to the Philosopher in Books 1 and 3 of the *Politics* and in Book 7 of the *Ethics*, and according to Saint Thomas and other doctors in various places.

First, barbarian in the loose and broad sense of the word means any cruel, inhuman, wild, and merciless man acting against human reason out of anger or native disposition, so that, putting aside decency, meekness, and humane moderation, he becomes hard, severe, quarrelsome, unbearable, cruel, and plunges blindly into crimes that only the wildest beasts of the forest would commit. Speaking of this kind of barbarian, the Philosopher says in the *Politics* that just as the man who obeys right reason and excellent laws is superior to all the animals, so too, if he leaves the path of right reason and law, he is the wickedest, worst, and most inhuman of all animals.

Boethius also speaks of these when he refers to the courtiers of the tyrant Theodoric as barbarians because of their savage and insatiable greed. "How often," he asks, "have I protected, by putting my authority in danger, such poor wretches as the unpunished greed of the barbarians abused with uncounted false accusations?"

The Second Book of Maccabees also mentions this kind of barbarian. For when Nicanor, a ruthless and savage despot, wanted to join battle with Judas Maccabaeus in Samaria on the Sabbath, some of the Jews who were with him said to him: "You must not massacre them in such a savage, barbarous way," that is, savagely and inhumanly. Both the Greeks and the Latins, and any others who live even in the most highly developed states, can be called barbarians if, by the savagery of their behavior, they are anything like the Scythians, whose country was regarded as singularly barbaric, as Isidore notes, because of the savage and inhuman practices of this race.

Indeed, our Spaniards are not unacquainted with a number of these practices. On the contrary, in the absolutely inhuman things they have done to those nations they have surpassed all other barbarians.

To this class of barbarian belong all those who, aroused by anger, hatred, or some other strong feeling, violently defend something, completely forgetful of reason and virtue. Gregory speaks of this in his *Letters*, and Gratian, when speaking of the uprising that occurred at Milan over the election of one of the bishops, says: "Many of the Milanese, driven by barbaric fury, come together." In his *Ethics*, the Philosopher calls this type of barbarian brutish when he writes: "It is found chiefly among barbarians, but some brutish qualities are also produced by disease or deformity; and we also call by this evil name those men who go beyond all ordinary standards by reason of vice."

The second kind of barbarian includes those who do not have a written language that corresponds to the spoken one, as the Latin language does with ours, and therefore they do not know how to express in it what they mean. For this reason they are considered to be uncultured and ignorant of letters and learning. Hence, so that his own people, the English, might not be regarded as barbarians, the Venerable Bede wrote in English on all the branches of the liberal arts, as we read in his life and as Saint Thomas notes. Likewise, Saint Gregory speaks in his *Moralia* as John Gerson quotes him:

> See how the tongue of Britain, which knew only how to grind out barbaric sounds, has long since begun to resound with Hebrew words in praise of God. See how the ocean, which before was swelling, is now calmed beneath the feet of the saints and is subject to them. Its barbarous motions, which the princes of the earth had not been able to control with the sword, the mouths of priests now bind with simple words through the fear of God.

In this sense he is called a barbarian who, because of the difference of his language, does not understand another speaking to him. Thus Paul, speaking of himself, says: "If I am ignorant of what the sound means, I am a barbarian to the man who is speaking and he is a barbarian to me." Saint John Chrysostom often calls the holy kings, the Magi, barbarians in this sense: "Indeed, because a star called the wise men from the east and barbarous men underwent the fatigue of so long a pilgrimage."

Barbarians of this kind are not called barbarians in the absolute but in a restricted sense; that is, they are not barbarians literally but by circumstance, as Chrysostom indicates in the same passage when he says: "The star which had gone before them only to desert them, leads to his worship not just any barbarians, but those among them who were indeed outstanding in the dignity of wisdom."

From these words of Chrysostom it is obvious that a people can be called barbarians and still be wise, courageous, prudent, and lead a settled life. So, in ancient times, the Greeks called the Romans barbarians, and, in turn, the Romans called the Greeks and other nations of the world barbarians. It is quite clear that in the first book of the *Politics* the Philosopher is not talking about this category when he writes that barbarians are by nature slaves and do not have the ability to govern themselves or others. However, he speaks of this kind of barbarian in the third book of the *Politics*, where, discussing the four kinds of kings and kingdoms, he places barbarian kingdoms in the second place. Although he says their rulers are rather like tyrants, nevertheless he holds that they are legal and hereditary rulers according to the usage of their country. Their subjects are so virtuous that they bear the exactions, taxes, burdens, and labors their rulers demand from them, even though they are burdensome. He also writes that these kingdoms are more stable and secure than others, for their subjects love and protect the ruler who governs them according to the practices of the country and who is the natural ruler whose children will inherit his kingdom.

This is what Aristotle says:

> There is another sort of monarchy not uncommon among barbarians, which closely resembles tyranny. But this is both legal and hereditary. For barbarians, being more servile in character than Greeks, and Asiatics than Europeans, do not rebel against a despotic government. Such royalties have the nature of tyrannies but there is no danger of their being overthrown, for they are hereditary and legal. For this reason also, their guards are such as a king and not such as a tyrant would employ. For kings are guarded by citizen-soldiers, tyrants, however, by mercenaries. For kings rule according to law over voluntary subjects, but tyrants over involuntary [subjects]; and the ones are guarded by their fellow-citizens, the others are guarded against them.

The third kind of barbarian, in the proper and strict meaning of the word, are those who, either because of their evil and wicked character or the barrenness of the region in which they live, are cruel, savage, sottish, stupid, and strangers to reason. They are not governed by law or right, do not cultivate friendships, and have no state or politically organized community. Rather, they are without ruler, laws, and institutions. They do not contract marriage according to any set forms and, finally, they do not engage in civilized commerce. They do not buy, they do not sell, they do not hire, they do not lease, they do not make contracts, they do not deposit, they do not borrow, they do not lend. Finally, they enter into none of the contracts regulated by the law of nations. Indeed, they live spread out and scattered, dwelling in the forests and in the mountains, being content with their mates only, just as do animals, both domestic and wild.

These are barbarians in the absolute and strict sense of the word, such as were perhaps living in the country that has been named Barbary. They lack the reasoning and way of life suited to human beings and those things which all men habitually accept. The Philosopher discusses these barbarians and calls them slaves by nature since they have no natural government, no political institutions (for there is no order among them), and they are not subject to anyone, nor do they have a ruler. Certainly, no one among such men has the skill needed for government, nor is there among them quickness of mind or correctness of judgment. As a result, they do not want to choose a ruler for themselves who would bind them to virtue under political rule. They have no laws which they fear or by which all their affairs are regulated. There is no one to evaluate good deeds, promote virtue, or restrain vice by penalties. Finally, caring nothing for life in a society, they lead a life very much like that of brute animals. Since they fall so far short of other men in intellectual capacity and behavior, they are inclined to harm others. They are quick to fight, quarrelsome, eager for war, and inclined to every kind of savagery. They live on their prey like wild beasts and birds. Hence they are not naturally free except at home, since they have no one to rule them.

Against these, the Philosopher cites Homer's reproach of a certain person whom he calls unsociable, because of his evil disposition, and isolated without anyone living nearby, because he has such traits that he would be unable to establish or continue any friendship or close association. He calls him lawless because he did not submit to the rule of law. He calls him restless and factious and, finally, wicked and criminal, since he cannot bring his acts into line with the dictates of reason, and hence, avid for battles and brawls, he became ready for and swift to every evil. We see all this in birds of prey that do not fly together in a flock. The saying of the Philosopher applied to these men:

> He who is without a state is either above humanity or a beast, so that he is contemptuously denounced by Homer as "the tribeless, lawless, homeless one"; for he is so by nature, craving war like one who is not restrained by any yoke, like vultures.

Barbarians of this kind (or better, wild men) are rarely found in any part of the world and are few in number when compared with the rest of mankind, as Aristotle notes at the beginning of the seventh book of the *Ethics*. So, too, men endowed with heroic virtue, whom we call heroes and demigods, are also quite rare.

The Philosopher makes the same point in his *On Heaven and Earth*, where he writes: "Nature always follows the best course possible," and somewhat further on: "Nature lavishes greater care on the nobler things," and again, in his work *On Old Age and Youth*, he says: "Nature makes the best possible things." Furthermore, in the *Rhetoric* he states: "Things which happen by nature have a fixed and intrinsic cause, since they occur uniformly, either always or in most cases." Therefore, for the most part, nature brings forth and produces what is best and perfect. Rarely do natural causes fail to produce the effects which follow from their natures. Seldom is a man born lame, crippled, blind, or one-eyed, or with the soles on top of the feet, as some were in Africa, according to the testimony of Augustine and others. Generally, fire generates fire; oil, oil; man, another man. Finally, every creature brings forth and generates perfectly what is like itself and is of the same species, and all men naturally understand and admit first principles.

The only reason for this, of course, is that the works of nature are the works of the Supreme Intellect who is God, as is stated in the *Book on Causes*. For this reason it is in accord with divine providence and goodness that nature should always or for the most part produce the best and the perfect, [and] rarely and exceptionally the imperfect and the very bad.

Therefore this kind of barbarian is savage, imperfect, and the worst of men, and they are mistakes of nature or freaks in a rational nature, as the Commentator on *The Soul* says in the following words: "What intellectual error and false opinion are in relation to the thinking process, so is the freak to bodily nature." And since a rational nature is provided for and guided by divine providence for its own sake in a way superior to that of other creatures, not only in what concerns the species but also each individual, it evidently follows that it would be impossible to find in a rational nature such a freak or mistake of nature, that is, one that does not fit the common notion of man, except very rarely and in far fewer instances than in other creatures. For the good and all-powerful God, in his love for mankind, has created all things for man's use and protects him whom he has endowed with so many qualities by a singular affection and care (as we have said), and guides his actions and enlightens each one's mind and disposes him for virtue in accordance with the ability given to him. Hence it necessarily follows that a rational nature, receiving its power from the Creator alone, should include men who, as a rule, are endowed with the best gifts of their nature and are rarely slow witted or barbarous. For if nature does this for beasts, why will it not do the same for man, whom God willed to stand above all other animals, chosen for himself and wonderfully endowed? And we must hold that nature makes man more perfect in no other way than by his intellect, by which he most specially stands above the other animals.

Who, therefore, except one who is irreverent toward God and contemptuous of nature, has dared to write that countless numbers of natives across the ocean are barbarous, savage, uncivilized, and slow witted when, if they are evaluated by an accurate judgment, they completely outnumber all other men? This is consistent with what Saint Thomas writes: "The good which is proportionate to the common state of nature is to be found in most men and is lacking only in a few. . . . Thus it is clear that the majority of men have sufficient knowledge to guide their lives, and the few who do not have this knowledge are said to be half-witted or fools." Therefore, since barbarians of that kind, as Saint Thomas says, lack that good of the intellect which is knowledge of the truth, a good proportionate to the common condition of rational nature, it is evident that in each part of the world, or anywhere among the nations, barbarians of this sort or freaks of rational nature can only be quite rare. For since God's love for mankind is so great and it is his will to save all men, it is in accord with his wisdom that in the whole universe, which is perfect in all its parts, his supreme wisdom should shine more and more in the most perfect thing: rational nature. Therefore, the barbarians of the kind we have placed in the third category are most rare, because with such natural endowments they cannot seek God, know him, call upon him, or love him. They do not have a capacity for doctrine or for performing the acts of faith or love.

Again, if we believe that such a huge part of mankind is barbaric, it would follow that God's design has for the most part been ineffective, with so many thousands of men deprived of the natural light that is common to all peoples. And so there would be a great reduction in the perfection of the entire universe—something that is unacceptable and unthinkable for any Christian. Saint Thomas says that for this reason God created immense numbers of angels, many more than material beings. He offers as the reason "that since it is perfection of the universe which God chiefly intends in the creation of things, the more perfect some things are, in so much greater abundance were they created by God." We can also cite on this point the teaching of the holy doctor that many more angels remained in heaven than fell. Saint Thomas is moved by the consideration that "sin is contrary to natural inclination. Those things which are against the natural order happen with less frequency for nature attains its effects either always or more often than not." . . .

As a result of the points we have proved and made clear, the distinction the Philosopher makes between the two above-mentioned kinds of barbarian is evident. For those he deals with in the first book of the *Politics*, and whom we have just discussed, are barbarians without qualification, in the proper and strict sense of the word, that is, dull witted and lacking in the reasoning powers necessary for self-government. They are without laws, without king, etc. For this reason they are by nature unfitted for rule.

However, he admits, and proves, that the barbarians he deals with in the third book of the same work have a lawful, just, and natural government. Even though they lack the art and use of writing, they are not wanting in the capacity and skill to rule and govern themselves, both publicly and privately. Thus they have kingdoms, communities, and cities that they govern wisely according to their laws and customs. Thus their government is legitimate and natural, even though it has some resemblance to tyranny. From these statements we have no choice but to conclude that the rulers of such nations enjoy the use of reason and that their people and the inhabitants of their provinces do not lack peace and justice. Otherwise they could not be established or preserved as political entities for long. This is made clear by the Philosopher and Augustine. Therefore not all barbarians are irrational or natural slaves or unfit for government. Some barbarians, then, in accord with justice and nature, have kingdoms, royal dignities, jurisdiction, and good laws, and there is among them lawful government.

Now if we shall have shown that among our Indians of the western and southern shores (granting that we call them barbarians and that they are barbarians) there are important kingdoms, large numbers of people who live settled lives in a society, great cities, kings, judges and laws, persons who engage in commerce, buying, selling, lending, and the other contracts of the law of nations, will it not stand proved that the Reverend Doctor Sepúlveda has spoken wrongly and viciously against peoples like these, either out of malice or ignorance of Aristotle's teaching, and, therefore, has falsely and perhaps irreparably slandered them before the entire world? From the fact that the Indians are barbarians it does not necessarily follow that they are incapable of government and have to be ruled by others, except to be taught about the Catholic faith and to be admitted to the holy sacraments. They are not ignorant, inhuman, or bestial. Rather, long before they had heard the word *Spaniard* they had properly organized states, wisely ordered by excellent laws, religion, and custom. They cultivated friendship and, bound together in common friendship, lived in populous cities in which they wisely administered the affairs of both peace and war justly and equitably, truly governed by laws that at very many points surpass ours, and could have won the admiration of the sages of Athens, as I will show in the second part of this *Defense*.

Now if they are to be subjugated by war because they are ignorant of polished literature, let Sepúlveda hear Trogus Pompey:

> Nor could the Spaniards submit to the yoke of a conquered province until Caesar Augustus, after he had conquered the world, turned his victorious armies against them and organized that barbaric and wild people as a province, once he had led them by law to a more civilized way of life.

Now see how he called the Spanish people barbaric and wild. I would like to hear Sepúlveda, in his cleverness, answer this question: Does he think that the war of the Romans against the Spanish was justified in order to free them from barbarism? And this question also: Did the Spanish wage an unjust war when they vigorously defended themselves against them?

Next, I call the Spaniards who plunder that unhappy people torturers. Do you think that the Romans, once they had subjugated the wild and barbaric peoples of Spain, could with secure right divide all of you among themselves, handing over so many head of both males and females as allotments to individuals? And do you then conclude that the Romans could have stripped your rulers of their authority and consigned all of you, after you had been deprived of your liberty, to wretched labors, especially in searching for gold and silver lodes and mining and refining the metals? And if the Romans finally did that, as is evident from Diodorus, [would you not judge] that you also have the right to defend your freedom, indeed your very life, by war? Sepúlveda, would you have permitted Saint James to evangelize your own people on Córdoba in that way? For God's sake and man's faith in him, is this the way to impose the yoke of Christ on Christian men? Is this the way to remove wild barbarism from the minds of barbarians? Is it not, rather, to act like thieves, cut-throats, and cruel plunderers and to drive the gentlest of people headlong into despair? The Indian race is not that barbaric, nor are they dull witted or stupid, but they are easy to teach and very talented in learning all the liberal arts, and very ready to accept, honor, and observe Christian religion and correct their sins (as experience has taught) once priests have introduced them to the sacred mysteries and taught them the word of God. They have been endowed with excellent conduct, and before the coming of the Spaniards, as we have said, they had political states that were well founded on beneficial laws.

Furthermore, they are so skilled in every mechanical art that with every right they should be set ahead of all the nations of the known world on this score, so very beautiful in their skill and artistry are the things this people produces in the grace of its architecture, its painting, and its needlework. But Sepúlveda despises these mechanical arts, as if these things do not reflect inventiveness, ingenuity, industry, and right reason. For a mechanical art is an operative habit of the intellect that is usually defined as "the right way to make things, directing the acts of the reason, through which the artisan proceeds in orderly fashion, easily, and unerringly in the very act of reason." So these men are not stupid, Reverend Doctor. Their skillfully fashioned works of superior refinement awaken the admiration of all nations, because works proclaim a man's talent, for, as the poet says, the work commends the craftsman. Also Prosper [of Aquitaine] says: "See, the maker is proclaimed by the wonderful signs of his work and the effects, too, sing of their author."

In the liberal arts that they have been taught up to now, such as grammar and logic, they are remarkably adept. With every kind of music they charm the ears of their audience with wonderful sweetness. They write skillfully and quite elegantly, so that most often we are at a loss to know whether the characters are handwritten or printed. I shall explain this at greater length in the second part of this *Defense*, not by quoting the totally groundless lies of the worst [deceivers] in the histories published so far but the truth itself and what I have seen with my eyes, felt with my hands, and heard with my own ears while living a great many years among those peoples.

Now if Sepúlveda had wanted, as a serious man should, to know the full truth before he sat down to write with his mind corrupted by the lies of tyrants, he should have consulted the honest religious who have lived among those peoples for many years and know their endowments of character and industry, as well as the progress they have made in religion and morality. Indeed, Rome is far from Spain, yet in that city the talent of these people and their aptitude and capacity for grasping the liberal arts have been recognized. Here is Paolo Giovo, bishop of Nocera, in praise of those people whom you call dull witted and stupid. In his *History of His Times* he has left this testimony for later generations to read:

> Hernán Cortés, hurrying overland to the kingdom of Mexico after defeating the Indians, occupied the city of Tenochtitlán, after he had conquered in many battles, using boats which he had built, that city set upon a salt lagoon—wonderful like the city of Venice in its buildings and the size of its population.

As you see, he declares that the Indian city is worthy of admiration because of its buildings, which are like those of Venice.

As to the terrible crime of human sacrifice, which you exaggerate, see what Giovio adds in the same place. "The rulers of the Mexicans have a right to sacrifice living men to their gods, provided they have been condemned for a crime." Concerning the natural gifts of that people, what does he assert? "Thus it was not altogether difficult for Cortés to lead a gifted and teachable people, once they had abandoned their superstitious idolatry, to the worship of Christ. For they learn our writing with pleasure and with admiration, now that they have given up the hieroglyphics by which they used to record their annals, enshrining for posterity in various symbols the memory of their kings."

This is what you, a man of great scholarship, should have done in ascertaining the truth, instead of writing, with the sharp edge of your pen poised for the whispers of irresponsible men, your little book that slanders the Indian inhabitants of such a large part of the earth. Do you quote to us Oviedo's *History*, which bears the approval of the Royal Council, as though Oviedo, as he himself testifies, was not a despotic master who kept unfortunate Indians oppressed by slavery like cattle and, in imitation of the other thieves, ruined a great part of the continent, or as though the Council, when it approves a book, appears to approve also the lies it contains, or as if, when the Council approves a book, it knows whether its contents are true? To this enemy you give your belief, as also to the one who is an interested party. For he possessed an allotment of Indians, as did the other tyrannical masters.

From this it is clear that the basis for Sepúlveda's teaching that these people are uncivilized and ignorant is worse than false. Yet even if we were to grant that this race has no keenness of mind or artistic ability, certainly they are not, in consequence, obliged to submit themselves to those who are more intelligent and to adopt their ways, so that, if they refuse, they may be subdued by having war waged against them and be enslaved, as happens today. For men are obliged by the natural law to do many things they cannot be forced to do against their will. We are bound by the natural law to embrace virtue and imitate the uprightness of good men. No one, however, is punished for being bad unless he is guilty of rebellion. Where the Catholic faith has been preached in a Christian manner and as it ought to be, all men are bound by the natural law to accept it, yet no one is forced to accept the faith of Christ. No one is punished because he is sunk in vice, unless he is rebellious or harms the property and persons of others. No one is forced to embrace virtue and show himself as a good man. One who receives a favor is bound by the natural law to return the favor by what we call antidotal obligation. Yet no one is forced to this, nor is he punished if he omits it, according to the common interpretation of the jurists.

To relieve the need of a brother is a work of mercy to which nature inclines and obliges men, yet no one is forced to give alms. . . . Therefore, not even a truly wise man may force an ignorant barbarian to submit to him, especially by yielding his liberty, without doing him an injustice. This the poor Indians suffer, with extreme injustice, against all the laws of God and of men and against the law of nature itself. For evil must not be done that good may come of it, for example, if someone were to castrate another against his will. For although eunuchs are freed from the lust that drives human minds forward in its mad rush, yet he who castrates another is not severely punished.

Now if, on the basis of this utterly absurd argument, war against the Indians were lawful, one nation might rise up against another and one man against another man, and on the pretext of superior wisdom, might strive to bring the other into subjection. On this basis the Turks, and the Moors— the truly barbaric scum of the nations—with complete right and in accord with the law of nature could carry on war, which, as it seems to some, is permitted to us by a lawful decree of the state. If we admit this, will not everything high and low, divine and human, be thrown into confusion? What can be proposed more contrary to the eternal law than what Sepúlveda often declares? What plague deserves more to be loathed? I am of the opinion that Sepúlveda, in his modesty, thinks Spain regards other nations as wiser than herself. Therefore she must be forced to submit to them according to the eternal law! And, indeed, the eternal law has arranged and determined all things in admirable proportion and order. It separated kingdom from kingdom and people from people "when the Most High gave the nations their inheritance, when he divided the sons of men." Also, each nation placed over itself, under divine guidance, a king and rulers: "Over each nation he has set a governor." For all kings or rulers, even among the barbarians, are servants of God, as divine wisdom teaches: "By me monarchs rule and princes issue just laws; by me rulers govern and the great impose justice on the world." And all kings and governors who fail to rule their subjects rightly, barbarians or not, are violators of the eternal law and face God, who is the avenging judge of that transgression. Since, therefore, every nation by the eternal law has a ruler or prince, it is wrong for one nation to attack another under pretext of being superior in wisdom or to overthrow other kingdoms. For it acts contrary to the eternal law, as we read in Proverbs: "Do not displace the ancient landmark, set up by your ancestors." This is not an act of wisdom, but of great injustice and a lying excuse for plundering others. Hence every nation, no matter how barbaric, has the right to defend itself against a more civilized one that wants to conquer it and take away its freedom. And, moreover, it can lawfully punish with death the more civilized as a savage and cruel aggressor against the law of nature. And this war is certainly more just than the one that, under pretext of wisdom, is waged against them.

Sepúlveda advances another argument: The less perfect yield naturally to the more perfect as matter does to form, body to soul, sense to reason. I do not deny this at all. Nevertheless, this is true only when two elements are joined by nature in first act, as when matter and the form that gives being to the thing unite in one composite, [for example] when body and soul are joined to each other and make an animal, and when the senses and reason exist in the same subject. But if the perfect and the imperfect are separated and inhere in different subjects, then imperfect things do not yield to the more perfect, but they are not yet joined in first act.

According to this distinction, if the wise and the unwise live in one and the same political community or under the same prince or ruler, then the unwise ought to submit themselves willingly to the wiser man who governs the state, for example, the king or his laws or his governors. If they refuse to do this, it is lawful to use force against them and they can be punished, since the law of nature demands this. On the other hand, no free person, and much less a free people, is bound to submit to anyone, whether king or nation, no matter how much better the latter may be and no matter how advantageous he may think it will be to himself [sic]. Augustine of Ancona teaches this conclusion in this very form, that is, when the imperfect yield to the more perfect. No free nation, therefore, can be compelled to submit itself to a wiser one, even if such submission could lead to [its] great advantage. When the Philosopher advances the argument that matter yields to form, he intends to assert only that nature has produced men fitted by an inborn talent for governing others who have not been endowed with so great a natural ability. And so he teaches that such wiser men are to be entrusted with the helm of government for its preservation and welfare. Others ought to be subject to them as matter is subject to form and the body to the soul.

Sepúlveda's final argument that everyone can be compelled, even when unwilling, to do those things that are beneficial to him, if taken without qualification, is false in the extreme. For Augustine, whom he cites, is speaking of those who had promised something useful for themselves and did not keep their promise, with damage or injury to others. Specifically, he is discussing heretics whom the Church compels to keep their baptismal vows, not only because they are useful for themselves but especially *because they have promised and vowed them to God and, from the promise, they are bound by a certain special obligation.* For it would not be enough to argue that the vows are beneficial to them. For we see that no unbeliever is forced to receive baptism. From the teaching of the above-mentioned Augustine the doctors conclude that one can and should be forced to do a good he has promised, but not one he has not promised. But many things will have to be discussed later concerning this.

There is a fourth kind of barbarian, which includes all those who do not acknowledge Christ. For no matter how well governed a people may be or how philosophical a man, they are subject to complete barbarism, specifically, the barbarism of vice, if they are not imbued with the mysteries of Christian philosophy. Now these vices can be cleansed only by the sacraments and the power of the Christian law, which is the only unspotted law that "converts souls" and frees and cleanses the hearts of men from every vice and superstition of idolatry, from which springs the source of all the evils that make both private and public life miserable and unhappy. "For the beginning of immorality is in seeking idols and the corruption of life is in finding them."

The Christian faith brings the grace of the Holy Spirit, which wipes away all wickedness, filth, and foolishness from human hearts. This is clear in the case of the Roman people, who sought to enact laws for all other nations in order to dominate them and who were, at one time, highly praised for their reputation for political skill and wisdom. Now this people itself was ruled by heinous vices and detestable practices, especially in its shameful games and hateful sacrifices, as in the games and plays held in the circus and in the obscene sacrifices to Priapus and Bacchus. In these everything was so disgraceful, ugly, and repugnant to sound reason that they far outdistanced all other nations in insensitivity of mind and barbarism. This is explained clearly and at length by Saint Augustine and by Lactantius when he speaks about the religion of the Roman and Greeks, who wanted to be considered wiser than all the other nations of the world. He [Lactantius] writes that they habitually worshiped and offered homage to their gods by prostituting their children in the *gymnasia* so that anyone could abuse them at his pleasure. And he adds: "Is there anything astonishing in the fact that all disgraceful practices have come down from this people for whom these vices were religious acts, things which not only were not avoided but were even encouraged?"

These are they who called all other nations barbarians, though no true barbarians could do anything more absurd or foolish. Perhaps the Romans excelled in quickness of judgment and mental expertise, so that they could make themselves tyrants over mankind and subdue foreign territories amid great destruction. But even if the Greeks and Romans did refrain from these horrible crimes and foul vices, where is the credit due if not to the splendor of the gospel, which, once it had spread throughout all the nations of the world, came to the notice even of that [sic] ambitious nation? Since, therefore, through their foul and corrupt way of life and the other detestable acts practiced by unbelievers (which arise especially from and follow on superstitious opinions about divine matters) they became like animals, certainly anyone who has not been initiated into the Christian mysteries is considered barbarous and unfortunate. And so note that the fourth kind of barbarian has been indicated.

The Turks and the Arabs are a people said to be well versed in political affairs. But how can they be honored with this reputation for uprightness when they are an effeminate and luxury-loving people, given to every sort of sexual immorality? The Turks, in particular, do not consider impure and horrible vices worthy of punishment.

Furthermore, neither the Greeks nor the Romans nor the Turks nor the Moors should be said to be exercising justice, since neither prudence nor justice can be found in a people that does not recognize Christ, as Augustine proves.

When, therefore, those who are devoid of Christian truth have sunk into vices and crimes and have strayed from reason in many ways, no matter how well versed they may be in the skills of government, and certainly all those who do not worship Christ, either because they have not heard his words even by hearsay or because, once they have heard them, reject them, all these are true barbarians.

This is obvious from the Acts of the Apostles, where, after telling about the Apostle Paul's shipwreck on Malta, Saint Luke adds: "The barbarians showed us no small courtesy." Malta is a port on the island of Lesbos, which gave us the lyric poets Alcaeus and Sappho, as well as Pittacus (called "the Maltese"), who was one of the seven sages of Greece, and Theophrastus, a disciple of Aristotle. Because of this reputation it is praised by Horace: "Others will praise famous Rhodes or Malta. Yet the Apostle calls the people barbarians, not because they were slow witted or wild but because they did not acknowledge Christ, although Lyra writes in this regard that they were called barbarians because they did not know Hebrew, Greek, or Latin. This is how Saint Jerome speaks. Speaking about barbarous nations, he says: "For Africa, Persia, the Orient, India, and all barbarous nations adore one Christ. They observe one law and rule of truth."

Now on Good Friday the Church prays against these barbarians, who are enemies of the Church, in these words: "Let us pray for the Most Christian Emperor, so that our God and Lord may make all barbarian peoples subject to him for our lasting peace," and later: "May all the barbarian peoples who put their trust in their fierceness be restrained by the right hand of your power." However, with regard to the barbarians who do not bother Christian people the Church does not pray that they be restrained but that iniquity be removed from their hearts so that they might abandon their idols and be converted to the one true God. And so, a little later:

> Almighty and Eternal God, you seek not the death of sinners but you always seek that they may live; graciously accept our prayer and free them from the worship of idols and bring them into the flock of your holy Church, for the praise and glory of your name.

Here there is a clear recognition of some distinction among barbarians, as the Church suggests in rather precise terms. Moreover, from everything that was brought forth above it is clear that there are four classes of barbarians and that the first, second, and fourth classes are based in some way on certain fierce practices and especially on their lack of faith. Now the first class can include even Christian men if, in some way, they manifest fierceness, wildness, savagery, and cruelty. It is on this basis that the Spaniards who have maltreated the Indians—harmless peoples who are far gentler than all others—with so many horrible defeats, so many massacres, and evils worse than hell itself are barbarians and worse than barbarians. They also showed that they are barbarians when they insolently took up arms and rebelled against the emperor. Now the fourth kind of barbarian refers to those who are outside the faith of Christ, and this includes all unbelievers.

Barbarians in the strict sense of the term, however, are those about whom we spoke in the third class, that is, those who are sunk in insensitivity of mind, ignorant, irrational, lacking ability, inhuman, fierce, corrupted by foul morals and unsettled by nature or by reason of their depraved habits of sin. And about such men the Philosopher speaks in a special way in the first book of the *Politics*. So let the ungodly men, and those who have enticed Sepúlveda to defend an evil cause by lies, stop citing the Philosopher in opposition to our position. They do not understand or do not want to understand the distinction the Philosopher and the holy doctors have shown in regard to barbarians. Let them take pity on their own souls and let them pray to Christ so that falsehood may die in them and truth live.

Sor Juana Inés de la Cruz (1651–1695)

In 1651 Juana Ramírez de Asbaje, known to us as Sor Juana Inés de la Cruz, was born in San Miguel Nepantla, a village south of Mexico City. Her father died when she was a young girl, so she was raised by her widowed mother. In 1660 Sor Juana was sent to Mexico City to live with her maternal grandfather, who shared the books of his impressive library with the young, intellectually inquisitive girl. By all accounts, the young Sor Juana was remarkably intelligent. In 1662 she entered the court of the viceroy's wife and was widely admired. In 1669 she entered the Order of the Jerónimas. In the convent she devoted herself to study and writing, remaining there until her death.

There has been much speculation regarding her motivation for becoming a nun. By all accounts, there was no shortage of available and willing suitors. Yet, for a woman of the time in New Spain (as Mexico was then known), there was little space for her participation in intellectual life. The convent offered a kind of refuge from society and, within its confines, women were able, even if still within all too narrow limits, to study and to write. Sor Juana's mind was attracted to all areas of knowledge, ranging from poetry and music, to science. Her room was filled with books and her work tables covered with instruments to measure the movements of the heavens.

Sor Juana's writing developed through her reading of authors from the sixteenth century; especially strong is the influence of the Spanish writers Luis de Góngora and Pedro Calderón de la Barca. Much of her work was done at the request of friends or her superiors. She produced poetry, drama, and philosophy. Her style ranged from the somber, serious tone of certain poems, to the fun word plays typical of *conceptismo* and *gongorismo*, which she used when writing for friends or to mask the

51

meaning of her work and keep authorities at bay. Irony became a kind of shield used by Sor Juana to protect herself from the censure of superiors.

Sor Juana continues to draw the attention of scholars today. Mexican writer and Nobel laureate for literature Octavio Paz dedicated a book and several essays to the contributions made by Sor Juana to the development of Mexican literature. And several contemporary feminists hail her as a path-breaking figure in creating an intellectual space for women. Sor Juana died in 1695, while tending to the victims of an epidemic in Mexico City.

Response to Sister Filotea

W ell, and what then shall I tell you, my Lady, of the secrets of nature that I have learned while cooking? I observe that an egg becomes solid and cooks in butter or oil, and on the contrary that it dissolves in sugar syrup. Or again, to ensure that sugar flow freely one need only add the slightest bit of water that has held quince or some other sour fruit. The yolk and white of the very same egg are of such a contrary nature that when eggs are used with sugar, each part separately may be used perfectly well, yet they cannot be mixed together. I shall not weary you with such inanities, which I relate simply to give you a full account of my nature, and I believe this will make you laugh. But in truth, my Lady, what can we women know, save philosophies of the kitchen? It was well put by Lupercio Leonardo [sic] that one can philosophize quite well while preparing supper. I often say, when I make these little observations, "Had Aristotle cooked, he would have written a great deal more." And so to go on with the mode of my cogitations: I declare that all this is so continual in me that I have no need of books. On one occasion, because of a severe stomach ailment, doctors forbade me to study. I spent several days in that state, and then quickly proposed to them that it would be less harmful to allow me my books, for my cogitations were so strenuous and vehement that they consumed more vitality in a quarter of an hour than the reading of books could in four days. And so the doctors were compelled to let me read. What is more, my Lady, not even my sleep has been free of this ceaseless movement of my imagination. Rather, my mind operates in sleep still more freely and unobstructedly, ordering with greater clarity and ease the events it has preserved from the day, presenting arguments and composing verses. I could give you a very long catalogue of these, as I could of certain reasonings and subtle turns I have reached far better in my sleep than while awake; but I leave them out in order not to weary you. I have said enough for your judgment and your surpassing eminence to comprehend my nature with clarity and full understanding, together with the beginnings, the methods, and the present state of my studies.

If studies, my Lady, be merits (for indeed I see them extolled as such in men), in me they are no such thing: I study because I must. If they be a failing, I believe for the same reason that the fault is none of mine. Yet withal, I live always so wary of myself that neither in this nor in anything else do I trust my own judgment. And so I entrust the decision to your supreme skill and straightway submit to whatever sentence you may pass, posing no objection or reluctance, for this has been no more than a simple account of my inclination to letters.

I confess also that, while in truth this inclination has been such that, as I said before, I had no need of exemplars, nevertheless the many books that I have read have not failed to help me, both in sacred as well as secular letters. For there I see a Deborah issuing laws, military as well as political, and governing the people among whom there were so many learned men. I see the exceedingly knowledgeable Queen of Sheba, so learned she dares to test the wisdom of the wisest of all wise men with riddles, without being rebuked for it; indeed, on this very account she is to become judge of the unbelievers. I see so many and such significant women: some adorned with the gift of prophecy, like an Abigail; others, of persuasion, like Esther; others, of piety, like Rahab; others, of perseverance, like Anna [Hannah] the mother of Samuel; and others, infinitely more, with other kinds of qualities and virtues.

If I consider the Gentiles, the first I meet are the Sibyls, chosen by God to prophesy the essential mysteries of our Faith in such learned and elegant verses that they stupefy the imagination. I see a woman such as Minerva, daughter of great Jupiter and mistress of all the wisdom of Athens, adored as goddess of the sciences. I see one Polla Argentaria, who helped Lucan, her husband, to write the *Battle of Pharsalia*. I see the daughter of the divine Tiresias, more learned still than her father. I see, too, such a woman as Zenobia, queen of the Palmyrians, as wise as she was courageous. Again, I see an Arete, daughter of Aristippus, most learned. A Nicostrata, inventor of Latin letters and most erudite in the Greek. An Aspasia Miletia, who taught philosophy and rhetoric and was the teacher of the philosopher Pericles. And Hypatia, who taught astrology and lectured for many years in Alexandria. A Leontium, who won over the philosopher Theophrastus and proved him wrong. A Julia, a Corinna, a Cornelia; and, in sum, the vast throng of women who merited titles and earned renown: now as Greeks, again as Muses, and yet again as Pythonesses. For what were they all but learned women, who were considered, celebrated, and indeed venerated as such in Antiquity? Without mentioning still others, of whom the books are full; for I see the Egyptian Catherine, lecturing and refuting all the learning of the most learned men of Egypt. I see a Gertrude read, write, and teach. And seeking no more examples far from home, I see my own most holy mother Paula, learned in the Hebrew, Greek, and Latin tongues and most expert in the interpretation of the Scriptures. What wonder then can it be that, though her chronicler was no less than the unequaled Jerome, the Saint found himself scarcely worthy of the task, for with that lively gravity and energetic effectiveness with which only he can express himself, he says: "If all the parts of my body were tongues, they would not suffice to proclaim the learning and virtues of Paula." Blessilla, a widow, earned the same praises, as did the luminous virgin Eustochium, both of them daughters of the Saint herself [Paula]; and indeed Eustochium was such that for her knowledge she was hailed as a World Prodigy. Fabiola, also a Roman, was another most learned in Holy Scripture. Proba Falconia, a Roman woman, wrote an elegant book of centos, joining together verses from Virgil, on the mysteries of our holy Faith. Our Queen Isabella, wife of Alfonso X, is known to have written on astrology—without mentioning others, whom I omit so as not merely to copy what others have said (which is a vice I have always detested): Well then, in our own day there thrive the great Christina Alexandra, Queen of Sweden, as learned as she is brave and generous; and too those most excellent ladies, the Duchess of Aveyro and the Countess of Villaumbrosa.

The venerable Dr. Arce (worthy professor of Scripture, known for his virtue and learning), in his *For the Scholar of the Bible*, raises this question: "Is it permissible for women to apply themselves to the study, and indeed the interpretation, of the Holy Bible?" And in opposition he presents the verdicts passed by many saints, particularly the words of [Paul] the Apostle: "Let women keep silence in the churches: for it is not permitted them to speak," etc. Arce then presents differing verdicts, including this passage addressed to Titus, again spoken by the Apostle: "The aged women, in like manner, in holy attire . . . teaching well"; and he gives other interpretations from the Fathers of the Church. Arce at last resolves, in his prudent way, that women are not allowed to lecture publicly in the universities or to preach from the pulpits, but that studying, writing, and teaching privately is not only permitted but most beneficial and useful to them. Clearly, of course, he does not mean by this that all women should do so, but only those whom God may have seen fit to endow with special virtue and prudence, and who are very mature and erudite and possess the necessary talents and requirements for such a sacred occupation. And so just is this distinction that not only women, who are held to be so incompetent, but also men, who simply because they are men think themselves wise, are to be prohibited from the interpretation of the Sacred Word, save when they are most learned, virtuous, of amenable intellect and inclined to the good. For when the reverse is true, I believe, numerous sectarians are produced, and this has given rise to numerous heresies. For there are many who study only to become ignorant, especially those of arrogant, restless, and prideful spirits, fond of innovations in the Law (the very thing that rejects all innovation). And so they are not content until for the sake of saying what no one before them has said, they speak heresy. Of such men as these the Holy Spirit says: "For wisdom will not enter into a malicious soul." For them, more harm is worked by knowledge than by ignorance. A wit once observed that he who knows no Latin is not an utter fool, but he who does know it has met the prerequisites. And I might add that he is made a perfect fool (if foolishness can attain perfection) by having studied his bit of philosophy and theology and by knowing something of languages. For with that he can be foolish in several sciences and tongues; a great fool cannot be contained in his mother tongue alone.

To such men, I repeat, study does harm, because it is like putting a sword in the hands of a madman: though the sword be the noblest of instruments for defense, in his hands it becomes his own death and that of many others. This is what the Divine Letters became in the hands of that wicked Pelagius and of the perverse Arius, of that wicked Luther, and all the other heretics, like our own Dr. Cazalla (who was never either our own nor a doctor). Learning harmed them all, though it can be the best nourishment and life for the soul. For just as an infirm stomach, suffering from diminished heat, produces more bitter, putrid, and perverse humors the better the food that it is given, so too these evil persons give rise to worse opinions the more they study. Their understanding is obstructed by the very thing that should nourish it, and the fact is they study a great deal and digest very little, failing to measure their efforts to the narrow vessel of their understanding. In this regard the Apostle has said: "For I say, by the grace that is given me, to all that are among you, not to be more wise than it behoveth to be wise, but to be wise unto sobriety, and according as God hath divided to every one the measure of faith." And in truth the Apostle said this not to women but to men, and the "Let [them] keep silence" was meant not only for women, but for all those who are not very competent. If I wish to know as much as or more than Aristotle or St. Augustine, but I lack the ability of a St. Augustine or an Aristotle, then I may study more than both of them together, but I shall not only fail to reach my goal: I shall weaken and stupefy the workings of my feeble understanding with such a disproportionate aim.

Oh, that all men—and I, who am but an ignorant woman, first of all— might take the measure of our abilities before setting out to study and,

what is worse, to write, in our jealous aspiration to equal and even surpass others. How little boldness would we summon, how many errors
might we avoid, and how many distorted interpretations now noised
abroad should be noised no further! And I place my own before all others,
for if I knew all that I ought, I would not so much as write these words.
Yet I protest that I do so only to obey you; and with such misgiving that
you owe me more for taking up my pen with all this fear than you would
owe me were I to present you with the most perfect works. But withal, it
is well that this goes to meet with your correction: erase it, tear it up, and
chastise me, for I shall value that more than all the vain applause others
could give me. "The just man shall correct me in mercy, and shall reprove
me: but let not the oil of the sinner fatten my head."

And returning to our own Arce, I observe that in support of his views
he presents these words of my father St. Jerome (in the letter *To Leta, on
the Education of Her Daughter*), where he says: "[Her] childish tongue
must be imbued with the sweet music of the Psalms. . . . The very words
from which she will get into the way of forming sentences should not be
taken at haphazard but be definitely chosen and arranged on purpose. For
example, let her have the names of the prophets and the apostles, and the
whole list of patriarchs from Adam downwards, as Matthew and Luke give
it. She will then be doing two things at the same time, and will remember
them afterwards. . . . Let her every day repeat to you a portion of the
Scriptures as her fixed task." Very well, if the Saint wished a little girl,
scarcely beginning to speak, to be instructed thus, what must he desire for
his nuns and spiritual daughters? We see this most clearly in the women
already mentioned—Eustochium and Fabiola—and also in Marcella, the
latter's sister; in Pacatula, and in other women whom the Saint honors in
his epistles, urging them on in this holy exercise. This appears in the letter
already cited, where I noted the words "let her repeat to you . . ." which
serve to reclaim and confirm St. Paul's description, "teaching well." For
the "let her repeat the task to you" of my great Father makes clear that the
little girl's teacher must be Leta herself, the girl's mother.

Oh, how many abuses would be avoided in our land if the older
women were as well instructed as Leta and knew how to teach as is com-
manded by St. Paul and my father St. Jerome! Instead, for lack of such
learning and through the extreme feebleness in which they are determined
to maintain our poor women, if any parents then wish to give their daughters more extensive Christian instruction than is usual, necessity and the
lack of learned older women oblige them to employ men as instructors to
teach reading and writing, numbers and music, and other skills. This
leads to considerable harm, which occurs every day in doleful instances
of these unsuitable associations. For the immediacy of such contact and
the passage of time all too frequently allow what seemed impossible to be

accomplished quite easily. For this reason, many parents prefer to let their daughters remain uncivilized and untutored, rather than risk exposing them to such notorious peril as this familiarity with men. Yet all this could be avoided if there were old women of sound education, as St. Paul desires, so that instruction could be passed from the old to the young just as is done with sewing and all the customary skills.

For what impropriety can there be if an older woman, learned in letters and holy conversation and customs, should have in her charge the education of young maids? Better so than to let these young girls go to perdition, either for lack of any Christian teaching or because one tries to impart it through such dangerous means as male teachers. For if there were no greater risk than the simple indecency of seating a completely unknown man at the side of a bashful woman (who blushes if her own father should look her straight in the face), allowing him to address her with household familiarity and to speak to her with intimate authority, even so the modesty demanded in interchange with men and in conversation with them gives sufficient cause to forbid this. Indeed, I do not see how the custom of men as teachers of women can be without its dangers, save only in the strict tribunal of the confessional, or the distant teachings of the pulpit, or the remote wisdom of books; but never in the repeated handling that occurs in such immediate and tarnishing contact. And everyone knows this to be true. Nevertheless, it is permitted for no better reason than the lack of learned older women; therefore, it does great harm not to have them. This point should be taken into account by those who, tied to the "Let women keep silence in the churches," curse the idea that women should acquire knowledge and teach, as if it were not the Apostle himself who described them "teaching well." Furthermore, that prohibition applied to the case related by Eusebius: to wit, that in the early Church, women were set to teaching each other Christian doctrine in the temples. The murmur of their voices caused confusion when the apostles were preaching, and that is why they were told to be silent. Just so, we see today that when the preacher is preaching, no one prays aloud.

Poem 92, Philosophical Satire

1 You foolish and unreasoning men
who cast all blame on women,
not seeing you yourselves are cause
of the same faults you accuse:

2 if, with eagerness unequaled,
you plead against women's disdain,
why require them to do well
when you inspire them to fall?

[handwritten: ironic: if women do well, they are submissive to what men desire, if the inverse, they are still falling victim to the standards of men.]

3 You combat their firm resistance,
and then solemnly pronounce
that what you've won through diligence
is proof of women's flightiness.

4 What do we see, when we see you
madly determined to see us so,
but the child who makes a monster appear
and then goes trembling with fear?

[handwritten: maternal instincts, post-partum depression]

5 With ridiculous conceit
you insist that woman be
a sultry Thais while you woo her;
a true Lucretia once she's won.

6 Whose behavior could be odder
than that of a stubborn man
who himself breathes on the mirror,
and then laments it is not clear?

*[handwritten: * Men made restrictions on women, then blame them for their faults]*

7 Women's good favor, women's scorn
you hold in equal disregard:
complaining, if they treat you badly;
mocking, if they love you well.

8 Not one can gain your good opinion,
for she who modestly withdraws
and fails to admit you is ungrateful;
yet if she admits you, too easily won.

[handwritten: there is no winning as a woman in society]

Reprinted from *The Answer/La Respuesta*, pp. 157, 159, copyright © 1994 by Electa Arenal and Amanda Powell, by permission of the Feminist Press at the City University of New York, www.feministpress.org.

9   So downright foolish are you all
    that your injurious justice claims
    to blame one woman's cruelty
    and fault the other's laxity.

10 How then can she be moderate
    to whom your suit aspires,
    if, ingrate, she makes you displeased,
    or, easy, prompts your ire?

11 Between such ire and such anguish
    —the tales your fancy tells—
    lucky is she who does not love you;
    complain then, as you will!

12 Your doting anguish feathers the wings
    of liberties that women take,
    and once you've caused them to be bad,
    you want to find them as good as saints.

13 But who has carried greater blame
    in a passion gone astray:
    she who falls to constant pleading,
    or he who pleads with her to fall?

14 Or which more greatly must be faulted,
    though either may commit a wrong:
    she who sins for need of payment,
    or he who pays for his enjoyment?

15 Why then are you so alarmed
    by the fault that is your own?
    Wish women to be what you make them,
    or make them what you wish they were.

16 Leave off soliciting her fall
    and then indeed, more justified,
    that eagerness you might accuse
    of the woman who besieges you.

17 Thus I prove with all my forces
    the ways your arrogance does battle:
    for in your offers and your demands
    we have devil, flesh, and world: a man.

Simón Bolívar
(1783–1830)

Simón Bolívar is one of the most important figures in the history of Latin America, both as a thinker and as a man of action. Born in Caracas, Venezuela, in 1783 to a wealthy family, he was orphaned at the young age of nine. Subsequently, he was raised by his maternal grandparents. He received a European education at home by private tutors and was familiar with the liberal and republican ideals of the French Enlightenment. Andrés Bello (1781–1865), one of Venezuela's most important intellectual figures, was Bolívar's tutor.

In 1799, with the death of his grandfather, Bolívar was sent to Spain and France to continue his studies. He returned briefly to Caracas and then, in 1803, traveled to Paris, where the revolutionary zeal of the city influenced him. On August 15, 1805, Bolívar is said to have announced in Rome that he would devote his life to the cause of independence. Before returning to Caracas in June of 1806, Bolívar made a brief visit to the United States, which served to invigorate his revolutionary goals. Napoleon's invasion of Spain in 1808 opened a space for the young revolutionaries of Venezuela, who used the instability of the Spanish Crown to move from ideas of a revolution to the first steps toward its realization. This revolutionary action led to Bolívar's imprisonment in 1808 and marked his official public entry onto the political stage.

In Venezuela, Bolívar worked as a diplomat, a statesman, and then, in his most important role, as a general in the revolutionary army that ultimately defeated the royalist Spanish troops and led to the establishment of the countries known today as Venezuela, Colombia, Ecuador, Peru, Bolivia, and Panama. Because of his pivotal and leading role in the independence movement, Bolívar is known as "*el Libertador*" (the Liberator). Between 1817 and 1826 Bolívar fought tirelessly to free and maintain the

61

independence of most of South America. He led the Viceroyalties of New Granada (which had Bogotá as its capital and consisted of present-day Colombia, Venezuela, Panama, and Ecuador) and Peru to independence. He then established present-day Bolivia (named after him), by separating Alto Peru from the rest of Peru and proclaiming it a separate territory.

Bolívar is the undisputed hero of the independence movements in Latin America and is respected as a great military genius. In 1819 he became the president of Gran Colombia. His dream was the establishment of a continental union. Yet, this plan never reached fruition and all attempts in the direction of unifying the newly independent regions were futile, leading Bolívar to believe that the project was impossible. As all hope of Pan-Americanism withered, Bolívar himself became disillusioned, claiming that "America is ungovernable. Those who served the revolution plowed the sea." He died in Colombia, of tuberculosis, in 1830.

Jamaica Letter

REPLY OF A SOUTH AMERICAN TO A GENTLEMAN OF THIS ISLAND [JAMAICA]

[Blanco y Aspurúa, V, 331–342]

Kingston, Jamaica, September 6, 1815.

My dear Sir:

I hasten to reply to the letter of the 29th ultimo which you had the honor of sending me and which I received with the greatest satisfaction.

Sensible though I am of the interest you desire to take in the fate of my country, and of your commiseration with her for the tortures she has suffered from the time of her discovery until the present at the hands of her destroyers, the Spaniards, I am no less sensible of the obligation which your solicitous inquiries about the principal objects of American policy place upon me. Thus, I find myself in conflict between the desire to reciprocate your confidence, which honors me, and the difficulty of rewarding it, for lack of documents and books and because of my own limited knowledge of a land so vast, so varied, and so little known as the New World.

In my opinion it is impossible to answer the questions that you have so kindly posed. Baron von Humboldt himself, with his encyclopedic theoretical and practical knowledge, could hardly do so properly, because, although some of the facts about America and her development are known, I dare say the better part are shrouded in mystery. Accordingly, only con-

From "Reply of a South American to a Gentleman of This Island [Jamaica]," trans. Lewis Bertrand, published by Banco de Venezuela (New York: Colonial Press, 1951), pp. 103–105, 109–11.

jectures that are more or less approximate can be made, especially with regard to her future and the true plans of the Americans, inasmuch as our continent has within it potentialities for every facet of development revealed in the history of nations, by reason of its physical characteristics and because of the hazards of war and the uncertainties of politics.

As I feel obligated to give due consideration to your esteemed letter and to the philanthropic intentions prompting it, I am impelled to write you these words, wherein you will certainly not find the brilliant thoughts you seek but rather a candid statement of my ideas.

"Three centuries ago," you say, "began the atrocities committed by the Spaniards on this great hemisphere of Columbus." Our age has rejected these atrocities as mythical, because they appear to be beyond the human capacity for evil. Modern critics would never credit them were it not for the many and frequent documents testifying to these horrible truths. The humane Bishop of Chiapas, that apostle of America, Las Casas, has left to posterity a brief description of these horrors, extracted from the trial records in Sevilla relating to the cases brought against the *conquistadores*, and containing the testimony of every respectable person then in the New World, together with the charges [*procesos*], which the tyrants made against each other. All this is attested by the foremost historians of that time. Every impartial person has admitted the zeal, sincerity, and high character of that friend of humanity, who so fervently and so steadfastly denounced to his government and to his contemporaries the most horrible acts of sanguinary frenzy.

With what a feeling of gratitude I read that passage in your letter in which you say to me: "I hope that the success which then followed Spanish arms may now turn in favor of their adversaries, the badly oppressed people of South America." I take this hope as a prediction, if it is justice that determines man's contests. Success will crown our efforts, because the destiny of America has been irrevocably decided; the tie that bound her to Spain has been severed. Only a concept maintained that tie and kept the parts of that immense monarchy together. That which formerly bound them now divides them. The hatred that the Peninsula has inspired in us is greater than the ocean between us. It would be easier to have the two continents meet than to reconcile the spirits of the two countries. The habit of obedience; a community of interest, of understanding, of religion; mutual goodwill; a tender regard for the birthplace and good name of our forefathers; in short, all that gave rise to our hopes, came to us from Spain. As a result there was born a principle of affinity that seemed eternal, notwithstanding the misbehavior of our rulers which weakened that sympathy, or, rather, that bond enforced by the domination of their rule. At present the contrary attitude persists: we are threatened with the fear of death, dishonor, and every harm; there is nothing we have not suffered at the hands of that unnatural step-mother—Spain. The veil has been torn asunder. We have already seen the light, and it is not our desire to be thrust back into darkness. The chains have been broken; we have been freed, and now our enemies seek to enslave us anew. For this reason America fights desperately, and seldom has desperation failed to achieve victory.

Because successes have been partial and spasmodic, we must not lose faith. In some regions the Independents triumph, while in others the tyrants have the advantage. What is the end result? Is not the entire New World in motion, armed for defense? We have but to look around us on this hemisphere to witness a simultaneous struggle at every point. . . .

I have listed the population, which is based on more or less exact data, but which a thousand circumstances render deceiving. This inaccuracy cannot easily be remedied, because most of the inhabitants live in rural areas and are often nomadic; they are farmers, herders, and migrants, lost amidst thick giant forests, solitary plains, and isolated by lakes and mighty streams. Who is capable of compiling complete statistics of a land like this? Moreover, the tribute paid by the Indians, the punishments of the slaves, the first fruits of the harvest [*primicias*], tithes [*diezmas*], and taxes levied on farmers, and other impositions have driven the poor Americans from their homes. This is not to mention the war of extermination that has already taken a toll of nearly an eighth part of the population and frightened another large part away. All in all, the difficulties are insuperable, and the tally is likely to show only half the true count.

It is even more difficult to foresee the future fate of the New World, to set down its political principles, or to prophesy what manner of government it will adopt. Every conjecture relative to America's future is, I feel, pure speculation. When mankind was in its infancy, steeped in uncertainty, ignorance, and error, was it possible to foresee what system it would adopt for its preservation? Who could venture to say that a certain nation would be a republic or a monarchy; this nation great, that nation small? To my way of thinking, such is our own situation. We are a young people. We inhabit a world apart, separated by broad seas. We are young in the ways of almost all the arts and sciences, although, in a certain manner, we are old in the ways of civilized society. I look upon the present state of America as similar to that of Rome after its fall. Each part of Rome adopted a political system conforming to its interest and situation or was led by the individual ambitions of certain chiefs, dynasties, or associations. But this important difference exists: those dispersed parts later reestablished their ancient nations, subject to the changes imposed by circumstances or events. But we scarcely retain a vestige of what once was; we are, moreover, neither Indian nor European, but a species midway between the legitimate proprietors of this country and the Spanish usurpers. In short, though Americans by birth we derive our rights from Europe, and we have to assert these rights against the rights of the natives, and at the same time we must defend ourselves against the invaders. This places us in a most extraordinary and involved situation. Notwithstanding that it is a type of divination to predict the result of the political course which America is pursuing, I shall venture some conjectures which, of course, are colored by my enthusiasm and dictated by rational desires rather than by reasoned calculations.

The role of the inhabitants of the American hemisphere has for centuries been purely passive. Politically they were nonexistent. We are still in a position lower than slavery, and therefore it is more difficult for us to rise to the enjoyment of freedom. Permit me these transgressions in order to establish the issue. States are slaves because of either the nature or the misuse of their constitutions; a people is therefore enslaved when the government, by its nature or its vices, infringes on and usurps the rights of the citizen or subject. Applying these principles, we find that America was denied not only its freedom but even an active and effective tyranny. Let me explain. Under absolutism there are no recognized limits to the exercise of governmental powers. The will of the great sultan, khan, bey, and other despotic rulers is the supreme law, carried out more or less arbitrarily by the lesser pashas, khans, and satraps of Turkey and Persia, who have an organized system of oppression in which inferiors participate according to the authority vested in them. To them is entrusted the administration of civil, military, political, religious, and tax matters. But, after all is said and done, the rulers of Ispahan are Persians; the viziers of the Grand Turk are Turks; and the sultans of Tartary are Tartars. China does not bring its military leaders and scholars from the land of Genghis Khan, her conqueror, notwithstanding that the Chinese of today are the lineal descendants of those who were reduced to subjection by the ancestors of the present-day Tartars.

How different is our situation! We have been harassed by a conduct which has not only deprived us of our rights but has kept us in a sort of permanent infancy with regard to public affairs. If we could at least have managed our domestic affairs and our internal administration, we could have acquainted ourselves with the processes and mechanics of public affairs. We should also have enjoyed a personal consideration, thereby commanding a certain unconscious respect from the people, which is so necessary to preserve amidst revolutions. That is why I say we have even been deprived of an active tyranny, since we have not been permitted to exercise its functions.

Address Delivered at the Inauguration of the Second National Congress of Venezuela at Angostura

Angostura, February 15, 1819.

Gentlemen:

Fortunate is the citizen, who, under the emblem of his command, has convoked this assembly of the national sovereignty so that it may exercise its absolute will! I, therefore, place myself among those most favored by Divine Providence, for I have had the honor of uniting the representatives of the people of Venezuela in this august Congress, the source of legitimate authority, the custodian of the sovereign will, and the arbiter of the Nation's destiny.

In returning to the representatives of the people the Supreme Power which was entrusted to me, I gratify not only my own innermost desires but also those of my fellow-citizens and of future generations, who trust to your wisdom, rectitude, and prudence in all things. Upon the fulfillment of this grateful obligation, I shall be released from the immense authority with which I have been burdened and from the unlimited responsibility which has weighed so heavily upon my slender resources. Only the force of necessity, coupled with the imperious will of the people, compelled me to assume the fearful and dangerous post of *Dictator and Supreme Chief of the Republic*. But now I can breathe more freely, for I am returning to you this authority which I have succeeded in maintaining at the price of so much danger, hardship, and suffering, amidst the worst tribulations suffered by any society.

From "Address Delivered at the Inauguration of the Second National Congress of Venezuela at Angostura," trans. Lewis Bertrand, Banco de Venezuela (New York: Colonial Press, 1951), pp. 173–77, 182–83, 191–92.

The period in the history of the Republic over which I presided was not one of mere political storm; nor was it simply a bloody war or merely popular anarchy. It was, indeed, the culmination of every disruptive force. It was the flood-tide of a devastating torrent which overran the good earth of Venezuela. What barriers could one man—a man such as myself—erect to stay the onrush of such devastation? In the midst of that sea of troubles, I was but a mere plaything in the hurricane of revolution that tossed me about like so much straw. I could do neither good nor evil. Irresistible forces directed the course of our events. To attribute these forces to me would not be just, for it would place upon me an importance that I do not merit. Do you wish to know who is responsible for the events of the past and the present? Consult the annals of Spain, of America, and of Venezuela; examine the Laws of the Indies, the one-time system of *mandatarios*, the influence of religion and of foreign rule; observe the first acts of the republican government, the ferocity of our enemies, and our national character. Do not question me about the effects of these ever-to-be-lamented catastrophes; for I am but a simple instrument of the great driving forces that have left their mark on Venezuela. Nevertheless, my life, my conduct, my every public and private action—all are subject to public censure. Representatives! You must judge my actions. I submit the record of my rule for your impartial verdict: I shall add nothing in its favor, for I have already said all that can be said in my behalf. If I obtain your approbation, I shall have achieved the sublime title of Good Citizen, which I prefer to that of *Liberator* given me by Venezuela, or that of *Pacificator* accorded me by Cundinamarca, or to any title the world at large might confer upon me.

Legislators! I deliver into your hands the supreme rule of Venezuela. Yours is now the august duty of consecrating yourselves to the achievement of felicity of the Republic; your hands hold the scales of our destiny, the measure of our glory. They shall seal the decrees that will insure our liberty. At this moment the Supreme Chief of the Republic is no more than just a plain citizen, and such he wishes to remain until his death. I shall, however, serve as a soldier so long as any foe remains in Venezuela. Our country has a multitude of worthy sons who are capable of directing her progress. Talent, virtue, experience, and all else needed to command free men are the heritage of many who represent the people here; and outside this Sovereign Body there are citizens who at all times have shown courage in facing danger, prudence in avoiding it, and the ability, moreover, to govern themselves and others. These illustrious men will undoubtedly deserve the support of the Congress, and they will be entrusted with the government which I now so sincerely and gladly relinquish forever.

The continuance of authority in the same individual has frequently meant the end of democratic governments. Repeated elections are essential in popular systems of government, for nothing is more perilous than to permit one citizen to retain power for an extended period. The people become accustomed to obeying him, and he forms the habit of commanding them; herein lie the origins of usurpation and tyranny. A just zeal is the guarantee of republican liberty. Our citizens must with good reason learn to fear lest the magistrate who has governed them long will govern them forever.

Since, therefore, by this profession of mine in support of Venezuela's freedom I may aspire to the glory of being reckoned among her most faithful sons, allow me, Gentlemen, to expound, with the frankness of a true republican, my respectful opinion on a *Plan of a Constitution*, which I take the liberty of submitting to you as testimony of the candor and sincerity of my sentiments. As this plan concerns the welfare of all, I venture to assume that I have the right to be heard by the representatives of the people. I well know that your wisdom needs no counsel, and I know also that my plan may perhaps appear to be mistaken and impracticable. But I implore you, Gentlemen, receive this work with benevolence, for it is more a tribute of my sincere deference to the Congress than an act of presumption. Moreover, as your function is to create a body politic, or, it might be said, to create an entire society while surrounded by every obstacle that a most peculiar and difficult situation can present, perhaps the voice of one citizen may reveal the presence of a hidden or unknown danger.

Let us review the past to discover the base upon which the Republic of Venezuela is founded.

America, in separating from the Spanish monarchy, found herself in a situation similar to that of the Roman Empire when its enormous framework fell to pieces in the midst of the ancient world. Each Roman division then formed an independent nation in keeping with its location or interests; but this situation differed from America's in that those members proceeded to reestablish their former associations. We, on the contrary, do not even retain the vestiges of our original being. We are not Europeans; we are not Indians; we are but a mixed species of aborigines and Spaniards. Americans by birth and Europeans by law, we find ourselves engaged in a dual conflict: we are disputing with the natives for titles of ownership, and at the same time we are struggling to maintain ourselves in the country that gave us birth against the opposition of the invaders. Thus our position is most extraordinary and complicated. But there is more. As our role has always been strictly passive and our political existence nil, we find that our quest for liberty is now even more difficult of accomplishment; for we, having been placed in a state lower than slavery, had been robbed not only of our freedom but also of the right to exercise an active domestic tyranny. . . .

Subject to the threefold yoke of ignorance, tyranny, and vice, the American people have been unable to acquire knowledge, power, or [civic] virtue. The lessons we received and the models we studied, as pupils of such pernicious teachers, were most destructive. We have been ruled more by deceit than by force, and we have been degraded more by vice than by superstition. Slavery is the daughter of Darkness: an ignorant people is a blind instrument of its own destruction. Ambition and intrigue abuse the credulity and experience of men lacking all political, economic, and civic knowledge; they adopt pure illusion as reality; they take license for liberty, treachery for patriotism, and vengeance for justice. This situation is similar to that of the robust blind man who, beguiled by his strength, strides forward with all the assurance of one who can see, but, upon hitting every variety of obstacle, finds himself unable to retrace his steps.

If a people, perverted by their training, succeed in achieving their liberty, they will soon lose it, for it would be of no avail to endeavor to explain to them that happiness consists in the practice of virtue; that the rule of law is more powerful than the rule of tyrants, because, as the laws are more inflexible, everyone should submit to their beneficent austerity; that proper morals, and not force, are the bases of law; and that to practice justice is to practice liberty. Therefore, Legislators, your work is so much the more arduous, inasmuch as you have to reeducate men who have been corrupted by erroneous illusions and false incentives. Liberty, says Rousseau, is a succulent morsel, but one difficult to digest. Our weak fellow-citizens will have to strengthen their spirit greatly before they can digest the wholesome nutriment of freedom. Their limbs benumbed by chains, their sight dimmed by the darkness of dungeons, and their strength sapped by the pestilence of servitude, are they capable of marching toward the august temple of Liberty without faltering? Can they come near enough to bask in its brilliant rays and to breathe freely the pure air which reigns therein?

Legislators, meditate well before you choose. Forget not that you are to lay the political foundation for a newly born nation which can rise to the heights of greatness that Nature has marked out for it if you but proportion this foundation in keeping with the high plane that it aspires to attain. Unless your choice is based upon the peculiar tutelary experience of the Venezuelan people—a factor that should guide you in determining the nature and form of government you are about to adopt for the wellbeing of the people—and, I repeat, unless you happen upon the right type of government, the result of our reforms will again be slavery. . . .

Having dealt with justice and humanity, let us now give attention to politics and society, and let us resolve the difficulties inherent in a system so simple and natural, yet so weak that the slightest obstacle can upset and destroy it. The diversity of racial origin will require an infinitely firm hand and great tactfulness in order to manage this heterogeneous society, whose complicated mechanism is easily damaged, separated, and disintegrated by the slightest controversy.

The most perfect system of government is that which results in the greatest possible measure of happiness and the maximum of social security [*seguridad social*] and political stability. The laws enacted by the first Congress gave us reason to hope that happiness would be the lot of Venezuela; and, through your laws, we must hope that security and stability will perpetuate this happiness. *You* must solve the problem. But how, having broken all the shackles of our former oppression, can we accomplish the enormous task of preventing the remnants of our past fetters from becoming liberty-destroying weapons? The vestiges of Spanish domination will long be with us before we can completely eradicate them: the contagion of despotism infests the atmosphere about us, and neither the fires of war nor the healing properties of our salutary laws have purified the air we breathe. Our hands are now free, but our hearts still suffer the ills of slavery. When man loses freedom, said Homer, he loses half his spirit. . . .

. . . Unless there is a sacred reverence for country, laws, and authority, society becomes confused, an abyss—an endless conflict of man versus man, group versus group.

All our moral powers will not suffice to save our infant republic from this chaos unless we fuse the mass of the people, the government, the legislation, and the national spirit into a single united body. Unity, unity, unity must be our motto in all things. The blood of our citizens is varied: let it be mixed for the sake of unity. Our Constitution has divided the powers of government: let them be bound together to secure unity. Our laws are but a sad relic of ancient and modern despotism. Let this monstrous edifice crumble and fall; and, having removed even its ruins, let us erect a temple to Justice; and, guided by its sacred inspiration, let us write a code of Venezuelan laws.

PART II
Philosophical
Anthropology

Introduction

THE ANTHROPOLOGICAL ISSUE

Western philosophy has always struggled with the concept of humanity, but it was only toward the latter part of the nineteenth century and the beginning of the twentieth that this issue came to a prominent position in philosophical thought. The latter part of this period, extending into the twenty-first century, is the primary focus of Part II of this collection of readings, and it seeks to provide a general overview of the way the anthropological issue has been confronted by Latin American philosophers.

The most striking characteristic of philosophical anthropology as encountered in Latin American thought is the variety of the approaches used in it. In contrast to the precision and the well-defined boundaries within which the problem of value is formulated (see the introduction to Part III)—with focus on the conflict between axiological objectivism and subjectivism—philosophical anthropology is approached in a multifaceted, complex manner. Positivists at the end of the nineteenth century and throughout the twentieth were concerned with the psychological description of humans in order to resolve the mind-body problem; neo-scholastics concentrated their efforts on the investigation of the universal and eternal essence of human beings; philosophers who were influenced by Bergson's vitalism (such as Antonio Caso, Vasconcelos, and Farias Brito) and by recently imported German ideas attempted to formulate a new interpretation of what is intrinsically human; whereas the existentialists denied any possibility of an essential definition, giving preference to an existential humanism. This pluralism is the reflection of the many facets assumed in European anthropological discussions, and it also stems from

75

the inherent ambiguity of the question that anthropological speculation seeks to answer, namely, "What does it mean to be a human being?"

The way in which this question is interpreted and the context in which it is raised seriously affect the nature of the answer. There are at least four separate problems to which the question can be taken to refer: the ontological problem of the status of human beings, the metaphysical problem of what constitutes the essence of human beings, the epistemological problem of what one knows as human, and the cosmo-ethical problem of the place of humans in the universe. Different philosophical traditions have approached the question of the human condition in keeping with their understanding of the context within which it is formulated. Scholasticism, whether colonial or contemporary, Latin American positivism—a mixture of naturalism, Comtism, and scientism—as well as most other traditional perspectives insist, although for different reasons, that the discussion of the ontological status of humans remain at the center of philosophical anthropology. Marxist and existentialist philosophers, however, engage in a well-defined attempt to clarify the metaphysical problem of the essence of human beings, whereas the vitalism of French origin and the German philosophy of the spirit, so popular in Latin America during the first half of the twentieth century, direct their principal efforts to the reinterpretation of the specific dimension that separates humans from the rest of the universe. All of them, moreover, give special attention to the cosmo-ethical consequences of their respective solutions, often announcing a new era of genuine humanism.

It must be pointed out, however, that in spite of the preference for approaching the anthropological question with a given emphasis, most of these philosophical perspectives have also developed views about its other dimensions. Each concentrates on a specific aspect of the problem, and the implications with respect to the other aspects are often less fruitfully and profoundly explored. That is to say, all of these positions, explicitly or implicitly, contain ontological, metaphysical, epistemological, and cosmo-ethical dimensions, although usually one of them dominates as a thematic center of gravity.

The ability of a philosopher or of a philosophical view to recognize the implications and interrelationships of each of these aspects of the anthropological question with respect to the others provides a criterion for determining the degree of originality and value of its contributions to philosophical anthropology. The more restricted the orientation, the more restricted is the contribution and the less valuable the solution offered. And, by the same token, the more each of these aspects is explored and proper attention given to its relations with the others, the more profound and lasting is the theory.

DIMENSIONS OF THE PROBLEM

The indispensable prerequisite for any philosophical anthropology, as has been pointed out by Frondizi in the preface to *El yo como estructura dinámica*,[1] is a theory of the self or, in keeping with the terminology used here, a solution to the problem of the nature and the ontological status of the conscious center of the human being. All major philosophers (Aristotle, Descartes, Hume, and others) have recognized the importance of the ontology of the self and thus have begun their anthropological discussion at this point. When we ask "What is a human being?" our answer must begin with an examination of the kind of being humans are and especially of the core, i.e., the self, that constitutes the basis for distinguishing humans from the rest of nature. Such a concern does not seek to set humans apart from the rest of the universe in our understanding, since it is not looking for criteria that would serve to help us distinguish humans from other things. The latter type of emphasis focuses on what we here refer to as "the epistemological aspect" of the problem. What is sought at this point is to classify humans, and particularly the self, within the ontological categories of reality. The question is *whether* the *self exists* and, if so, *how* it exists, not primarily *what* and *how* I know it.

Philosophical anthropology in Latin America was shaped by a positivist approach to this cluster of issues concerning the self and its existence. The most direct expression of this approach led thinkers to claim that the self was an epiphenomenon of matter. With the dismantling of positivism and the vitalist-spiritualist reaction to it that emerged in the second half of the twentieth century, diverse theories concerning the self emerged. For the most part these theories reflected a partial return to an ontologically autonomous concept of the self in which the self regains some of the attributes lost in late nineteenth-century scientism. With the exception of neo-scholastic developments, however, this tendency stopped short of substantialism. The new theories use the dynamic terminology of function, activity, and structure rather than that of substance.

The problem of human essence is perhaps the second most important problem in philosophical anthropology. This issue has two clearly distinguishable aspects, each of which has important implications. Although the 'what is' of humans is no longer interpreted as a 'whether it is' or 'how it is', but rather in the sense that is appropriate to the question to be answered by a definition of the essence, this 'what is' opens up into an initial introductory moment in which one investigates *if* humans *have* an essence in order then to understand *what* the essence *is*. The first corresponds to what we have called the metaphysical aspect of the issue and the second to its epistemological aspect. The metaphysical problem is similar to that of the ontological status of the human being already considered, but in this case it refers to an abstract rather than a concrete reality.

As is to be expected, this issue follows a development parallel to that of the ontological question in the history of Western philosophy. It begins with the essentialist perspective of the Greeks in which the particular and mutable human being is subordinated to its universal and immutable essence. This extreme position, taken by Western philosophy in its initial stages, begins to weaken with the growing awareness of the reality of concrete existence. The doctrine that gives it the final blow is the Hegelian identification of the essence of humans with their activity. Owing to this development, it is possible to conclude that the essence of humans is not some immutable universal but rather that it depends upon what humans do. In short, humans create themselves.

Nevertheless, in the nineteenth century the identification of humans with what they would make of themselves is not complete and therefore the human essence is not thought to be completely determined by human activity. The *homo faber* of the 1880s still has an essence, albeit one that is dependent upon a particular type of activity—work in Marx and the libido in Freud—but nevertheless an essence. Only in twentieth-century existentialism does the eroding effect of a radical nonessentialism that denies every essence to humans come full cycle, identifying humans completely with their particular existence and activity. This trend has continued, gathering force as philosophers pay increasing attention to the identities of groups, favoring a definition of humans in terms of ethnicities and races rather than in terms of universal humanity. (For more on this, see the selections from Alcoff and Schutte in Part IV.)

As these intellectual developments reached Latin America, they were incorporated into its thought and guided it toward an understanding of human essence as active and dynamic. The concrete human being takes the place of the abstract human and hence human essence is conceived as created in particular circumstances and oriented toward a future. Nevertheless, there have been very few thinkers, even among those influenced by existentialism—perhaps Astrada is the only exception—who have gone so far as to deny completely that there is a human essence. The tendency in Latin America has been to conceive this essence as dynamic, rather than to eliminate it altogether.

In examining the issue of *whether* humans have an essence, we come to the third issue that constitutes the nucleus of the anthropological problem. In it the meaningfulness of the question itself is raised. This investigation can be regarded as epistemological insofar as it includes the following two dimensions: the identification of criteria whereby humans can be effectively distinguished from other beings and the understanding of such criteria. For example, if one accepts the Aristotelian view that humans are rational animals, then the first aspect consists in establishing the criterion of rationality as effective in distinguishing humans, whereas the second consists in understanding what is meant by this criterion. The answer to this twofold question properly resolves the problem of whether we can meaningfully speak of a human essence. Of course, as we saw in Part I of this volume, during the colonial period of Mexican philosophy, for example, there were radically divergent interpretations of the answers to this question. Both Sepúlveda and Las Casas used an Aristotelian model to answer the question of whether the natives were human or not, yet their answers were in complete opposition to one another. Las Casas argued that the Indians were humans, but Sepúlveda objected that they were barbarians and therefore not entitled to have human rights.

Given the strong influence of positivism in Latin America, many philosophers of the region have devoted considerable time to combating the scientistic view that reduced humans to something purely physiological, destroying all qualitative distinctions between humans and nature. In this reaction, the Latin American philosophers of the twentieth century were in the company of European philosophers such as Scheler and Cassirer.[2] However, the fight against what were perceived to be the ills of positivism often involved a neglect of some of the ontological and metaphysical dimensions of the human problem.

In contrast, the cosmo-ethical status of humans has seldom been neglected, and contributions by Latin American thinkers to this dimension of philosophical anthropology have been consistently impressive. With rare exceptions, all the Latin American thinkers who have given serious attention to philosophical anthropology have also examined the place that humans occupy in the universe and the consequences for the moral, social, and political life. This concern is especially evident among those committed to a practical ideology, such as Marxists, and is, perhaps, a direct result of the critical situation that continues to confront Latin America, a region rife with political instability and economic problems.

Simply put, this aspect of the anthropological question is central to humanism, insofar as it concerns how to understand humans in light of their particular relationships to nature and society. The pertinent question becomes in this context: "What is a human being in a given region and in relation to specific socioeconomic realities?" Again, in their search for an adequate answer, Latin American philosophers have followed the lead of Western thinkers who have always given great importance to this matter. The Greeks began to treat this problem effectively when they placed humans at the cosmological and ethical center of the universe. But classical humanism does not recur in its fullness at any time in the subsequent history of Western thought, not even in the Renaissance. With the death of Greek culture, humans ceased to be considered the absolute center of the universe and became subordinate to a greater or lesser degree to other realities. Parallel to the development that gradually deprived humans of their traditional attributes such as substantiality, essence, and reason, they became deprived of their cosmological and ethical preeminence to such a degree that in the nineteenth century they were even denied a moral conscience. Positivism's crude scientism converted moral conscience into a mere illusion reducible to instincts that function mechanically.

The inadequacy of such a view engendered an adverse antiscientistic reaction with which the twentieth century opened in Latin America. Inspired particularly by the perspectivism of Ortega y Gasset and later by existentialism, Latin American philosophers, as had been the case with their European counterparts, turned again to humans and restored them as the measure, indeed the center, of the universe, though no longer in the absolute sense of the ancients. A return to the Greek cosmogony and its essentialist ethic was impossible. Scientific and philosophical discoveries of the nineteenth and twentieth centuries, advancements which continue into the present, prevented such a return. Humans became only the relative center of the universe. They were no longer the universal entities who judged the cosmos, but concrete and historical beings who constructed their world. Rather than an essential center, in this more radical contemporary humanism, humans become the transcendental condition of all things. The centrality of humans, therefore, is relative to individuals and eminently subjective.

POSITIVISTIC ANTHROPOLOGY

Latin American anthropological thought in the twentieth century takes root in the major philosophical current of the nineteenth century, namely, positivism. Positivism was nurtured on such heterogeneous elements as the evolutionistic naturalism of Herbert Spencer, the positivism of Auguste Comte, and the utilitarianism of John Stuart Mill. The unity of Latin American positivism, therefore, is more a matter of perspective than of content, since it reduces ultimately to an attitude that exalts the explanatory value of science to the detriment of metaphysics and other theoretical disciplines. All genuine knowledge must be based on empirical experience and not on speculation. As a result, the anthropological problem within this perspective is reduced to the study of psychic phenomena, and philosophical anthropology becomes empirical associationist psychology or biology.

However, one must take note of positivism's philosophical wisdom in recognizing the fundamental importance of the ontological problem mentioned earlier. Positivists begin by raising the problem of the self's existence, even though the answer is negative in that they analyze the self in phenomenal terms. In positivism, the self ceases to be an existing and substantial entity and is conceived as a set of phenomena that, because of the interrelationships, contiguity, and succession of the pertinent individual phenomena, gives the impression of including something that sustains them. This empirical phenomenalism is used to explain the subject-object, mind-body dualism of human experience, a dualism resolved by maintaining a parallelism between these phenomena considered as correlative but irreducible as Enrique José Varona (1849–1933) did, or by accepting a biomechanistic monism in which the phenomenal duality is reduced to the real unity of a common, energized substratum as was proposed by José Ingenieros (1877–1925).

As already stated, most positivists begin their investigation of the human being by focusing on the question of ontological status, but their solution to this precludes the possibility of continuing the investigation along metaphysical and epistemological lines. If individual human selves are reduced to bundles of phenomena, then it is superfluous to speak of a human essence or its definition and interpretation. Some positivists, like Varona and Ingenieros, however, do attempt to offer solutions to the cosmo-ethical problem, although their attempts are lamentable failures. The presuppositions of positivistic anthropology do not permit the construction of a normative ethic. If humans are no more than collections of phenomena strictly ordered according to deterministic laws, then human freedom is an illusion and ethics becomes a purely descriptive science. Ingenieros understands and explicitly accepts the consequences of his psychological position: "The term *to choose* is badly used and has the false connotation of an entity that chooses: the supposed choosing is simply *a natural selection* among different possibilities, in the sense most appropriate to the conservation of life and the least expenditure of energy."[3]

VITALISTIC ANTHROPOLOGY

These implications, devastating for ethics, were instrumental in engendering the anti-positivistic reaction in Latin America. A group of thinkers influenced principally by Bergson began to attack those presuppositions of positivism that destroy human freedom. The concern with the problem of freedom emerged early in the twentieth century and continues to shape many of the contributions to philosophical anthropology to this day. In 1903 Carlos Vaz Ferreira started work on his book *Los problemas de la libertad*, and published it in unfinished form in 1907. The first serious criticisms of positivism, however, were made by Alejandro O. Deústua in Peru and Antonio Caso in Mexico. They were followed by those of Enrique Molina, Alejandro Korn, and others.

Deústua argued persuasively in *Las ideas de orden y libertad en la historia del pensamiento humano* (1917–22) that the idea of order, which is the basis of positivistic determinism, is logically posterior to the idea of freedom and that both are necessary to explain intellectual history. Freedom is necessary for any change in order and, therefore, order is subordinate to freedom.

With the ethical limitations of positivism made explicit, Latin American thought was free to explore new philosophical horizons. Philosophical anthropology abandoned its interest in the ontological status of the mind, which had been the foundation of positivistic psychology, and turned toward the epistemological problem connected with the criteria of distinction of human beings and its understanding. The philosophers who established the foundations of the new anthropology were, principally, Caso and Vasconcelos in Mexico.

Antonio Caso (1883–1946) and José Vasconcelos (1882–1959) were the two major figures who shaped contemporary Mexican philosophy. Born only one year apart, they were charter members of the Ateneo de la Juventud, which was the point of departure for new philosophical thinking in Mexico. Both became presidents of the National University of Mexico at some point in their careers, and both were intensely concerned with the destiny of their country, an issue about which they wrote at length.[4]

Caso's philosophical anthropology, as developed in *La existencia como economía, como desinterés y como caridad* (1919), can be characterized as a personalism. Humans are differentiated from the rest of the universe because they are persons. The physical realm is constituted of things, that is, beings without unity that, as a consequence, are highly divisible. The organic realm consists of individuals that constitute a level of being superior to a divisible thing, although still inferior to humans. It is only in humans that the highest level of the spirit—the person—appears in nature. When individuals become persons, they acquire unity, identity, and substantial continuity, only then becoming fully human. The person is the complete fulfillment of human essence because it is a creator of values. "It is proper to man to fulfill his essence continually and the essence is the person creating values."[5]

Humans, however, are also individuals, and the tension between individuals and persons creates moral conflict. Individuals are egotistical and interested only in their own biological survival and welfare. The law that governs human existence is essentially economic: "life = maximum gain with minimum effort."[6] Persons, on the other hand, exist toward others and tend to unbind their biological interests, choosing freely the ethics of disinterest and love. The law that motivates them is that of charity: "sacrifice = maximum effort and minimum gain."[7] The highest expression of this free and disinterested activity is art.

Caso's trilogy "thing-individual-person" is reformulated in Vasconcelos's *Todología* (1952) as "quantic wave-molecule-cell-person." However, the significance of the elements is completely different. In Vasconcelos's aesthetic monism each of the elements represents a different stage in the constant struggle of the cosmos to maintain its existence and to contain the tendency toward dissolution and dispersion present in every being. The quantic wave is the first elemental structure to restrain the process of universal dissolution. The molecule is the second cosmic effort to restrain the disintegration; the third and fourth cosmic efforts constitute, successively, the cell and the human person. In the fourth one finds the maximum degree of coordination of the heterogeneous, namely, consciousness. By means of consciousness, humans reflect and unify within themselves the heterogeneous multiplicity of the universe, becoming true microcosms.

The 'self', 'consciousness', and 'soul' are equivalent terms for Vasconcelos. The nature of the reality that they represent is known to us through their coordinating activity, but their being "is an unfathomable abyss."[8] The self always escapes any analytical scrutiny. We know it only through its effects.

For Caso as well as for Vasconcelos, the primary concern is to characterize our place in the universe. They both point to personality as the essential constitutive element of our humanity. For the first, the person is the center of free, disinterested activity. Vasconcelos, on the other hand, identifies the person with consciousness and characterizes it as a coordinating element of the cosmos. Both thinkers, therefore, tend to neglect the ontological and metaphysical problems involved in philosophical anthropology.

ANTHROPOLOGY OF THE SPIRIT

When the philosophical supremacy of positivism was broken through the work of Deústua, Korn, Caso, Vasconcelos, and Farias Brito, among others, the study and acceptance of new European philosophical tendencies became more widespread. In 1916 Ortega y Gasset came to Latin America for the first time and introduced contemporary German thought to audiences throughout the continent. The generation of thinkers that followed "the founders" were inspired by him and his mentors, Husserl, Dilthey, Scheler, and Hartmann.

Philosophical renovation took root with such thinkers as Samuel

Ramos in Mexico and Francisco Romero in Argentina, followed by Risieri Frondizi, Francisco Miró Quesada, and Leopoldo Zea. Ramos and Romero focused attention on the characterization of the relation of humans to the universe and also explored the ontological implications of their views. As the selections included in this volume indicate, Frondizi and Miró Quesada develop different lines of thought. And Zea's interests, as we shall see in Part IV, grew into a quite different direction, which although having roots in philosophical anthropology gave rise to new developments in Latin American philosophy, the search for cultural identity. Frondizi is the only thinker of his generation to work extensively with the ontological question, and Miró Quesada investigates the metaphysical problem from an epistemic perspective.

Francisco Romero (1891–1962)

According to Romero, "duality is the constituting fact of the full man."[9] The elements of this duality are intentionality and spirit. The first in itself is a human element, although animals possess a rudiment of intentionality. Humans, however, possess intentionality in a full and essential sense. Human "consciousness is organized as a differentiated structure in which there exists a subjective pole which grasps objects and projects itself actively toward them."[10] The subjective pole is the individual self that, in Romero's view, distinguishes human consciousness from the pre-intentional psychism characteristic of animals.

The "intentional man" or self, however, is not the "full man." The intentional self is "a mere human." His humanity is completed with a second element: spirit. Structurally, there is no difference between the intentional man and the spiritual man. Both are human beings and both are structured as a self-world pair. The difference is in their direction. In the first, the direction is subjective, toward the self. In the second, it is objective. The purely intentional act always returns to the subject, whereas a spiritual act comes to rest on the object.

The intentional man is part of nature and acts in accord with its laws. The spiritual man, on the other hand, is not a natural entity. The direction toward the other indicates that he has broken with nature, giving him the freedom of action that constitutes man as an axiological being.

Transcendence is the metaphysical basis of man's being as well as of all reality. For Romero reality consists of four orders: the inorganic, the organic, intentionality, and spirit. Each of these is structured on the level that precedes it, which in turn serves as a foundation to the level above it. Each level transcends its preceding level and is transcended by the level that follows it. Humans, therefore, consist of a dual transcendence: as intentional selves, they transcend toward the objects which they take to themselves, and as spirits they transcend toward the object and rest in it. The highest level of transcendence is spirit.

Romero's theory is profound and fruitful. However, it tends to ignore a fundamental problem in the anthropological question, namely, that concerned with ontological status. In the same year in which Romero published his major work, Frondizi brought out his *Substancia y función en el problema del yo*, a book that gives special attention to the very issue that Romero neglects.

Risieri Frondizi (1910–1983)

Frondizi rejected the two traditional solutions to the problem of the existence and nature of the self: the substantialist position that conceives the self as a transempirical entity and the atomist position that dissolves it into a collection of lived experiences.

The basic error of the traditional substantialism originating with Descartes is to suppose that all activity requires a subject. This sort of approach leads to the conclusion that thinking presupposes a something that thinks. Empirical atomism, finding its origins in Hume, erred, according to Frondizi, through "the sophism of reduction," i.e., the metaphysical postulate that seeks to reduce wholes to their component parts. The outcome of both perspectives is disastrous; the substantialist creates an artificial entity whereas the atomist destroys the self.

Frondizi finds the solution in the concept of structure (*Gestalt*). The self is a quality that lived experiences possess when they are taken as wholes. Immutability, simplicity, and independence, characteristics that substantialism sustained in a transempirical entity, are changed to mutability, complexity, and dependence. At the same time, however, Frondizi avoids the atomist reduction of the self to its component parts. As a structural quality, the self depends upon the members of its structure, the lived-experiences, but it cannot be reduced to them. In virtue of this condition, the self is one and permanent in spite of being mutable and complex.

Francisco Miró Quesada (b. 1918)

For Miró Quesada the basic problem in philosophical anthropology is what we characterized above as the metaphysical question, and he approached it from an epistemological perspective in *El hombre sin teoría* (1959). The problem is not the status of the human essence but rather the possibility of formulating an adequate theory of man.

On the one hand, it is a fact of human experience that we cannot live without theory and that all theory concerning the world that surrounds us implies a theory concerning us. On the other hand, man is a reality so complex that every theory of man is destined to inevitable failure. What, then, is one to do? One solution is to cast aside or modify unacceptable theories in favor of more truthful ones. But this procedure is unsatisfactory, in that "whatever we do, our theory concerning ourselves will have the same outcome as the others."[11] The only way out, therefore, is to desist from theorizing about man. But is this not impossible? Is theory not necessary for our practical life and even implicit in our language?

Miró Quesada claims this is not necessarily the case. To be sure, we cannot dispense with the theory implicit in language, but this theory is different from scientific-philosophical theories about the world, life, and human destiny. The first is primitive, spontaneous, collective, and practically unconscious; the second, however, is created for the specific purposes of knowledge. It is the latter that we must abandon in order to pay attention to the facts, since scientific and philosophical theories about human beings are artificial dividers among us. True humanism must be founded on fact and not on theory.

EXISTENTIALIST AND MARXIST ANTHROPOLOGIES

Existentialism began to influence Latin American philosophy in the 1930s. Its impact was extensive, but few Latin American philosophers accepted existentialism uncritically. Among those most influenced by it, the more prominent are Carlos Astrada of Argentina and Vicente Ferreira da Silva of Brazil. The work of the former reflects the reading of *Being and Time*, although in about 1950 Astrada abandoned the Heideggerian perspective and adopted a Marxist outlook. Ferreira da Silva (1916–1963), not included in this collection, was inspired principally by the works of Heidegger's later period. Both of these philosophers were concerned in particular with the metaphysical problem of the essence of human beings.

Carlos Astrada (1894–1970)

In *La revolución existencialista* (1952), Astrada identified the essence of human beings with their historic humanity. Heidegger's error, according to Astrada, consisted in the ambiguity latent in his thought, an ambiguity couched in the debate between the old ontological objectivity and existential-historical transcendence.

Properly speaking, man is not a determinate thing. Human essence is temporal existence and, therefore, it is more a possibility than a given reality. "Man never *is* in the sense of something conclusive and formed in the ideal mold of a goal that was to be achieved; rather he is an eternal *coming to be* suspended in the effort in which he is projected toward historical concretions."[12] The mission and nature of humans is dramatic, says Astrada in terminology reminiscent of Ortega. Human beings can be remolded and changed because they are nothing definite. Men do not depend on the idea of man; rather the idea of man depends upon men.

Once humanity is accepted as a mere possibility, humans are able to develop free of the limitations imposed by eternal truths and essences. This is the basis of a true humanism centered upon the identity of existing man. As for Marx, Astrada maintains that the only limitation imposed upon human beings is their concrete existence. This does not condemn us to subjectivism, however, because our objectivity is given in our history.

NOTES

1. R. Frondizi, *El yo como estructura dinámica* (Buenos Aires: Paidós, 1970), p. 11.

2. See, for example, Scheler's *Man's Place in Nature* (1928) and Cassirer's *Essay on Man* (1944).

3. J. Ingenieros, *Principios de psicología*, in *Obras completas*, vol. 3 (Buenos Aires: Mar Océano, 1962), p. 148.

4. See, for example, A. Caso: *Discursos a la nación mexicana* (1922), *México y la ideología nacional* (1924), *Nuevos discursos a la nación mexicana* (1934), and *México, apuntamientos de cultura patria* (1943); and J. Vasconcelos: *Estudios indostánicos* (1920), *La raza cósmica* (1925), and *Indología* (1926).

5. A. Caso, *La existencia como economía, como desinterés y como caridad*, in *Antología filosófica* (Mexico City: Ediciones de la Secretaría de Educación Pública, 1943), p. 190.

6. Ibid., p. 51.

7. Ibid., p. 61.

8. J. Vasconcelos, *Todología*, in *Obras completas*, vol. 4 (Mexico City: Libreros Mexicanos Unidos, 1961), p. 905.

9. F. Romero, *Teoría del hombre*, 3d ed. (Buenos Aires: Losada, 1965), p. 193.

10. Ibid., p. 127.

11. F. Miró Quesada, *El hombre sin teoría* (Lima: Universidad Mayor de San Marcos, 1959), p. 24.

12. C. Astrada, *Existencialismo y crisis de la filosofía* (Buenos Aires: Devenir, 1963), p. 190. This text is an expanded reedition with substantial changes of *La revolución existencialista*.

Francisco Romero
(1891–1962)

Romero was born in Seville in 1891 and as a child came to Argentina, where he remained the rest of his life. He was educated as a military engineer and attained the rank of major in the army. During his youth he began to explore the bounds of his professional training, tending first toward literature and then toward philosophy. In these areas he was his own teacher. His philosophical interests and self-discipline led him to study philosophy on his own during long nights in the barracks after he had completed his professional duties. He began by reading Spencer and later turned to the study of German philosophy. Husserl, but principally Scheler and Nicolai Hartmann, were major influences in the formation of his philosophical perspective. His close friendship with Alejandro Korn was also a guiding factor in his life.

In 1939 he resigned his commission in order to work full time in philosophy. He was promoted from assistant professor to full professor of epistemology and metaphysics at the University of Buenos Aires, replacing his friend Korn who had retired the previous year. He was also professor at the University of La Plata. In 1946 he resigned from all his positions but returned to them in 1955. In 1962 he was appointed professor emeritus and traveled to Europe. Upon returning, he suffered a cerebral hemorrhage and died on the seventh of October that same year.

His creative work ran concurrently with the teaching he carried on both in and out of the university. From 1937 until his death he was director of the philosophical library of the Losada Publishing House. He was the organizer of the chair of philosophy in the Colegio Libre de Estudios Superiores, and he published numberous popular essays that came to create an environment favorable to the development of philosophy as a "normal task." Romero was the last Argentinian philosopher to live in a heroic age, when philosophical activity was carried on in the face of public indifference or official opposition.

Until 1952 he had not published a systematic work, although for more than twenty years he had developed his philosophical ideas and published articles sketching his thought. His most important essays were "Vieja y nueva concepción de la realidad" (1932); "Filosofía de la persona" (1935); "Programa de una filosofía" (1940); and "Trascendencia y valor" (1942). The last two were published in *Sur*, numbers 73 and 92, and were incorporated in *Papelas para una filosofía* (1945). The majority of his important essays were also incorporated into books.

If we leave aside his *Historia de la filosofía moderna* (1959), his only systematic work is *Teoría del hombre* (1952), in which he develops a philosophical anthropology "within the context of a metaphysics of transcendence."

The concept of "transcendence" is fundamental for his thought. Hierarchical levels depend on the degreee of transcendence, with the least to be found in the physical and the most to be found in the spiritual level. The intermediate levels are those of life and intentional psychism. What is human is found on the third level, that of intentional psychism, and this is perfected in the spirit, which is "absolute transcendence." The first most important characteristic of the spirit is "absolute objectivity" and the second is "universality." To these must be added freedom and historicity.

If the numerous works published throughout a period of twenty years had not been enough to ensure that Romero would be an outstanding philosopher, his *Teoría del hombre*, considered by many to be one of the most solid works in Latin American philosophy, secured his position as an original thinker.

Theory of Man

INTENTIONAL CONSCIOUSNESS

Preintentional Psychism and Intentional Consciousness

It is best to conceive of psychism[1] in its earliest stages as an undivided succession of states, a kind of psychical repercussion of life. No distinction between subject and object exists in such psychism, nor can one properly speak of it as consciousness. Life is recorded psychically; it resounds and multiplies in a clouded psyche. This psychism is, so to speak, inherent in life from its beginning, being a direct echo of life and the instrument of the living entity to be used for its internal coordination and external conduct. The superior or intentional psyche is based on this foundation, and its distinguishing characteristic consists in the objective direction of its acts. Also resting on this foundation, though in less direct fashion, is the spirit, the principle whereby man passes beyond the natural realm.

Our sole concern at this point is to make clear the nonintentional character of animal psychism, yet at the same time, conceding to some species of animals a vague rudiment of intentionality that is limited and detained in its first stages. As a normal function, true and complete intentionality carries with it, of necessity, both nomination and objective communication, in preparation, as we shall see, for that inversion of interest of which the spirit consists. If intentional consciousness actually operated in animals, it would manifest itself in a language of objective content; it

From Francisco Romero, *Theory of Man* (Berkeley: University of California Press, 1964), pp. 3–4, 6–7, 33–35, 83, 96–97, 122–23, 133–37, 139–42, 162–65, 167–74, 177–78, 180–81, 207–209. Originally published by the University of California Press, reprinted by permission of the Regents of the University of California.

would give rise to the beginning of self-consciousness, and that being would not then be an animal, but the sketch of a man. Provisionally, we accept Max Scheler's conclusions concerning the psychism of animals as it pertains to affective impulses (which would seem to be apparent in plants), instinct, and associative memory. We do not share his opinion concerning what he calls practical intelligence. We disagree with his supposition that practical intelligence is similar in animals and in man—that there is only a difference of degree between a chimpanzee and an Edison (as inventors of technical artifacts). We believe that the difference—or the primary difference—between man and the animals must be sought in this aspect, yet without denying the statement that it is the spirit that completes and perfects human nature. . . .

It is proper for man to perceive objects, to recognize reality as a conglomeration of separate entities endowed with existence and consistency. Man is, in the first place, an intentional consciousness—without it he is not man. What is characteristic of intentional consciousness consists in a cluster of intentions or acts projected toward objects in the function of cognitive, emotional, or volitional apprehension. "States" or psychical acts without intentional character, that is without objective direction, occur in man as in animals, but it is man's prerogative that many of his states lose their condition as such by becoming the content of intentional acts. Of these, the cognitive acts enjoy an undoubted priority and preeminence in the shaping of human nature, for they are what establishes intentional consciousness. Simultaneously these acts create or distinguish the object and present it to us as perceivable, for they have the concealed ability to give objective form to sensible material and the evident capacity to present this outcome to us as objects existent in themselves. The common observations concerning the priority or superior strength of the emotions or the will with respect to the intellect do not succeed in invalidating the former assertion, as will be seen later.

Intentional activity transforms the states into objects. The exploration and description of the mechanism and function that produce that transmutation are the concern of the theory of knowledge. We use the word "object" in its most inclusive sense—it takes in everything that comes into the cognitive glance, everything that is apprehended by the subject. . . .

We are able to conceive the attribution of objectivity only as an act similar to judgment. The state is merely lived, endured. It is neither accepted nor rejected; it is not apprehended and, properly speaking, there is no consciousness of it. When one turns toward a state, it automatically becomes an object, and the "turning onward" is a becoming aware that the state is there, that it is, and subsequently that it is of this or that form. To perceive, to apprehend something, is to attribute being and consistency to what is apprehended. The subject, therefore, is born as the ability to assign presence to states, to judge that they are. This objectifying judgment, however, is not conscious, formulated, and explicit, since we are not conscious of it. Yet this judgment provides us with the consciousness of objects. Further, the lack of consciousness of this act of judgment does not argue against it, because, even in the ordinary activity of the intelligence, we are not conscious of the major part of our judgments.

The objectifying judgment is similar to the existential judgment dealt with in logic, and though this similarity has been noted more than once before, there is considerable difference between the two. One must keep in mind that for both the characteristic of judgment is assertion and not the attribution of predicates. Yet we do not become trapped in insurmountable difficulties if we insist—contrary to the opinion of Meinong and others—in maintaining predication as a sine qua non of judgment, since what constitutes the object may be thought of as the predication of existence, or, as we prefer to state it, of presence. The objectifying act may be conceived according to the formula "that is an existent" or "that is present," whereby one expresses that "that" (which was a state until the intentional glance fell on it) is an existent or something of the class of that which is placed before a subject. . . . As has been previously stated, man is the being for whom there are (or who perceives) objects, and he is the being who is a subject. Let us now add with equally strong emphasis that man is the being who judges. For, as we have seen, the subject unfolds as the being capable of judging, of attributing objectivity to states. In fact, we might say that this capacity to judge becomes substance or is structured into an entity. The subject is the judging entity, but he himself seems to appear in order to embody the judging attitude, as though awakened or called up by an obscure power in the preintentional psyche which would assert itself and thereby rise to the level of consciousness—the level it achieves as soon as it forges an adequate instrument.

To dwell on problems limited to the sphere of knowledge would lead us astray from our primary aim—the elucidation of the idea of man—so we will add only those comments that seem indispensable to our purpose. For us, as has been firmly asserted, the essential activity of the subject is judgment. This is not the only function in which the subject is engaged, yet it is the function which, so far as he is a subject, bestows being on him, and which through reiteration confirms him as a subjective entity and increases his stature as such. . . .

The subject-object structure is not only essential and determinative in man—in what might be called his individual constitution; it is also essential in the community or collection of men and in man's objective product, that is, his culture. The capacity of this basic structure to provide a satisfactory explanation of everything human is precisely what assures us of its truth.

What is proper to the human community derives, without exception, from the fact that man is a subject and that he perceives or conceives a world of objectivities. Social life, as such, is not exclusively human. Not only do many species of animals live in societies of diverse kinds, they also reveal some of the conditions investigated in human society by sociologists—positive and negative tensions, leadership, stratification, division of labor, and so forth. The parallel can be drawn with particular reference to family complexes. No animal grouping, however, regardless of the aspects which it may have in common with human society, can reasonably be equated with it; only human society is a grouping of subjects, each with its own world of objects, and each one, therefore, capable of objectifying the group and of objectively conceiving each of his companions. . . .

CULTURE

Our primary intention is to show how culture stems—one might say by necessity—from the objectifying capacity and, therefore, is a part of the fact that man is a subject who grasps and conceives an objective world. The unity of man and culture is manifest in many ways, and we are especially interested in pointing out, in the correlation between them, culture's influence on man.

Let us first define the distinction between objective culture and cultural life. Objective culture includes all of man's creations that achieve substantiality and autonomy with reference to their creator and thus have a relatively separate existence, such as institutions, works of art, theories, and customs. By cultural life is understood the life that man lives in the midst of the objects he has created. If the merely organic—in which man coincides with other living beings—is left aside, then the whole of man's life is cultural life. What continues to be purely organic in man is not clear, for, since man is immersed in culture, much in him that originally was organic has taken on cultural implications. For example, the digestive functions are modified by diet and regularity, which are the products of culture; sexual activity stems in part from peculiarly human motives occurring within a framework in which the agents are subjects, and their activity takes place in specifically defined situations usually under strict social regulation.

The reference to culture at this point provisionally sets aside its spiritual aspect. From our point of view, culture is not necessarily spiritual, even though throughout it seems to be dominated from above by spiritual motives, and even if in effect it is spiritual in many of its expressions. The spiritual implications in culture will be discussed later.

All specifically human activity is cultural. It presupposes cultural objectifications and it manipulates them in the processes of creation, modification, comprehension, and development. Human life is inconceivable apart from culture. The notion of culture includes, then, every human product and all human conduct. The strictly organic is not human, just as the physical is not organic. Yet weight, a physical trait, is something no living body can escape. . . .

THE SELF AND THE WORLD: THE NATURAL MAN

In the previous chapters we have tried to describe the fundamental structure of man. We have shown that this structure presupposes a judging attitude, that it introduces into the most profound levels of man what later becomes the explicit judgment. We have attempted to show that intelligence and significative language, just as much as the human community and culture, are based on that fundamental structure; and we have referred to the role of intentionality in the acceleration of activity and in the process of individualization which seem to provide the essential directions to the cosmic process. The problem of the spirit has remained a separate one thus far, since it is to be the theme of Part Two. But it has been indicated that intentionality leads to the spirit and is perfected in it, and that intelligence, society, and culture, if indeed they can be maintained on the level of pure intentionality, take on the forms in which they are familiar to us as well as their characteristic human dimension when they are integrated with the spiritual dimension.

To be constructed on the intentional structure yet to be deprived of the spirit, is neither to be an animal nor, strictly speaking, to be a man in the full sense of the word. It is not legitimate, on the other hand, to deny absolutely a human condition to such a being. Perhaps we might say that we should attribute that condition to him in the light of the promise of the spirit which is latent in his intentionality. Such a being has undoubtedly existed in the inferior stages of humanity, perhaps existing normally in minimal cultures and, perchance, in isolated instances, enduring in the superior cultures. We refer to it as *natural man* and, as we have stated, characterize it by the total lack of the spiritual factor. We do not preclude that the spiritual attitude may arise suddenly and unexpectedly in intentionality, influenced by inner motives, by an example, or by some external appeal. The natural attitude is maintained only until the first spark of spirit appears. Habitual persistence in overtly natural attitudes, if in some way one has assented or assents to the spiritual attitude, does not constitute a true natural attitude, but rather a special situation related to the duality peculiar to man. This duality is discussed in Part Three.

Let us consider the principal traits of the natural man—that is, man so far as he is deprived of spirit.

This man, built on the subject-object structure, is a self surrounded by a world of objectivities. The self-world pair represents a step up from the subject-object pair. The subject is converted into a self through the reiteration of intentional acts which organize the subjectivity, granting it consistency, continuity, and identity with itself. The world is the result of habitual objective experience.

The self can be dissolved into the "we" or affirmed individually. The consciousness of the self is just as natural when the individual incorporates himself into a natural complex with which he identifies himself as when he sharply distinguishes his own natural individuality from that of his fellows. The universal projection, the turn toward the "other," exclusively constitutes the nonnatural or the spiritual attitude. . . .

THE SPIRIT IN GENERAL

Intentionality and Spirit

In preintentional psychism, the individual lives his states obscurely, without referring them to a subjective center. In intentional psychism, consciousness is organized as a differentiated structure in which a subjective pole exists that grasps objects and projects itself actively toward them. The subjective pole, in keeping with its normal function, is constituted as a self surrounded by a world, that is, an environment of objectifications linked together objectively. The acts of the self—cognitive, emotional, volitional—flow into this world, which determines them in part, both by the situations that it presents to the self and by what the latter owes to the accumulated experiences of that world with respect to its own constitution. In merely intentional psychism, the world is only the objective field in which the self affirms and develops its existence, governed entirely by practical interests, by incentives of an individual sort which are referred to the concrete and unique being of the self. The situation does not change fundamentally, as has been said, when these interests are referred to complexes or groups with which the individual is concretely identified rather than directly to a single individual. This is true only to the extent to which the identification with the group stems from concrete and practical motives and not from ideal intentions, for in the latter case one crosses over from the natural to the spiritual attitude.

Merely intentional activity creates objectivities for the subject but subordinates them at once to the immediate goals of the percipient, who catalogues them under the earmark of interesting or indifferent, useful or useless, agreeable or disagreeable, attractive or repugnant, and so on. The emphasis on some of these objectivities and the blurring of others, the direction and energy of the objectifying glance, depend on practical factors. These concrete incentives are at work, primarily, in subsequent cognitive activity, in intellectual elaborations. The emotional and volitional acts are oriented in the same manner, depending on and yet to the advantage of the psychophysical reality of the agent. Thus, intentional acts are launched toward given objectivities, but a return to the subject is within them.

The principal characteristic of the spiritual act is the lack of this return. The spiritual act is projected toward the object, and it remains there. In cognitive, emotional, and volitional activity, the self is concerned with the objectivities for what they are in themselves. In merely intentional activity the subject places the objects and then takes them to himself, whereas in the spiritual act he places the objects and then yields himself to them. In order to give profile to the spiritual act at this point, let this provisional and incomplete definition be offered: the spiritual act is that intentional act in which the subject yields himself to the object. A more precise specification of this kind of act requires that one determine its what, why, and how—that is, its internal nature, the presumed motive of its appearance, and its manner of functioning.

Because the spiritual act is an act of a special nature, of a superior kind, hereafter, when we refer to nonspiritual intentionality, we will say "mere intentionality" or "pure intentionality," or we will use some other expression distinguishing it from intentionality made spiritual.

At first glance, according to the preceding summary description, the spiritual act seems more simple, more direct, and less complex than the act of mere intentionality. Actually, one element in the nonspiritual intentional act is lacking in the spiritual act—the subjective return, the practical reference of what is objectified to the individuality of the agent. When the naked acts are taken in themselves, they undoubtedly present this difference. But this is not so if, as is only just, attention is focused on the self and its corresponding behavior in mere intentionality and in intentionality made spiritual. In the first, the self lives its natural state spontaneously, leaning over the object and bringing to bear its own reality as a concrete individual who takes himself as the universal and ultimate point of reference. As can now be well seen, what we have referred to as subjective return is not something that can be superimposed on its act by the self; rather, it is an intention operative within the act itself—it is the final polarization of the act toward the agent which is inherent in the "natural" attitude of the agent. In the spiritual act, on the one hand, this intention is suppressed, but what occurs is not, properly speaking, a simplification, but a purification of the act. On the other hand, the spiritual act enlarges its radius with respect to the nonspiritual act, because, in freely turning to its object, it finds a more extended area than that circumscribed by the relatively limited register of the practical interests of the agent. Mere intentionality redirects reality to the midst of man's natural state, whereas, in the spiritual attitude, man turns to whatever is and participates abundantly in totality. The self, particularistic in the first attitude, rises above itself and is universalized in the second.

The difference between the psychism of states and intentional psychism is self-evident if one accepts the proofs or assumptions we have previously set forth. The first is a flux of psychic matter with no clear distinction between cognition, emotion, and the will, and without a subject before whom objectified instances might appear. Intentional psychism is an intimate aspect of the activity of a subject to whom objectivities are presented, who recognizes them intellectually and projects on them, as objectivities, his acts of emotion and will. The difference between these two psychical realities is enormous in itself, even if one considers only their internal structures. Such a difference is increased when one considers its mode of functioning. Preintentional psychism finds itself inevitably at the command of organic life. It is an instrument of regulation and adaptation for the individual, in that it adapts the individual to the surroundings and also in that it partly adapts the surroundings to the individual—so far as it limits the environment and makes it functional in view of the implicit demands in the constitution of each species. High as one may ascend the scale of this psychism, though occasionally and exceptionally the rudiments of intentionality may be found in the individual, such an individual never passes beyond the level of the purely vital, it does not come to be a self surrounded by a world that it can recognize and within which it conducts itself with a free choice, taking into consideration the wide perspective of objects extended in space and time. Intentional psychism, however, draws the individual out of the strictly organic level, converting the individual into a self gifted with a world in which he develops an action overcoming the biological levels to the extent that the incentives of this order are partly transformed into motives of another kind. It is essential not to ignore that intentionality entails cultural objectification whereby a realm of a new kind is constituted around the individual, the realm of culture, thus creating a complex, untested situation; for the subject lives simultaneously in the world of the spontaneous natural state and in that of culture, and he works in virtue of them both. Even in the lowest levels of civilization, however, a notable preeminence of the cultural influx exists, an influx that defines his evaluation of basic, natural reality and his behavior in its presence. The distance between the nonintentional and the intentional entity, from the point of view of structure and activity, is sufficiently large to justify a strict ontological separation.

The preintentional psychic field and the intentional psychic field differ profoundly. No structural difference between the merely intentional and the spiritual exists, however, because the foundation, the self-world pair is the same in the second as in the first. Intentional consciousness is the common field of the purely intentional and the spiritual acts, so that one cannot speak accurately of a spiritual consciousness that could be opposed to the other. The spiritual act is an intentional act of a special kind, an act that not only turns toward objects but is governed by them and is exhausted in them, though this should be said with the reservations that will emerge later. What is essential in it is the full objective direction. In functioning as the agent of such an act, the subject does not change in what we might call his subjective makeup but rather in his implantation within reality, in his meaning, in his posture or attitude. One cannot say, however, that for the subject the spiritual state is only a mode of working and not a mode of being, because the subject is constituted by his acts, and what he is depends on the character of his acts, with reference both to actuality and to acquired habit. The differences to which we have been referring find support in the awareness that nonintentional acts are easily distinguished from intentional acts on the basis of external factors, whereas an intentional act may appear spiritual without being so and vice versa. At times one may be in error about the nature of one's own act.

From one point of view, then, the difference is minimal, from another, and undoubtedly more justified standpoint, however, it is immense. The difference between the merely intentional act and the spiritual act seems minimal because many times the two are confused, and the only difference between them may rest in the final subjectivist intention of the former and the objectivist intention of the latter—nothing more. But with the step toward radical objectivism which defines the purely spiritual act, the natural level is abandoned, and even a particle of the divine—nothing less—is restored in humanity.

It follows that between the purely intentional and the spiritual there is an identity of real contexture, but a difference of intention or purpose. In other words, we might say that there is an identity of matter or content, but a difference of relation or form. The same occurs in the two previous strata of reality—the inorganic or physical and the organic or living. The constitutive matter of the inorganic and the organic is the same. Not one single component can be discovered in the organic level that cannot be reduced to elements existing in the physical order. But the relation or form differs, and, with its functional consequences, it serves in each case to define the entity, to locate it in the level of organic reality or that of life. . . .

Passing from pure intentionality to spirituality not only carries with it a distinction capable of giving shape to a new ontological species, but it produces one of the greatest separations imaginable. This separation is between the two great orders into which reality is divided, that of nature and spirit, concerning whose heterogeneity something has already been said and which will be treated extensively in the following pages.

The great distance—a truly unbridgeable abyss—open between nature and spirit, however, does not hinder our attempt to understand the motive for the appearance of the latter, with the former serving as a foundation. The meaning of that appearance will be discussed when we attempt to establish the relation between spirit and transcendence.

Removed as spirituality may be from natural intentionality, basic though the novelty be that it introduces into the picture of totality, one must recognize that it was already present as a possibility, even as a seed, in the first intentional attitude. What we have referred to as mere intentionality is an imperfect intentionality. In the light of spiritual demands it even appears as frustrated because the subjective return does not emerge as a *plus*, but rather as a decrease in the objectifying intention. In general, intentionality characteristically constructs objectivities, perceives them, thinks them, and directs itself toward them in emotional and volitional movements. The objective direction is thus inherent in intentionality. What happens before the appearance of the spirit is that the objective direction, not entirely fulfilled, is delayed by a ballast that hinders its free advance. That ballast is the structure of the self as a sheaf of individual interests. Mere intentionality, therefore, is revealed to us as something incomplete and mutilated, as an impetus of the subject toward what he is not—an impetus that later weakens and returns to the subject, bringing to it, one might say, the usable spoils of the object. Basically, the intention of the subjective return, the "vested or interested interest," constitutes the purely intentional act and defines it from the beginning, although this return may indicate an obstruction of the objectifying impulse. The naturalness of the nonspiritualized intentionality is rooted specifically in the final reference or the redirecting of the acts toward the self as a particular center, whereby it shares the particularism that, as we shall soon see, characterizes everything natural in contradistinction to the radical universalism of the spirit. With its vested interests in the world, the nonspiritualized subject shares in its own way the condition of the organic entity, which is only interested organically in its surroundings, for its own specific and individual goals. The attitude is the same, although the actors and the stage may change. One must admit, however, that although particularism is the general law of nature, its forms allow for degrees of extension and dignity, and that intentional particularism at times approaches spiritual universalism, as when the objectified world is enlarged and the self broadens into a "we" which may come to include all humanity and even elements in addition to man which are accepted for purposes of an interpenetrating sympathy. Many times, no doubt, the self is enlarged and ennobled when it is broadened into a "we," but any act ultimately referred to that "we" is purely intentional—though of a superior intentionality—because the open and cleanly objective direction is basic to the spiritual act, a projection toward something as "other."

Thus mere intentionality, which in itself is on a high level in the scale of reality, on occasions comes to border on the spirit through the broadening of the subject into a "we"—to which, for all practical purposes, the subject's acts are referred. The "we" of which we speak here is not the social complex to which the primitive refers his behavior before he has lived as a true and individualized subject. Rather, it is the "we" that is constituted after there has been an actual subject; it is the "we" that presupposes the self. Yet this bordering with the spirit does not suppress the enormous difference in level between the two. One need only keep in mind that with the self broadened into a "we" the subjective return is the same as it was before, except that the center to which the action is directed has changed. The particularism acquires a much broader base, but it does not cease to be particularism.

What defines the spiritual act is not that the subject swells and is enlarged, but that it gives up the subjective return of the act. The notion of the "we" is always relative: we, the living human beings, Americans, those of our class, our family, the doctors, the athletes, the contributors, the pipe smokers—we, who now agree in something and feel bound by that tie, which can be fundamental or accidental, permanent or temporary. The notion of pure objectivism, however, which is the mark of the spiritual state, is absolute. It is the absolute projection toward the other, conditioned only by the mode of being and of the other (and of the objectified subject itself as an other). In the spiritual state, as well, the subject has become larger, but in a special sense that is not akin to the broadening of the circle of concrete interests of the "we." The subject has become larger because he has turned loose of his battery of individual interests and has converted otherness as such into his own interests. He has not evaporated as a subject, as one might imagine; he has only annulled himself as a subject who functions as a single unit, which, for all practical purposes, redirects every existing thing toward himself. The purely intentional subject works naturally. Nothing is more natural than this: that each one work according to, and as a function of, what he is with intentions that terminate in himself because he is a self. The spiritual subject is no longer a natural entity. It is not *natural* that a self yield itself definitely to the other. The spiritual state is freedom, it is evasion. This freedom, this evasion, is above all the destruction of the walls of particularism that enclose each self in a private enclosure and, generally speaking, enclose every natural instance in the special regulation that pertains to it. . . .

THE UNIQUENESS AND SIGNIFICANCE OF THE SPIRIT

Traits of the Spirit

The central, founding event of the spiritual act—the projection in this act of the subject toward the object—has certain consequences and is manifest in certain modes that can be considered as the principal traits of the spirit. These traits, however, are not to be considered as independent properties that meet in the spiritual act, as something added to it, forming part of it, or making it complex; rather they are to be considered as different expressions of its most genuine and profound character, as diverse aspects of a single reality.

The first of these traits is *absolute objectivity,* which is the fundamental condition of this kind of act. The merely intentional act is also of objective scope because it gives form to objectivities and manipulates them in various ways; all intentionality is a working with objectivities. But this objectivity is not absolute. In it the subject functions with the particularism of a living, intentional being, keeping continuously in mind his particular concrete being; and this gives a highly subjective quality to his act. The subjective interest imposes its direction on the intentional glance: heightening some aspects of the object and darkening others, it circumscribes the realm of objectivities according to its own standard. In addition, the object is given in a modified form because the practical intention of the subject is included in it. It is understood as "something for the subject," and to the extent that this occurs, it diminishes or annuls the autonomous condition of the object, which is an undeniable part of it and on occasion the fundamental aspect, since the object can signify its own unchangeable meaning, its very heart. In spiritual or absolute objectivity, the *whole* object is objectified, without its being altered with subjective innovations, and without neglecting the ultimate and independent significance of anything that is not the object itself. Knowledge of a spiritual kind is concerned with what is only because it is; the interest thus projected toward the object deserves the characterization "disinterested," because it is not governed by any interest peculiar to the agent, but rather by an interest engendered in the agent by the mere fact of the object's existing or by its being given. In ethical behavior, a given objective situation may be disvalued in a moral judgment, or the attempt may be made to correct it through actual intervention. But this is not equivalent to an interference of subjective particularism in the objective situation; rather the subject, facing a complex situation characterized by a conflict or an encounter with something given as real and something considered as an objective value or duty, decides for the latter—that is, for an order he recognizes as justified and valuable above the given reality.

Absolute spiritual objectivity does not permit the elimination of the subject as the terminal for its acts, but it does permit the elimination of the subject as a complex of subjective interests. The spiritual subject does not deny itself; rather it recognizes in itself an objectivity parallel to others. It is doubtlessly concerned with itself, but only as its being and meaning are conceived objectively.

Universality is another trait of the spirit; it has already served to distinguish the spirit from nature because of the particularism that is akin to everything natural. The spirit is universal in various ways, and all these stem from total objective projection. The subject, deprived of actual reference to itself, of the intention of redirecting everything to its own concrete being, feels universalized, cleansed from any existential particularism. This universality does not mean self-denial, as was indicated previously; on the contrary, the subject lives with a new intensity in this new situation, which, at the same time that it opens him to reality, in a sense brings the whole of reality to him. . . .

The *freedom* characteristic of the spirit, which Max Scheler considers to be one of the three traits that define it, is only the evasion of natural particularism; it is autonomy with regard to the interests and incentives of the living human being as a single concrete entity. Freedom, therefore, is absolute objectivism and universalism as viewed from the relation of the spiritual subject to the nonspiritual subject that sustains it and with which it lives. One should keep in mind that, properly speaking, it is not a matter of the spirit's independence from "life" in the biological sense—from the strictly organic and animal complex—because the section of nature most closely related to the spirit is not organic nature, but intentional nature. The freedom of the spirit is affirmed against the propensities and attitudes of what we have called the natural man—the man subject to intentional, nonspiritualized acts. It is not opposed to some animal-man who does not exist in the human race. The essential duality of man is rooted precisely in the difference and the frequent conflict between the natural conditioning of what is merely intentional and the freedom of the spirit or, what amounts to the same thing, between full subjectivism and full objectivism, between particularism and universalism. . . .

From this radical objectivism also stems a *unity* of the spirit, which is primarily perceivable in the most general and consolidated spiritual attitudes, such as the cognitive and the ethical attitudes. . . .

The *historicity* of the spirit has been previously discussed. The spirit has a historical source; it emerges in a determined season, probably when the merely intentional function has been consolidated. Spiritual acts are absolute—that is, they either have the distinctive features or they are not spiritual acts. But their "habitualness," their frequency, is undoubtedly a historical conquest. . . .

Respect and interest (the "disinterested interest") are the secondary traits of the spirit. The spirit respects everything and is interested in everything, and obvious signs of the absence of spirit are lack of respect and indifference with regard to beings and things. The pragmatic stamp that mere intentional consciousness imposes on its objectifications is a lack of respect for what they are in themselves and a lack of interest in their own, nontransferable character. From a certain point of view, to behave spiritually is to be aware that everything is worthy of respect and everything is interesting. Philosophy, pure science, and art are born of a disinterested interest in things, of a respect for what is and for what is imagined. It is not difficult to discover in the moral attitude the confluence of the high potential of interest and respect. For common eyes the only hierarchy of beings and things is that given by reasons which pertain to the practical order. . . .

Responsibility is a trait of the spirit that has received little attention. There is a feeling of responsibility that tends to reach very elevated forms and, though not belonging to the sphere of the spirit, almost borders on it. We do not refer to the responsibility that primitive man experiences toward his group, for he is hardly individualized; rather it is that felt by the subject when he lives as an identical and continuous self. This responsibility to one's own individuality, to one's own life as reality, whether as fictionally imagined or as projected, at times reaches the heroic and the sacrificial. The same is true of responsibility with respect to others when a solid nexus of interests and affection exists. Spiritual responsibility has special characteristics. The responsibility of the subject to himself as a spiritual subject, as a person, presupposes responsibility to other persons conceived as entities of equal worth. The spirit, as we have repeatedly stated, is an absolutely objective projection, and it feels, as an intimate obligation, that it must act as such. . . .

Self-consciousness has been considered by Max Scheler as one of the three principal traits of the spirit. But self-consciousness is not an exclusive attribute of the spirit. In nonspiritualized intentionality, self-consciousness is to be found as soon as the subject is firmly constituted as a self. An unprecedented intensification of subjective interests tends to reinforce self-consciousness without taking into account that there are more or less morbid psychic dispositions that turn the subject toward himself and stir up a watchful and even exasperated self-consciousness. In general, the adolescent, the timid person, and the introvert turn toward their own inner reality. There is also a frankly pathological complacency in self-contemplation in some psychic types (the one who analyzes himself, the one who feels sorry for himself, the one who suffers from an excess of intense scruples, the one who feels inferior) that leads to a constant probing and, as a result, an exaggerated self-consciousness which abounds in erroneous interpretations and a defective appreciation of the context in reality in which the self is found. . . .

Finally, we hold *absolute transcendence* to be the essential trait of the spirit.

Spirit as Absolute Transcending

As we have repeatedly asserted, the fundamental difference between the spiritual act and the merely intentional act consists in the fact that the former is directed toward its object without a subjective return, whereas the latter has a subjective intent, a subordination of the object to the particular goals of the subject. Such a difference may also be expressed by saying that the nonspiritual act is transcendent to the extent that it has an undeniable, objective direction inseparable from its intentional character. Yet it partly denies or shifts its transcendence by referring the object, in one way or another, to the interests of the subject. The spiritual act, however, is absolutely transcendent because it goes out to the object and remains with it, in no way actually referring the object to the existential uniqueness of the subject.

The spiritual act thus achieves pure transcendence. Its reference to the subject is only the inevitable connection between the subject and his act. . . .

The absolute transcendence and the full objectivism of the spiritual act come to be the same thing. But the introduction of the notions of transcendence and immanence makes possible the sounding of the spiritual act to its very depths, the placing of it in relation to metaphysical hypotheses that help in understanding its place and meaning in totality. It also offers a new interpretation of values that recognizes their objectivity without falling into the error of disconnecting the realm of values from that of being, an error incurred by most axiological systems of an objectivist bent.

Although, as we have indicated, absolute transcendence and complete objectivism come to be the same thing, strictly speaking they are not identical. In our opinion, absolute transcendence is primary, basic, and original in the spiritual act. Thus, one should not say that an act is fully transcendent and objective, rather that it is completely transcendent; and, as a consequence, it is completely objective, because absolute transcendence is what provides the foundation for complete objectivity. In the merely intentional act the transcending toward the object is accompanied by the domination of the subject as a cluster of interests which leads to the modification of the object, its practical subordination to the subject. The transcendence is, therefore, weak and incomplete, and it is ultimately defeated by the subjective demands. In the spiritual act, transcendence works without obstacles or limitations; its strength yields to no opposition. The spiritual subject is the one who is identified and the one who coincides with the transcending impulse of the act. The objectivity is a direct expression of that transcendence, of the lack of subjective return; and all other qualities of the spiritual act, as they have been previously set forth, can be equally understood as manifestations or consequences of absolute transcendence.

Something will be said later concerning transcendence in general and freedom. Transcendence is always a setting free and, in its turn, freedom is a mode or an aspect of transcendence. The constitution of the intentional order undoubtedly points to the appearance of a regime that is much freer than the organic order. The intentional individual enjoys an autonomy superior to that of the animal. . . .

As for self-consciousness, lived though its content may be, it is only conceivable through "reflection," by the return of the subject to itself. The subject goes out of itself in order to fall back on itself; it is the point of departure and the destination of the act. Self-possession confers on the self a dual role, as possessor and as possession. However it occurs, it presupposes that the subject steps out of himself in order to return again, to himself. This going out of oneself is a transcending of oneself. And in the same manner as we have already done for freedom, we must distinguish here between restricted and total transcendence, between a transcendence that later becomes immanent and a pure or spiritual transcendence. There is a transcendence accompanied by a tendency to immanence when the reflection which grants the self-consciousness does not take the subject out of the natural level; when in it and through it the subject continues to live, in an absolute sense, as the supreme reality to which everything else, for all practical purposes, must be subjected. There is spiritual self-consciousness when the subject, as he transcends in his reflection of himself, perceives himself in full objectivity—which is close yet at the same time distant—and therefore can possibly refer to himself with that "disinterested interest" of which full objectivity consists. The reflective transcendence that this self-consciousness affords is obviously absolute.

Spirit in the Context of a Metaphysics of Transcendence

Reality is arranged on four different levels or orders: the physical or inorganic level; the level of life; the level of intentional psychism; and the level of the spirit. Each is the foundation of the level that follows it, emerges from it, feeds on it, and surpasses it. A notable increase in transcendence is evident in this succession of levels. One can best imagine a pure immanence on the physical level here, transcendence is least visible. It is at this point that the attempts at a strict rationalist interpretation have felt the preference for "downward explanations," that is, for the idea that the physical order is the only one with substantial or metaphysical worth and that all the rest is a manifestation of the physical, a mere accidental result of the interplay of matter. Transcendence is quite evident in life. Living beings are active centers of transcendence, not only as individuals and species but, above all, as they make up the whole current of life, multiplying on the inorganic level as they colonize it. Living beings succeed and reproduce through the series of generations in which the progenitors transcend themselves and seem to continue to transcend themselves, even after they have disappeared, through the continuity of a vital message entrusted to the farthest reaches of time. In intentional psychism transcendence is even more evident: intentionality consists precisely in the transcendence toward the object. The subject is the point of departure of innumerable, continuous transcending acts, and the horizon for such acts is practically unlimited because everything is objectifiable—everything is or may be the target of intentions. The whole of reality with all its elements, real and nonreal, has been converted into a stage where the intentional individual acts out his role, which consists of nothing other than acts of intentionality, of transcendence. This transcendence, however, is not complete. The intentional individual refers his acts to himself; as an existing individual, he holds himself to be the ultimate concern to whom all his acts are tied by the bonds of his own interest. Such a limitation or relativization of transcendence disappears in the spiritual attitude, so that all actual reference of the act to the subject is severed—except that the act still remains that of the subject. The subject, we might say, is the point of departure of the act but not its goal; this is true, however, of the purely intentional act, because of the concrete and individual interest in the purpose of the act. The spiritual subject, therefore, is a focus of pure transcendences; in him transcendence reaches its highest possible attainment. The animating thrust of the whole of reality thereby achieves its triumph and functions with total autonomy, free from any remainder of immanence. This functioning consists in reaching out to the whole of reality, unhindered by bonds or compulsions; it consists in turning in a special way toward oneself as the informing principle of reality, in cognitively apprehending oneself and in achieving an ethical wholeness with oneself. . . .

The three orders of reality that form an echelon above the physical level reveal a gradual increase in transcendence. There is more transcending on the organic than on the physical level, on the intentional than the organic level, and on the spiritual than the merely intentional level. Spiritual transcendence indicates the apex and does not allow for a higher level; it is absolute and total transcendence. Spiritual acts are defined by their completely objective direction, and the spiritual focus—the subject—is immediately identified with his acts. As self-consciousness, the subject is constituted through acts of pure, reflected transcendence, which do not form kernels of immanence. Spiritual self-consciousness is fully objective, and the only "lived" factor found in it is the direct impression of transcendence, which is the specific feeling that accompanies every spiritual act. One might conclude from this that when the concretely immanent disappears from the subject, all effective individuation also disappears. But we have already made clear that transcendence is not the annulling of the center that transcends, rather it is action that stems from that center, a going beyond oneself without ceasing to be that self. Spiritual individuality is assured by the unity and continuity of the subject, by its reflexive reference to itself, and by the distinctness of the spiritual processes, so far as they form an organic complex that constitutes the activity and experience appropriate to each self. . . .

DUALITY

Duality is the constitutive event of the complete man. The being we properly refer to as man, who has a destiny, who develops historically and is determined by individual and group motivations—yet he also obeys certain demands that are foreign to these motivations which shape an ideal order—this being, we say, is fundamentally a dual entity. In principle we have maintained that man is created when the intentional function is normally organized, bringing with it the appearance of the subject, the constitution of an objective world for him, and the elaboration of culture with the indispensable, objectified creations. All this carries with it something new with respect to the animal kingdom, and it is sufficient to provide for man's separation from the zoological scale, justifying that a new section within the bounds of reality be marked out for him. If what is human rested solely on intentionality,[2] as defined in Part One of this book, that special section kept apart for man would be within the natural sphere. When intentionality is dispossessed of spiritual demands, it is no more than the highest expression of natural activity. From his beginning, however, man is capable of spirit, and he seems to be gifted with spirituality from the first stages of history. Perhaps what we currently call history is the human process beginning with the emergence of the spirit. The man we know, and the one to whom we attribute the characteristics which define the species, is man with the spirit, though we do not absolutely exclude the existence of men lacking in spirituality. The complete, finished man, not some fiction or idealized image, but a historical reality, is he who comes to us as a complex in which mere intentionality and spirit alternate and are joined together. Man permanently deprived of the spirit may subsist in the lowest levels of the species, in the midst of embryonic cultures or even sporadically located in middle and high cultures. In any case, at least in some degree, the spirit is indispensable if we are to recognize what it is in man that we call human in the full sense.

Without spirit, man is already something more—rather, much more than an animal. He is a subject who through his continued, subjective activity is converted into a self; he contemplates and conceives a world of objectivities which is extended in space and time and which leads him to live, taking into consideration what is present, what has happened, and what is foreseen, and is thus in keeping with the past and the future. He makes use of the rich accumulation of objectifications of the community, which he receives through significant language, and he creates and uses culture, which in its elemental forms does not necessarily presuppose the spirit. There is nothing similar to this in the animal kingdom. Natural man, or man without spirit, is, then, a being different from any organic entity, because he encloses his organic life in, and makes it conform to, intentional lines, in keeping with the general situation traced by the enumerated elements whose extraorganic character seems quite evident. Demanding as the biological requirements may be for natural man, they echo throughout a structure which imposes its own special mode of being upon them. Preintentional psychism comes to be an echo or a psychical modulation of the organic realm. Intentional psychism responds to its own laws and is governed by them, strong as the organic ingredients may be that are introduced in it.

As was stated, spiritual projection is latent in intentionality. Intentionality perceives objectively, it recognizes what is perceived as subsisting. The spirit radically strengthens the objectification, showing that what is objectified enjoys a fullness of being and autonomy when confronting the objectifying subject, making it possible for the latter to act without the subjective return. In order to understand the significance and scope of spirituality in man, one must keep in mind that it does not consist of a principle completely alien to his primitive nature. It does not consist of an element which comes to primitive human reality from the outside and is inserted into it in some mysterious manner. We might say that it is the fulfillment of the promises contained in the most unpretentious intentional attitudes; it is the completion of what was already present as a seed in the first objectifying acts.

However, this does not set aside the radical difference between mere intentionality and spirituality, for this difference points to a profound break between the spirit and all natural reality. With the spirit, a new order in reality is established; the enclosure of each part of reality within itself, which is characteristic of nature, is broken, and centers heedful of totality are organized, centers which lean toward totality, receiving it in keeping with their universality. Stated in another way, they are centers which transcend themselves and radiate to every horizon, giving whole-hearted attention to whatever is, through different spiritual attitudes yet without being dissolved or even weakened thereby, but rather purifying and strengthening their condition as personal centers. Spirituality, as we have already seen, imposes a complete inversion in the direction of the interest of the subject, whose behavior changes, through the work of the spirit, from subjectivism to full objectivism, from particularism to universalism, from partial to absolute transcendence.

The duality of man is a fact widely recognized in religious and philosophical concepts. . . .

NOTES

1. [Romero uses the word "psychism" and its adjectival form "psychical" with a meaning similar to that developed by Brentano. Husserl's discussion on pp. 249–50 of his *Ideas* (New York: Macmillan, 1931), clarifies the use of this terminology.—Trans.]

2. Personal spirituality is always intentionality. For the sake of convenience, when we use the word "intentionality" by itself, we are referring to what at other times we have called mere intentionality—that is, an intentionality not spiritualized.

Risieri Frondizi
(1910–1983)

F rondizi belonged to that generation of Latin American philosophers
born around 1910 whose contributions to philosophy began in the
1940s. His writings are not extensive, but his work was sound, original,
and stated in a meticulously clear style. This last characteristic was the
result, at least in part, of the contact he maintained with Anglo-Saxon philosophy.

Frondizi was born in Posadas, Argentina, in 1910. His education, however, took place in Buenos Aires, where he received the degree of professor of philosophy in 1935. He also received a master of arts from the
University of Michigan in 1943 and the doctorate in philosophy from the
National Autonomous University of Mexico in 1950. Some of his graduate
work was done at Harvard, where he studied under A. N. Whitehead, C. I.
Lewis, and R. B. Perry, among others. In 1933 he studied in Buenos Aires
with Romero, with whom he maintained a close relationship until
Romero's death.

His teaching career began at the University of Tucumán in 1938, where
he also served as chair of the department of philosophy and letters for two
years (1938–40). In 1946 he was forced to abandon the country for political reasons. During this period he was visiting professor of philosophy at
the Central University of Venezuela (1947–48) and the Universities of
Pennsylvania (1948–49), Yale (1949–50), Puerto Rico (1951–54), and
Columbia (1955). He returned to Argentina in 1955 and resumed his
teaching responsibilities as professor at the Universities of La Plata
(1955–56) and Buenos Aires (1956–66). In the latter university he was
elected dean of the Faculty of Philosophy and Letters (1957) and president
of the university for two terms (1957–62). His heavy involvement in university reform forced him to relinquish his philosophical work for a time.

When the military government of Onganía put an end to the autonomy of the university, he resigned from his positions in protest, and accepted positions at the University of California in Los Angeles (1956–68), the University of Texas (1968–69), and the University of Southern Illinois at Carbondale. He retired in 1979, but subsequently was appointed distinguished visiting professor at Baylor University, a post he held until his death.

The importance of Frondizi's work both within Latin America and internationally was recognized on various occasions. He was elected president of the Inter-American Society of Philosophy and of the Argentine Philosophical Society as well as a member of the executive council of the International Federation of Societies of Philosophy and of the International Institute of Philosophy in Paris. In addition he was a member of the Institute of Advanced Studies at Princeton and lectured at several of the most important universities in both Americas and at leading European universities. In 1980 twenty philosophers from around the world presented him with a volume in his honor entitled *Man and His Conduct* and published by the University of Puerto Rico Press.

His main works were published in several editions: *El punto de partida del filosofar* (1945–57); *Substancia y función en el problema del yo* (1952–70, also under the title *El yo como estructura dinámica)*; and *¿Qué son los valores?* (1958: 5th ed., 1972). The last two works also appeared in English as *The Nature of the Self* (1953, 1971), and *What Is Value?* (1963, 1971). In addition, he published approximately fifty articles on various philosophical topics and several books on the mission of the university in Latin America (1971).

In Frondizi's first work we are able to find a general sketch of his thought. He maintains that philosophy is the theory of human experience constituted by the self, its activity, and objects. In the book devoted to the problem of the self, he is opposed to Descartes's substantialism as well as Hume's atomism, and develops a concept of the self as a dynamic structure. Later he applied this approach to the study of values, taking a position opposed to both axiological subjectivism and objectivism. For Frondizi, value is a structural quality that emerges in the relationship between the subject and its objects and is present in every situation. His axiology leads to a situational ethics, although in his judgment this does not imply an ethical relativism. On the contrary, the existence of an axiological hierarchy for every situation strengthens ethical feeling as well as human creative activity.

The Nature of the Self

THE BEING AND THE DOING OF THE SELF

Experience shows us that the self does not depend upon any obscure or hidden substantial core but depends upon what it does, has done, proposes to do, or is able to do. The self is revealed in its action; it reveals itself and constitutes itself by acting. It is nothing before acting, and nothing remains of it if experiences cease completely. Its *esse* is equivalent to its *facere*. We are not given a ready-made self; we create our own self daily by what we do, what we experience. Our behavior—in which both our actual doing and our intentions should properly be included—is not an expression of our self but the very stuff which constitutes it.

What holds experiences together, what gives us personality, is not, therefore, a substantial bond but a functional one, a coordinated structure of activities. The self is not something already made but something that is always in the making. It is formed throughout the course of its life, just as any institution is formed—a family, a university, a nation. There is no aboriginal nucleus of the self that exists prior to its actions; the self arises and takes on existence as it acts, as it undergoes experiences. The category of substance must be supplanted by that of function if we wish to interpret adequately the nature of the self. The concept of function connotes, in this case, the concepts of activity, process, and relation.

The functional link by no means includes only our past experiences. The self is memory, but it is not memory alone. Our personality depends upon what has happened to us, but it cannot be reduced to our personal history; the self is not the blind aggregate of our experiences. We get the

From Risieri Frondizi, *The Nature of the Self* (Carbondale: Southern Illinois University Press, 1971), pp. 145–47, 158–63, 170–77, 181–84, 188–93, 197–200. Reprinted by permission of the author.

push of the past, but we also get the pull of the future. There is, in the self, a note of novelty and creativity, a free will, an ability to control the eventual course of our experiences. Activity, therefore, contains an element of novelty; it cannot be grasped or comprehended by referring exclusively to its past. The self is not inert matter, deposited on the shore by the tide of experience, but creative will, plotting its own course for itself. It depends upon its past history but is able to mold its own history-to-be, to orient its life according to new courses. It is memory but memory projected toward the future, memory hurled ahead. The future conditions the nature of our self not only as it merges with the present but also while it is still more distantly future. What we plan to do, even if we never get to do it, gives sense to our activities. The future, however, is not a part of our self merely as a system of ideas and intentions; it also enters into the formation of the self through our emotions. In times of confusion and disaster the thought of the future of our country, our child, our own lives grieves us. Though it is true that this suffering is a present and not a future experience, its object is the future. It is like the pain caused by a splinter; the pain is not the splinter, but it could not exist without the presence of the splinter. Hope, despair, and many other experiences would be impossible if the future were not an element in our lives.

The self is a function already performed but also a function to be fulfilled, a capacity, a potentiality. Our being consists of what we have done but also of what we intend and are able to do. The past creates ability; the ability gives a sense of direction to the past. Even the capacity that was never realized, the potentiality that never had the chance of becoming actual, forms an integral part of our self.

The past and the future of the self are not, strictly speaking, separable parts; they form an indissoluble whole. The past acquires meaning in the light of the future; the future, in turn, depends upon the past. We cannot do whatever we want; our abilities depend upon our past experiences.

Some people have denied the dynamic character of the self or have relegated it to a position of secondary importance, thinking it to be incompatible with its unity. Unable to conceive of the unity of a changing being, they have considered that the process of alteration of the self only scratches its surface and that the self keeps an immutable central core. It is true that there is only one Ego for each experiential stream, but it is also true that the self is not immutable. We have seen that the self is constantly changing, that everything that happens to us enriches and modifies our self. But change does not mean substitution; rather, it means an alteration of the inner pattern. Thus, former experiences never quite disappear completely, though they can change their nature and meaning with the development of the self.

ANALYSIS AND ANALYTICISM

As is well known, the method that is used conditions the nature of the object under observation. If, blinded by the prestige acquired by the scientific method, we commit the stupid blunder of the modern tourist who tries to examine under the microscope a city which he is visiting for the first time, we shall not succeed in seeing the houses, the people, the plants, and the flowers. It would imply an even greater blindness to maintain that in the city there are neither houses nor people nor flowers, without realizing that they have disappeared as a consequence of the instrument chosen. The naked eye, in such a case, is a better instrument than the microscope, which, though it shows us the detail, keeps us from seeing the whole.

The analytic method has often worked like a microscope. It has revealed details which no one had ever seen before, but it has impeded our view of the whole. Again, the naked eye and the free-ranging glances of the spirit are superior to the intellect provided with the perfected technique and instruments of analysis. We need only to glance within, if we hold no prejudicial theories, to see what is hidden from the philosophers using analytic methods and blinded by the postulates of their theory and by their technique of observation.

Why should we be surprised that the wholes are not perceived if it has already been accepted in advance that analysis is the only form of apprehension? That which has been previously eliminated cannot be discovered, and it is impossible to reconstruct what should never have been destroyed.

The analytic philosophy which sprang from Hume's atomism is subject to an almost demoniac desire for destruction—destruction by reductions. When confronted by a whole, these philosophers make no effort to comprehend its nature and find the sense of the whole. They proceed immediately to chop the whole into as many parts as possible and to submit each part to the thoroughgoing test of analysis. It is like the little boy who wants to find out what makes his toy work and ends up defiantly facing a heap of loose nuts and bolts.

This destructive drive is based upon a metaphysical postulate from which another postulate, an epistemological one, is derived; these two postulates support what we might call "the fallacy of reduction." The metaphysical postulate may be stated thus: elements have a more actual reality than wholes. The epistemological consequence is obvious: the goal of philosophic knowledge is to come to grips with the basic elements which constitute reality.

From these two postulates a series of principles is derived and conditions the whole attitude of the analytic philosophers. There are two principles which particularly concern us in the study which we are making: (a) that the "parts" or elements can be separated from the "whole" without undergoing any change; (b) that these elements can be discovered by analysis and defined in such a way that leaves no room for doubt. . . .

I am not proposing, of course, the abandonment of analysis as a philosophic method. It is not clear how analysis could be abandoned without falling into an attitude of contemplative mysticism, which would bring as its immediate consequence greater confusion and obscurity to the field of philosophy. What I am criticizing is *analyticism, if we may so call it*, which attempts to reduce to analysis every philosophic task and actually analyzes away what is really important.

Analysis involves the disarticulation of a complex reality whose unity is destroyed when its component members are separated. It can be used in the realm of psychic life with a great deal of profit and very little danger, provided that one is constantly aware of its limitations and consequences and never loses sight of the fact that the elements which have been separated by analysis are members of a totality which must, of necessity, remain united. Analysis should therefore be used—always, of course, keeping the totality in mind—only in order to make clear the meaning of the whole and to comprehend its inner mechanism, not in order to eliminate the whole or reduce it to a heap of disjointed pieces. Hence analysis should be applied to a structure only after the structure has been taken in and recognized as a whole; reality should not be sacrificed to the method used. . . .

The analytic attitude is moreover complemented by a mechanical conception of the psychic life which tries to "explain" everything by means of simple elements and the forces that move them. When the psychic life has been put together again in this way, it has lost its organic unity, its spontaneity, its very life—all that characterizes the human being. Hence the final result seems more like a robot than a man: the parts that make it up remain unalterable, and the forces that move it are completely mechanical. The process of reconstruction cannot give us what analysis has previously destroyed—the organic coherence of the inner life. Reconstruction is neither necessary nor possible, for this organic unity is a primary reality and not the conclusion of a system.

THE CONCEPT OF *GESTALT*

What is the self before its unity has been broken down by analysis? In what does its organic or structural unity consist?

Let us first make clear that this unity is not one that transcends the empirical world, the world of experiences. It is a unity derived from the very experiences themselves. There is nothing under or above the totality of experiences. If one overlooks the word "totality" or interprets it in an atomistic sense, this statement would be equivalent of subscribing to Hume's theory. But we should never interpret the totality or structure of experiences as a mere sum or aggregate of the same. The experiential totality has qualities which are not possessed by the members which constitute it. Consequently the characteristics of the total structure of the self cannot be deduced, necessarily, from the characteristics of each of the experiences taken separately. . . .

What is it that characterizes a *Gestalt?* Like any other fundamental concept, that of *Gestalt* presents a degree of complexity which does not allow one to enunciate in a few words all the richness of its content. Nevertheless, there are certain characteristics which seem to be fundamental. First, there is the one that has already been emphasized: a structural whole—a *Gestalt*—has qualities not possessed by any of the elements which form it. In this sense, a *Gestalt* or structure is set in contrast with a mere sum of elements. The physical and chemical qualities of a cubic yard of water are the same as those of each gallon that makes it up. The whole, in this case, is no more than the mere sum of its parts. In the case of a structure, on the other hand, this is not so, as we have seen in considering the character of a melody; it possesses qualities which cannot be found in any of the notes, for it can be transposed without being changed into another melody.

The above-mentioned characteristic does not mean, of course, that a *Gestalt* is completely independent of the members which constitute it. In the first place, there can be no structure without members. But the dependence of structure upon members does not stop here—the removal, addition, or fundamental alteration of a member modifies the whole structure, as can be seen in the case of an organism. Any important alteration or suppression of a member alters the totality of an organism and may even cause its disappearance. This does not happen in the case of a sum. We can remove one, two, thirty, or forty gallons of water without causing the rest to undergo any important change in quality.

But not only does the structural whole suffer alteration when one of its members is taken away, the member that is taken away is also basically altered. A hand separated from the body is unable to feel or to seize an object—it ceases to be a hand—whereas the gallon of water separated from the rest retains practically all of its properties. This characteristic, taken along with the foregoing one, will suffice for the definition of a member of a structure. A member of a structure is that which cannot be removed without affecting the whole structure and losing its own nature when separated from the "whole." Conversely, we can characterize the "mere sum" as something made up of "parts" or "elements" that undergo no change when joined to other "parts" and which can be removed without producing any change either in itself or in what remains. The relationship between the parts is that of mere juxtaposition.

The difference between structure and mere sum does not stem solely from the fact that the parts of the latter are independent of the whole and that the members of the former are conditioned by the structure. There is also the fact that the parts may be homogeneous, whereas the members must offer diversity and even opposition of characteristics. One gallon of water is just as much water as any other gallon or measure. The same is true of one brick in a pile of bricks or of each grain of sand in the desert. On the contrary, in an organism each member has its own specific nature—the heart is the heart and cannot perform the functions of the liver or kidneys. There is not only diversity among the members but also opposition; and this opposition is subsumed into the unity which organizes them. The unification and organization of the members which make up a structure do not come about at the expense of the peculiar and distinctive qualities of each member. Organization is not the equivalent of homogenization, and unity does not contradict the multiplicity and diversity of the elements. This multiplicity and diversity must always be maintained as absolutely essential. Thus we find structure to be the result of a dialectic play of opposites, of a struggle between the members; it seems to hang by the thread which establishes a dynamic balance. But this unity is not of an abstract sort. A concept which organizes different members into a unity by grouping them in agreement with a common note does not constitute a structure. One essential aspect of the structure is lacking: its unity must be concrete. For that reason I use the term "structure" rather than "form" or "configuration" to translate the German word *Gestalt*, which, besides carrying the connotation of these two latter concepts, designates a unity that is *concrete*.

THE STRUCTURAL UNITY OF THE SELF

When we considered the applicability of the category of substance to the self, we noticed that none of the three classic characteristics of this concept—immutability, simplicity, and independence—belonged to the self. We obtained a similarly negative result from the consideration of the atomistic conception. In the first place, the supposed psychic atom is a poorly defined unit which, when one attempts to fix it with any precision, vanishes into thin air, becoming a mere arbitrary instant in an uninterrupted process. In the second place, the aggregation of atoms, which can have only a relationship of juxtaposition one to another, looks like a grotesque caricature of the real organic unity of the self. Let us now see if the category which we have called *Gestalt* or structure is any more successful.

It seems unquestionable that the psychic life is not chaotic, that each state or experience is connected to all the rest. This connection, however, is not of experience to experience, like the links of a chain, for if this were so there would be a fixed order of connections and in order to get to one link we should necessarily have to go by way of the preceding ones. But in the same way that Köhler showed that there is no constant relation between stimulus and response, it would be easy to show that in like manner there is no constant relation between one experience and another. No laboratory experiment is needed to prove this, for our daily experiences supply all the material we require—the sound and sight of the sea is exhilarating one day and depressing the next; the same piece of music arouses in us different reactions according to the situation in which we hear it; our arrival at the same port and in the same ship can start altogether different trains of reflection in us, depending on whether we have arrived to stay for the rest of our life or only for a short vacation; the memory of a disagreement with a friend, which irritated us so much when it happened, may now provoke only an indifferent smile. The relations of experiences to each other resemble the relations between stimuli and responses in the fact that they arise within a given context.

These undeniable data of the psychic life are founded on the fact that the self is not a sum of experiences or an aggregate of parts in juxtaposition but a structure—in the sense defined above; whatever happens to one of its elements affects the whole, and the whole in turn exerts an influence upon each element. It is because the whole reacts as a structural unity and not as a mechanism that a stimulus can provoke consequences in an altogether different field from the one in which it has arisen. Thus, a strictly intellectual problem can give rise to emotional torment, and a fact of an emotional sort can have far-reaching volitional consequences. The self is not departmentalized—like modern bureaucracy—but constitutes an organic unity with intimate, complex, and varied interrelations.

The self presents itself, then, as an organized whole, an integrated structure, and experiences are related to one another not through but within the whole. For that reason, when the structure is modified the nature of the experiences and of the relationships between them are also modified. The interdependence of the different experiential groups shows that the self is a structure which is organized and "makes sense" and that each member occupies its proper place within the structure.

This does not mean, of course, that the structure which constitutes the self cannot be analyzed and broken down, theoretically, into less complex structures. It does mean, however, that we are in fact dealing with a unity that is formed upon substructures and the intimate and complex interrelation of these substructures.[1]

And here we notice another characteristic of the concept of structure which is directly applicable to the self: the members of a structure are heterogeneous in contrast with the homogeneity of the parts of a non-structural unity. Let us state, first of all, that the structure which constitutes the self, being a very complex structure, is made up not of "simple members" but of substructures; it is consequently to the heterogeneity of these substructures that we are referring. It must also be kept in mind that the substructures are not of an abstract nature, like concepts, and that we are not trying to reconstruct a reality by juxtaposing abstractions such as the so-called faculties of the soul.

The complexity and heterogeneity of the structure are twofold: on the one hand there is the complexity which we may call transversal; on the other there is the horizontal or, better, the temporal complexity. In actuality the self embraces the combination of both complexes, which do not and cannot exist in separation. . . .

This diversity and opposition among the elements which constitute the self should not lead us to forget the unity which characterizes every structure. The self is no exception. Its multiplicity does not exclude its unity or vice versa. And this is not the abstract unity of a concept which points to what is common; it is a concrete unity, of "flesh and blood" as Unamuno would say, for there is nothing more real and concrete than our self. Diversity underlies the structure but is in turn lost within it, for the elements uphold each other mutually in an intimate sort of interweaving in which it is impossible to distinguish warp from woof. This is not because the three types of substructure have equivalent strength and no one of them dominates the other two—as in the theory of the so-called balance of power—but because they vary constantly. At a given moment one element stands forth as the figure and the others form the ground; after a while there is a change of roles. These changes are explained by the fact that the self is a dynamic structure and thus resembles a symphony rather than a painting.

We should perhaps stress the point that the changes undergone by the self are not due exclusively to a different distribution of the members, for the members themselves are of a dynamic nature. Moreover, the self is constituted not only of members but also of the *tensions* produced by the reciprocal play of influences. The breakdown of the equilibrium of tensions is what generally produces the most important changes.

It now appears obvious that the relations between the experiences are not fixed, for each experience as it is incorporated into the structure modifies its former state. This member in turn undergoes the influence of the whole, which is another characteristic of a *Gestalt* easy to find in the self. Thus, the perceptions which we have at this moment depend upon our former state. The new experience immediately acquires the coloration given it both by the basic structure of the self and by the particular situation in which it finds itself at that moment. If we are happy and in pleasant company, for example, the color of the spectacles we happen to be wearing has very little effect upon the emotive state of our spirit. This is not because visual perception ceases to have emotional tonality but because a greater affective tone—the happiness which results from a different cause—completely overshadows it. What is more, the stable nature of the self colors the transitory state. There are people who give the impression of seeing the world in the rosiest colors, whatever the tint of the spectacles they wear, and there are others who see clouds in the clearest sky.

This is the influence of the whole upon the member which is incorporated, but there is also an influence of the member upon the whole. We must not forget that a structure is not suspended in thin air but rests solely upon the members which constitute it. A symphonic orchestra is something more than the sum of the musicians that go to form it, but it cannot exist without the musicians. A self without the experiential structures that go to make it up would be the same as an orchestra without musicians, that is, a pure fantasy, the fantasy of a spiritual entity that would be unable to love, hate, decide, want, perceive, etc., and would pretend to be immutable substance. Such a concept would be immutable without doubt, but it would have the immutability of nothingness.

In the same way that the total suppression of the experiential structures would mean the suppression of the self, any change or alteration of a member has repercussions on the whole structure. By this I do not mean a man lacking in emotional life, for example, for it is obvious that he would not be a man but a mere caricature, or projection on a plane of two dimensions, of a three-dimensional reality. I am referring to the alteration of a structural subcomplex. Abulia, for example, is a disease of the will, but the changes which it provokes are not limited to the volitional—it has immediate repercussions in the emotive and intellectual spheres and consequently in the total structure. Its intellectual repercussions are easily seen, for the person suffering from abulia is unable to concentrate his attention, and thus his intellectual processes break down completely. And the emotional sphere is impaired, too, for the sufferer is unable, by an act of the will, to get rid of the emotion which has taken control of him, so he lets himself be so possessed by this emotion that it changes his whole personality.

Of the characteristics of the structure that are applicable to the self we have only to consider now the first and most important, that is, the fact that the structure possesses qualities not possessed by the members that make it up. At this stage in our inquiry it seems a waste of time to insist that this is one of the characteristics of the self. Let us consider only the most obvious reasons. The self has a permanence—in the sense of constant presence—and a stability that the experiences and experiential groups do not have. Experiences are totally unstable; transiency is their characteristic. The self, on the other hand, remains stable in the face of the coming and going of experiences. If experiences do not have stability, even less can they have permanence, which is the fundamental characteristic of the self. And this is not all. The structure of the self is such that the members that make it up cannot exist in separation from it. There is no experience that does not belong to a particular self. The self depends, then, upon the experiences, but it is not equivalent to their sum. It is a structural quality. . . .

PROBLEMS SOLVED BY THE STRUCTURAL CONCEPTION

A. Permanence and Mutability of the Self

At the beginning of this chapter we saw that both substantialism and atomism were unable to give an adequate picture of the self because they could not comprehend how its permanence and continuity could be compatible with the changes that it undergoes. Substantialism emphasized the permanence and atomism the mutability.

The structural conception that we are here proposing allows us to see that the two characteristics are not only compatible but also complementary. The historical survey of past thought on the subject, which occupied the first part of this book, showed us that substantialism could not understand the changing nature of the self because it held fast to an irreducible and immutable nucleus and that Hume's atomism, in its effort to destroy the doctrine of a substantial nucleus, confused it with the very real permanence and continuity of the self.

If we free ourselves of the limitations of both historical positions and observe reality just as it presents itself, we shall see that the permanence and continuity of the self are based upon its structural character, for it is a dynamic structure made up not only of the elements which we can isolate in a cross section of our life but also of the substructures that form the complex longitudinal bundles that constitute the self. And change occurs each time a new element is taken in, which alters but does not destroy the structure.

In this way the constant alteration of the self insures its stability. It is undeniable that a new experience modifies, or can modify, the structure of the self. The loss of a child or a friend, a war, a religious experience, etc., can produce such an inner commotion that they may alter the total structure. From that time on we are not the same person as before. We act in a different way, we see life in a different perspective, and it may be that not only the future but also the past is colored by the new attitude. But it is just this experience causing us to change which gives endurance to the self. From now on we shall be the man who has lost his son or his friend or who had this or that religious experience. Other children that we may have or the new friends which we may take into our hearts may cover up but can never completely obliterate the existence of an experience that at one time shook us deeply and persists in the structure of our spirit despite all that may happen to us in the future.

What happens on a large scale in the case of experiences that are profoundly moving happens on a smaller scale in all the other experiences of our life. Each new experience alters the structure or substructure to which it is connected, and thus it is incorporated "definitively," so to speak. Whatever happens afterward may alter the meaning of the experience within the whole—increasing it or diminishing it—but it can never erase the experience completely.

An analogy of a physical sort, even though inadequate to characterize our psychic life, may perhaps make clear the meaning of what I am trying to put across. The self resembles, in this respect, a mixture of colors. If we add to the mixture a new color—for example, blue—the mixture will be altered to a degree that will depend upon the quantity and shade of blue added and upon the combination of colors that were there before. This quantity of blue which produces a change in the former mixture is incorporated definitively into the whole, and however many more colors we add we shall never be able completely to counteract its presence.

The nature of the whole and the influence of the element incorporated into it are controlled, in the case of the analogy, by certain stable physical laws in which quantity plays an important role. This is not the case with psychic structures, in which quantity gives way to equality. Psychic structures obey certain principles, carefully studied by the *Gestalt* psychologists in the case of visual perception, which also exist in all the other orders of life and in the constitution of the total structure of the self. These general principles governing the organization of our total personality are what the most psychologically acute educators use as the basis for their choice of one type of experience rather than another in their endeavor to devise a system of corrective education for an aberrant personality.

Every self has a center or axis around which its structure is organized. When the personality has already developed, this axis is what gives direction and organization to our life, not only in that new experiences do not succeed in dislodging it from its route but also in that it chooses the type of experience that it finds to be in tune with it. But it is not a nucleus immutable in itself or fixed in relation to the rest of the structure. In the first place it undergoes an evolution which we can consider normal. The axis that predominates changes at the different stages of our life. In our earliest childhood the predominant experiential substructure is that related to alimentation, later it is play, and so on through life.

What is more, the center undergoes sudden displacements caused by new experiences that shake and modify the total structure. This is the case with the soldier who, according to war records, after devoting his life to the acquisition or intensification of his capacity for destruction and after exercising this capacity for years at the cost of many lives, suddenly discovers "the truth," "finds himself," decides that "we are all brothers." The center of his personality is completely displaced. His technical capacity as a killer, in which he formerly took pride—and centered his whole personality—is now a source of humiliation and shame. His personality must retrace its steps and choose another route.

These changes are due to many varied and complex reasons. Usually they have a long period of germination, as it were, in the world of the subconscious and burst forth full blown at a propitious moment. I recall the case of an American pilot who fought for several years in the Pacific; all of a sudden "the truth was revealed to him" while he was reading, more or less by chance, certain passages in the Bible. At other times the change comes about because of the intensification of the means of destruction; the explosion of the atomic bomb produced a psychological shock in many of those who had launched 200-pound bombs under the same flag. Most commonly it comes about because of the shock of contrast; the soldier, in the midst of hatred, destruction, and death, comes across people who are devoting their lives to healing, in a spirit of disinterested love, the physical and moral wounds that other men cause. These external situations usually act as the immediate cause for the eruption of subterranean currents; at other times they stir up for the first time currents that burst forth later on, if a propitious situation presents itself.

We should not be surprised that an apparently insignificant fact may be able to change the total structure of our personality after it has been stable for many years; in the psychological realm quantities are of no great importance. The principle, *causa aequat effectum,* is not valid in the interrelations of the different elements. *Gestalt* psychology has shown us how the constitution of the structure and its alteration are governed by principles that have nothing to do with the principle of causality in its simplistic interpretation as the equal of cause and effect. . . .

B. Immanence and Transcendence of the Self

Another apparent paradox—similar to that of permanence and mutability—which is resolved by the structural conception is that of the immanence and transcendence of the self. For both atomism and substantialism, immanence and transcendence are incompatible. Either the self is equivalent to the totality of experiences—and in this sense is immanent to them—or it is something that transcends the experiences. Atomism holds the first position and substantialism the second.

According to the theory that I am proposing, the self is immanent and transcends experiences at the same time, though admittedly the terms have different meanings from those attributed to them both by atomism and by substantialism. The self is immanent because it is, indeed, equivalent to the totality of experiences; but this totality, in turn, should be interpreted not as the sum or aggregate of the experiences but as a structure that has properties that cannot be found in its parts. According to this interpretation of the concept of totality, the self transcends the experiences and becomes a structural quality, in the sense in which Ehrenfels used this expression. Nevertheless, this is not the transcendence defended by the substantialists when they affirm the existence of a being that supports states or experiences. Mine is a transcendence that not only does not exclude immanence but actually takes it for granted.

Let us look at the problem from another point of view. The relation between the self and its experiences is so intimate that every experience reveals some aspect of the self; what is more, every experience forms part of the self. In this sense, the self seems to be represented in each one of the experiences, to be nothing but them. No experience, however, is able to reveal to us the self in its entirety. Not even the sum of all the experiences can do that. The self is able to transcend its autobiography; hence the possibility of a true repentance, a conversion, a new life. In the first instance the self seems to be immanent; in the second it is seen to be something that transcends its experiences.

The problem is clarified considerably if one turns his attention to those two propositions which Hume, and many others after him, considered to be incompatible: (a) that the self is nothing apart from its experiences; (b) that the self cannot be reduced to its experiences. I, of course, affirm that both propositions are true. When Hume maintained that the self should be reduced to a bundle of perceptions because it could not exist without them, he let himself be misled by the substantialist prejudice in favor of the so-called independence of the self. But the self, though not independent of the perceptions, is not reducible to the mere sum of them.

The paradox of the immanence and transcendence of the self, just like the paradox which we examined before, has arisen as a consequence of the way in which substantialists stated the problem of the self, a statement that the atomists accepted without realizing its consequences. The problem, as stated, presupposes a metaphysics and a logic which our conception rejects. First, it conceives of real existence as substance, independent and immutable; and second, it interprets the principles of identity and of noncontradiction in a very rigid way. My concept, on the other hand, gives a very dynamic interpretation to both principles, to the point of seeing in contradiction much of the essence of the real. What is more, I believe that there is nothing independent and immutable. I can hardly believe, therefore, in the independence and immutability of the self, the stuff of which is relationship and the essence of which is creative process.

C. Unity and Multiplicity

A variant of the preceding paradoxes is that of unity and multiplicity. When atomism took over the analysis of the self, its unity was destroyed forever and the self was turned into a great mosaic of loose pieces. Each perception became a reality in itself, independent, separable, sharply delimited. With this conception of the elements it proved impossible to rewin the lost unity. Atomists maintained, therefore, the plurality of the self, even though they sighed from time to time for the unity that they themselves had destroyed. When atomists—and men like William James who criticized atomism without being able to free themselves from the source of its confusion—ask what unites the different parts constituting the self, one must simply answer that the self never ceased to constitute a unity. Atomism's difficulties in reaching the unity of the self are merely a consequence of the arbitrary way in which it was dismembered. First they build a wall; then they complain they cannot see beyond the wall.

Substantialism, on the other hand, takes as its point of departure the postulate of unity and relegates multiplicity to accidents. The self is only one, although many different things happen to it.

With the importance that these "happenings" have for us—the self is made up of what it does—the whole statement of the problem collapses; the self is one or multiple according to how one looks at it. It is one if one focuses on the whole; it is multiple if one focuses on the members that constitute it. The self is the unity of the multiplicity of its experiences. . . .

NOTE

1. By substructure I mean any of the structural parts that constitute the total Gestalt that makes up the self.

Carlos Astrada
(1894-1970)

Astrada can still be considered one of the outstanding representatives of Heideggerian existentialism in Latin America, although he shifted to a Marxist orientation toward the end of his life.

He was born in Córdoba, Argentina, February 26, 1894, and died in 1970. He completed secondary education in the Colegio Monserrat and then began the study of law in his native city. In 1926 he obtained a scholarship to study in Germany for two years, later renewed for an additional two years. He studied at the University of Cologne and Freiburg with Scheler, Husserl, and Heidegger.

Upon returning to Argentina, Astrada was designated associate professor of the history of modern and contemporary philosophy in the University of Buenos Aires (1936–47) and professor of ethics in the University of La Plata (1937–47). He assumed Francisco Romero's position as professor of epistemology and metaphysics when the latter resigned in 1947 in protest against the Perón government. Romero then replaced Astrada in 1956 when the government of Perón fell. Astrada traveled to Moscow in 1956 where he gave lectures and in 1960 he traveled to Peking for the same purpose.

He wrote extensively and produced several works. His writing began with an article in 1931 and continued until his death. His main works are: *El juego existencial* (1933); *Idealismo fenomenológico y metafísica existencial* (1936); *La ética formal y los valores* (1938), which has an incisive criticism of the axiological absolutism of Scheler; *El juego metafísico* (1942); and *Temporalidad* (1943). After this there is a tendency to abandon existentialism and turn toward Hegel and Marx as is evident in *La revolución existencialista* (1952). The second edition of this work bears the title *Existencialismo y crisis de la filosofía* (1963) and has a "Conclusion" in which there is an even sharper turn toward Marxism. He also published *Hegel y la dialéctica* (1956), *El marxismo y la escatología* (1957), *Marx y Hegel* (1958), *Humanismo y dialéctica de la libertad* (1960), *La doble faz de la dialéctica* (1962), and other books that were collections of important essays. Unfortunately, in his later publications there is a decrease in the intellectual rigor that characterized his early work and he often falls into political rhetoric of a noble inspiration but lacking in theoretical foundation and significance. He proclaims that "Western culture" is crumbling inevitably and religious fervor, so modestly and ingeniously praised, can do nothing to counter this phenomenon. The downfall is due to the demise of capitalism.

Astrada was a passionate man who placed his thought at the service of his convictions. His philosophical training was wholly German. He relied primarily on Hegel, Nietzsche, Marx, phenomenology, Heidegger, and to a lesser degree on Scheler and Hartmann.

Astrada's conception of human beings is primarily Heideggerian, and takes on a strong social concern when his thought is reoriented under Marxist influence, as can be seen in the selections included in this anthology and in the passage quoted below, which is taken from the "Conclusion" of the 1963 edition of *Existencialismo y crisis de la filosofía*.

> We have therefore, on the one hand, an existential ontology (Heidegger) that is anchored in an irrationalist solipsism and, on the other hand, an existentialism (Sartre) that can be reduced to an ontological phenomenonalism without any foundation. . . . Within western, class-oriented philosophy, although they did not intend to do so, these two positions . . . have actualized the vigorous, radical problematic of dialectical materialism, giving emphasis by contrast to the perceptive insight of the philosophy of Marx.

This turn toward Marxism is reminiscent of Sartre, whose existentialism Astrada criticized on numerous occasions.

Existentialism and the Crisis of Philosophy

[THE PROBLEMATIC OF MAN]

Within the diversity of positions included in the common meaning of "existentialism," within its points of contact and divergency, one should take note of a perspective of great philosophical breadth and rigor represented primarily by the thought of Heidegger, in which the rhythm and direction of the new problematic is to be found.

One of the most significant dimensions of the phenomenological analysis of human existence *(Dasein)* focuses on that existence as it is present in this world in its naked facticity, as a temporal process that in itself is conclusive. Thus, *Dasein* is no longer conceived as mere transition, as a function of some other world of blessedness to which it might be destined. Within this focus emerges the affirmation of concrete existence with its socio-historical environment and of man's destiny as ground of being, making clear for man the way that leads to full humanity without transcendentalist interference or calls from the beyond.

Since man comes to existence in virtue of the ability to accede to the truth of being, what is at stake is nothing less than the actualization of the human essence of man as a being in this world, consigned to the world's finite dimensions. Man can be conceived only in his *humanitas* and is able to tend toward it because he thinks the truth about being and becomes the ek-sistent through accession to his own being.

Man's essence is in what he actually is, and not something beyond that, therefore he only wants to be what he can be, but this essence of man—his *humanitas*—is historical and not an ontological structure or nucleus of a supratemporal character. This is to say that the being of man

From Carlos Astrada, *Existencialismo y crisis de la filosofía* (Buenos Aires: Edit. Devenir, 1963), pp. 42–43, 65–69, 110–12, 128–30, 189–203.

129

must be accomplished in history through all its contingencies, necessities, and changes. In the midst of these, immersed in historical time, man will always be bound to his unpredictable earthly adventure: becoming human. To become human he directs himself toward the fullness of his own being in virtue of the relationship that in the midst of his own self-hood, that is, the temporal environment of his ek-sistence, he establishes with *being*, as the permanent dimension in the process of his historic humanity.

Being and Transcendence

Dasein possesses a structure that is both open to other things yet also endowed with a comprehension of them. The comprehension characteristic of *Dasein* draws a sketch in which things (the entity) are discovered in their possibility. To the things thus discovered, it attributes a *meaning*. "When the intra-mundane entity is discovered with the being of *Dasein*, when it is comprehended, we say it has meaning."[1] Therefore, what is articulated in a reference filled with comprehension we call meaning; meaning is that in which full comprehension of something is maintained. However, what is comprehended in the ultimate instance is not meaning but the entity itself, the thing to which we grant meaning and, correlatively, *being*. On this basis Heidegger says "meaning is an existential dimension of *Dasein*, not a property which, adhering to it, resides behind it or floats in an intermediate domain somewhere."[2] *Dasein* thus has meaning. This indicates that to ask for the meaning of being is to ask for being itself, since being can be understood by *Dasein*.

In following the two roads headed in opposite directions, which is a quest that Heidegger pursues, a difficulty or one might even say an ambiguity emerges that affects the direction and the ultimate consequences of the investigation. The outcome of this situation brings us to deciding on the possibility of a fundamental ontology in one of two directions: either in the direction of a transcendence that ends up in the objectivity of the old ontology (with the danger of falling back into the naturalist idea of being or into a theologically personalist idea of the same, with the added alternative of a mythical conception of being); or in the direction of an existential-historic transcendence, beyond the subject-object relation and the idea of being as the predicate of a suprasensible object. Such an ambiguity in Heidegger's thought, with its oscillation between two directions, gives rise to an ambivalent idea of being as well as of the historical essence of man.

The thread of all questioning, including questioning about being, begins with *Dasein* and returns to it.[3] When the problem of being is focused on its ontological root, that is, on the temporal structures of

Dasein, it can only be stated on the basis of the ontic as well as ontological preeminence of *Dasein,* of all the possibilities embedded within it. The problem of being is the philosophical radicalization of the understanding of being appropriate to *Dasein.* The problem is that philosophical thinking, ontological thematization, in straying from this root tends to hypostasize in a naturalistic direction or in that of a personal entity, the latter being the *summum esse* of religions, the understanding of being that is articulated in the unified concept of *being* as the unity of all existential things. All predication of being, all truth is relative to the being of *Dasein,* to its existence. In saying that it is relative, however, we are far from affirming that it is subjective, since its relativity is not bound to subjective will or discretion. "being-there" someone who lives concretely

Dasein, as discoverer of things, is not placed in an empty happening without a world, like a "subject" facing a correlative "object," rather because it is in the world it places itself through understanding itself in its own existence, in the presence of its own factual objectivity. The interrogation concerning being will be formulated beginning with the concrete situation of the entity that interrogates. That is to say, that "we interrogate here and now for ourselves."

Transcending in the comprehension of being, *Dasein* sketches its own being and the being of things through the articulation of the concept implied in an existential unity that permits it to predicate *being.* Such a concept is implied in the comprehension of being. This particular transcendence in which the comprehension of being moves is not a flight into the "objective," rather it is the way that conduces to an ontologico-existential interpretation of the objectivity of the *Dasein,* which is located *objectively* because of its de facto placement in the world, this side of "objectivism" and "subjectivism." That is to say, that the effective transcendence of *Dasein* is transcendence in existential immanence. The direction toward which this transcendence points is not the ontic polarity that stems from the subject-object relationship, but being as a relation installed through existence. Its horizon is temporality.

Transcendence is thus interwoven with the elemental temporality of *Dasein* within which all being is constituted. However, it is not appropriate to affirm of *Dasein,* as classical ontology did, that it is a *constancy* in the *present* or permanent presence indicative of an extratemporal "now," conceived as *eternity.* As the horizon of the comprehension of being, time can no longer be considered the "moving image of eternity" as is said in Plato's *Timaeus.* On the contrary, "eternity" is the *crystallization* or stagnation of a now that is absolutized in an artificial manner, segregated from finite temporality, that is, from originating time.

Being as Finite Temporal Progression

If a fundamental ontology, one with foundations in ek-sistence, were limited solely to explaining what has been stated above without exploring its ultimate consequences, it would be an ontology in every way inoffensive, stationary. However, the step forward is the incisive possibility of thinking of *being* in the sense of a temporal-finite progression, centered in the ek-sistent man, in virtue of which it is given to him to actualize himself in his own being, that is, in his historical essence. For man to be able to maintain himself in ek-sistence, he must accede to his being, that is to say to *being*, through remembering and through a prospective thinking that is inserted into the future as a mode of primary temporality. In these two temporal dimensions ek-sistence moves in its own realm—*being*—because if the present procures for *Dasein*, through its being-in-the-world, openness toward being and thereby its accession to ek-sistence also to forget *being*, since, through the primacy that the perceptive and representative contents in this mode of temporality have, the present is scattered in the entity. The temporalization of being occurs, thus, primarily in the past and the future, and it is thus that the "instant" can be actualized as present or as a mode of primary temporality, which permits us to recover the "instant" (maintaining the unity of the three modes of temporality) and to distinguish it from the "now," which is absorbed and scattered in the entity. In its historicity such an event is remembering what abides, which has neither passed by nor been completed but is at the same time an exploration, that is, an inserting into the future, wherein the existential decision is anticipated, attentive to *being* and to the plenitude of ek-sistence. This decision is not the anticipated decisiveness of which Heidegger speaks and through which *Dasein* reaches its limit in order to take hold of itself as a whole, rather it is a decision that is more elementary, in which that decisiveness finds its foundation, a decision that governs man (and here the *ethos* is revealed, the root of all ethic), as ek-sistent, to be and to maintain himself in ek-sistence, in the home of *being*. It governs him in the degree that his remembering and his thinking are primary acts, laden with his historical essence, with his human destiny.

The Rescue of Man from Alienation

The humanism of freedom is defined above all as the affirmation and rescue of the being of man. Therefore, it is founded on an existential ontology, directed toward a conception of human life as ek-sistence, and concerned with all of life's essential aspects, ethical, political, and economic, as well as others.

Such a rescue of man can be effected only by the forces residing within the human being himself. If this recuperation of his being implies that man has the nontransferable task of saving himself, then the humanism that leads him to salvation is opposed to Christianity that, in defining man in relationship to the *Deitas,* conceives salvation only as a work of God. The humanism of liberty begins with what man effectively is, excluding as spurious and contrary to its basic presuppositions everything from which man has alienated himself through the influence of the dominating powers in historical evolution. These powers also determine the type of man developed historically in the different ages, as well as the particular anthropological views of each age.

The objection made against so-called pure humanism, i.e., that it falls into naturalism, cannot be made against the humanism of liberty, except in error, because the latter neither recognizes nor accepts the artificial and unfounded separation of man from nature. Centered as it is in existence, which is the essence of man, humanism of freedom thinks of him as leaning toward *humanitas* without abandoning the entitative or psychophysical support of his *Dasein.* Only in the latter does one find through its accession to existence, i.e., the opening toward being, the opening that presupposes man's coming to his being. There is a traditional type of humanism that only accentuates a "properly human" nature derived from the separation in man of the body from the soul, of a will and a self that are superior from a will and a self that are inferior, that is to say, on the supposition of the separation between human nature and animal nature. This humanism rests on presuppositions of Christian dogma and therefore derives inspiration from the duality of body and soul, of terrestrial life and celestial life. Herein man is conceived in relationship with the *Deitas.*

The humanism of liberty, however, affirms the being of man over against what alienates him from himself, whether this be subjection of his spirit to supposed truths, essences, eternal values, or superhuman powers, all of which reduce him to an infrahuman level by seeing him primarily as a means for the production of goods and riches, as is the case in capitalist economies.

For Christianity, therefore, man is at the same time nature, since his body is a natural entity, and supernature, since his soul has been infused by divine creation, granting him a free immortality. For existential humanism or humanism of freedom on the other hand there is no split in man's being in the fashion described above, rather man is a natural entity, an individual in a biological species with the functional ontological possibility of raising himself, an entity that has already yielded to its being, selfhood, and freedom, even to its *humanitas.* However, he raises himself to *humanitas* without annulling his nature or pretending to escape it, because to exist and to exist as a person impelled in that direction by the spirit implicit and generated in *humanitas,* presupposes the ontic conditionality of *Dasein* (of the human entity).

We must concede to Heidegger that the humanism or humanisms referred to as such thus far, because they are under the dominance of metaphysics, focusing only on the entity, on defining man as a rational animal, and not on the being, think about man beginning with *animalitas* and not in the direction of *humanitas*. They claim that existence can never be thought of as a specific mode among other modes, and that the body of man is something different (but not "essentially different," as Heidegger affirms) from an animal organism. This distinction does not prevent existence from conditionally supposing and requiring the ontic of the "being there" (*Dasein*). Man, to the degree to which he is humanized, makes of his body an instrument for his humanity. His humanity is preformed, as Herder maintains, in the biological organization of man. Therefore, this humanity does not make its appearance in man as if it were blown in from the essential truth of an extraexistential being, for in that case existence would emerge ecstatic in man.

Man in the Crisis of Philosophy

Man has changed the direction in which he searched for himself; his demands have become radical and the process of becoming human has become more profound in all aspects. This being the case, the philosophy of existence, now in the process not only of giving complete expression to this change but also of opening the way and making its acceptance genuine, proclaims and embodies a *crisis of philosophy*. It is now clear that man's fundamental struggle can be understood in terms of rescuing his being from its alienation in the Platonistic categories and products of every kind; in recuperating his being from its alienation in "eternal" essences, values, and "absolute" truths and to rescue him also from the alienation he suffers from infrahuman conditions that reduce him to a mere means for the production of material goods and wealth. With due attention to affirming his selfhood and the fullness of his *humanitas,* he leaves behind as a *caput mortuum* the philosophy of the past and the image it forged of him, which he no longer recognizes. Thus, turning his back on conceptual transcriptions of his being and his potentialities and possibilities offered in that philosophy, he pursues the path indicated by his most intimate human needs and desires.

If man finds himself in crisis and in the midst of it asserts himself in his own being and freedom, of necessity he must nourish the new life germinating within him from the substance, resistance, weakness, and even the vital forces remaining in these last stages of the past. Therefore, in its determination to recover, and even though it is pulled along in the flow of contemporary events, his thought must frequently revert in its polemic, denial, and criticism to the philosophical jargon of the conceptions from which he seeks to be separate and free. To give human shape to this image in gestation, the image of a man with viscera, blood, and historic and earthly substance, he must still refer to the philosophy of the past, to its conceptual instruments. That is to say, he must engage philosophically and therefore debate combatively with the ideals concerning himself that were left to him by the worldviews of the great systems, in which he was included as just one more element.

Philosophy of existence has brought to the forefront the crisis in which contemporary man is debated. While struggling and divided, contemporary man tries to free himself from the ontologically hypostasized structures of the "objective spirit" (the technical term coined by Hegel), within which he has been transcribed, schematized, and pressured to conform to a rigid system of values, to a cultural ideal, and to a specific cosmic image. In this struggle to return to himself, man discovers, through the progression of his being as he seeks to direct himself toward the fullness of his *humanitas,* the possibility of giving a new turn to historical becoming.

THE HUMANISM OF LIBERTY AND ITS IMAGE OF MAN

Man in the Unexpectedness of His Becoming

The age in which we live, with its thrust toward the mutation of economic and social structures and of the qualitative content of life, gives an accelerated tempo to human becoming in the individual as well as the collective dimensions.

Before our very eyes, with the pressure of an intense desire and of a need for change, a transformation, revolutionary because of its extensiveness, is at work in the whole political order. Activating this process and at the same time impelled and shaped by it, the individual, concrete man, begins to emerge with traits of life and spirit that proclaim his commitment to another style of life and differentiate him basically from men of the previous age. Historically, there is an intrinsic correlation between the essential characteristics of a determined age and the typical traits of the individuals who belong to it. In these individuals appears a scale model of the structural characteristics of their age.

When there comes a change such as the one of which we are a part, there is also the formation of a new concept, of another image of man that begins to stand out and proclaim its own dynamics, to outline its life-spirit content on the horizon of the age under consideration.

Future days will be responsible for filling out the new idea of man, whose existential profile is already emerging from the convulsing present.

Man is a pilgrim who through all the incarnations of his precarious and ephemeral humanity searches for man, anticipating the exultation of the full affirmation of himself. For man never *is*, in the sense of something finished and formed in the ideal mold of a goal that he proposed to reach; rather he is an eternal *coming to be,* suspended in the effort in which he projects himself toward historical concretions and temporal fulfillment of his *humanitas,* a *desideratum* never reached nor possessed in its total fullness.

Impelled by his temporal destiny, by his intrinsic making of himself, which is consubstantial with and even defines his being, his "essence" as *humanitas,*[4] he tempers and refines his soul in the uncertainties of becoming. According to the temper of the times, man's pilgrimage goes through calm and sunny regions or those that are stormy and dark. Sometimes to live is to be confident and serene; but at other times historical development is torrential, and to live is a dramatic mission to force destiny and hasten the rhythm of the march one's heart feels in a burning fever.

In the present man travels a dangerous stretch to the true crossroads of his destiny. And if vision and will are lacking, he may lose the way and forsake the task that history proposes for him: to remodel his essence, to give new form to being, a being both constant and changing, in whose successive thrusts of historic accomplishment his exhausted humanity is restated.

In turning toward a new image of himself, man seeks above all to rescue the meaning of his essential humanity from the prison of dead forms and from styles of life that are already perishing. After being formed by the Greek *logos*, after being deluded in the Christian netherworld and getting lost in the rationalist impasse of the modern period, man aspires to raise his humanity to a lordly height.

Man, Sketched by Reason

The Christian image of man reaches its culmination and end in the Middle Ages and with it the possibility that this man, fearful of everything terrestrial, should continue considering himself a candidate for peaceful existence in the life beyond. From the Renaissance comes the so-called idea of modern man. With the dawn of the Renaissance comes nothing less than the rediscovery of man himself, he who like a terra incognita offers himself to the obscured vision of that age. Thus, when the unifying norm of the Middle Ages was broken there emerged from its midst, as Jacob Burckhardt so aptly stated, the imponderable world of the human personality. The geographical horizon had already been expanded with the discovery of the New World.

European man therefore begins to feel himself the master of his destiny. Obstacles that hindered the free development of his vital forces were eliminated and he turned toward the Earth, dedicated to the unfolding of immanent possibilities. Stirred by new passion, he searches through nature, looking for a pattern that would harmonize with his own designs. Through this exercise of his intellect new scientific disciplines took form. New discoveries fed his increasing curiosity and, filled with faith in the power of the instruments he was making, he dreamed of being lord of the material universe. One more step toward the dawn of the Enlightenment and "science now becomes an idol, a myth," says Paul Hazard. "There is a tendency to confuse science and well-being, material progress and moral progress."

With the apogee of the Enlightenment spirit, the image of man begins to bear the highly schematic seal of rationalism. Later there emerges the conception of History as a unified process, whose stages, oriented toward a predetermined end, must conform to the demands and modes of an all-powerful reason. Thus, for Hegel, the philosopher to whom the spiritual hegemony belongs in the first half of the nineteenth century, History is the dialectical process of the *Idea.* The conception of History as progress emerges as a skillfully drawn system in Hegel. Its first manifestation is found in Pascal, who imagines humanity as "a single man who always subsists and continuously learns through the course of the centuries."

The perspective holds that man as a rational being is not a psychological given, but a being in process turned toward becoming, who emerges as a historical task. He participates in universal reason and in the universality of reason only as a historical being (Hegel's correction of the Enlightenment concept of man); that is to say, man is conceived specifically and individually as developing, as in a process tending toward actualizing his essence, which as *humanitas* is a possibility that is achieved only in the concrete singular man and apart from him lacks meaning.

In these stages, the image of man becomes an image that is entirely schematized by reason, conforming to the demands of its postulated universality. This is the man who comes from nowhere, who has neither blood nor earthly roots, an anonymous being of utopian political constructions. Given this idea as the goal of his self-realization, man is constrained to imprison his essence, to shrink it into a simplistic rational scheme from which his vitality and intrinsic possibilities of historic progression are eliminated. This man, with no biological roots or temporal dimension, to the extent that he is an atomic element and a supposed constant, rational factor of a type of civilization, is dissolved into an entirely impersonal entity.

Toward a New Image of Man

The rationalist concept of man is dogmatically constructed on the peripheries of concrete humanity, of individual historic man, and of vital reality. Over against this rationalist concept, a real, living image of man is being raised, an image with blood and viscera, with earthly fluids and air to breathe.

A new image of man, man conceived according to other necessities and purposes, necessarily presupposes a new social order, a new hierarchical order of values to which the historical sensitivity of the age gives allegiance. The concept of man of rationalist humanism with its parallel postulate of progressivism is embedded in all the instances and sectors wherein it was able to gain preeminence, but even now, it is dead, though still hauled around on a declining verbal rather than mental plane on which are placed all the survivors of individual liberalism and its residual doctrinaire expressions.

This type of man, purely rational, antihistorical, and anonymous, is a ghostlike entity that eludes reality and struggles along a retreating front against the great events the future is preparing. It cannot be ignored, however, that this image of man has reigned for almost three centuries in the cultural and political life of the West, having shown that in the past it was an efficient reagent in the multiple aspects of this life. However, for the past three decades, this image of man is in obvious decline. It is barely a vanishing shadow that those adrift in the historical present vainly attempt to seize.

The completed man, conceptually constructed by rationalist humanism, that is to say, the isolated, completed, purely ideal man, without roots in a specific soil, with no vital ties to a nationality, with no connections to an instinctive and emotional repertoire of historically conditioned preferences—such a man does not exist. Neither is there an essential equality of all men based solely on universal reason as a constant and unalterable factor that would act independently in the psycho-vital, historical reality of national communities, classes, and racial constellations.

Having surpassed it, we are also far beyond the pseudoantinomy of *individualism* and *collectivism*. Our age no longer knows the individual as a social atom nor over against him the collectivity, considered as an aggregation of such atoms and billed as the leading actor of social and political history. It does recognize, however, opposing classes whose struggle, undoubtedly, is the crux of the economic-social process. There is also a growing awareness of the concrete historical man, the man who, without turning loose the bonds and surroundings in which he is implicated, stands out as a personal, psycho-vital unit, who affirms and gives life to his humanity as a function of his real goals, which are immanent in his particular becoming.

The Extinction of Modern Man

The unbalanced society of our age, especially the capitalist and mercantile commanders who are the possessors of political power, attempt in vain to live off the remains of the rationalist idea of man embodied in so-called modern man, an image already in a state of dessication. These commanders are the crusty bark oppressing and retarding the buds of a new idea of man of great historical significance that have been germinating rapidly in the deeper levels of contemporary life. Suppressed forces that are emotionally and historically articulated by a generation destined to place its seal on the future give added thrust and life to this idea of man with which the coming generation will impose a new *ethos,* affirming a particular political will and instituting also a different scale of evaluation for the culture, economy, and society.

Modern man is a cadaver that senescent human groups, adrift in the storm of these days, attempt vainly to galvanize, appealing to slogans and incantations that no longer have meaning. In a letter to Dilthey, Count Yorck von Wartenburg said: "Modern man, the man who began with the Renaissance and has endured until our time, is ready to be buried."

This type man, the man of individualistic liberalism, the ultimate, valedictory expression of "modern man," imbued with vestiges of the rationalist ideals of the nineteenth century is the corpse to be buried. The present age is responsible for carrying out this task so the new man can cover the whole surface of history and thus affirm and give full meaning to the spiritual and political orders now germinating.

History has no compassion for values in decline nor for human types that are repositories of endangered sensibilities and ideals, inanimate modules of a destiny that has made its rounds and can no longer swell history with new hope or give it new impetus. History takes into its flow only the vital ascending force, the *ethos* in which a new message for men is given form, the promise of accomplishment that is the incentive for renewed effort. History—the matrix of all possibilities—yields itself only to those generations capable of engendering the fullness of a new age, that is, to that type of man capable of implanting an ascending meaning in history and of proposing to it new and valuable goals.

Historical Becoming and Objective Goals

According to Dilthey, ages differ from each other in their structure. Each age contains a nexus, a correlation of similar, related ideas that govern the different realms of cultural life, the so-called objective spirit. It is the common repertoire that defines the character of an age. However, the ultimate foundation of this organic repertoire of ideas is constituted by the powers of the historical life, in whose nourishing soil all the objective spiritual structures, all the forms of culture take root. "The facticity of race, of space, of the relationships among powers constitute everywhere the foundation which can never be spiritualized. It was a mere dream of Hegel that different ages represent stages in the development of reason."

The remains of this dream, sifted through liberal rationalism of the nineteenth century, were thought to be unending sources of life and strength for the order of things that today is drawing near to its dissolution because its foundation has been undermined.

To affirm the spiritual personality and uniqueness of each age does not imply dissolution into a historical relativism concerned only with the pure, autonomous flow of these disconnected spiritual worlds. Such a relativism would never see in history anything firm that would serve as a point of reference, nothing that would tie these spiritual worlds together so they could establish an objective and transcendent nexus as a norm for change, as the goal of the historical process itself. Ranke saw this perfectly well, when in formulating his concept of the meaning of historical ages and in criticizing the idea of linear progress, he said "each age has its own particular tendency and its own ideal. . . . Its value does not reside in what emerges from it, but in its own existence, its own selfhood"; that is, in its identity with itself.

Neither does Ranke allow any given generation to be reduced in rank for the sake of successive generations, since "all generations of humanity appear with equal rights." Contemplating universal history as a whole, as a supreme process that includes every individuality and all spiritual realms, he thinks of States "as individualities, analogous to each other, but essentially independent of one another . . . original creations of the human spirit."

The same can be said of the individual, who in his historicity is not given to a bare flowing, a becoming with no meaning, that recognizes nothing firm in the midst of mutation and does not transcend toward anything objective, such as ideals, goals, and values, though such an objectivity would be functional and not ontologico-hypostatic. Objective truth as well as objective structures do not reside in a transcending moment nor in a transcending world of reason that has no tie with human historical becoming, rather they belong to such becoming, to its primary existential temporality, since they have been formed by its flowing.

Sameness, Otherness, and Humanitas

To be sure, there is a realm of ends, norms, and values structured on an objective plane that transcends individual consciousness. One may also conceive and accept the effectiveness of an objective spirit as a structured whole that has emerged from the historical process, but this process is a far cry from being the domain of pure contingency and subjective irrationality. For it is precisely man's ability to establish an objective realm of the spirit that permits him, in each moment of his becoming, to be himself, to apprehend his own self-sameness.

Although man aspires to fulfill himself in his being, to affirm himself in his humanity, to feel identical with himself in each moment of temporal transition, the personal identity to which he aspires leads him to postulate time, a transcendence in the sense of otherness, as a guarantee of his identity and as the goal of his efforts. Stating this problem as a function of the finite-infinite, historicity-eternity antinomy, Kierkegaard tells us that man in his sameness, in his desired self-existence, always finds something, the Absolute, before which he is his own self-sameness.

While the sameness of man lives and exists, in the proper sense of these terms, through his becoming this sameness, it is bound to a concrete self-consciousness that, because it is expressed in temporality, is also becoming and thus never crystallizes, since there is no crystallizing in the existing man. This concrete-self-consciousness gathers man into the lived experience of its own identity, anchored to the temporal structures of existence. This is because man, in everything (ideals, values, objective norms of life) toward which he transcends and projects himself from his concrete historicity—which is the ineradicable moment of his being, of his being made in time—in all this transcending, man searches only for himself, he attempts only to seal his identity in the midst of mutations and change, shaping it into a consistent and stable image of himself, into an idea of his "humanitas."

He now strives toward a new actualization of his being, a new image of himself. He aspires to actualize and conceive himself in all his immanent possibilities, to integrate himself with his potentialities, to reencounter himself, at last, in the full concretion of his essential humanity.

Magnetizing its thrust, which is historically conditioned and limited, the ideal of the *full man*—as proposed by Max Scheler—is lifted up as the goal that at the same time that it transcends pure becoming, receives from it its meaning, which is latent, to the degree it is *existential*, in the immanence of the temporal structure. Although "this full-man, in an absolute sense, is far from us, . . . a relatively whole-man, a maximum of full humanity, is accessible to each age."

For the concrete, existing man, this ideal of the whole-man as a goal and model is an index of transcendence, a mediating synthesis of all objective structures. These structures represent the other, not in the sense of the naturalist idea of being or of an absolute conceived as a personal God, but of an other that, as a transcending instance toward which what is human is projected, permits man in each moment and stage of his temporal passing to know his concrete sameness. It is the apparently fixed limit that as an ideal point of reference hovers above historical becoming. Ultimately, however, existence activates and gives meaning to historical becoming, for existence historically determines and actualizes the humanity in man.

Conclusion (After a Decade)[5]

Within the structure of bourgeois philosophy and with respect to its doctrinal perspectives, the ontology of existence and existentialism have had a revolutionary impact, laying open the false suppositions and the state of crisis to which this philosophy had come. This ontology of existence and existentialism have served as true antidotes to the usual emphases of a sterile *Erkenntnistheorie* and of an absolutist axiology of Platonic heritage. At the same time, however, Heideggerian existential ontology and Sartrean existentialism—the latter derived erroneously from the former—in their encounter with the doctrines of bourgeois philosophy have revealed their own insufficiency and are implicated, as opponents of that philosophy, in its crisis and decadence.

We have, therefore, on the one hand an existential ontology [Heidegger] anchored in an irrationalist solipsism, and on the other hand an existentialism [Sartre] reduced to a phenomenalist ontologism with no foundation. Above all, the first, with its solipsistic *Dasein* and its "onto-theology," has shown its own frustration, its lack of authenticity in the analysis of historicity. In its own formulation and development, it has been incapable of surpassing the radical, solipsistic individualism of Kierkegaard. Both positions, the ontologico-existential and the existentialist, have actualized, though without saying so, the vigorous and radical problematic of dialectical materialism within Western classical philosophy, accentuating by contrast the immense foresight of Marx's philosophy.

Earlier we pointed out that existentialism, although it is a "philosophy of crisis," is fundamentally the proclamation of the crisis of philosophy. It is such in that it sums up the breakdown of the ideological structures of bourgeois philosophy. Further, it is crisis on a deeper level, since the type man that is dominant—the bourgeois and the petit bourgeois—is involved inthe actual decadent stage of Western capitalist civilization. Aside from this, the ecumenical man, struggling to rescue himself, from above and at the cost of concrete life, from the alienation in all the socially superstructured forms—from the fetish of consumerism to supposed eternal values and essences—this universal man searches for himself, searches for his own humanity along a path different from the one designated by historical humanisms, which up to the present, as ideas that have dominated successively, express only the ideas of the ruling classes, which gave to these humanisms their philosophical imprint. Thus, the crisis of one type of man—the so-called modern man who dates from the Renaissance—stems from the historical situation of the civilization in which he finds himself, which gives rise to the crisis of bourgeois philosophy and of its ideological structures. Basically, our concern here is not a temporary "philosophy of crisis" but the crisis of a particular philosophy, a superstructural expression of the crisis of a whole economic system, that inevitably follows the descending curve of its decadence to its dissolution and fall.

NOTES

1. Martin Heidegger, *Sein und Zeit*, p. 151.
2. Ibid.
3. Ibid., p. 38.
4. We can speak of the essence of man (with absolute exclusion of the "realist" presupposition of the doctrine of "universals") conceiving it only as an idea of a living individual, a specific individual, who is precisely the one who has or actualizes the idea. This essence or idea does not constitute an independent being that has primacy with respect to the concrete existing man, but as *humanitas*; it is realized only in individuals, in specific men. Outside of them, it does not occur nor does it have meaning. Hence we must avoid all absolutizing of the concept of "man," of hypostasizing the idea of man as well as the idea of "humanity," as if we had under consideration something distinct and above the totality of men. Since the idea of man is constituted in the existing individual, this idea, *humanitas*, is subject to the mutation that is imposed upon it by historical becoming, by the very historicity of concrete man.
5. This is part of a section added by Astrada to the last edition of this work.—ED.

Francisco Miró Quesada (b. 1918)

Born in Lima in 1918, Miró Quesada attended elementary school in Peru and France and completed secondary education at the Italian School in Lima. He received doctorates in mathematics and philosophy from the University of San Marcos, in Lima, where he also received a degree in law. At twenty-one years of age, he was appointed to the chair of contemporary philosophy at the University of San Marcos and subsequently to the chair of the philosophy of mathematics and to that of political science. He has given lectures in several Latin American universities—Buenos Aires, La Plata, Córdoba, México, Chile, Central Venezuela, and others—in European universities—Oxford, Cambridge, London, Rome, the Sorbonne, and the College de France—as well as the University of New York at Buffalo.

He is a member of the Peruvian Academy of Language as well as a corresponding member of the Royal Spanish Academy of Language. In 1942 he was one of the founders of the Peruvian Philosophical Society and has been its president several times.

Miró Quesada's principal interest has been in the theory of knowledge, but this interest has assumed a variety of expressions. He worked first of all in the phenomenology of Husserl as is reflected in his work *El sentido del movimiento fenomenológico* (1941). Later he became interested in mathematical logic and wrote the first book in this field published in Spanish America, *Lógica* (1946). Later he turned to juridical logic and wrote *Problemas fundamentales de la lógica jurídica* (1956) and *Apuntes para una teoría de la razón* (1963), in addition to many essays and books.

His principal aim has been to achieve a systematic perspective of the principles that govern rational knowledge. He claims that classical positions such as rationalism, positivism, pragmatism, dialectical philosophy, and historicism have been surpassed by advances in scientific knowledge. Miró Quesada uses the methodological procedures of modern logic and recent metatheory to formulate a model of the structure of rational thought that enables one to account for the result and the modalities of the formal sciences as a first step for a general theory of rational knowledge. More recently he has worked on the problem of synthetic a priori judgments and has used Gödel's theorem to prove the existence of this type of judgment in mathematics.

In later years Miró Quesada's attention was turned toward political theory. In 1959 he published *La otra mitad del mundo*, the diary of a long trip through the USSR and continental China. In 1970 he published *Humanismo y revolución* in addition to many other essays.

Miró Quesada's political philosophy seeks to find a foundation for political praxis that is more rigorous than that offered by Marxism, Christian socialism, and other contemporary views. In order to do this, he attempts to formulate a concept of humanism independent of every metaphysical position.

Miró Quesada's view may be characterized as a neorationalism or "dynamic rationalism" which is different from classical, Hegelian, and phenomenological rationalism. This difference rests on the methodology employed to establish conclusions as well as the views he has developed, such as his theory of synthetic a priori judgments and his theory of evidence and intellectual intuition.

Man without Theory

[THE FAILURE OF ALL THEORIES OF MAN]

Man cannot live without theory, for he is the theoretical animal par excellence. Ancient wisdom characterized him as "rational animal," because theories were formulated by reason. No longer does anyone hold that there are theoretical men and practical men, men dedicated to thought and others dedicated to action. All men are theoretical, only some know it and are distinguished by their determination to develop theoretical perspectives, whereas others are satisfied to live submerged in the theory and to use it to obtain pressing needs. Our life, however, is surrounded by theory. From our confidence in the firmness of the earth we walk on, all is the fruit of theory, of scientific thought, of our capacity to think about events and to interpret them. Thanks to theory we are able to confront the world, to have a world, to predict events, manage them, direct them, and take advantage of them. It is because there have been men dedicated to discovering how the world is that the "practical men" can dedicate themselves to modifying it through technology, a late and secondary product of theory.

Theory, the knowledge of things and events, emerges as a necessity in man's defense against the assault of the world. Theory is born as a function of man and for man to find a perspective within the endless labyrinth of events as he orders his world. He structures the world so he can reach his self-proposed goals. He must know himself to know what he pursues and what the true relationships to his world are. This is to say that every theory concerning the world, concerning the things that surround him,

From Francisco Miró Quesada, *El hombre sin teoría* (Lima: Universidad Mayor de San Marcos, 1959), pp. 14–31. Reprinted by permission of the author.

necessarily implies a theory concerning himself, for to think about the world is to think about one's self, since the world is only the terminus of action. Furthermore, it is to think that thought has particular possibilities, that it is capable of dominating specified situations. It is to think about what is going to be done with the knowledge acquired about the world, and to think about one's own destiny.

However, at this point by their very nature things begin to be quite different, because the reality of man is infinitely more complex than that of the world. To theorize about the world is much easier than to theorize about man. In the surrounding world, simple patterns are more or less common, like the successions of various cyclical states such as day and night, tides, and movements of the stars. Given this simplicity and regularity, all theory can be verified, elaborate as it may be. One need only deduce the various consequences implicit in the presuppositions. As long as the consequences coincide with the facts one can continue to accept the theory as true, but if the facts contradict it, then one will have to reject, modify, or adapt the theory; otherwise it becomes untenable. This process of verification is the foundation of all possible knowledge of realities and is what has permitted man to evolve from the most primitive and infantile theories to the present elaborate systems of physics, astronomy, and biology.

The more complicated a segment of reality, the more difficult it is to elaborate a theory that will account for it and allow man to know it. It is more probable, also, that one will find a theoretical consequence that does not coincide with the facts and will make the theory fail. However, by means of corrections and reelaborations, it is always possible to improve it and to adapt it to the new demands of the facts, achieving thereby a knowledge of nature that is more or less uniform and progressive. When we are concerned with human beings, however, this procedure is practically impossible. Because man's complexity is such and the intertwining of the facts that characterize him is so great that to elaborate a reasonably acceptable theory concerning his nature, it becomes necessary to rely on a dense skein of concepts and hypotheses. From this theoretical mire an endless series of consequences unfold that must be correlated with the facts about man. And in the long run the facts ruin the theory because, unfortunately, some and often many of the consequences of the theory contradict the facts. In addition to this insuperable difficulty, there is another that is perhaps even greater, the phenomenon of freedom. Human freedom is not a theory, it is a fact—the fact of the unpredictability of our actions. Whereas in nature the smooth, simple recurrences of phenomena permit astounding predictions, the possibility of man making decisions that go counter to what is foreseen makes it impossible to achieve rigorous knowledge of what we are. In principle, every man can show any theory concerning man to be inadequate. All he has to do is act so as to contradict what the theory permits one to predict concerning his actions. In some cases, of course, the predictions are fulfilled, but it is on a superficial or pathological level. Ultimately, no one can predict anything concerning what a human being will do. Yet, the essence of theory consists in deriving consequences, that is, making predictions.

However, if formulating theories about man is such a difficult and demanding task, all our other theories concerning the world and life also incur a subtle, grave danger. For, as we have seen, to formulate a theory concerning nature one must presuppose something about man himself, about his capacity to formulate theories and about life's purpose that is his lot to pursue. Every radical change in the theory of man leads inevitably to change in our way of seeing the world, and this produces insecurity and distress. For, to change a theory concerning the world forces us to recognize that what we believed is not so certain, that the earth we walk on has suddenly become moving sand in which we may sink. Further, to have to change our perspective on ourselves forces us to recognize that we were in error, that what we believed was eternally true about our possibilities and destiny has been seriously questioned. Suddenly, as with the psychopath, we are strangers to ourselves, we no longer recognize ourselves. Nothing is more terrifying to man than to discover that he is not what he believed he was. For years, centuries, perhaps even millennia, he struggled for security only to have it dissolved in a gust of mysterious theoretical wind. Hence the furor, the resentment, and the hatred toward those who dare attack this security, for without it we are not able to live. . . .

The process in which theories concerning man dissolve is inflexible and its successive stages are easily describable. The first step is the general elaboration of the theory. In a majority of cultures this step has been simple and spontaneous. In the modern world it is conscious and has scientific and philosophical pretensions, as for example in Nazism, fascism, and Marxism. In all cases, however, the point of departure is the same: a tangled mass of extremely complicated hypotheses that are taken to be the sublime, incontrovertible, and definitive truth. For some people this truth is of a divine origin and in some cases these hypotheses seem quite simple when first proposed. . . .

In order to understand these issues, it is important to have a clear concept of what a theory is, especially of the relationship between a theory and its logical implications. As we have seen, a theory is a series of hypotheses about some aspect of reality, and it may be restricted or broad and encompassing. Once the hypotheses have been formulated a series of consequences can be derived logically. The fundamental aspect of this logical derivability is the immensity of its range, since, beginning with a small number of hypotheses one can derive innumerable consequences, so many, in fact, that they are practically infinite. This is the main characteristic of any theory whatever, constituting its greatness as well as its limitation, its usefulness as well as its terrible danger. Through the power of derivation, atomic energy has been developed, so that it will be possible within a few years to improve the world in unforeseen ways or to destroy it by pressing a button. Through this strange and almost magical power we have made airplanes fly, we have burned witches, invented the telescope and the microscope, committed atrocious genocides, saved millions of lives, and made martyrs of millions of human beings.

A theory's power of derivation is so immense that it is difficult to understand without a concrete example. If we take arithmetic as an example, it will be sufficient to clarify what we want to say. Those who know what mathematical theories are and how they are organized know that all, absolutely all arithmetical knowledge can be derived from the seven postulates of Peano. These hypotheses are extraordinarily simple and can be understood by a child. However, in spite of being only seven, an immense number of conclusions is derived from them, a number so great that, although our knowledge of arithmetic has been increasing for 2,500 years, it still continues to increase, and will continue to increase in the coming centuries. Aside from being numerous, the consequences are so complicated that no one can foresee where they will eventually lead. This example permits us to see clearly the incalculable power of a theory, for, once hypotheses are formulated, we can deduce an incalculable number of conclusions from them by means of logic.

This example demonstrates that from a few, simple hypotheses one can derive an infinite number of consequences that because they are so rich and numerous are unforeseeable, for once the hypotheses are formulated, no one can foresee what the future consequences will be. These consequences follow a rigorous, logical line and as the investigators continue to deduce them, their derivation follows necessarily from the hypotheses. However, no one can foresee what the consequences will be or where they will lead. If this is true in the case of a theory that has only seven, very simple hypotheses, what would happen with a theory concerning man that, as we have seen, consists of a great number of complicated hypotheses?

Let us turn now to a third dimension of all theories about man, their strange quality and inevitable failure. To obtain security in the world and to make headway through life's complexities, man elaborates a complicated theory concerning himself. The complication is inevitable because man, the subject of the theory, is the most complicated being in the universe. Due to the inextricable complications of being human, every theory concerning man is incomplete, in spite of its inevitable complication.

Because of this incompleteness and because the theory is so complicated, the number of consequences derived from it is overwhelming. The liability, however, is not found in the number of the consequences, but in their unpredictability. Thus, in the case of arithmetic, or for that matter all mathematical theories, even though the hypotheses are few and simple, the consequences are so numerous that they become unforeseeable and leave the most perceptive minds stupefied. In the case of theories as complicated as those concerned with man, however, this impressive array of consequences must be multiplied to infinity. And this has always been true. Due to the complexity of the theories he has elaborated concerning himself, man has drawn very odd, strange, and stupefying conclusions concerning his own being. Beginning with hypotheses that for him were more or less evident, man has come to conclusions that in the beginning were quite foreign to his thought. We only need to review history to support the claim that the doctrines man has elaborated concerning himself have carried him to unanticipated extremes. Calvinism, for example, begins with ascetic principles but comes to the inevitable conclusion that wealth is a sign of having been chosen by God for salvation. From this perspective to modern colonialism is only a small step, a step that naturally was taken in the most sincere conviction of its being just. Think for example of the strange character of funeral rituals, of human sacrifices, of the auto-da-fé, of the differences of sexual morality that exist in diverse cultures, of religious wars. One must recognize that all these actions that seem so foreign to the points of departure are only their inevitable consequences. They lead to the failure of the theory, because given their great quantity, there comes a point at which the theory is obviously opposed to the facts. And then man ceases to believe in them or he tries to adapt them, if he can, to new demands. We must recognize that every theory concerning man is incomplete and thus has inherent limitations. However, because the theory is so complex it allows for the derivation of unexpected consequences, and in the long run one of the consequences will be evidence in support of the limitation or imperfection of the theory. Since man is such a complex reality, in the first theorizing efforts consequences usually coincide with the facts, but even if they do not one can pretend they do. The theory however, like Pandora's box, continues producing consequences that are added to the initial hypothesis, in turn leading to other more complex and wondrous consequences until it would seem the whole theoretical machinery had gone wild. A theory, however, is inflexible, the most inflexible thing in the world, much more so than machines or the will of man, and once placed in motion it has a terrifying force, like a monster that devours everything and can be detained by nothing. In a spontaneous manner as generally happens, or in a conscious manner, once the primitive hypotheses have been formulated, the consequences unfold and continue to do so without stopping, falling like grenades on a battlefield with increasing precision and explosive potential. It is as if man were a spider and the theory were his web, but a web that continued to expand unceasingly until it had imprisoned him in its own strands and slowly, inevitably asphyxiated him. When this happens, he realizes for the first time that the complicated theory that he created concerning himself is betraying him. Man does not create theories for his pleasure. He creates theories as a fundamental way of life, for it is his method of overcoming the chaos of existence. When consciously and often implicitly in secular pursuits, he elaborates a theory concerning himself, his nature, his relationship to the universe, or his ultimate destiny, it is in order to handle in a more adequate fashion the dangerous complexity of his existence, in order to feel more secure and well grounded. However, if the contrary occurs, it means that this theory is inadequate, that it must be amplified, restructured, or perhaps radically changed. . . .

The history of humanity is an impressive succession of complicated, yet false theories that man has woven around himself. Along the millennial pathway of history, theories lay semidestroyed and rusted like military equipment left behind by an army in retreat. Each great theoretical crisis, each great change, each new development marks the shift from one culture to another, from one age to another. In earlier days men were not sufficiently aware of what was happening, although they were aware that something was happening and expectantly waited the new. At times their desires were implemented in a conscious, more or less rapid manner. At other times, however, the restructuring process lasted centuries. Intuitively men grasped the significance of the situation, but the mechanism for restructuring was not grasped for two reasons: the lack of historical consciousness, that is, awareness of the relationship between their worldview and historic era, and the lack of understanding of what a theory is. In the nineteenth century a great movement began that culminated in our day and overcame both limitations. For this reason, in the present, in this modern, troubled atomic era, the era of the machine and technology, we are aware nevertheless of what is really happening. We have a clear understanding that history is a succession of ways of conceiving the world and man, of ways considered absolute by men of different ages but that today are no more difficult to understand than vague shadows. Our civilization, therefore, is the most philosophical of all, because none has had as clear an awareness of its limitation and relativity. In truth, our age is characteristically an age of search, of disorientation, and of acute consciousness of its negative traits. Contemporary man is one who experiences in his own flesh the failure of a great theory concerning himself: European rationalism, in all its facets, from the liberalism of "laissez faire" to Nazism and Marxism. Ortega has said of our age that it is an "age of disillusioned living," but to be more precise we should say, "an age of disillusioned theorizing." Scheler begins one of his books, perhaps his best, with the celebrated phrase, "Never has man been such an enigma to himself."

Given this situation the inevitable question is "What shall we do?" The depth of the question does permit a dogmatic answer. Indeed, perhaps this essay should end here. However, to be human means to try unceasingly to overcome every "non plus ultra" and since we do not wish to deny our human condition, we have no alternative but to forge ahead. Yet, before continuing we wish to emphasize that what follows is no more than the point of view of a particular individual who, along with all other individuals in this age, is faced with an immense problem that by its very nature transcends any purely individual response.

The first thought that might come to mind, and perhaps a majority already favors it, is to commit our efforts to the reconstruction of the old theory, making it more comprehensive and adapting it to the demands of our modern circumstance. Or, should this not be possible, to elaborate a new theory that may or may not be related to the old or to earlier theories, but would constitute an organic system, capable of providing answers to the most pressing questions and have the scope and flexibility necessary to permit men of our day to work with the total range of their problems. In actual experience, the normal or spontaneous attitude always develops a theory. So we, although disillusioned by theories, in seeing ourselves in a bind, think of amplifying or creating theories, like men of other ages. In this day, however, there is a difference: men of previous ages were not aware of the relativity or limits of their theories, nor of the horrible dangers implicit in creating a complicated theory concerning man from which unforeseeable and mortal consequences were derived. Furthermore, they did not suspect that their theories ran the same risks as all preceding theories. Therefore they created under illusion, but in faith, and so their theories had "vital force" and served to resolve human problems since men believed in them and were convinced that all previous ages had been in error whereas they were in the truth. In this day, however, we are not convinced our position is unique, true, or definitive. Indeed, we know that whatever we do, our theory about man will suffer the same end as the others.

Yet, instead of searching for a new theory and instinctively following the destiny of Sisyphus, what if we assume a completely different attitude? Instead of inventing a new and dangerous theory, why not simply give up formulating theories about ourselves? Now this proposal may well produce a scandal and for two good reasons. First, because man is so accustomed to formulating theories about himself, to taking for granted that he knows what he is, to feeling himself at the helm of a world of structures and hierarchies, to renounce theory leaves him with the impression that he is giving up the possibility of finding solutions, that he is spineless and morally decadent, that he has given up the struggle for good and against evil. Second, because it is believed, more for theoretical than practical considerations, that no matter what man does he is condemned to theorize and that he can give up everything except formulating a complete concept of the world, of things, and of himself. It is believed that man needs theory to live, that without it he flounders and does not know what to hold on to, he is a lost soul on a ship without a rudder. For, although he may deny theory, implicitly he is always constructing a system of concepts for clarifying the meaning of his life.

To be sure, this second argument is much more powerful than the first. Its strength, however, lies in its inclusive breadth, for its detailed analysis of situations is slipshod. For example, if one analyzes all the elements constituting the world within which man includes himself, one sees there are various dimensions. One dimension is the surrounding world. This dimension, naturally, is undeniable. If man does not possess a well-formulated theory concerning the surrounding world he is not even able to walk down the street. The simple act of dodging an automobile indicates the possession of a rather clear concept of the principles of causality and the laws of dynamics. Further, our cultural crisis is not a crisis in knowledge of the natural world. The cosmic world, our surrounding environment is known with increasingly greater certainty and vigor. It is perhaps the only part of our general vision of the world that at present follows a linear evolution. We have reached such a comprehension of what physical theory is, that the elaboration of that type theory is carried out in the awareness that in time it will be surpassed, and that it will be necessary to amplify it to include new facts. For this reason, it is possible that the nuclear emphasis of the old theory may be preserved intact and that it may be possible to consider it as a special case of a new theory. Some might believe that this procedure is applicable to the theory about the nature of man, but, given the complexity of all anthropological theory, this is not possible. Physical as well as mathematical theories are very simple, since they are based on broad abstractive processes. Therefore, this approach is not adequate for anthropological theory. However, if we do not make use of it, we encounter the earlier objection, namely, that every theory concerning the surrounding world presupposes an integrated theory of the human being. Here we come to the crux of the issue, for if this affirmation is true, then we will never be able to free ourselves from a theory concerning ourselves and we will always return to that monotonous, well-beaten path. This we believe to be false, because even though it is undeniable that every theory concerning the cosmos presupposes a theory concerning man, it does not presuppose necessarily that the theory of the cosmos is complete. In order to grant validity to a theory about the cosmos, we must presuppose certain epistemological postulates, certain beliefs concerning the structure and organization of our consciousness, but in no way does such a theory necessarily include hypotheses about the moral life or destiny of man. The most to be said is that from these epistemological presuppositions, one can derive many consequences as to the possibilities of knowing the world in general and even ourselves and that these consequences may be positive or negative in some or in many aspects. However, this does not invalidate our point of view because what we are specifically trying to do is place brackets around our cognitive faculties insofar as these are applied to ourselves.

Man is so accustomed to living on the theoretical level that he does not conceive the possibility of refraining from decisions about his own nature and fundamental relationships with the surrounding world. Thus he always finds arguments that justify his use of theories. In the present case, those who deny the possibility of avoiding theory about man adduce that this avoidance is impossible because determining one's orientation in the world without language is impossible. To establish interhuman communication, whatever it may be, is impossible without speech, but speech is in itself a theory. The philosophical analysis of language shows unequivocally that every expressive system acquires its ultimate meaning from theoretical presuppositions about the nature of the world and of man. Thus the very possibility of language implies the immersion of the human being in a complete theory concerning himself, a theory that refers not only to his objective relationship with the environing world, but also to his norms of action and destiny. Philological analysis of the most trivial words reveals, in a surprising way at times, the immense background of cosmological, metaphysical, and ethical theory upon which all possible language rests. The argument, then, would seem to be definitive: man cannot live without an orientation in the world and to seek an orientation in the world requires a specific theory concerning the physical structure of the cosmos. This theory, however, cannot be elaborated without language, but language is the great, universal theory, the expression of what in the ultimate, collective, anonymous, and therefore inevitable sense man believes about the world and himself. Thus, it is impossible to live as a human being without presupposing certain theoretical axioms concerning our nature and our destiny.

The inference from this last bulwark of the theory is sound. The error, however, is not found in the conclusion but in the point of departure. The error is found in the lack of theory as to what a theory is. For if one analyzes what a theory really is one sees immediately that it is always possible to do without it. Better said, there are two classes of theories, one that is implicit and spontaneous, formulated by the primitive collective mind that creates language, and the other is conscious, elaborated and created for specific purposes of knowledge. *The first cannot be avoided, but the second can and this is our concern.* The first cannot be avoided because it is implicit in language and it is impossible to do without language. Even if it is a theory that decisively influences our manner of seeing the world and of being ourselves, it is an implicit, practically unconscious theory, a theory so remote that we have forgotten its true meaning. Words that in a primitive beginning embodied terrifying revelations about nature, about the world, and about ourselves are now applied mechanically to specific, concrete objects. "To exist" signifies etymologically, "to place oneself outside himself." Enormous theoretical ranges are implicit in this meaning. Nevertheless, for the man who is not specialized, who does not meditate philosophically on the meanings of words, "to exist" means simply "to live" if he refers to a human being and "to be real" if he refers to things. "Devil" meant "slanderer" for the primitive man. Much feeling is wrapped up in this meaning. However, in modern Western languages when speaking of the devil, one does not think specifically of a slanderer in spite of the biblical passage in which the devil tempts Eve, slandering God. In pursuing the analysis of the primitive meaning of language, one comes to the following conclusion: as constituted, language is an original theory about the world and ourselves, a theory containing ethical and metaphysical principles. In an indirect and inevitable manner it influences our manner of being. This influence is weakened by distance and by forgetting the primitive meanings. With the passage of time, with the progress of expressive flexibility, in the coming of the scientific spirit words acquire a new seal, a precise meaning of associative reference to things, persons, and actions over their primitive, vague, and metaphorical meaning. Therefore, in spite of the theoretical "pressure" of language, we are quite capable of overcoming the primitive worldview. Thus, any of our Western languages of Indo-European origin presupposes in its beginning a theological vision of the world, a special conception of "being" and a specified taxonomy of moral values and disvalues centered in a paternalistically organized society. These meanings are so worn by time and so covered with semantic accumulations that it is perfectly possible for a Western man to see the world in a completely different manner. To be sure, the liberation can never be complete, although it is sufficiently radical that the Indo-European origin of our languages does not oblige us to consider a man a scoundrel who does not believe in God or who believes, with respect to sexual morality, that men and women have equal rights. This shift is the focus of our concern. •

Let us now take a look at the other type of theory, *conscious theory* or if one prefers "scientific-philosophical" theory in a very broad sense. *Every theory formulated by man about the world, life, and its destiny belongs to this type of theory.* Every human being, in addition to the theoretical background imposed by language, lives subsumed in some scientific-philosophical theory, although an analysis of the human situation shows quite readily that it is also possible to avoid this type theory. To do this only a clear concept of the epistemological significance of the word "theory" is needed. Every theory presupposes the existence of "facts" and although facts cannot be interpreted without a theory, this does not prevent them from existing as such. A completely convincing example is that in spite of the change in theories, facts remain the same. Thus, the orbital path of Jupiter can be explained by Newton's theory as well as by Einstein's theory of generalized relativity. Nevertheless, in spite of the difference between these two theories, Jupiter's orbital path, as fact, remains the same. It can be explained also by primitive concepts, for example, as the movement of a lamp carried by a nocturnal god as he travels his circular path through the firmament. Still, all men will inevitably see Jupiter in the same manner, and in seeing it they will consciously or unconsciously formulate some theory about it. The facts are nevertheless undeniably there; the blue of the sky, the white of the clouds, the brilliance of the light, the green of the fields are facts that are seen alike by all men in spite of the theories.

Just as in nature, in spite of the change of theories or perhaps precisely because of this change, one can clearly identify the facts, so in the human realm the facts remain stable over against the changes in the understanding of life. Between the theory whose consequences lead to the sacrifice of human lives and the theory that interprets such action as intolerable there is, to be sure, a significant distance. Nevertheless, all men who lived with these theories have undeniable characteristics in common. All were capable of suffering and rejoicing, all wept and laughed at least once in their life. All spoke, all felt emotions, all loved and hated at one time or another. One might object that in these affirmations we are formulating a theory, for to affirm that all were men is to universalize a concept of man. For among savages there are many groups that do not consider others to be human, but see them as animals, and some tribes even see themselves as dispossessed of the human condition. To this, however, we respond that what presupposes a theory is not the description of the facts, but dividing men into men and other things. For one must have a theory that is thoroughly elaborated and proclaimed with zealous fanaticism in order to come to believe that a person that speaks as we speak and communicates with us is not equal to us. In such interpretations of the facts, complicated ethico-metaphysical theories of the totem and the taboo are at play. If one insists that the universal application of the word "man" is the direct or indirect implication of some theory, we can dispense with the term. We only need observe the facts directly: there is something animated that laughs and cries, sings and shouts, hates and loves, suffers and rejoices, and above all speaks and communicates with others by means of symbols. And this type of animated something we decide to call "man." We presuppose nothing concerning its nature, origin, destiny, or obligations. There it is before us with curious demeanor, mysterious gestures, and different looks. Its history develops through the centuries, elaborating strange theories for which it has strong attraction, an attraction that is so strong that in support of their truth it is capable of anything, even of killing and torturing a fellow man. However, just as some men are capable of killing and torturing to support a theory, others are incapable of doing so in spite of all theories, in spite of all the demands and pressures of their environment. There are men who love other men and there are others that do not feel any special love but nevertheless rebel and draw back in the face of suffering and injustice. Within the range of these attitudes of cruelty and brotherhood man displays all his possibilities. All human life is tinted with these two attitudes that are like the two ultimate but opposing colors of an infinite spectrum. When man takes hold of a theory to justify his desire to make others suffer, he descends to the level of the demonic. When he rises to the level of self-sacrifice in order to prevent the suffering of others, he attains sainthood. Between these two extremes are all other men. This is the great fact, the formidable fact of the human condition down through history. Through all changes and ages, all cultural cycles and crises, all great achievements and catastrophes, we find the same fact: there are men who make others suffer and there are men capable of suffering so that others will not suffer. There are men who struggle against man and there are men who struggle for man. This fact follows two possibilities, two ways *from which to choose:* One can decide either to exploit man or to defend him. These are the fundamental attitudes. All others belong in some degree to these two, for even indifference is the zero point at which one attitude shifts into the other. The course of history is guided by the way men have organized to implement some gradation of these two activities.

PART III
Values

Introduction

Toward the end of the nineteenth century, the problem of values acquired special prominence. Since then, this importance has continued to increase because of the impact this problem has had on other areas of philosophy, especially ethics, aesthetics, and the philosophy of law.

In Latin America, interest in the problem of values emerged, in great part, as a result of the impact of works by French and German authors. The earliest influences came through the French sociologism of Durkheim and Bouglé and led eventually to social subjectivism. However, with the rejection of positivism, which came to be associated with the French sociologism of Durkheim and Levy-Bruhl, social subjectivism suffered a gradual decline, and new philosophical currents from Germany—Husserl, Scheler, and N. Hartmann—replaced it. The *Revista de Occidente* and in particular its editor, José Ortega y Gasset, exercised an influential role in this change. "What Are Values?" an article published in the *Revista* in 1923, is the point of departure for the objectivist, absolutist conception of value in the Hispanic world.

With insight and enthusiasm, Ortega summarized and supported Scheler's position. Scheler was heavily influenced by Husserl's phenomenology and in particular by his doctrine of essences. However, whereas Husserl maintained that essences are grasped through intellectual intuition (*Wesenschau*), Scheler emphasized the role of emotional intuition in grasping essences. Ortega maintains that values, like triangles, "are *transparent* natures. We see them immediately and as a whole. . . . For this reason, mathematics is an *a priori* science of absolute truths. Therefore, evaluation or the science of values, also will be a system of evident and invariable truths, of a type similar to mathematics."[1]

Ortega's support of a theory of immutable essences and a priori,

161

absolute forms of knowledge is surprising. When writing this article on values, existentialist and historicist thinkers were already important for him, and he had begun to elaborate his "perspectivism," which led eventually to his notion of "vital reason." And "vital reason" necessitates the rejection of immutable and absolute essences in favor of concrete dimensions of human existence, as these are conceived by historicism and existentialism.

Even at this early stage, Ortega enjoyed an enviable reputation in Latin America and his views on axiological issues were not taken to constitute a mere theory among others but rather as the indisputable truth. That value was an essence that could be grasped through emotional intuition was accepted as fact and very few questioned its a priori and absolute nature. A similar attitude was taken toward the hierarchy of values espoused by Ortega that had been derived from Scheler's a priori, absolute stance. There were a few isolated instances of rebellion, as in the case of Korn and Caso, but they did not have significant influence. Absolute objectivism was the accepted truth in university courses and textbooks. Husserl's criticism of psychologism and of John Stuart Mill in particular had a profound effect on Latin American thought, particularly since positivism was being rejected in all its forms.

In addition to the above, another important development supported the interest in values and their objective interpretation. Positivism tried to separate values from human reality in order to apply freely the methods of natural science to the study of humans. Thus, the German philosopher R. H. Lotze (1817–1881) maintained that values are independent of nature and summarized his views in a proposition that maintained its influence for many years to come, namely, "values do not exist, rather they are valuable." This separation prepared the ground in Germany for insisting on the radical distinction between the natural sciences (*Naturwissenschaften*) and the human sciences (*Geisteswissenschaften*). Windelband, Rickert, Dilthey, and other German philosophers insisted on this distinction, a distinction that was accepted and taught in Latin America without major opposition or criticism. The natural sciences, it was argued, are value-free whereas the human sciences are value-oriented. In this way, the theory of values or axiology is converted into one of the principal instruments for understanding the human world. Axiological typologies such as those of E. Spranger emerged and value, in addition to the defining role it played in aesthetics and ethics, became indispensable in the fields of cultural anthropology, sociology, law, philosophy of religion, and history

The introduction of value into the aforementioned fields complicates those fields, because the nature of value is complex. Even the most basic questions concerning value are difficult to answer. For example: Do we desire things because they have value or do they have value because we desire them? Do we confer value on things because we like them, desire them, or have some interest in them, or do all our reactions arise from qualities found in the object that we perceive—as occurs with primary qualities in visual perception? When we do not look at an object, we suppose that its qualities remain in it, ready to be seen as soon as we look again at the object. So-called axiological objectivism supports this principle, i.e., values depend on the object and the subject merely grasps the value. Subjectivism, on the other hand, claims that values are the result of our individual and collective responses.

The subjectivist asks: Can something have value if no one has perceived it nor can perceive it? Real or potential valuation seems to be an indispensable element in the concept of value, for it is unthinkable that something should have value without reference to any kind of subject.

Objectivism recognizes that valuation is subjective, but this does not imply that value itself is subjective. In the same way that perception is subjective whereas the object perceived is not, because the primary qualities remain intact when no one perceives the object, the value of a given object remains intact independently of the subject who is judging that object to be of value, or evaluating it. Just as we should not confuse the perception of a given object with the object itself, we must not mistake the valuation of a given object with its value.

Between the extremes of a radical subjectivism and an a priori, absolute objectivism that converts values into entities similar to mathematical entities, there are many different views. Among them is the social subjectivism of Durkheim that had its origin in France toward the beginning of the century. According to this view the isolated individual does not confer value on an object, for this is the task of a specific community or society. Individuals acquire valuations from their cultural environment. Bouglé, Levy-Bruhl, and other French sociologists developed Durkheim's ideas in order to establish the social character of morality that for them is rooted neither in a priori forms nor in individual caprice. This view is represented in Latin America by Antonio Caso, who preferred to call it social objectivism because the value is objectified in the collective consciousness. The truth is that it is a form of subjectivism that is social rather than individual. Objectivism presupposes the recognition of qualities that are found in the objects.

Axiology had its beginnings toward the end of the last century in Austria and Germany. At that time, Meinong and von Ehrenfels, supported by the psychologism of the day, gave axiology a decidedly subjectivist bent. However, their axiological studies did not have great influence in Latin America. It was the French sociologism referred to above, as presented in the work of Durkheim, Bouglé, and Levy-Bruhl, that took root in Latin America and shaped the development of value theory there.

As psychologism lost its predominant role in Europe, and Husserl "refuted" it in his *Logical Investigations* (*Logische Untersuchungen*, 1900, 1913), philosophical views with a phenomenological orientation, which considered values as essences, came to the fore. Scheler was the first to present this view in *Der Formalismus in der Ethik und die materiale Wertethik*. The first part was published in 1913 in the *Jahrbuch* edited by Husserl and the second part was published in 1916. This lengthy, important work was translated into Spanish in 1941 under the title *Ética*, making absolute objectivism more widely known. Scheler's perspective found additional support in Nicolai Hartmann's *Ethik*, published in 1926. Although the latter was not translated into Spanish until much later, it was influential in Latin American university circles.

The views of these two German philosophers created the environment in which the problem of value was discussed in Latin America. However, through the influence of Heidegger's historicism and Sartre's existentialism, the absolutist and a priori conceptions of value based on the views of Scheler and Hartmann began to lose their prestige. The Argentine Carlos Astrada was one of the first Latin American followers of the existentialism of Heidegger, under whom he studied at Freiburg. He formulated an incisive criticism of Scheler's axiology in his book *La ética formal y los valores* (1938). The Uruguayan Juan Llambías de Acevedo, however, defended Scheler in an article written in 1952. The article reflects both a sound grasp of Scheler's position and enthusiastic adherence to it. The supposed refutation of axiological objectivism by existentialism was one of the main themes of the Third Inter-American Congress held in Mexico in 1950.

After that, the discussion became less intense and the problem was approached from other perspectives. Logical empiricism and subsequently analytic philosophy became more prevalent, although both traditions are contrary to an objective, absolute understanding of value and are oriented toward semantic analysis. Given these shortcomings, discourse ethics in the style of the German philosopher Jürgen Habermas has taken root, with many contemporary Latin American ethicists having spent time in Germany studying under Habermasian ethicists. Another important influence upon contemporary currents of value study has been Ernst Tugendhat.

The authors included in this section share a rejection of positivism and the development of value theories suited to the Latin American context. Thus they have helped to develop a Latin American philosophical tradition. The purpose of this section is to introduce the figures who shaped Latin American value theory in the particular fields of ethics, aesthetics, and philosophy of law.

Alejandro Korn

Korn is the only Latin American philosopher who openly defends a subjectivist position. He maintains that "value is the object of valuation" and "valuation is the reaction to an event" and an event is "a manifestation of the will." In his discussion, aesthetic values are not considered.

Korn affirms that absolute, universal values exist only in an act of thought or imagination, since the only values we actually have are historical, changing, and relative. The same fact is evaluated differently by different subjects, and it is natural that this should be the case since each person responds in his own way. Valuations are therefore individual and vary with the changing stages and circumstances of life. There are also social, communal, and national evaluations.

He claims that the historical transmutation and the differences among contemporary values prove there are no fixed values. The supposed immutable values are no more than projections of one's ideals and desires or those of our society or historical age.

Since values are subjective, so is the hierarchy of values. Throughout history, the supreme value has changed from time to time. "In reality, no objective hierarchy exists, although we have the right to establish one on our own," that is, arbitrarily.

One might object to Korn's thesis by pointing out that what he has described is true as a psychological or sociological description of valuation. However, there are erroneous evaluations and, if this is the case, one cannot reduce value to valuation. Inevitably, one must consider the qualities of the valued object, since the adequacy of the evaluation depends on these qualities.

Alejandro Deústua

The Peruvian Alejandro Deústua did not develop a theory of value, but chose to analyze a specific axiological experience, in this case, aesthetic experience. In *La idea de orden y libertad en la historia del pensamiento humano* as well as in *Estética general*, from which the selection in this collection has been taken, Deústua evaluates human activity on the basis of the fundamental concepts of liberty and order. He sees aesthetic activity as free creation in which one achieves the highest degree of freedom. Freedom, however, does not exclude order, for it is an ideal order. Furthermore, there can be no beauty if there is no freedom. Art thus becomes the highest expression of human activity. In all other human activities, such as economics, science, and religion, freedom is subordinate to principles, norms, or laws. As an intrinsic value, aesthetic value is "essentially disinterested" and is, therefore, the highest of all values. Its freedom rests upon the emancipation from ends that might restrict it. Aesthetic activity embodies the "value of values."

Carlos Vaz Ferreira

The extensive work of Vaz Ferreira, a leading Uruguayan philosopher, does not provide a systematic analysis of fundamental problems in axiology. In the reprinted passages from *Fermentario* he refers indirectly to moral value with the term "optimism of value" that is opposed to the "optimism of succes." His approach is a condemnation of moral pessimism. For Vaz Ferreira there is undeniable moral progress. The view that denies such progress, pace Ferreira, stems from an erroneous evaluation according to which the past is idealized by the imagination and purified through a forgetting of all that is objectionable.

With the passage of time, humanity has multiplied its ideals, and dissatisfaction with some of those ideals creates a pessimistic outlook on the present. The conflict of ideals is difficult to resolve. Therefore, according to Vaz Ferreira, we must resign ourselves at the present to conflicting moral demands, which stem from a conflict in values.

Miguel Reale

The Brazilian philosopher of law Miguel Reale approaches axiology by way of law. In his *Filosofia do direito* (1953), he distinguishes between judgments of existence and judgments of value. The former refer to being and the latter to what ought to be. He rejects Hartmann's interpretation that value is an ideal object. Ideal objects are independent of space and time whereas values are linked to valuable things. In addition the former are quantifiable and the latter are not. He believes that value, like being, cannot be defined because it is a fundamental category, and he repeats with Lotze that "value is what is valuable." According to Reale, the characteristics of value are: bipolarity, implication, referrability, preferability, incommensurability, and hierarchical ordering. He carefully unpacks the meaning of each of these terms in the selection included here.

NOTE

1. José Ortega y Gasset, "Qué son los valores?" *Obras completas* (Madrid: Revista de Occidente, 1947), 6:333.

Alejandro Korn
(1860–1936)

I n spite of having written relatively little, Korn was the philosopher of the greatest prestige in Argentina during the first half of the twentieth century. His influence was personal and Socratic. He made his impact not only in the world of ideas but also in that of action. Pedro Henríquez Ureña referred to him correctly as "a teacher of knowledge and virtue."

Korn was born in San Vincente, in the province of Buenos Aires, in 1860. He was the son of a German doctor who had emigrated for political reasons. He died in La Plata in 1936 in his house on Avenue 60, surrounded by friends and disciples. He received a degree in medicine at the age of twenty-three in Buenos Aires. After practicing medicine in several towns, he settled in the city of La Plata, which had recently been founded. He limited his practice to psychiatry and became the director of the State Hospital of the Alienated in Melchor Romero. In 1916 he resigned this position and retired, setting aside his medical career.

In 1906 he had been designated assistant professor of history of philosophy in the College of Philosophy and Letters at the University of Buenos Aires. In 1909 he was named full professor. Some years later he also was appointed to the chair of epistemology and metaphysics, and after the university reform of 1918 he was elected dean of the faculty. He retired from these responsibilities in 1930.

Although Korn's early orientation was positivistic, he soon overcame this perspective through his interest in literature and metaphysics and his reading of the works of German and Spanish mystics. *The Critique of Pure Reason* convinced him of the impossibility of any knowledge of metaphysics, but he remained torn by a deep inclination toward metaphysics that he knew he could not satisfy. His theoretical caution and his critical spirit prevented his falling into philosophical utopias and hypostasis, as can be seen in his theory of knowledge and in the passages from his axiology that are incorporated here. This attitude also gave an ironic quality to his terse, limpid prose.

His principal works are *Influencias filosóficas en la evolución nacional* (1912–14); *La libertad creadora* (1920–22); his fundamental work, *Axiología* (1930); and *Apuntes filosóficos* (1935), where he summarizes his thought in a clear form and in a simple style. He wrote many articles and bibliographical reviews that were published in journals, principally in *Valoraciones* of La Plata.

Korn was a major influence in overcoming the theoretical limitations of positivism, the predominant philosophy in Argentina at the beginning of the century. However, he did not limit himself to criticizing it, as was the case with many others; rather, he developed a theory that went beyond it.

The problem of freedom attracted him not only for its theoretical importance, but also because of its impact in ethics and politics. The influence of Kant is evident at this point. Korn affirms that the objective world obeys necessary laws, whereas the subjective world lacks such laws and is free, hence the desires and resolutions of the subjective world cannot be foreseen. But the freedom of the self is that of wanting, not that of doing. The self aspires to actualize freedom, with science and technology as the instruments of that liberation. Korn refers to this process of liberation as "economic freedom." Man must also free himself from his own impulses, appetites, and passions and he does this by means of the moral law that he imposes upon himself in free choice. For Korn, there is no possibility of ethics without freedom. Economic liberty and ethical liberty are not opposed to each other, rather they interpenetrate. Nevertheless, one must distinguish between them because the useful is not always good nor is the good always useful. United, however, they constitute human liberty. "To actualize absolute freedom through economic dominion's conquest of nature and through ethical self-dominion and therefore submit necessity to freedom" is the goal of the process of liberation that is creative. Hence, this can be called a "creative freedom."

In axiology he was the main representative of subjectivism, to which he adhered when the absolute and a priori objectivism of Scheler was predominant, since Scheler's view had been introduced into the Spanish-speaking world by Ortega y Gasset. Korn's position can be summarized in his affirmation: "Value is the object of an evaluation." He refers to the existence of absolute and universal values in an ironic tone, since he believed that they have only a changing, historical existence.

Korn's influence remains alive through his writings and his followers. The greatest of these, without a doubt, was Francisco Romero, who succeeded to Korn's chairs in epistemology and metaphysics at the University of Buenos Aires. Romero wrote, "In Argentine philosophy, the significance of Korn is exceptional and allows for no comparisons."

Philosophical Notes

[VALUE AS THE OBJECT OF A VALUATION]

Valuation is the human reaction to a fact or an event. This subjective reaction, which grants or denies value, is the manifestation of the will: it says, "I want it" or "I do not want it." *Value is the object—real or ideal—of an affirmative valuation.*

We use the term "will" to designate a psychological function, without hypostasizing it. It is not an autonomous faculty, and still less is it a metaphysical entity. It is the outcome of the psychic process and should, more properly, be called volition. And it would be better yet to use only the verb "to want" or "to desire," in referring to the final act of affirming or denying. Psychological analysis shows us, though not completely, the multiplicity of elements that take part, consciously or unconsciously and more or less strongly, in the act of volition: biological needs, inherited atavisms, acquired habits or prejudices, persistent memories, emotive, ethical, or aesthetic impulses, weighty reflections, odd suggestions, practical interests, and the like. But the final synthesis is not so much the mechanical addition of such various factors, as it is the culmination of a vital process, in which individual personality is revealed in its unprecedented and unrepeatable uniqueness. Once achieved, this synthesis comes to dominate and direct the whole complex of psychical activity. Thus we have a vicious circle. Wanting or desiring emerges from the psychical complex, not as a servant, but as a master. It is like the way a historical personality arises from the nameless mass, on which he imposes his

From Alejandro Korn, *Apuntes filosóficos*, in *Obras* (La Plata: Universidad Nacional de La Plata, 1938), 1:244–34.

169

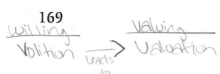

authority, at the same time that he represents collective tendencies. The will—which disintegrates under analysis—grasps the elements that make it up so as to give them structure, unity, and meaning.

Volition is explained as much by its causes as by its aims. It is supported by the past but is directed toward the future. It is not moved by the facts themselves but by the valuation of them. The will can override the claims of instincts and interests; it can counteract violent passions or set aside wise, rational counsel. It postulates its own values—that is, its own ends—and requires logical operations to provide it with appropriate theory and suitable means. This is when it is strong, since when it is weak it goes begging. Masterworks of fiction and drama serve better than psychological treatises to reveal these happenings. And history, in offering concrete and lively examples of the rule of will, shows us how it triumphs or fails.

Will is neither the complete master of judgment nor the slave of external forces. Here we leave the realm of theory to confront practical problems of life. There are still those who dispute whether the act of volition is compelled or spontaneous. It is the old quarrel over determinism and indeterminism, necessity and freedom. Too much time has been wasted on it. In each case we certainly know in what way our will feels restrained or free. We know when an oppression binds us and when we follow our own impulses. *Coercion and freedom are subjective states. If we were to speak objectively, it would be of necessity and contingency.* We only create confusion when we use these terms where they do not belong; to give them absolute value is to exceed the limits of experience.

Coercion is the basic fact; liberty is the absence of coercion. In an act—rare, to be sure—in which coercion is reduced to zero, we experience the full delight of liberation. When, on the contrary, the act is entirely compelled and opposed to our desires, it pains and oppresses us, until we suffer the consciousness of servitude. We find an intermediate condition in the normal course of life in which the degree of freedom one can acquire is the measure of personal dignity. When an energetic will strives to fulfill itself completely, it is overtaken by tragic conflicts.

It is only when people are conscious of coercion that they strike out for freedom. Coercion does not pain us when it does not bother us or we are not conscious of it or do not even feel it, or when we tolerate or even approve it. Human beings have often tolerated, and still tolerate, coercions that arouse protests, whether successful or not, in others. Coercion means different things to different people. Great numbers of people may agree at times, while at others a solitary voice hears no echo. A cave dweller may well feel himself coerced if he has to exchange his cave for a hut. The survival of troglodytic atavisms at least permits us to imagine this. Even now, many millions of the most oppressed and disinherited people do not feel the weight of their chains. They have neither consciousness of servitude nor desire for freedom. Their reaction is the same as that of the person who, not experiencing the tyranny of his instincts, follows them like an animal. Our tightest bonds are those within us.

One encounters coercion in all areas of human activity—whether those areas be physical or biological, political or economical, emotional or spiritual. Thus, man has to conquer freedom in combat with nature, with his fellowmen, and with himself. But this assumes the goals of mastery of the physical world, adequate organization of human coexistence, and personal autonomy. In each concrete case, the will has an affirmative or negative attitude, explicitly or implicitly, thoughtfully or impulsively, and well or badly advised.

We need general concepts to examine, classify, and systematize the indefinite number of valuations arising from all the shadings of individual reactions. This is the mission of the theory of values—or axiology. Various such efforts have been made with different criteria; they come to be evaluations of valuations and, like them, have a personal character. Evaluations necessarily differ, since each subject reacts in his own way. Different subjects value the same fact in unexpected and contradictory ways; what is good for one is bad for another. The fact itself is innocent of any such bickering. It is hard to argue over the empirical reality of things: one observes, one proves. But people dispute their valuations interminably, without agreement. There is great wisdom in the bumpkin's remark: "You can't convince me with reasons." A psychiatrist would be mad to try to cure madness with arguments. And the same rule applies to those who are sane: each to his own tastes. People are always confusing the fact and the valuation of it. Political economy is not concerned with the physical and chemical properties of gold as they are scientifically determined; it just endlessly discusses the value of gold. So it is with all axiological theories: law, ethics, and aesthetics—above all history. Philosophy itself, the theory of subjective action, is nothing other than axiology, once we separate it from science and metaphysics. Thus there is no way to reduce philosophy to a single expression.

Valuations are above all individual; each person is free to accept or reject them. But the gregarious community of the species, the community of psychological structure, the community of interests, the community of historical antecedents—all these, more or less extensively, determine collective valuations. One finds local, guild, and national valuations, just as one finds personal valuations. But valuations also change in the same person at different stages of his life and under different circumstances. It is useless to recall historical mutations, not to mention that fads change the current valuations every six months. Fads are not limited to clothes.

Are there then no absolute, universal, obligatory, and unchanging values? They seem to exist, but as creations of naive idealism. They exist insofar as we think them or imagine them. But in spatiotemporal reality, there are only perpetually changing, relative, historical values. The abstract concepts, which we use to put the world of values in order, are always double: they set an unreal fact against a real fact. They imagine in the distance the illusion of an end that is pursued but not reached; they suppose that we have already fulfilled our desire. Let us take a concrete example of what we see as an injustice. We immediately try to correct it. If we generalize the case, we begin the process of mental abstraction, at the limits of which we encounter the dualism of injustice and justice. But the first term is abstracted from reality, and the second is only its negation. The just state would be one in which there were no injustices. Is there anyone not eager for that? But we live in disagreement about what is just and what is unjust. Only the will decides; only historical power establishes the legal formula. And that for little time.

Humanity expresses its highest values in symbolic concepts; we do not have to defame them with a contemptuous epithet. It is not fair to deny satisfaction to the demands of feeling and faith, to deprive rhetoric of its preferred expressions. They are not tall tales; they are myths. The effective elimination of but one concrete injustice is worth more than all digressions about the perfect state. And yet, myth is an emotive factor that helps guide the historical process, when it is not used to avoid modest daily chores.

In the following table of values there are nine pairs of basic valuations, each of which has a historical fulfillment and an ideal concept. The table is only an attempt; the number of fundamental valuations can be increased or decreased.

VALUATIONS	BASIC CONCEPTS		HISTORICAL FULFILLMENT	IDEAL GOAL
Biological	I Economic	Useful-Useless	Technical Skill	Well-Being
	II Instinctive	Agreeable-Disagreeable	Pleasure	Happiness
	III Erotic	Lovable-Hateful	Family	Love
Social	IV Vital	Select-Common	Discipline	Power
	V Social	Permitted-Prohibited	Law	Justice
Cultural	VI Religious	Sacred-Profane	Worship	Holiness
	VII Ethical	Good-Bad	Morality	Good
	VIII Logical	True-False	Knowledge	Truth
	IX Aesthetic	Beautiful-Ugly	Art	Beauty

It has been assumed that values form a hierarchy in which some are subordinated to others, and all of them, perhaps, to a supreme value. Of the nine basic affirmative values, there is not one that has not been put in first place by some thinker. Economic, historical, vital, religious, logical, ethical, and aesthetic values have been and still are the crux of certain philosophical systems. Utilitarianism, hedonism, empiricism, rationalism, mysticism, stoicism, aestheticism are all philosophical positions under the hegemony of a value. There has never been a truly uniform evaluation in the history of philosophy; they are all one-sided. There really is no objective hierarchy, although each of us has the right to decree one on his own account.

Historically speaking, biological values have been the most urgent for primitive man, when not the only ones. This is obvious. Other kinds of values have been added—shall we say, superimposed?—little by little. Nothing prevents us, if we like, from rating them higher. When man is freed from economic servitude, higher values will probably impose themselves. But as each day dawns, people nowadays, exactly like their remote ancestors, find themselves in the presence of the problem, not of existence, but of subsistence; economic value retains its rights. The anguish of life is real, although it sets us empirical, rather than metaphysical problems. It requires us to act. . . .

Action is will set to work in proportion to our power. The complex process of psychic activity ends in a material goal. The arm carries out the volition. By action man breaks his isolation, takes part in his world, conquers his well-being, repels aggression, and traces the limits of his authority. Action is communion of subject and object, conjunction of the ideal and the real. Action reestablishes psychophysical unity.

Theoretical examination of our knowledge of reality leaves us perplexed: we never hit upon certainty. Empirical facts, pure concepts, poetic myths—all these, alike, dissipate under analysis. The ultimate nature of things eludes us. Faith is a subjective conviction; logic ends in antinomies; evaluations are contradictory. Neither the secret of the cosmos, nor the secret of the soul, surrenders itself to us. Instead of solutions, we are offered problems; doubt is our intellectual inheritance.

But action cuts the Gordian knot. It cuts it after meditative reflection or by violent impulses, but in any case as a matter of life and death. Thus the problems evaporate. Action does not take place in a fictitious world; it confronts what is present and concrete. Our space-time environment is real: it both resists us and gives way to our effort. Because action is efficacious, we do not argue in limbo. Existence is real because we conquer it day by day. Conflict with our neighbor is real because it constrains and threatens us. The unknown is real because it limits us at each step. The fist that knocks down the obstacle is also real.

Action is justified by success, condemned by failure, and judged by its goal. It is subject to our valuation. Heroic actions have been carried out in the name of superstition, and base actions in the name of high ideals. Life does not depend on a theorem or creed; life is action. But action depends on will; man is responsible for his acts; he is on target or misses, triumphs or yields. If he accepts life, he accepts its risks bravely or pusillanimously, clearheadedly or stupidly. His sovereign will decides. Once done the act is irrevocable; no god can erase it; it happened once and for all; it is woven into the future for all eternity. One must accept and endure its inexorable consequences.

Action is unavoidable. We have not sought the gift of existence. It is by chance that we are born in a certain time and place, in a bare and fluffy cradle, into hardship or luxury. We choose none of it. For better or worse we find ourselves in our world. Those who are responsible for us redeem the sin by helping us get started. Then we are abandoned to our efforts. We have scarcely sensed the happiness of living when we feel its pain. He who takes account of it can reject his ambiguous destiny, or resign himself to it, or confront it boldly. There is an appropriate theory for each of these attitudes, but the problem can only be resolved, negatively or affirmatively, by action. Not to do anything is an action as heroic as to do something. How can we escape the dilemma? The animal, and thus the animal willfulness in each of us, chooses life at all costs. Perhaps man discovers higher values in his consciousness or in the work of his predecessors than those that are merely biological, perhaps the life for fulfilling higher purposes. The values a man chooses express his personality, his own value. And then perhaps his own life acquires worthwhile contents, is justified, and comes to be appreciated.

Both history and personal experience prove that the instinct of self-preservation requires one to affirm life, in spite of pain, and in spite of the sentence we receive in bitter hours. Not even pessimistic negation spares us action. We have no alternative but to choose our place in the contest. We can do without theories, but not without action. "In the beginning was action." Not at the beginning of things, but at the beginning of human redemption. The species has forged its technical, human, and spiritual culture through action; and it is culture that enables us to pursue our emancipation from all servitude. Culture is the work of will; will desires liberty. Be it: *Creative Liberty.*[1]

NOTE

1. Reference to his own work, "La libertad creadora," *Verbum* (1920), revised and reedited several times.—ED.

Axiology

[VALUATION]

Valuation is a complex process in which all psychical activities participate in various proportions, as part of a whole, until they are synthesized in a volition. Psychological analysis can identify the confluence of the most elemental biological impulses, the most instinctive appetites, the most refined sensibility, the most prudent reflection, the most remote memories, the most headstrong faith, the most idealistic or mystical vision—all of which come together in the act of valuation, in the movement of will that approves or repudiates. The genesis of valuation is influenced by the historical moment in which we live, the collective atmosphere—cultural, ethnic, and associational—that envelops us, and the more or less social features of our character. In short, there is a slippery, personal dimension to valuation, which eludes all logical coercion. Although psychological analysis, armed with the intuition of a Dostoyevski, may penetrate to the murkiest depths of the human soul, there will always remain something, an undecipherable x. And this is to say nothing of those professional psychologists who are condemned to skim the surface.

If we judge another person's valuation to be naive or stupid, wise or brilliant, this is a valuation in its own right. Even valuations that are personally repugnant to us—that strike us as paradoxical, cynical, or extravagant—originate in a conscience that can declare them whenever it assumes the responsibility. They do not bind us, to be sure; they cannot even command our respect since we accept or reject them according to our own judgment. A universal conscience can deny the most pampered

From Alejandro Korn, *Axiología*, in *Obras* (La Plata: Universidad Nacional de La Plata, 1938), 1:129–44.

valuation, however attired in dogmatic authority. So many valuations, originally scorned and vilified, come to win general assent. Many others become silent, without echo, because they were isolated occurrences. We should realize not only that the valuations of our contemporaries disagree among themselves to infinity, but also that there is a continuing transformation of values throughout successive generations. How strange, indeed, if even in the course of our own brief existence we change our minds as we do!

We should not be led into error by the apparent existence of valuations that seem to be supported by indisputable evidence, as well as by our own assent. They would vanish as soon as one barely squeezed them. There is no need to choose a trivial example. Let us take the fifth of the Ten Commandments, but with its tacit qualifications: you shall not kill, if you are not a warrior, judge, or priest; you shall not kill, except for members of another tribe; you shall not kill but those who profess a different creed; you shall not kill, except in defense of your life, your honor, or your property; you shall not openly kill, although you may exploit the life of your neighbor; you shall not kill, as long as you have no motive for it. The author of this commandment was never concerned with living up to it; he must have been a very word-minded person. History is the history of human slaughter. Thinkers have justified it; poets have glorified it.

There is no need to multiply examples; they all lead to the same conclusion. Normative valuations may assume airs of universality, but that claim can be, and is, converted into a lie by historical reality. Effective valuation dwells in our inner authority; there is no judge outside the conscious will. We insist: it is impossible to point out a universal, permanent, or constant valuation that is esteemed by all people in all times. Conscience always reserves the right to choose or refuse the presumed obligation. I like it when someone else agrees with my evaluation; but I am not disposed to submit mine to an extraneous authority, whether that of the overwhelming majority of men or that of the highest magistrate. The decision is in the last resort that of the autonomous person. This is the common root of the infinite number of concrete valuations, and also the reason for their divergence.

Well, someone may say, these conclusions reflect historical and empirical reality, and in this sense they are beyond attack. And yet, valuations are not arbitrary: the will does not adopt them capriciously, nor can it ignore the existence of values independent of human whim—indeed, of human valuation. In other words, we do not create value, we are limited to discovering it, and the concept of it is independent of the psychological or historical process. Let us now examine this new problem.

Value, we have said, is the object of an affirmative valuation. It has to do with real or ideal objects. No one should attribute intrinsic value to real objects. Neither natural nor made objects have value if no one appreciates them, if they are unrelated to human interest. There are no values for science; there are only equally interesting or equally indifferent facts. When we attribute value to a thing, it is a shaky title; it is not the same for me as for another, nor the same today as yesterday. The Arab who was lost in the desert found what he took to be a sack of dates in the track of a caravan. He looked inside, and threw it away in disgust. They're only pearls, he said. The conditional value of real objects depends on our estimation of them. But let us leave the case of real objects: it is too simple.

We have examined the historical creations that pertain to the different order of valuations. The value of these creations depends on our evaluation. We can withhold it. The religious dogma, the work of art, the judicial formula, the practical advice, the philosophical truth—what other value should they have than what they receive from our assent? Has not the protest of the martyr or of the reforming genius always come under the scrutiny of the dominant valuation, armed perhaps with material power? When a secular value ceases to rule, first in one conscience and then in many, it ends by disappearing or by being replaced. Each person can bring this about, individually, within the jurisdiction of his own conscience, and he will do it if the dominant value strikes him as coercive. Historical, like material values, remain subject to our personal valuation.

Let us, then, get down to a discussion of the most important concepts: the great ideal values. Positivism manages to convert them into subjective postulates derived from the cosmic mechanism. The current metaphysical reaction classifies them as absolutes. In either case they are regarded as constant and immutable values, set apart from any act of will. They would continue to exist, whether or not any human mind conceived or esteemed them. Their own authority is enough to establish them; they cannot be denied: who would dare deny justice, beauty, truth?

It is commonsensical that such values do not exist. One does not find them in spatiotemporal reality. In what superreality or in what unreal limbo can one place them? They are the abstract name for still unrealized ultimate aspirations, and they put us in contact with the transcendent as we think about their fulfillment. They are pure ideas; they come to be but are not. Word on our lips, ideal concept in consciousness, they only become effective and efficacious when, through action, they are objectivized in concrete, relative, and deficient form, destined to be a historical episode in the evolution of human culture. These creations of will symbolize its ultimate aims. We cannot conceive of purposes as part of the mechanical process of nature as it is interpreted by science; only will proclaims them. Causal and teleological conceptions cannot be reconciled; they constitute a basic antinomy that is deepened, rather than avoided, by rational analysis. Let this be said for the naturalists.

Those axiological theories that make use of objective, unreal, and atemporal values represent a shamefaced metaphysics scarcely disguised by its mask of logic. We are by no means denying metaphysical need. Man keeps trying new roads to escape the greatest of his anxieties. Unfortunately, reason is no help. We deny the possibility of a logical and rational metaphysics and we require philosophies to set a neat boundary between empirical reality and metaphysical poetry. The "Great Demolisher" did his work to give the neorationalists a chance to hide amid the ruins of their miserable shacks. Any rational metaphysics is a sin against logic. We have no words—hardly even metaphors—to express the eternal—that is, the ineffable. There is no scholastic technique for finding the *coincidentia oppositorum*[1] of irreducible antinomies. That can come only from the great creations of art and mystical vision, aesthetic and religious emotion.

The authors who are committed to discovering absolute values, valid a priori, have already invented an ad hoc gnoseology. They will not discuss the historical and psychological consequences of valuations; they will maintain, however, that this process arises from values and does not create them. This assumes that our axiological knowledge transcends empirical reality and arrives at the notion of timeless values. In effect, they rely on a theory according to which spatiotemporal objects are only one kind of object within a multiplicity of objective orders. The unreal as well as the real can be an object. This is another effort to open the royal road to metaphysical truth.

It affirms, first, the autonomy of logical values, and then the autonomy of ethical values. They are objective and not subjective. They are born following a psychological gestation but, once the umbilical cord is cut, they have their own destiny. We know the offspring: the "substantial forms" of scholasticism, the old "rational entities," which prudent criticism, not daring to hypostasize, deprives of "being" and reduces to vague nonsense in a kingdom where they neither are, exist, nor act. If this paradox does not captivate us, it is, according to Rickert, because our mental habits are deficient.

We are dealing with wordplay, in which talented men waste their great erudition in byzantine discourse, a marvelous mixture of logical subtlety and essential intuitions (*Wesenschau*). They claim to have captured the unreal object, but they have only lost contact with reality. . . .

But now some terrified soul will break in: "In this case we are without fixed and binding values!" And indeed, we never had them; they do not exist. Is not the historical change of values an obvious fact, along with the incompatibility of contemporary values? One finds different values at each geographical latitude, in each ethnic group, in each political alliance, and with each social interest. Within each group, however homogeneous it may seem, we find persons who resist the current valuation. There is always some dissent on the way to triumph or failure. Is it not amusing how the satisfied bourgeoisie try to turn their profit into a timeless value, or how the true believer hawks the promptings of his fanaticism like dogmas?

Philosophers are no better; indeed, they provide the most disconcerting spectacle. It is the very nature of philosophy, they say, to aspire to universality. Philosophical truth must be one. It is impossible to conceive it as circumscribed by geographical limits, or determined by the historical moment, or by the interests of a social level. Nevertheless, this is what happens. As in so many cases, the paradox is the real. We know of a Western philosophy and of another that is Eastern; of a Greek philosophy and of another that is modern, of an empirical position opposed to rationalism, skepticism to dogmatism, realism to idealism. All systems are logical, but their pied multiplicity simply shows how ineffective logical argumentation is. Each different philosophy is the expression of a different valuation. Thus it has to run the same risks as all valuations. Each philosophy is systematized as a legal brief for the will that inspires it. Sometimes, though, in periods of decadence, the professor's poor and empty pedantry reveals a lack of will, a lack of vital conviction.

People should not be so afraid of subjective valuation. Humanity has not fallen into anarchy just because valuations have always been subjective. Aristotle alerts us, with his usual sagacity, by his observation that man is a gregarious animal. An isolated individual is a rare event; as a member of a group, his personal impulses are toned down by the rule of the gregarious instinct. Without feeling himself restrained, he will recite the liturgical formula that he has been taught, he will revere the established legal norms, he will respect the hallowed commonplaces, and will dress according to the current fad. No one rebels against an oppression he does not feel. Satisfied souls do not change collective values.

If rebellious evaluation appears, it will take its chances. Only a closed mind would object to it; while if many experience the same coercion, the rebellious judgment will be generalized. But a subjective valuation will be extinguished without consequences if, after a short or long conflict, it comes to have no historical dignity. Expressions of the general will, to be effective, should at least express the will of a more or less large group.

How, then, are we to choose from among the available valuations those that ought to prevail? The historical process does this; those that triumph prevail. It is not always the most just valuation—namely, ours—that triumphs. So, to conciliate them, we have recourse to argumentation, to persuasion, to the coincidence of interests, or to authority—if we have it. And yet, let us not forget that valuations represent our reaction to a physical or historical reality that is given to us, that common setting within which the individual and the collectivity act. . . .

NOTE

1. Scholastic term popularized by Nicholas of Cusa in the fifteenth century. The Mexican José Vasconcelos borrowed the term from Cusa and made it the foundation of his "Aesthetic Monism."—ED.

Alejandro Octavio Deústua (1849–1945)

Deústua belongs to the group of thinkers Francisco Romero has called the "founders" of Latin American philosophy. This group is characterized by its rejection of the dogmatic positivism in which its members were educated and by a turn toward a more spiritual perspective. The "founders" had long careers as educators and molders of a generation of young people dedicated to the serious study of philosophy. Deústua's merit rests more in his career of over fifty years as a dedicated teacher than in the originality and depth of his thought, which found its inspiration primarily in the idealism of Krause and the vitalism of Bergson.

Born in Huancayo, Peru, in 1849, Deústua received his degree in philosophy at the age of twenty-three and was named assistant professor of history in the University of San Marcos. Three years later he received a doctorate in philosophy (1872) and a year later a degree in law and a doctorate in jurisprudence. In 1882 he was named associate professor of literature and aesthetics and in 1884 professor of philosophy in the same university. In addition to his teaching responsibilities he also held high offices within the university and in public life. Among his more important positions were director of justice, culture, instruction, and welfare in 1895, senator from Lima in 1901, dean of the faculty of philosophy and letters in 1915, and president of the university from 1928 to 1930. On three occasions, in 1898, 1909, and 1924, Deústua visited Europe in order to study modern pedagogical methods to be incorporated into the Peruvian educational system. Widely respected and appreciated in his country, he died in Lima on August 6, 1945.

Because of his interest in the education of Peruvian youth, Deústua dedicated a significant portion of his writings to pedagogical themes. Nevertheless, it was in the areas of ethics and in aesthetics that he made his more important contributions. The strength and originality of his own ideas are evident in his discussion of the thought of European authors, especially in the volume on aesthetics, *Estética general* (1923). To a lesser degree, one also finds elements of his personal philosophy in the last chapters of *Los sistemas de moral* (1938–40) and in one of his earlier works, *Las ideas de orden y de libertad en la historia del pensamiento humano* (1917–19). In the last work he formulates the view that is developed more fully later on within the axiological context of his *Estética*. The thesis is that order as well as freedom are basic ideas in social development and although the first has dominated in the history of human thought, the second has priority over it, since it constitutes the positive expression of the spirit. In addition, freedom is the necessary condition of all change of order.

In the chapter from the *Estética* reprinted here, Deústua develops the position that aesthetic value is the source of all value. This "value of all values" as he calls it is the product of free activity whose essential function consists in the creation and the contemplation of the ideal aside from any practical intent. In contrast to the essentially instrumental character of other values, aesthetic value constitutes its own end, generating a completely disinterested activity, the creation of beauty.

> Free activity never gives up its essential and supreme function: the creation and contemplation of the ideal with no practical intent whatever. This is pure aesthetic function, the production of beautiful art in which the spirit aspires to achieve its creative ambition which is capable of producing something that the coercion of the environment makes impossible. This function constitutes, therefore, the fount from which other values derive their aspirations.

General Aesthetics

AESTHETIC EXPERIENCE

Even if we grant that all creation has aesthetic value, this still does not settle the question of the nature of beauty: the creative imagination takes different forms, aside from those classified as beautiful or ugly; they make up orders of phenomena distinguished by their subjective and objective natures; and they aspire to be treated with the same respect as other human values. In fact, all the normative sciences have an independent end, which seeks to become a value created by imaginative intuition. Logic, economics, ethics, law, and religion strive to achieve the values or ideals of truth, utility, goodness, justice, and holiness. Imagination is active in each of those disciplines. It performs an aesthetic function, which is nevertheless different from the creation of the beautiful, since this last has to do exclusively with what would, strictly speaking, be called the aesthetic emotion. The phenomenon of the beautiful, fully understood to include the ugly as well as the beautiful, both in nature and in art, is based on free activity, whether or not the activity is conscious. And yet we find that same kind of activity in logical, economic, moral, legal, and religious creations. Like artistic creations, they take on both psychic and social aspects; they tend also to set norms for thinking and willing, criteria for distinguishing and judging, and motives for conscious actions.

It is often discussed whether truth and utility are final values, true values like the others mentioned, or whether they are merely means to attain human ends considered as supreme. We have to exclude them if we look only at the question of the end; and we must also exclude them if we

From Alejandro Octavio Deústua, *Estética general* (Lima: Eduardo Rávago, 1923), pt. 2, chap. 2, pp. 424–40.

consider them in relation to the feeling of liberty, whether pleasant or painful, which is a necessary element in value.

Logic, like economics, proceeds with the rigorous determinism of science, without feeling or freedom. We can think of the demonstration of truth and the calculation of interest as purely intellectual functions, as means to final values although distinct from them. But this is pure abstraction and it neglects the intuitions of imagination in the discovery of new truths that, here, have the character of true values, even when they do not have all their traits. As instrumental values they differ radically from other values, and especially from aesthetic value, which can be classified as the *value of values*.

The dichotomy set by contemporary philosophy between science and art—which is different from Aristotle's distinction between theory and practice or thought and action—is a distinction between two activities: the ordering activity and the free activity; and this marks the difference between truth, as instrumental value, and beauty, as final value. Orderly, logical activity, which eliminates freedom for the sake of science, is auxiliary to the free activity that shapes the work of art, or that results from its aesthetic contemplation. Unlike truth, the beautiful cannot be demonstrated. One understands its nature by intuiting or feeling it, because the inspiration that engenders it or results from it escapes the exclusively logical process of deduction. Neither the concrete origin of the work of art, nor the aesthetic state, suffused by freedom and feeling, can be explained logically.

Intelligence can indeed collaborate in both: it can prepare the elements of inspiration, and it can support the efforts involved in making them objective; but it can in no way substitute the imaginative and free function of the beautiful creation. To suppose otherwise is to include norms antagonistic to freedom within aesthetic activity; it is to disregard the nature of imagination; it is to assume arbitrarily that there are innate types of beauty that function like axioms in logic; or to attribute to the action of physical and social media a dominating power that psychology disproves by the infinite variety of artistic works and, also, by the infinite possibilities of aesthetic emotion. The great error of intellectualism has been to assign thought a contemplative, primordial, and theoretical function, like the aesthetic, while subordinating art to it by placing art in the realm of practical activity. But contemporary voluntarism has reduced thought to its proper role in the psychic synthesis: to be an instrument auxiliary to freedom in its effort to become effective. Such are the real relations between the true and the beautiful, between logical and aesthetic phenomena, between pure art and pure science.

These relations are analogous to those between economic and aesthetic phenomena, and between the useful and the beautiful. So it is seen by those who have rejected the hedonistic or eudaemonistic theory of the beautiful, according to which aesthetic value is based on human happiness which, in turn, is based on pleasure. The aesthetic phenomenon is essentially disinterested. It pursues no end exterior to itself, whether economic, moral, or religious; its end is within itself; this is its essential characteristic, on which both its disinterest and its freedom are based. Thus it is, as Kant says, a "purposiveness, without purpose." The economic phenomenon is subject to the imperative of desire, which destroys its autonomy completely; the useful depends exclusively on desire. Even when desire is present in the development of aesthetic emotion, it is not there as a necessary element. Aesthetic emotion can and should exist apart from the desire to appropriate the contemplated work, the benefits that its author hopes to receive, or even those ends of artistic utility that are part of the work. Once desire is eliminated, the beautiful does not disappear, although the aesthetic emotion may lose or gain intensity. The so-called aesthetic congruity is an associated, but not necessary element. The freedom with which the artist produces his work can be limited by the need for congruity or fitness. Aesthetic feeling can be integrated with it without being dependent on it. On the other hand, if freedom is suppressed, the beautiful disappears, although the economic phenomenon persists.

Although the aesthetic phenomenon is radically different from logic and economics, it is analogous to the moral phenomenon. Freedom is essential in both. The moral ideal may indeed be regarded as an aesthetic creation, and, in the same sense, the actions to attain that ideal may be regarded as aesthetic. An action of great moral value becomes beautiful; beauty and goodness interpenetrate to such an extent that any effort to separate them would drastically change the nature of the action. For all their similarities, they are different, because freedom plays a different role in each. Moral phenomena involve the coercion of duty, imposed by a norm that moral consciousness finds superior to its will. There is no avoiding this imperative quality of law, whatever character we may attribute to it and whatever influence it may exercise over freedom. Whether categorical, hypothetical, or persuasive, it remains an imperative that imposes a duty, to which moral consciousness feels the need to submit, even when it rebels. The moral norm, like the logical norm, is an inescapable condition, which spirit ought to follow. Without fulfilling the first, the goodness of an action disappears; without obedience to the second, there is no truth in thinking. None of this applies to the aesthetic phenomenon, in which freedom is all and any norm is subordinate to it. Properly speaking, there are no norms in the aesthetic order, since the feeling of liberty can create or feel beauty within a unique and original psychic state. Originality is precisely the basic characteristic of the great work of art. A genius can alter or destroy existing norms, creating new ones, as he offers new models of artistic production. If he does not always do so, if he uses canons established by technical tradition, he does so freely because he considers them useful to the production and for the intelligibility of his work. Furthermore, since those canons are the results of the free activity of spirit, they can oppose it only when they come to set narrow limits to its expansion, by crystallizing forms that do not respond to freedom's greater ambitions. Unlike morality, aesthetic judgment is not content to establish absolute and eternal dogmas; nor does it feel the need to preserve them; nor is it troubled by substituting some ideals for others even when they are opposed. It is, on the contrary, eager for diversity as an essential condition for what it is and does. When the ideal, in the process of unification, takes the abstract form of universality—which is what ethical judgment constantly aspires to—aesthetic judgment rejects unity as anti-aesthetic.

Aesthetic emotions are closely related to moral emotions, but they spring from different causes in their contemplation of beautiful actions. Aesthetic consciousness enjoys what it has of free action, while moral consciousness enjoys what is appropriate to the norm. The moral act is based essentially on the power to inhibit consciousness, and even in regard to positive acts it supposes the absolute inhibition of opposing acts. Not so with the aesthetic act, which is essentially expansive. Aesthetic enjoyment is based on intuition of the ideal; moral appreciation, on the comparison of the deed with the precept, in such a way that reflection surpasses intuition to the extent of rendering it useless. Thus moral beauty has intuition and reflection at the same time; one feels its beauty and its morality can be demonstrated as a logical consequence of the universal and abstract precept.

Such demonstration presupposes an invariable principle, a dogma, an imperative norm that is superior to the will. But as I have said, there is no such norm in aesthetic activity, however much the aesthetic sociology of Lalo may want to claim it for technique. Whatever influence one may attribute to traditional rules, they cannot go beyond the freedom of spirit that creates the artistic work, nor can they condemn passive aesthetic feeling to a particular form of pleasure, nor can they explain its existence and evolution without reference to freedom, which is its source.

On the other hand, the idea of order performs a different role in each area. In morals it is the transcendent end of freedom, which ought to submit to it. The norm here creates an order in its own likeness. Such order is imperative, necessary, absolute, eternal. It is the very perfection of human life, which the individual does not create, although he freely accepts it as an ideal; it constitutes, even in the hedonistic concept of the moral law, an external and superior end for the will. Freedom does not create that order, because if it did the norm would no longer be external and superior; it would no longer impose a system of duties on conduct. The morality of the act is, at bottom, just such a submission to the norm. Freedom is connected with it at all only as the postulate for the sanction of the act, and because, in a spiritualist conception of man, only free actions are human, whether freedom be understood in an intellectualist or voluntarist sense. With the aesthetic phenomenon everything is the other way around: freedom creates its own order; it is an end in itself; it has no transcendent goal. The aesthetic order is that which best satisfies the expansion of spirit, and which best eliminates the coercion that is opposed to its nature. The whole aspiration of the aesthetic will is to achieve that order and ideal. The moral order and the aesthetic order thus have very different characteristics. The moral order, at its best, is a system of relations, of concepts, established by a normative law, even when it may originally have been an order of images. The second has been and always is a system of images. Systematization in the first is a logical process, which pursues the unity of the ideal and of the norm external to the individual, as in science. In the second, systematization is an intuitive process that finds unity and variety simultaneously in the individual's imaginative activity. In the first, one seeks universality in the extension of the norm, while in the second one finds it in the extension of aesthetic activity and in the depth of its intuition. The moral order presupposes the existence of an ideal of perfection, which it dogmatizes and imposes on the will in its relation with other wills; the aesthetic order is the ideal that is created by the spirit in the exercise of its freedom. Without that creation there would be no other than the biological imperatives; the moral imperative could not be explained. The moral order is thus based on the aesthetic order, because only the latter is a creation.

The religious phenomenon is even more closely analogous to the aesthetic phenomenon. They were born together in the creation of myth, as Wundt says, and they have never been completely separated. The religious phenomenon has always sought its most effective and complete expression in aesthetic form. But their difference is clear, when we consider the role that freedom plays in each. The religious state is one of liberation or emancipation from the world, but of absolute submission to divinity. The aesthetic state is absolute freedom. In the religious phenomenon, the norm, dictated by the divine will and known by revelation, is all. In the aesthetic phenomenon, whether in the work of art or in aesthetic enjoyment, inspiration is not subject to any norm. The work of art does not suffer its imposition, and aesthetic enjoyment does not adjust to it. The feeling of liberation is profound in both, but their causes and tendencies differ radically. They coexist in the original myth, but myth is above all the work of the creative imagination and is therefore an aesthetic phenomenon par excellence. Revelation is either aesthetic inspiration or an inexplicable mystery. Without that inspiration myth would never have existed. Within the limits of philosophical investigation, we must presuppose the primacy of aesthetic activity in religion as in the moral order.

But the differences we have noted between aesthetic value and other values do not permit us to deduce that the aesthetic phenomenon exists in a pure state, isolated from other social events, with which it is obviously closely related.

Such parity would be another mere abstraction. In living reality, to the contrary, the different phenomena are so closely associated that the effort to analyze them gives rise to different theories of the beautiful—and of art, which is its most perfect expression.

The assumption that there is a directing *Idea*—which guides spirit in the slow process of artistic execution, or which permits aesthetic contemplation to discriminate beauty already achieved, whether to enjoy it or to criticize it—has given logical value a great importance in aesthetic evaluation, to the point that the very nature of the beautiful and the basis of our judgment of it depend on the realization of the *Idea*. To know that idea and to realize it, or to appreciate it after realizing it, has been the fundamental problem for those who have confused the aesthetic phenomenon of the beautiful with the logical phenomenon of the true. They have attributed to reason what properly belongs to imagination and have erroneously supposed that the aesthetic function is reflective rather than intuitive, that reason has a dynamogenic power that it lacks, and that the aesthetic problem is solved by knowing the beautiful, rather than by feeling it and producing it freely.

The influence of intellectualism in the development of aesthetic ideas has led to the dispute between idealists, who emphasize *content,* and realists, who emphasize *form* in the aesthetic phenomenon. Idealists are dominated by panlogism, which hinges its doctrine on the idea of *order,* in spite of their sympathies for the principle of liberty. The realists are subject to the powerful influence of artistic technique, which looks for the laws of its execution in scientific methods. Since both groups are more logicians than aestheticians, they have looked at the problem of the beautiful in terms of truth, as a theory of knowledge, as a logical explanation of harmony, taking it to be the essential characteristic of the beautiful and therefore subject to the methods of discursive knowledge.

This mistaken point of view derives from the systematic orientation of all philosophy toward the central idea of order, which is essentially a matter of logic, and from the reduction of all knowledge to that exclusive form and of all logic to the logic of thought. It ignores the intuitive activity of imagination, although it is intuition that penetrates into reality with all the energies of spirit, discovering what there is of the essential that exists through the forms accessible to sensory experience and in the very depth of the ideas elaborated by thought. The "divining sympathy" that Bergson speaks of, which explains aesthetic inspiration, is not an idea in the Platonic or Aristotelian sense, nor is it the fruit of a fragmentary consciousness that mutilates or eliminates reality; it comes from the whole consciousness, freely projecting itself toward an ideal that it has formed and tries to fulfill, or toward an ideal already gained that satisfies the drive for creative expansion. We cannot do without logic in this activity; it has a necessary role, but as a means, not as an end. Instead of imposing unity and direction on aesthetic life, logic is subordinated to the *élan* of spirit, which pursues a freer reality in a world forged by imagination, as a result of which it can guide the intellectual efforts that are directed toward practical matters. It is at this point that the directing idea, already an aesthetic creation, gives importance to logic—to conscious reflection—as it develops effective means to the established practical end.

Economics, too, in spite of its external goal, has an auxiliary role in aesthetic activity. Aesthetic activity does not altogether exclude the idea of utility, derived from the feeling of sensory pleasure, which is the basis of economics. Utility does not, to be sure, enter into aesthetic activity with the overwhelming force of human egoism, which destroys all solidarity in the name of a false liberty. This liberty is false because, concentrating entirely on effects, it ignores the slavery of the passion that causes it. To be sure, the economic phenomenon can be openly opposed to the aesthetic phenomenon. A disinterested activity having an end in itself is not conceived in a state of consciousness reduced to egoism, following a unilateral direction, and excluding any affective element that might sidetrack it or attenuate its destructive force. But of course, such a purely economic state would be abnormal, just as pure avarice would be; it would have no value, except as a pure abstraction; it loses its extreme character in normal experience. The useful and the disinterested are combined in ways that demonstrate possible harmony between the aesthetic and the extra-aesthetic. Useful coordination can favor aesthetic value by placing or disposing of beautiful objects effectively—as, for example, when different artistic objects come together in architecture, in drama, and in beautiful objects in nature. Even a simple, useful coordination of coexistence or succession can produce aesthetic emotion, if it can also present to the spirit the appearance or symbol of freedom. The useful, then, offers the illusion of a free life. It no longer seems to be an external goal to the person who contemplates it. It has the appearance of fertile spontaneity, from which it borrows an illusory aesthetic value—as illusory as the spontaneity on which it is founded. Guyau, unlike Spencer, finds an aesthetic element in the useful. Instead of destroying the disinterested character of the beautiful by assimilating the aesthetic phenomenon to the economic, it deprives utility of its special character in order to relate it to aesthetic form. Guyau thus confirms the belief that the useful and the beautiful can help each other without losing their own natures: thus utility conserves its practical end, while the beautiful preserves its intrinsic liberty from any objective end. Architecture and oratory give proof of how beauty and utility compenetrate, so that utility attains beauty, while beauty makes utility more efficacious.

The cooperation of moral experience is still closer. And it is necessary when the aesthetic object is a human action, whether it is now being carried out, or has been, or will be; or whether the imagination invents it, reproduces it, or intrudes only to make the action plausible. In each case the beautiful is inseparable from the good; they tend to fuse, so that aesthetic judgment becomes moral; there is a tendency to alter the nature of art, imposing a pedagogical end on it as an essential ingredient. The theories of *didactic art* and *of art for art's sake,* which are equally exclusivist and inexact, arise from that confusion. As they do so, they affirm these two theses, respectively: the powerful influence of moral value in the appreciation of aesthetic value, and the autonomy of art. Yet, far from being mutually exclusive, the theses complement each other, theoretically and practically: the moral phenomenon, for all its concern with order, supports aesthetic freedom; and aesthetic activity, for all its freedom, favors moral order. The full integrity and depth of the ideal feeling of both factors come together. Even when the feeling of moral value is extra-aesthetic and merely associated with what is aesthetic, it participates so much in the phenomenon of the beautiful that, without it, beauty would lose objectivity, leaving only aesthetic representations that are very different from those expressed by conscious acts of will. All poetry, especially dramatic poetry, would become merely sculpturesque, picturesque, and musical if moral value were excluded from aesthetic content. Even outside of art, human action would be beautiful only because of its practical form. In the other arts, with the exception of architecture, the exclusion of moral value would alter the nature of that beautiful action as long as the feelings that arouse expressions of the human spirit do not always enter the domain of moral value. This explains why immoral symbolism hurts the efficacy of aesthetic emotion, working against it and weakening it, and why the opposite happens when the symbol is not contrary to the moral beliefs of the aesthetic spectator, but is changed into a symbol of those same beliefs. And yet that fusion does not prevent one from feeling the hegemony of beauty, even finding and feeling it in the symbol as it expresses a powerful freedom that resolutely opposes morality and perishes in the struggle or remains in opposition as the aesthetic principle of freedom.

Religious values are related to aesthetic values in providing content for the feeling produced by the work of art. The highest aesthetic forms of art have sought to express the principle of divinity. The temple, the statue of the god, the religious painting, the mystic depth of music and lyric poetry—all of these, revealing what is divine in the human soul, have more or less directly and intensely expressed a religious content. The feeling of emancipation, which characterizes both aesthetic and religious values, relates them in the artistic expansions of spirit. On the other hand, religious feeling could not emerge from human consciousness if it did not clothe itself in forms produced by the imagination, and it would not purify itself if those forms were not idealized by art. Pure thought could never have understood the divine principle. Logic could never be a substitute for inspiration in creating religious ideas and feelings. God becomes man is the most perfect aesthetic symbol of the religious idea.

But just as we can analytically distinguish aesthetic from moral value in experience, so can we also distinguish it from religious value. Symbols opposed to art have had and still have a great religious value for mystical contemplation, while art may express the divine principle in aesthetic forms that leave religious sentiment inactive. The only aesthetic forms that are generally influential amid the many types of worship are those that are in harmony with the beliefs that people actually hold. It is only aesthetically that they can be admired by those who hold different religious beliefs. On the contrary, among people of the same religion, the religious symbol, united to religious form, can be adored as a symbol of divinity, even though it is not understood, or even judged, as an expression of the beautiful. Aesthetic form can even be condemned if it is opposed to religious belief—and in this respect, too, the situation is comparable to that between aesthetic and moral value.

In reality, then, the aesthetic phenomenon is not isolated, but is combined with other phenomena that are derived from the same creative activity and concur in attaining the aesthetic ideal of freedom. It is the nature of spirit to act and to be limitlessly fertile. But if free activity is so conceived as, logically, to eliminate all resistance, we would find that we could not create, or even subsist, without that coercive reality that helps produce consciousness of the self in our psychological development. It has been said that birds would believe that they might fly more freely if there were no atmospheric resistance, because they do not know that they could not fly without that resistance. The same is true of the flight of spirit. If there were no external coercion to provide resistance that one must take account of and control for the sake of greater freedom, a wider and more effective creation, psychic potentiality would be exhausted in an instant; it would stop being activity and would become merely inertia; it would not be spirit but matter—as Bergson holds.

Free activity fights the obstacles set by its surroundings. It can conquer the opposition of external nature by using intelligence to obtain the material means necessary to its ideal. Thus is born the close partnership of logic and economics. This is also why science was born: to destroy our slavery to physical reality and to enhance the production of riches. But it is all too easy for this utilitarian ideal at last to absorb inner freedom, so as to make egoism the exclusive criterion of happiness.

Free activity has another battle: it triumphs over the social medium pervaded by egoism by means of the moral solidarity that abandons the biological process of conquest. In doing so, it finds in the free association of free beings a network of unlimited flexibility, which organizes the function of will, together with the pure expansiveness of freedom. The ideal of expansion without norm, which is the essence of the creative imagination, becomes the ideal of joint activity; it creates morality in human coexistence, in the service of interior freedom; and legal and political values, which are values of the same sort, grow out of morality.

Free activity finally makes the aesthetic ideal, which is beyond human morality, incarnate in a divine personality. It erases the limits of all human work and raises creation to an infinite and absolutely free power, located in the region of the mysterious and inexplicable, wherein it generates religion, which feeds on supernatural inspiration.

Notwithstanding these expressions, free activity never renounces its essential and supreme function, the creation of the ideal and its contemplation without practical purpose, its pure aesthetic function, the production of beautiful art, in which spirit aspires to attain that creative ambition capable of producing what cannot be done by coercing the medium. This function is the spring from which the other values drink their inspirations. There is therefore no exaggeration in calling this disinterested activity the "value of all values."

Carlos Vaz Ferreira
(1872–1958)

Vaz Ferreira is the teacher par excellence in twentieth-century Latin American philosophy. The biographical note that introduces the publication of his complete works reads, "The professor prevailed over all other forms of expression of his creative spirit," and we might add, even at the expense of the originality and philosophical depth of his thought. He possessed a spirit that was eminently antisystematic, preventing him from accepting any school of thought and leading him to fight against all philosophical dogmatism, beginning with the positivist perspective in which he was educated. As a result of this iconoclastic attitude and the germinal character of his thought, his views are best expressed in short essays and in aphoristic notes based on concrete experience. Theoretical analyses are not suitable to his approach.

Vaz Ferreira was born in Montevideo, Uruguay, in 1872. He enrolled at the School of Law in the University of the Republic and graduated as a lawyer in 1903. He began teaching in 1897 when he obtained a position teaching philosophy in the University of the Republic. Due to his success as a professor and to the unprecedented reputation he acquired, a special position was created for him, "Maestro de Conferencias," which permitted him to express his ideas with complete freedom (1913–57). From 1924 until 1929 he also assumed a professorship in the philosophy of law. In addition to his teaching responsibilities he held important positions as dean of preparatory schools (1904–1906), president of the university on three occasions (1929–30, 1925–38, 1938–43), director of the College of Humanities and Sciences (1946–49), and later (1952) dean of that college until his death. Shortly before his death on January 3, 1958, the House of Representatives of Uruguay authorized a complete edition of his works in special honor of his life's work.

193

Vaz Ferreira's extensive publications reflect ethical, social, and educational concerns grounded in a pervasive humanism. Beginning with his first works, *Conocimiento y acción* (1907) and *Lógica viva* (1910), and continuing through his more mature works, such as *La actual crisis del mundo desde el punto de vista racional* (1940) and *Racionalidad y genialidad* (1947), Vaz Ferreira consistently attacks the narrow, purely rational concept of knowledge that excludes the dynamic vitality of reality. This "philosophy of experience," as described by Ardao, is based on the analysis of the concrete human situation, and finds its most adequate expression in *Fermentario* (1938). This work is a collection of aphorisms and short philosophical essays touching on a variety of human themes that were of concern to Vaz Ferreira from his youth. One finds topics such as "Men of Thought and Men of Action," "Reason and Experience," "To Search for the Truth," "Concerning Systems," and many others. As might be expected, this is the final statement of his moral perspective that, according to him, stems from the conflict of ideals, an irreconcilable conflict that leads to an uneasiness in man but does not condemn him to philosophical pessimism. On the contrary, the awareness of this conflict opens the way to an axiological optimism.

Fermentary

WHAT IS THE MORAL SIGN OF HUMAN ANXIETY?

There are two meanings to "optimism" and "pessimism": optimism (or pessimism) of success, and optimism (or pessimism) of value.

The optimism or pessimism of success and the optimism or pessimism of value: better than a definition is an example. In evaluating an adventure of Don Quixote, we could be, and in many instances reasonably will be, pessimists of success, but optimists (in the other sense) with respect to moral value, with respect to the sign "good" or "bad." And we would declare that adventure generous or noble, we will judge that it is good. This optimism concerning the moral sign is the optimism of value.

The optimism or pessimism of value is intertwined with the moral sign: good or bad.

To continue: as to a certain great adventure, begun and carried on, with all its efforts and aspirations, by a certain species on a given planet, the optimism of success could be risky and one might even say illusory. (We shall see, in addition, that this is an unfortunate way of stating the problem, for insofar as partial success is concerned, optimism is adequate. And to be truthful, a reasonable discussion would focus on the particular cases and the degree.) However, the optimism that seems to me should be upheld against the superficiality of some of the theories and states of spirit predominant today is the optimism of value, even though these theories and states of spirit have held fast in times of pain and hopelessness. I say this because perhaps they have engendered and reinforced the pain and lack of hope.

From Carlos Vaz Ferreira, *Fermentario*, in OBRAS (Montevideo: Homenaje Cámara de Representantes, 1957), 10:196–207, 41–44.

By way of preparation I need to summarize something that I have attempted to demonstrate for many years and in a long series of lectures: Generally it is thought and said that intellectual progress has not accompanied or is not correlated with moral progress. The claim is even made that there is no such thing as moral progress and again, some say this is an age of decadence. I have tried to maintain that this is not the case.

Let us begin by setting aside the issue of whether progress is or is not necessary. In fact, with respect to progress, one can question whether intellectual progress occurs. Moral progress, however, cannot be questioned.

Intellectual progress can be debated. It has been said, and perhaps correctly, with respect to progress, that what differentiates man's present from his beginning is the mere accumulation of intellectual acquisitions, for it has not been established that the discoverer of the theory of gravity was more of a genius than the one who invented the wheel or fire . . . perhaps, but that other progress, moral progress, cannot be questioned. . . .

Now the primary question is why does the contrary seem to be the case? Why does it appear that there is moral degeneration in human history? For reasons that only go on to create more illusions.

Some of these illusions are historical. For example, history isolates events and schematizes them. I was going to say that it turns these events into heroic acts and makes men heroic, but that is not the truth either since real heroism is something more than this fictitious heroism. Real heroism, the valuable heroism always comes with pain, it conquers cowardliness, and is accompanied by hesitation and moral doubt. History makes these acts appear more sensational and it gives men this same appearance. Then on top of it comes the educational process that goes to work on all of this. . . . Hence the first illusion of ancient supermorality. The effect is such that even in the multiple cases in which History itself reveals the inferiority of men, the historico-pedagogical cliches continue to act. The typical case, for example, is that of Cato, whose name is cited in multiple examples, and in great numbers of speeches even when history teaches us that he was cruel and avaricious, that he mistreated his slaves, and that he changed wives in order to obtain the wealth of the dowries. . . .

Furthermore, the men who carried out these acts were specialists, if we may use the expression. For example, there were specialists in patriotism who were capable of nothing else and even the specialists in saintliness or love may have lacked the relevant feeling for their country, family, work. . . .

However, none of this is essential, because there is something much more important for which I ask special attention. This, indeed, is essential: *in the human adventure, ideals are continually added.*

You have heard speak of the problem of the three bodies. Celestial mechanics calculates with ease the reciprocal attraction of two bodies, but when a third is introduced, the problem becomes so complicated that it is very difficult to solve satisfactorily. Nevertheless what has been introduced is only one body. If many more others were added the solution to the problem could not even be attempted.

This, then, is what had to happen and what has happened in morals. It is difficult to recognize what the addition of a single ideal could have meant, of what it had to mean in human moral evolution. We speak of adding, not substituting.

Let us look at the societies of Greece and Rome that were based on slavery, an institution natural for them and to which, to tell the truth, all other institutions were bound. Now let us consider the effects of the suppression of this institution alone, namely, the addition of only one idea, that of freedom for all men.

However, in resolving this situation, humanity, as if it were one, was not satisfied. It wanted a hundred, a thousand, indeed everything. Not only was slavery suppressed but humanity was not even satisfied that there should be less fortunate classes. It wanted to equalize and lift up all men. . . .

Given this perspective two conclusions are to be drawn:

The first is *the conflict of ideals.* These ideals can be reconciled only in part, in part they conflict. As to affections and feelings, the ideals of personal life, of the family, and of humanity are in part harmonious but in part conflicting, in part they have to be sacrificed to one another. Scientific ideals and artistic ideals conflict in part with one another. The ideals of work and those of the benefits of work, the ideals of material well-being and the ideals of spiritual perfection conflict with each other in part and in part are reconcilable. The ideals of reason and those of feeling, the good of the majority as an ideal and the conservation and preservation of superior beings. . . . In part, these ideals struggle with one another and are not reconciled.

There are ideals of love, but also ideals of justice. We have ideals of a positive, earthly life, but also those of a transcendent afterlife.

Furthermore, correlative with those conflicts of ideals there is another fact upon which we do not insist sufficiently nor reflect adequately and which is not discussed in treatises and books on morals, namely, that humanity has thus been creating a type of *conflictual morality.* This is to say, that few moral problems can be resolved in a completely satisfactory manner and if one senses all the ideals, generally one will have to sacrifice some in part, or perhaps even all of them.

On this issue I have been accustomed to refer in a special sense to possible "obscure Christs." One could conceive of a man that had as much love as the saints of old, as much patriotism as ancient heroes, as much love for science as the martyrs had for truth, indeed, had all the feelings in their historic maximum and, in addition, the nonhistorical feelings in their maximum also, that is, the feelings for family, friendship, and all the rest. Only with great difficulty could such an attitude be of importance to history. After all, what goes into history is what certain great men did. It does not record what others, perhaps even greater, were inhibited from doing. And above all the conflicting dimensions do not go into history or, if they do, they go in as "contradictory" or as a "weakness." Humanity, however, will nevertheless receive the warmth of these obscure Christs. . . .

In fact, no one will be this perfect, but what is coming to be a specialty in modern life *is the increase in the number of men who, although they do not have every feeling to the highest degree, have them all.* This is not sensationalism, for there it is—if you please, in this *our mediocrity*—there is our moral superiority as well as the cause of the illusion of our inferiority. This is essential, my friends: *what was added was not evil, but the increasing resistance, although yet small and poor, still a growing resistance to evil. This is essential* with respect to moral progress. What has been added, for example, is not war but an increased suffering because there is war and because one has to make war, there is more psychological resistance to it. What has been added is not that the less-favored classes should suffer, but the increasing suffering of humanity because of their suffering with the consequent reforms at least partially effective, leading to their betterment or relief.

When one takes this point of view, and these are only two examples to which many others could be added, one perceives the moral betterment of mankind down through history.

This remembering of ideas that I have defended so stoutly suggests an attitude of spirit I have always wanted to suggest as the most truthful and the most just and, it is, indeed, an optimistic attitude. But let us take a look at its two meanings.

The optimism of success can only be relative. Human pretension taken as a whole exceeds by far what is possible, namely, to reconcile all ideals yet let each develop to its fullness. . . . Adding more and more ideals before satisfying those at hand cannot be resolved even in the imagination. . . . But there is always some optimism for obtaining something and then a bit more, in each case and in each of the different directions.

The above can be stated objectively. However, with respect to value, the moral sign of our human adventure, there is no need for restrictions.

Yet, to be fair in our discussion, there is one possible restriction. If there is a transcendent power that works in support of what is good, as is proposed by some religious and metaphysical hypotheses, then all evil is conquered. However, I set aside and in reasoning with me I ask that you also set aside these possibilities that are part of one's personal beliefs.

So, on such an adventure, the rash and absurd and touching human adventure that is all these adventures taken together though individually each is no longer possible. . . perhaps I might repeat and say, in this rash and absurd and touching human adventure which is all the adventures taken together though individually each is no longer possible, deflection would only be natural: it would be "human," if it were not precisely the human that is so heroic!

Here we need to point to a possible error. Someone may have in mind the horrors of today, the horror of war and the terrible character that war has taken on. However, that there has been a change for war is merely the means, the technique, but this change is not of a moral nature, for had the ancients had access to this technique they would have exterminated each other more ferociously than we, for they did it right well with the elemental "putting to the sword." . . . No, the technique is not *what is added, it is not the new. The added* is the increase of our horror of war; that there should be more moral resistance, more repugnance, so much feeling, so much effort. It may be little as yet, weak and overcome thus far, but it is growing and it is more intense and present in more people. The same thing happens in other orders of events: the technology of modern economy may have provoked new sufferings for the worker but what is *morally* added is the suffering, the sympathy, and the growing effort to alleviate or suppress these evils. And this is what determines the moral direction of progress. . . .

So let me repeat more clearly and simply, without any complicating hypothesis or interpretation. The direction of moral progress is seen in the course of human history.

What is surprising is that man's adventure becomes increasingly impossible, but to his own honor. Don Quixote had only one adventure at a time, but for us all occur at the same time and they are ever more far-reaching. With each new dimension new ideals are added and in every case we want to fulfill each ideal more completely.

We have referred to those ideals added as we left the ancient world, when slavery was suppressed. But humanity was not satisfied, since it wanted the well-being of all classes and of all men. This humanitarian tendency and the concern for poverty has become increasingly intensified.

In other ages patriotism was a narrow sentiment. Now humanity, its better part at least, increasingly wants to reconcile patriotism with humanitarianism.

Furthermore, one must incorporate happiness and progress into the ideal, although they are in part contradictory, since progress brings with it an element of suffering. One must also incorporate happiness and culture that are also in part contradictory. One must include religious feeling and practice, consolation and hope, but reason as well. The afterlife with all its possibilities and its hopes along with life on this our earth must be woven in, along with feeling and logic, art and science. And one might say, in passing, that it is easy to rail against science and reason and logic, but even those who do, know that science, reason, and logic continue to work through them and for them.

Another enormous conflict and one of the most tragic is the ideal of goodness, yet one must struggle against evil.

"Reconciliation" in the common sense, "reconciliation" in the sense of satisfying all ideals is impossible. These ideals struggle against each other in part but we want to satisfy them all.

Another conflict: the health of the human race and compassion for the sick person. They are in part contradictory.

And yet, another conflict: intellectual and moral perfection, along with preservation of those that are inferior. To develop the elite, even to the level of a "superman," but also to raise the general level.

And all this together! Each one of these ideals is impossible, but even more impossible when all are taken together and more yet because of their interference with each other since in part they are contradictory!

From this perspective then *comes the optimism of value.*

There are many sincere human beings, whether among them fanatics for an ideal such as nationalists or humanitarians, sages or saints, practical men or mystics, yet all of them are "specialists."

Above all, however, *what grandeur for him who feels all these ideals, which in part contradict each other, and gives himself to all, or to many, without being able to satisfy any one of them completely and even less his own conscience!*

To summarize then, there are two ways of approaching history and the human adventure:

One can emphasize the evil or sad aspect, the impossibility of realizing everything, the impotence, the proportion of evil, and those that fall by the wayside.

Or one can measure the grandeur of the adventure and of the effort precisely because of the inferiority of the point of departure and because of the noble exaggeration of the whole group of ideals that we pursue.

I am not going to add more examples. I do not even have time to develop those that I have chosen. This is no more than a direction of ideas and feelings that I commend to you in every case as a spiritual exercise.

And now do these ideas and feelings bring some consolation?

Perhaps none but perhaps it is not a good thing that humanity console itself. But even though they may bring none, they should teach us and in teaching us to interpret the true feeling of human anxiety, they should teach us not to add to the pain and the inevitable horrors, the pain and the supreme horror of moral pessimism.

ON MORAL CONSCIOUSNESS

It has been observed and written that remorse is not inseparable from immorality nor proportionate to the immorality of the person or his acts. However, there are other errors and even some mystification concerning moral consciousness; for example, to believe, to make another believe or make oneself believe that peace of mind is a natural possession of good people, that it is their normal state, and even that it is a criterion or measure of their moral superiority. Here is a mixture of error and mystification, that pedagogical mystification in which at times it is so difficult to distinguish the sincere from the hypocritical, although the latter is more or less unconscious.

To be able to live with an undisturbed conscience, far from being a criterion of moral superiority, normally reflects some inferiority, usually an insensitivity, except in some cases of mental simplicity, in which case the inferiority would be intellectual.

There is more than one reason for this.

In the first place, the option, as made available for our action by the real circumstances of life, is ordinarily between acts or rules of conduct, each of which contains some evil. Only in exceptional cases, exceptions from real life, does one have the choice between good acts and one or more evil acts. In any case it is quite frequent that the only option we have is among acts, all of which are in part evil and of which, if one can say that one is better than the others, it is only because one produces or contains less evil.

Thus, even in the life of the most refined and pure man, evil is achieved, damage is caused, and pain is produced. And although logically or intellectually this should not give rise to suffering and even less to remorse, as a matter of fact, in the sensitive man it does.

And further, there is moral doubt. Even supposing a man who had resolved all the moral difficulties of his life in what we might call an objectively good fashion, if his moral psychological perspective is refined, he will have doubts: moral doubts about the past, about the present, and concerning the future. Now moral doubt is suffering and it is also an unpeaceful mind. So the absence of moral doubt, except in the case of singular mental simplicity, is not a criterion of moral superiority but of inferiority.

The illusion of peace of mind can be produced from the outside also, as with some historical types in which, even though one supposes they had the peace of mind attributed to them in their biographies or that the historians have ascribed to them, we still find some insensitivity or deficiency even in the most noble characters. To take a prime example: if

Marcus Aurelius had the peace of mind described in his *Memoirs*, we still feel that there was in him a deficiency akin to insensitivity in the soul of a man responsible for the persecution and death of many Christians. The insensitivity to which I refer would be twofold: insensitivity to the evil actually done and insensitivity to scruples and moral doubt.

Another absurd state or attitude related to "moral consciousness" is the pretense to "console" through appeal to peace of mind, to console a man in some specific circumstance or to console the human soul in the midst of evil, injustice, or suffering. For example, some employee, a man of action who has completed a good project and then sees it destroyed, is a man who suffers. He feels and suffers because he loved the project not through vanity or not so much through vanity but because good was accomplished through the project. To pretend, then, to console him with peace of mind would be as absurd as pretending to console a father who had lost his son by reminding the father that he had done everything possible, such as calling the doctor in plenty of time and giving his son all required aid.

It is true that the father would suffer if he had not done what should have been done, but that is all that suffering has to do with "peace of mind."

However, on this foundation certain pedagogical mystifications, more or less well intentioned, are organized, but their effects in the end are counterproductive, even from a pragmatic point of view. For that mystification is precisely the unfortunate aspect of a certain kind of book that in preaching truth and justice promises happiness as an automatic reward. There is no need to name authors since any one of them can be substituted for another, for the tendency is the same in them all. Those who write this kind of book are either insensitive or pretenders or perhaps they do not feel the pain of inevitable evil and injustice, of inevitable moral doubt and remorse. Perhaps they are hypocrites or write with mere words.

Furthermore and even more important, these books show a lack of respect for suffering and for the victims of the injustices of nature and of men. For if it has been possible to write these books, books for which peace of mind always accompanies the good, so that good finds its prize and recompense, again, if it has been possible for these books to be written (in the sense intended here, but not on the much more profound level in which it is all true, but in another sense), it is because their authors do not have a proper fellow feeling or sufficient understanding of human suffering. Their mental state proves they have not adequately experienced the pain of those who suffer unjustly or the pain of evil and injustice itself. The true books on moral issues, the good books had to be written by those capable of feeling pain and injustice and of recognizing its partial inevitability.

As for those phrases such as "to have no guide or judge other than one's conscience," and with its approval to live satisfied and happy, let us not forget that the conscience adjusts to situations. If there is any kind of man to be feared in this life, it is that kind who has managed to train his conscience and at the same time has no judge other than his conscience.

Miguel Reale
(b. 1910)

The continuing labor as educator and as supporter of philosophical activity that Reale carried out in his country for many years, together with voluminous published works in philosophy, has gained for him an outstanding reputation among Brazilian thinkers in the second quarter of the twentieth century. His interests have been focused primarily on the philosophy of law. However, this did not prevent him from making important contributions to axiology and philosophical anthropology from the general historicist perspective that he calls "cultural realism."

Born in 1910 in São Bento do Sapucai, in the state of São Paulo, he concluded his secondary studies in the Dante Alighieri Institute in that city. He placed first in a class of over a thousand members with an essay entitled "O valor da previdência na formação do carater," in which he formulates themes that were basic to his later work. He entered the faculty of law the year after his graduation from high school and received his degree in 1934. In the same year he published his first book, *O estado moderno*. He decided to give teaching his major attention and taught Latin, Portuguese, law, and psychology. In 1940 he obtained the chair of philosophy of law in the University of São Paulo on the basis of *Fundamentos do direito*, his first important theoretical work, in which he laid the foundation for his well-known "tridimensional theory of law." From this moment on he began his tireless efforts to promote philosophical thought. With the assistance of a distinguished group of Brazilian philosophers, among whom were Ferreira da Silva, Washington Vita, Euríalo Canabrava, and others, he established the Instituto Brasileiro de Filosofia in 1949 and the following year the *Revista Brasileira de Filosofia*. As president of the institute he assisted in organizing several national and international congresses of philosophy (São Paulo, 1950–56, 1959, 1972; Fortaleza, 1962),

205

and in 1954 he assisted in founding the Inter-American Society of Philosophy, of which he was president. In addition, he had other important administrative positions in academic and political institutions, holding the position of president of the University of São Paulo in 1949 and on two occasions secretary of justice. In later years, concerned with the destiny of his country, he joined the opposition to the leftist government of President João Goulart, playing an important role in the revolution of March 1964. In 1969 he again assumed the presidency of the University of São Paulo.

Reale's work is extensive, including more than twenty books and numerous articles and essays. Among the books, the most outstanding are: *Horizontes do direito e da historia* (1966), *Teoria tridimensional do direito* (1968), and *O direito como experiência* (1968). However, it is in his *Filosofia do direito* (1953) and *Pluralismo y liberdade* (1963) that his thought acquires a greater maturity and strength and his conception of the person as "the value-source of all values" was formulated. He states,

> what is certain is that man . . . the more he sounds the depths of the mysteries of the cosmos, the more he feels the urgency to turn toward himself, toward the inwardness of his consciousness, in toward the *deep self*, whose *being* is its *ought to be*, where freedom and value, *being* and *ought to be*, individual and society, existence and transcendence are interwoven, only when this occurs does man experience plenitude of being as a person, as a value-source of all values, aside from which the most rigorous and verifiable conquests of the sciences would have no meaning.

Philosophy of Law

VALUES AND THE REALM OF OUGHT TO BE

Some authors acknowledge only the sphere of objects or determinations of reality seen thus far, namely, that of natural and ideal objects, because they include within the latter what seem to me ought to constitute a third fundamental category under the designation of values. They maintain that values also are ideal objects.

I disagree with that point of view, because, although there are elements of contact and similarity between values and ideal objects, there is no lack of other essential elements of difference. Values as such possess a reality that is also aspatial and atemporal—in other words, they display a mode of "being" that is not bound to space and time. But already here a great difference arises. Insofar as ideal objects have value independently of what happens in space or time, values can only be conceived in terms of something existing, that is, of valuable things. Furthermore, ideal objects are quantifiable; values allow no possibility of quantification whatsoever. We cannot say that Michelangelo's *David* is five or ten times more valuable than Bernini's *David*. The idea of numeration or quantification is completely alien to the valuative or axiological element. It is not a matter, then, of mere absence of temporality and spatiality, but rather of *absolute impossibility of measurement*. The valuable cannot be numbered or quantified. Sometimes we measure it by indirect, empirical, and pragmatic methods, as happens, for example, when we express the "utility" of economic goods in terms of price; but these are mere references for prac-

From Miguel Reale, *Filosofia do direito*, 4th ed. (São Paulo: Saraiva, 1965), pt. 1, chap. 12, pp. 167–72; pt. 1, chap. 16, pp. 213–15; pt. 2, chap. 27, pp. 332–34. Reprinted by permission of the author.

tical life. Values as such are immensurable and not subject to comparison in terms of a unit or common denominator.

At first sight, it seems that we have started out with a definition of value. In fact, however, it is impossible to define value according to the logico-formal requirements of proximate genus and specific difference. In this sense, however legitimate the purpose of a rigorous definition might be, we agree with Lotze that about value we can only say that it has value. Its "being" is its "having value." In the same way that we say that "being is what is," we must say that "value is what has value." Why so? Because *"being" and "having value"* are two fundamental categories, two primordial positions of spirit in the face of reality. Either we see things insofar as they *are* or we see them insofar as they have value; and because they have value, they *ought to be.* No eqiualent third alternative exists. All other possible alternatives are reducible to those two or are governed by them. When we say, for example, that things "evolve," the "evolving" is nothing more than an unfolding or modality of "being"—it is being unfolded in time. We often say, using a metaphor, that to be and *ought to be* are somewhat like the left and right eyes, which together allow us "to see" reality, discerning it in its regions and structures, which are explained in terms of two fundamental principles: *causality* and *purpose.*

The distinction between *to be* and *ought to be* is an old one in philosophy, but it begins to take on a more pronounced importance with Kant's *Critique of Pure Reason.* It is in this major work that the distinction between *to be* and *ought to be,* between *Sein* and *Sollen*, is established with clarity and with the full weight of its significance.

Reality—the consistency of which in itself constitutes a problem that transcends the particular area of ontognoseology to find its place in metaphysics—reality unfolds, thus, into a multiplicity of "objects," according to a double perspective corresponding to the distinction between *judgments of fact* and *judgments of value.*[1] If, as we have said, *an object is anything that can be the object of a judgment,* then we can distinguish two orders of objects according to the two prisms cited, as follows:

TO BE
{
  natural objects { physical
                psychic
  ideal objects
}

OUGHT TO BE—*values*

}
  cultural objects
  (they *are* insofar as
  they *ought to be*)

As we shall see in the following pages, values are not to be confused with *cultural objects.* The latter are derived and complex objects, representing a form of integration of *to be* and *ought to be,* which means that we do not conceive *culture* as "value" in the way that Windelband, Rickert, or Radbruch do. Rather, *culture* is first and foremost an integrating element, inconceivable without the *to be–ought to be* correlation; and if culture marks a perennial reference of what is natural to the world of values, it is no less true that without it nature would have no meaning and values would not even be possible. . . .

CHARACTERISTICS OF VALUE

Value is always bipolar. The *bipolarity* possible in the realm of ideal objects is only *essential* in values; this alone would be sufficient not to confuse the two. A triangle or a circumference *are*, and nothing is opposed to this manner of being. On the contrary, bipolarity is inseparable from the realm of values, because a negative value is opposed to each value: an evil to a good, the ugly to the beautiful, the vile to the noble; and the meaning of one demands that of the other. Positive and negative values contradict and imply each other in a single process.

The dynamics of right result, as a matter of fact, from estimative polarity, since right is the concretion of axiological elements: there is a "right" and a "wrong," a licit and an illicit. The contradictory force that characterizes juridical life in all its areas reflects the bipolarity of the values that shape it. It is not by mere coincidence that there always is a victim and a culprit, a contradiction in the revelation of right, since the juridical life develops in the tension between positive and negative values. Right promotes certain values that it regards as positive and suppresses certain acts that constitute negations of values. It could be said that to a certain extent right exists because there is the possibility that values regarded by society as essential to living together might be violated.

If values are bipolar, it must be added that they are also *reciprocally implied*, in the sense that they are not realized without influencing, directly or indirectly, the realization of the remaining values. Nicolai Hartmann makes very clear the expansive and exclusivist force of values, each one tending to subordinate the rest of its estimative schemes. The realm of culture is a realm of *solidarity*, in the sense of the necessary interdependence of its elements, but not in the sense of a pacific or harmonious coexistence of interest and values. In this light, the total ethical solidarity implied by objective justice is a living tension in the quadrants of history and, in that way, as we shall see, right represents the fundamental force of the ever-confined social composition of values. Although the characteristics of *polarity* and *implication* are observed in values considered in themselves, or in the relation of some to the rest, we must remember that they lend themselves to the same situation in reality. Every *value* is opposed to the *given*, that is, to that which is presented as a mere *fact* here and now, as pure phenomenal reality. Value, in short, is opposed to *fact*; it is never reduced to fact. At the same time, moreover, every value *implies* a fact as condition of its realization, although it always transcends it.

Bipolarity and *implication* are qualities of value that reflect or translate the very nature of human conditionality, of spirit that is only conscious of itself and realized insofar as it is inclined and objectifies itself "to be as it ought to be." This brings us to consider the third characteristic of value, namely, its *necessity of direction or reference*.

Besides bipolarity, value always implies a taking of position by man and, consequently, a direction, a reference in existence. All that has value, has value for something or in the *direction of something and for someone.* We usually say—and we find that expression also used by Wolfgang Köhler, although in a slightly different way[2]—that values are *vectorial entities*, because they always point toward a direction, they are directed toward a determinate, recognizable point as an end. It is precisely because values have a direction that they determine conduct. Our life is nothing spiritually but a perennial experience of values. To live is to take a position with respect to values and to integrate them in our "world," perfecting our personality in the measure that we give value to things, to other men, and to ourselves. Only man is capable of values, and only in virtue of man is axiological reality possible.[3]

Value involves, then, an orientation and, as such, presents a fourth characteristic, *preference*. It is for this reason that, for us, every theory of value has as a logical, not causal, consequence, a teleology or theory of ends. Thus we say that an *end is nothing but a value insofar as it is rationally recognized as a motive of conduct.*

Every society has a table of values, so that the physiognomy of an epoch depends on the way in which its values are distributed or ordered. It is there that we find another characteristic of value: *the possibility of its ordering or preferential* or hierarchical *gradation,* though such gradation is incommensurable, as we have already stated.

Bipolarity, implication, reference, preference, incommensurability, and *hierarchical gradation* are, clearly, characteristics that distinguish the realm of values.

There is a possible ordering of the valuable, not absolutely, but rather in the cultural cycles that represent human history, while it is also true that there is something *constant* in the realm of estimations, something that conditions the historical process as a fundamental axiological category. This is man himself seen as value or spiritual source of all axiological experience.

Values represent, consequently, *the realm of ought to be,* of ideal norms, according to which human existence is realized, reflecting itself in *acts* and *works*, in forms of behavior, and in the achievements of civilization and culture, that is, in *goods* that represent the object of cultural sciences.

We have already said that from *to be* one cannot pass to *ought to be*, but the reciprocal is not true; if values were never realized, at least relatively, they would mean nothing to man. There is a vast field of experience whose existence results from the historical objectification of values: it is the *historico-cultural realm*, or the realm of "cultural objects," which are distinguishable *"by being insofar as they ought to be."* This, then, is a distinct category of objects, whose special nature requires the solution of some problems raised above. . . .

Only then will it be possible to clarify other aspects of value, such as, for example, its *objectivity* and *absoluteness,* understanding it as a quality not susceptible of revealing itself without something on which to support itself and without one or more consciousnesses to which it may refer.

The characteristic of *objectivity* of value, by which is recognized the necessity of distinguishing between *value* and *valuation* or *value* and *interest,* that is, that values are objectively imposed upon our subjective experiences, requires that we make a reference, though short, to the principal doctrines on the origin and binding or normative force of values. Only then shall we be able to understand one of the fundamental characteristics of value, which consists in never coinciding entirely with the awareness that we may have of them, always superseding it in a dialectical process that involves the historical dimension of man. . . .

[CLASSIFICATION OF VALUES]

For our purposes, we shall prefer a simple distinction, from the point of view of content, generally accepted, with this or that variant, by writers on this subject matter:

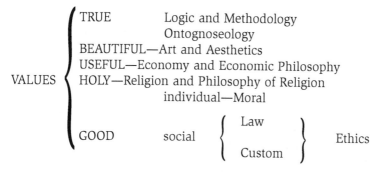

This is more an illustration of values than a classification pretending to satisfy all logical requirements. We could say that, within the fundamental values, we emphasize the above mentioned, because it is around these that subordinate values are gathered, constituting true "axiological constellations," which control, at times completely, collective and individual behavior. However, we must repeat, all of these gravitate around the fundamental value, which is that of man as *person*, in virtue of which and through which all values have value.

In the first place, we have the value of the *true*, to which some authors refer purely and simply by the word *truth*, giving to this term an axiological meaning.

The truth, as such, is not properly a value, but rather an objective relation. The true is the axiological expression of truth, that is, the attitude of spirit or spiritual dimension in the face of truth. The true only concerns knowledge, whether its *structure*—and thus we have logic—or its method—and thus we have gnoseology or, to use a more comprehensive term, ontognoseology. . . .

The second value is that of the *beautiful*, which is the basic value of the arts and gives origin to aesthetics.

Is the beautiful an autonomous value or is it reducible to some other value? The Socratico-Platonic definition of the beautiful as the splendor of the true is well known. There are some who deny full significance to the beautiful, conceiving beauty as an instrument for the realization of something true, the good, the useful, or the economic—taking the last adjective in its broadest sense.

Thus arises the problem of the autonomy of art, the problem of knowing whether there is a possible realization of the beautiful in itself, in its full significance, or whether the beautiful should be considered merely as an instrument at the service of an ideology, of any social or individual end. We believe the beautiful to be irreducible to other estimative foci, and although it shines more in conjunction or harmony with the remaining values, it does not lose its specific nature for this reason.

The third value, better known as a result of already available studies of political economy, is the value of the *useful*. Political economy, in its broadest sense, is the science of the useful, that is, of goods that can satisfy the desires and needs of man in society and that, as a consequence, are destined for exchange and consumption.

The *useful* is the founding value of economic, commercial, industrial, or agricultural activity. It poses at the same time a series of problems that economic science tries to solve, involving itself in investigations that constitute the object of economic philosophy.

As is well known, there are many who attempt to transform the value of the useful in value par excellence, the value characterizing the dominant line of the historical process, to such an extent that all other values, including the ethical and religious, would be simple consequences of technical processes of production, dictated by the increasing needs of social life.[4]

In the fourth place, we have as fundamental value the value of the *holy* or *religious*; the value of the transcendent, of the human destiny to what is beyond existential contingency. This is the basic value of religion as well as the cause of the philosophy of religion.

We would have, in the fifth place, according to some authors, the value of *life*, which is not to be understood in the biological sense of the term, but rather as indicating the full realization of individual or social existence.

Life is even presented as the fundamental value, considering as science par excellence that which is concerned with the life of man in the totality of its expressions, whether psychical or sociological, spiritual or material. Our times feel, in fact, a very strong attraction for the problem of life or existence. This should not cause surprise in a historical moment in which nothing seems so endangered as life itself or so precarious as existence.

The appearance of the philosophy of existence, of which existentialism is one expression, as well as the flowering of the philosophy of life, is understandable in the present historical coordinates and circumstances, because philosophy is never a series of conjectures formulated by some men eradicated and separated from the social and historical medium to which they belong. In those trends there is a correct insistence on the thesis that all philosophical systems or thinking is conditioned by historical experience, being impossible to conceive the attitude of a thinker without taking into consideration his existence, according to Ortega's formula: "I am myself and my circumstances."[5]

We think, however, that *life* as such is not a fundamental value, except in the sense that it contains or can contain the condition of the material realization of all values. All values, in a certain sense, refer to life, the vehicle of estimatives.

On the other hand, the life value can be considered as reducible to the *useful,* taking the latter term in a broad sense, since the useful is such only in the measure in which it enters in harmony with the fundamental needs of existence. Under this aspect, one can speak of the *useful-vital,* pointing to a unique axiological integration.

It is still left for us to deal with the value of the *good,* whose consideration, however, involves the whole problem of the philosophy of law. . . .

ACT AND VALUE

Only man educates because only man conducts himself. The problem of education is linked to the problem of self-determination. I educate because I conduct myself—"*educo, quia duco*": I educate because I am capable of conducting myself. If I were simply led, without awareness of the determinant motives of my acts, I would have no right to transfer or transmit values to others. Man, insofar as he is merely caused, is no different from other animals except for the awareness of his determination, due to which he carries out the same acts in which all other beings belonging to the same genus participate.

What is specific to man is to conduct himself, to choose ends and consequently means to ends. *End-directed action* (the *act* properly called or the *action* in its proper and specific sense) is something belonging only to man. One cannot speak, except metaphorically, of the action or the act of a dog or a horse. "Act" is something pertaining exclusively to the human being. Other animals move themselves; man alone acts. Action presupposes awareness of ends, possibility of option, singular projection in the seal of the species, excellence of attitudes, perfecting in the ways of being and acting. This problem is linked to that of culture, and, as the latter has its roots in freedom, in the *power of synthesis* that allows man to establish new processes while conscious of being integrated in nature and the vital complex conditioned by culture.

Let us emphasize now the problem of action in order to examine its constitutive elements.

Action in its strict sense, or *act,* is energy directed toward something that is always a *value.* Value, therefore, is that toward which human action tends, because it recognizes itself in a determined moment, to be motive, positive or negative, of action itself. We do not investigate here the nature or species of values, but only confirm that every time man acts he *objectifies or opposes something valuable.* To act without motive is proper to the alienated. The alienated is one who is alien to his conduct. It is one who loses the sense of his direction and dignity.

We posit here the problem of *alienation,* of the state of the man who finds himself divorced from his essence, an alien or stranger to himself, with all the consequences that are being pointed out from Hegel and Marx to Gabriel Marcel. These consequences should always be present to the spirit of the jurist or politician, whose main difficulty consists in conceiving and realizing a social order *in which men, groups, and classes do not become alienated.*

To say that man is a rational being is the same as saying that he is a being who directs himself. Action, therefore, always implies a valuation.

Every value, consequently, is an opening to ought to be. When one speaks of value, one speaks always of a solicitation of behavior or of a direction for action.

Value and ought imply and need each other reciprocally. Without the idea of value, we have no understanding of ought. When ought originates in value and is rationally received and recognized as the motive of action or act, we have what is called an *end*.

End is the ought to be of value, rationally recognized as the motive of action.

This distinction between *value* and *end* is not made with precision in classical thought. Many times it is spoken merely of ends, but every doctrine of ends hides an axiological theory in its bosom.

Here is a very delicate problem: the relation between axiology and teleology. For us, every teleology presupposes a theory of values. It is possible to speak of ends because the problem of the valuable has been posed before. . . .

In our view, the notion of end is derived from the notion of value. End is value insofar as it can be rationally grasped and recognized as motive of action. We have already seen that we climb to the world of values through emotional roads, and that value always transcends our rational ways of understanding. Beauty, justice, and all other values are not exhausted in rational formulas or schemes. What we declare as *end* is but a moment of value comprehended by our limited rationality, while its realization involves a problem of adequate *means*.

The nexus or relation of *means* to *end* is, and cannot stop being, of a rational nature; but the reference or adherence to a value can be dictated by motives that reason does not explain. Human history is a dramatic process of conversion of values into ends, and of cultural crises resulting from the loss of axiological force verified in ends that new generations refuse "to recognize."

NOTES

1. A literal translation would be "judgments of reality" and "judgments of value."—TRANS.

2. See Wolfgang Köhler, *The Place of Value in a World of Fact* (New York: n.p., 1938).—TRANS.

3. Ibid., p. 104.—TRANS.

4. The reference is to Marxism, a strong movement at the time Reale's book was published.—TRANS.

5. Ortega y Gasset, *Obras completas* (Madrid: n.p., 1947), 2:19.—TRANS.

PART IV
The Search
for Identity

Introduction

DEFINING LATIN AMERICA:
NATIONAL VERSUS CONTINENTAL APPROACHES

The selections included in Section A of Part IV deal with the problem of determining what it means to speak of "Latin America" and "Latin Americans" and the peculiar problems facing thinkers who analyze Latin American social reality, both within the countries of Latin America and in the United States. The nations and the people of the region that has become known as Latin America are not homogenous, as the umbrella term might lead some to think. The countries that constitute Latin America have different political systems, different currencies, different languages, and significantly different histories. Simón Bolívar was "the Liberator" of most of the countries of South America, including Venezuela, Colombia, Panama, Bolivia, Ecuador, and Peru (and British Guiana), but he did not liberate Mexico or Argentina from the clutches of Spain, for example. Obviously, each of the nations of Latin America shares a common past of colonization and an ensuing struggle for independence, but Brazil's relation to Portugal was quite unlike the relation that the Spanish colonies had to Spain. The nations of Latin America did not deal with the condition of colonization in identical ways, nor were they colonized in the same way.

Nevertheless, there are common themes that tie the philosophers of the region together at particular times. In dealing with the problem of defining the identity of Latin American philosophy, some philosophers favor what can be called a national approach whereas others favor a continental approach. For example, Sarmiento deals in particular with Argentina and the special problems besetting that nation. Likewise, Mariátegui addresses Peruvian reality, not Latin American reality, and Ramos turns his attention to the problem facing Mexicans. In contrast, Martí addresses issues of *nuestra America* (our America), emphasizing what is common to all the nations that compose Latin America, and Vasconcelos speaks of a *raza cósmica* (a cosmic race), not of a Mexican race.

Which approach makes more sense? Certainly, if the main question facing Latin American philosophers is that of cultural identity, given the fact that there is great variety among the populations of different countries within Latin America, answers to the question might be substantially different from country to country or even within the same country, and so national or regional approaches might be more appropriate to capture the identity of these peoples. Consider, for example, the Mayan population of Chiapas, Mexico, and the Náhuatl-speaking weavers of Guerrero, as compared to the cosmopolitan population of Mexico City. (The radical differences between the lifestyles of the *criollos* or American-born Spaniards, the *mestizos*, or peoples of mixed indigenous and Spanish heritage, and the *indios* are still evident today.) Mexico, Guatemala, Peru, Bolivia, and Paraguay have large indigenous populations, whereas countries such as Argentina, Chile, and Venezuela, for example, do not.

So, one may ask whether this difference might not give rise to a substantially different response to the question: Who are we? Is it not the case that a Peruvian philosopher concerned with capturing or attempting to provide an analysis of Peruvian social reality has to take the Amerindian culture into consideration, whereas a philosopher in Argentina with the same philosophical task might legitimately be more concerned with the ways in which various waves of European immigration have influenced the social reality of Argentina? The popular and rather humorous saying that "The Mexicans descend from the Aztecs, the Peruvians from the Incas, the Argentinens from the ships, and the Venezuelans from the oil" has some truth in it insofar as it points to the unique historical circumstances of each of these nations. And this truth might be overlooked when we approach the issue of cultural identity by attending merely to Latin America.

The issue of identity has also a political dimension, for it is clear that the nations of Latin America have varied political pasts. Therefore, something important is lost when we generalize in our philosophical investigation of identity and speak of the identity of all Latin Americans as if it were the same, whether one is concerned with a Náhuatl-speaking weaver in Mexico or a cattle rancher in Argentina.

In order to arrive at a definition of Latin American identity, we would do well to pay close attention to both the national and the continental approaches to this problem. There is something like *nuestra América* that is worthy of philosophical attention and, therefore, it behooves philosophers to go beyond national boundaries and to take something like a *raza cósmica* seriously. It does indeed make sense to speak of a Hispanic/Latino identity, yet this must be done with the awareness that the *gauchos* are particularly Argentine and an important element in understanding the particular breed of Latin American reality that is not only Latin American but also Argentine. Likewise, the problems of the indigenous populations in Peru and in Mexico are particular to those nations and are not representative of any continental problems besetting the entire region. In short, to capture accurately the social reality of Latin America, we must adopt *both* a continental and a national approach, for when we deal with the problem of the nations and the peoples of Latin America, certain aspects of social reality can best be addressed continentally and others are best dealt with via a national or regional approach. We uncover certain aspects of the social reality of the nations of Latin America if we approach the reality of postcolonial Latin American countries one by one, giving each their proper place of cultural, historical, and political significance, which otherwise would be missed.

A NEW DIMENSION OF THE PROBLEM OF IDENTITY: HISPANICS/LATINOS IN THE UNITED STATES

The problems facing philosophers as they grapple with the issue of the identity of Latin American nations and peoples become even more complicated for philosophers who deal with these issues in the context of the United States. What happens to the identity of Mexicans (whether of European, indigenous, or *mestizo* descent), Cubans (of Spanish, African, or mixed race descent), Colombians, Dominicans, etc., who immigrate to the United States? Can we speak meaningfully of these groups with one single term? If so, what term would capture the identity of this group? Or is the group so diverse that no single term can adequately capture its identity?

These issues become particularly relevant when the question of rights is raised. In particular, do groups of immigrants from Latin America have special rights and should they receive special benefits because they belong to those groups? To shed light on this problem, we have included three selections from contemporary philosophers who have dealt with these issues. Selections from the work of Jorge Gracia, Linda Martín Alcoff, and Ofelia Schutte show that the discussion of the identity of Hispanics/Latinos in the United States is complicated precisely because the group comprises a variety of ethnic, religious, and racial strains. And it is no easy task to find a term that will do justice to this diversity, while capturing the underlying unity of the group.

Latin American philosophers have discussed and developed views of the identity of the nations and peoples of Latin America, but their discussion of identity does not end there. They have also posed questions concerning the identity of Latin American thought and philosophy itself. There are many different approaches to this problem. Let us begin by considering the traditional ways in which this problem has been addressed by Latin American philosophers.

THE SEARCH FOR IDENTITY IN LATIN AMERICAN THOUGHT AND PHILOSOPHY: UNIVERSALISM, CULTURALISM, AND THE CRITICAL VIEW

In spite of the fact that Latin American philosophers have expressed many positions on the subject of what constitutes Latin American thought and philosophy, their opinions can be classified under three basic headings: universalist, culturalist, and critical. The first refers to a view inspired by a long tradition that goes back to the Greeks. According to this view, philosophy is a science (be it of concepts or of reality); as such, the principles it adopts and inferences it draws are meant to be universally valid and, consequently, it makes no sense to talk about a Latin American philosophy, just as it does not make any sense to talk about Latin American chemistry or physics. Philosophy, as a discipline of learning, cannot acquire idiosyncratic characteristics that may, in turn, make it Latin American, French, or Italian. Philosophy, strictly speaking, is simply philosophy, or philosophy "as such."[1] In spite of the fact that normally one may speak of "French" and "German" philosophy, this does not mean that philosophy as such is any different in the two cases. Categories like "French" and "German" are used as *historical* designations to refer to historical periods that include the thinking of the time or place one wishes to discuss. This does not mean that philosophy in a particular period is in itself any different from philosophy in another period. What may be considered idiosyncratic to the philosophy of a given period is not an essential part of philosophy, but simply the product of circumstances surrounding the development of the discipline at the time. As a result, then, such idiosyncrasies, which could also be called accidents, are not part of the discipline and are not included in its study; they are only part of historical studies concerning the period in question, just as a mathematical error is not part of mathematics, and just as the study of Egyptian physical theories is not part of physics. Philosophy, like mathematics and other disciplines of human learning, consists of a series of truths and methods of inquiry that have no spatiotemporal characteristics. Its application and validity are universal and therefore independent of the historical conditions in which they are discovered. The conclusion, for instance, that rationality is part of human nature is intended as a claim that is true or false anywhere and at any time.

Consequently, the answer to the question of whether there is a Latin American philosophy is, from this perspective, negative. Furthermore, this view not only denies that there is a Latin American philosophy, but it also rejects that there could be one, for it sees an intrinsic incompatibility between the nature of philosophy as a universal discipline of learning and such particular products as culture.

To this, the culturalist responds by contending that the universalist makes a serious mistake. Philosophy, as everything based on human experience, depends on specific spatiotemporal coordinates for its validity. There are no universal and absolute truths. Truth is always concrete and the product of a viewpoint, an individual perspective. This can be applied even to mathematical truths, as Ortega, a philosopher followed by many culturalists, suggests.[2]

Orteguian perspectivism, introduced in Latin America by many of Ortega's disciples, particularly José Gaos, is to a great extent responsible for the popularity of the culturalist view in Latin America. A philosophy that emphasizes the value of the particular and idiosyncratic lends itself quite easily to support the views of culturalist thinkers.[3] Consequently, many of them adopted this view without hesitation, adapting it to their conceptual needs. This is how the idea of a Latin American philosophy as a philosophy peculiar to the continent came about, a philosophy different from that of other cultures and particularly opposed to Anglo-Saxon culture and philosophy. This philosophy is supposedly the product of Latin American culture, which is in turn the product of the perspective from which Latin Americans think. This view has given way to the search for an autochthonous philosophy that can unambiguously reflect the characteristics of Latin American culture.

From this perspective, it is not only possible to find a Latin American philosophy, it is actually the case that any genuine philosophy produced in Latin America *must* be Latin American. If it is not, then it is simply a copy of philosophies produced elsewhere, imported and imposed on the continent. As such, these alien ways of thinking do not constitute a genuine or authentic philosophy when they are adopted in Latin America, since they do not have any relation to Latin American culture, being as they are the product of perspectives and conditions completely foreign to those of the continent.

Many of the thinkers who adopt this view conclude that, at present, there is no Latin American philosophy because the only philosophy that has been practiced in the region is imported. But at the same time, while accepting this, they trust in a different future. Others, on the contrary, point out that there are some Latin American philosophical perspectives that can be classified as Latin American, and although they may be few, they are sufficient to justify the use of the term "Latin American philosophy" with a culturalist connotation.

A third view adopted by Latin American philosophers in relation to this problem may be described as critical; it has been put forward as a reaction against both universalism and culturalism, although it takes some elements from both. This view, like universalism, rejects the existence of a Latin American philosophy not because the term "Latin American" is incompatible with the term "philosophy," but rather because until now philosophy in Latin America has had an ideological character, that is, it has not been a free pursuit. Philosophy has been used and continues to be used, *pace* the adherents of the critical view, to support ideas conducive to both the continuation of a status quo and the benefit of certain groups. To support this charge, those who adhere to the critical view point to scholasticism and positivism as philosophical developments that thwarted the development and progress of Latin American philosophy.

With regard to scholasticism, these critics point out that the Spanish Crown made use of scholastic philosophy to maintain its political and economic control over the New World. Scholastic philosophy, they suggest, became an instrument to sustain an otherwise ideologically untenable position.

In the case of positivism, they emphasize how certain Latin American governments used this philosophical school to justify both their notion of social order and supremacy of a ruling elite. The most frequently cited case is that of Porfirio Díaz's government in Mexico, which adopted positivism as the official doctrine of his dictatorship. The inference drawn, on the basis of this and other examples, is that until now there has not been, and in the future there cannot be, a genuine and authentic Latin American philosophy so long as present social and economic conditions prevail. Only when this situation changes and philosophy is no longer used ideologically to justify the modus vivendi can there be an opportunity for a genuine and authentic Latin American philosophy to develop. Some of those who defend this view think that this Latin American philosophy will be the product of a particular Latin American perspective, adopting therefore a culturalist view with respect to the future. Others, on the contrary, take a universalist position and suggest that this nonideological philosophy will be universally valid and not relative to the particular circumstances of Latin America. They all coincide, however, in viewing the role of philosophy in Latin America in a critical light.

HISTORICAL DEVELOPMENT OF THE PROBLEM

Explicit questions about the existence of a Latin American philosophy were first explored in the writings of Leopoldo Zea and Risieri Frondizi in the 1940s. The growth of philosophical literature until then seemed to justify and perhaps even require an investigation into the nature, themes, and limits of the philosophical activity. The proliferation of specialized journals, the creation of philosophy departments in various universities, and the foundation of international associations that had started to coordinate philosophical activity in the continent made possible the raising of an issue that continues to concern Latin American philosophers until today.[4]

Even before Zea and Frondizi, however, the Argentine Juan Bautista Alberdi (1810–1884) had raised the problem of the character and future of Latin American philosophy.[5] An outstanding member of the thriving liberal movement of his time, Alberdi put forth his ideas under the influence of a liberalism very closely related to the philosophical rationalism, the anticlericalism, and the optimism about industrialization that were so characteristic of nineteenth-century Latin America. His view of philosophy, consequently, is not alien to the basic tenets of this movement. Alberdi, however, had a high degree of awareness with respect to the connection between philosophy and cultural identity that, for good reasons, has drawn the attention of many philosophers who have subsequently focused on the theme of Latin American philosophy.

According to Alberdi, a Latin American philosophy must have a social and political character intimately related to the most vital needs of the continent. Philosophy is an instrument that can help to introduce an awareness of the social, political, and economic needs of Latin American nations. This is why Alberdi categorically rejected metaphysics and other "pure and abstract" philosophical fields, for he viewed them as alien to urgent national needs.[6]

As the selections from Part A indicate, since the independence of the Latin American territories from the Spanish and Portuguese colonial yoke in the nineteenth century, the issue of the identity of the nations and peoples of Latin America has been explored in great depth by a wide variety of philosophers. This search to define the nations and the peoples of this vast and variegated region continued to shape the history of ideas in the twentieth century. The more rigorous philosophical discussion of identity took longer to be developed and sustained.

Our discussion of Alberdi's early comments attests to one of the intellectually rich ways in which this search for Latin American identity was carried out. Yet, in spite of Alberdi's reflections on the character of Latin American philosophy, it was not until the fifth decade of the twentieth century that the problem of the philosophical identity of Latin America was explicitly formulated and fully explored. The decade of the 1940s was a period in which intellectuals looked back on Latin American culture and attempted to use it as the basis for philosophical thinking. A generation of Mexican authors inspired in Orteguian perspectivism, introduced in Latin America by the *transterrados*, or Spanish exiles, and particularly by José Gaos, suggested that the cultural "circumstances" of the continent provided the basis for the development of an original Latin American philosophy.[7] Leopoldo Zea, the leader of these intellectuals, asserted that any type of philosophical reflection emerging on the continent could be classified as "Latin American philosophy" by virtue of the intimate relationship between philosophy and culture.[8] He also suggested that this philosophy had a historical foundation, owing to the fact that Latin Americans had always, in Zea's judgment, thought of their situation from a vitally Latin American perspective.[9] Zea categorically affirms the existence of a Latin American philosophy which springs from the unique historical circumstances of Latin American social reality. Following Ortega, Zea has a conception of philosophy as a historical product, emerging from particular perspectives, but not ending there. As he claims in the selection included below, "The Actual Function of Philosophy in Latin America": "When we attempt to resolve the problems of man in any spatiotemporal situation whatever, we will necessarily have to start with ourselves because we are men; we will have to start with our own circumstances, our limitations, and our being Latin Americans, just as the Greeks started with their own circumstance called Greece. But, just like them, we cannot limit ourselves to our own circumstances. . . . [We] must also be aware of our capacities as members of the cultural community called humanity." The problem that remains is how to bridge the gap between the particular cultural circumstances from which we begin and the universal circumstance of humanity toward which we strive.

Zea's culturalist perspective has won many adherents. His supporters find in his approach to defining philosophy a way of opening space for contributions that do not fall under the umbrella of the European and Anglo-American philosophical traditions and hence tend to remain marginalized. Abelardo Villegas, Diego Domínguez Caballero, and Guillermo Francovich are just a few of the philosophers who support Zea's view.[10]

A common criticism of this way of defining philosophy is that it amounts to a kind of philosophical nationalism, and that moreover, it leaves out of the group of Latin American philosophers those who work in logic, theory of action, ethics, and similar traditional, philosophical fields. A philosopher who does not specifically address the Latin American circumstance is not a *true* Latin American philosopher. Risieri Frondizi was a leading critic of Zea's way of conceiving Latin American philosophy. According to Frondizi, philosophy must be distinguished from cultural nationalism and should be considered independently of geographical boundaries. One should speak of philosophy *in* Latin America rather than of a philosophy *of* Latin America.[11] Philosophy, as Francisco Romero pointed out, has no last names, that is, it must be understood as a discipline with universal characteristics.[12]

Even Vasconcelos, whose work exerted a strong influence on Zea, while sympathetic to a culturalist perspective, adopted a universalist position when discussing the nature of philosophical activity. Vasconcelos went so far as to deny explicitly the existence of a peculiarly Latin American philosophy on the grounds that the discipline was universal in character, although he conceded that it was the prerogative of each culture to reconsider the great themes of universal philosophy. Philosophical nationalism had no place in his thought.[13]

The polemic that suddenly surrounded the question of the existence of a Latin American philosophy in the 1940s had the effect, in many cases, of undermining the focus on identity in general that had characterized Latin American philosophical thought prior to the dispute, and which in many respects had prompted it. The controversy set a precedent for discussions of culture that became increasingly separated from the actual analysis of cultural phenomena. The culturalists themselves, who based their conception of a Latin American philosophy on a cultural perspective, have left few detailed accounts of the continent's cultural *ethos*, and frequently refer to culture in very general terms.

The controversy continued to grow and attracted much attention among members of practically every philosophical tradition, with the exception of philosophical analysis. Existentialists, phenomenologists, Thomists, Kantians, Orteguians, etc., all felt compelled to explore this issue. But since none of the different interpretations of the cultural identity of the continent has become widely accepted, it became impossible in turn to establish a consensus on the notion of Latin American philosophy. This is the reason why during the 1960s a number of authors re-addressed this problem, although this time not in terms of universalism and culturalism. It was at this time that the critical position took shape. Augusto Salazar Bondy, for example, argued for the view that philosophy in Latin America is the province of intellectual elites. These elites borrowed European cultural forms uncritically, and they lacked an identifiable and rigorous method and awareness of other social groups. Viewed in this light, the problems of culture and philosophy have been the problems of only a small minority of intellectuals alienated from the rest of society, and from the economic, social, and political problems of the continent.[14] This position, which has also been shared by Juan Rivano and others, suggests that the history of the controversy concerning the existence and nature of Latin American philosophy epitomizes the lack of concern with the most urgent problems of their respective communities on the part of the region's intellectuals.[15]

It is in this context that the (so-called) philosophy of liberation appears. For philosophers like Enrique Dussel, Horacio Cerutti Guldbeg, and Arturo Andrés Roig, the fundamental task of philosophy in Latin America consists in the social and national liberation from the unjust relations such as that of dominater-dominated which have traditionally characterized it. For Roig in particular, this implies the integration of the Latin American peoples based on the consciousness of the historicity of the American "man" and of the history of philosophy in Latin America. He rejects the formalism and ontologism characteristic of traditional academic philosophy, favoring instead a philosophy of commitment that seeks integrating concepts in Latin America. This area of philosophy is rooted in the political discourse of the marginal and exploited segments of society, and given the enduring political and economic instability that plagues the countries of Latin America, liberation philosophy continues to be of great social relevance.

In spite of the strong disagreement voiced by the various authors discussed and in the works included below, most of them would agree that philosophy has historically provided one of the most important vehicles for the expression of cultural concerns in Latin American society. Not always listened to, and at times suppressed by regimes of the Right or the Left, philosophy in many ways reflects the very situation of Latin American society today. And given that the region does not enjoy the stability of its Northern neighbor, its philosophy will continue to reflect the general turmoil of the region, a place where the *caudillo* is not a ghost of the past, where tanks still roll onto the streets when problems become too threatening, and, in short, a place where the philosophers have no ivory tower in which they can hide from the distractions of the world.

NOTES

1. Risieri Frondizi, "Is There an Ibero-American Philosophy?" *Philosophy and Phenomenlogical Research* 9 (March 1949): 355. See also a slightly different use of the expression in Fernando Salmerón, "Los problemas de la cultura mexicana desde el punto de vista de la filosofía," in *Cuestiones educativas y páginas sobre México*, p. 137; originally published in *La palabra y el hombre* 6 (1958).

2. José Ortega y Gasset, *El hombre y la gente*, chap. 13, in *Obras completas*, 3:115.

3. See Samuel Ramos, *Historia de la filosofía mexicana* (Mexico City: Imprenta Universitaria, 1943), p. 149.

4. One of the most useful bibliographical tools for the study of Latin American philosophy is the *Handbook of Latin American Studies*, which has been publishing a section on philosophy since 1939. The Web site maintained by José Luis Gómez-Martínez, *Repertorio Americano*, is also an excellent resource, with contributions from leading scholars on major Latin American philosophers. Gómez-Martínez's *Anuario Bibliográfico de Historia del Pensamiento Ibero e Iberoamericano* (published in five volumes, 1989–1993) is also a good resource.

5. A prolific writer and one of the outstanding members of the generation of Argentinean intellectuals who criticized the regime of Juan Manuel de Rosas,

Alberdi spent many years in exile in Uruguay, Chile, and Europe. The piece of writing that most specifically addresses our subject of concerns here is "Ideas para presidir la confección del curso de filosofía contemporánea," in *Escritos póstumos de Juan Bautista Alberdi*, vol. 15 (Buenos Aires: Imprenta Europea, Moreno y Defensa, 1895–1901). This essay was originally published in 1842.

6. Alberdi, "Ideas," p. 613.

7. José Gaos, *En torno a la filosofía mexicana* (Mexico City: Porrúa y Obregón, 1952), 53–54, 88. An excellent study of the impact and importance of the Spanish contributions to Latin American philosophy is provided by José Luis Abellán's *Filosofía española en América* (Madrid: Ediciones Guadarrama, 1967) and José Luis Abellán and Antonio Monclús, eds., *El pensamiento español contemporáneo y la idea de América*, especially vol. 2, *El pensamiento en el exilio* (Barcelona: Anthropos, 1983).

8. Zea, *Ensayos*, p. 166.

9. Ibid., p. 201.

10. Abelardo Villegas, *Panorama de la filosofía iberoamericana actual* (Buenos Aires: Editorial Universitaria de Buenos Aires, 1963); Diego Domínguez Caballero, "Motivo y sentido de una investigación de lo panameño," in Zea, *Antología*, 157–69; Guillermo Francovich, *El pensamiento boliviano en el siglo 20* (Mexico City: Fondo de Cultura Económica, 1956), and "Pachamama," in Zea, *Antología*, pp. 79–87.

11. Frondizi, "Hay una filosofía iberoamericana?" p. 166.

12. Ibid., p. 167.

13. Vasconcelos, *Indología: Una interpretación de la cultura iberoamericana* (Paris: Agencia Mundial de Librería, 1926), pp. 109–10.

14. Augusto Salazar Bondy, *Existe una filosofía de nuestra América?* (Mexico City: Siglo XXI, 1968), sec. 8, "Una interpretación."

15. Juan Rivano was born in Santiago, Chile, in 1926 and taught philosophy at the University of Chile until the Chilean military regime imprisoned him in 1975 and forced him into exile in 1976. Trained in logic, he has written mostly on the subjects of theory of knowledge and philosophy of science. Rivano addressed the problem of Latin American philosophy in his *El punto de vista de la miseria* (Santiago: Facultad de Filosofía y Educación, Universidad de Chile, 1965), pp. 145–72. Some of his publications include *Entre Hegel y Marx: Una meditación ante los nuevos horizontes del humanismo* (1962), *Lógica elemental* (1970), and *Introducción al pensamiento dialéctico* (1972).

A.
The Nation and the People

Domingo Faustino Sarmiento (1811–1888)

An outstanding public intellectual from Argentina, Domingo Faustino Sarmiento was born in 1811 in the western town of San Juan de la Frontera. Owing to the political upheavals that plagued his native country, Sarmiento spent much of his life in exile in Chile. He was a fierce critic of Manuel de Rosas, the military dictator who ruled Argentina from 1815 to 1852. Indeed, his resistance to this dictatorship and his dedication to improving education in Argentina shaped his intellectual project.

Sarmiento came of intellectual age during the period of positivism (1850–1910). This period immediately followed independence. Positivism was in part a response to the social, financial, and political needs of the newly liberated countries of Latin America. Other leading figures of the time included Juan Bautista Alberdi (Argentina, 1812–1884) and Andrés Bello (Venezuela, 1791–1865). These thinkers shared the belief that experience was more important than theoretical speculation and a primary interest in issues of social justice, educational reform, and progress.

Sarmiento's life was greatly disrupted by the military rule of Rosas, as he was forced into exile time and again for his opposition to this dictatorship. In 1839 he returned to Argentina and opened the College of Santa Rosa in San Juan. He also became the editor of El Zonda, and the political nature of an article he published there landed him in jail and eventually back in Chile for another period of exile. In 1941, while in Chile, he began writing for El Mercurio, thus maintaining ties with the literary and journalistic world of the period. During this period he developed a deep and lasting friendship with Manuel Montt who became president of Chile in 1852. In 1843 Sarmiento became a faculty member of the newly opened Universidad de Chile. He traveled to the United States and Europe during 1845–47 to undertake a comparative study of educational systems.

In 1852 Rosas was finally thrown out of office, and in 1855 Sarmiento returned to Argentina, serving as Minister to the United States in 1865. Sarmiento became president of Argentina in 1868.

The selections included here come from *Facundo, or Civilization and Barbarism* (1845), which was ostensibly a biography of Juan Facundo Quiroga, a provincial dictator, but in fact is a study of the destructive influence of dictatorship in civilized life in Argentina. Sarmiento is particularly interested in the role that *gauchos*, uneducated men of the pampas, play in the traditions of dictatorships in Argentina. He equates the *gauchos* and the entire interior of the country with the barbaric elements that are responsible for undermining the progressive, liberal, civilized plans of those from the cities. According to Sarmiento, the *gaucho* develops only his physical skills, while all intellectual powers are neglected, hence the horse and the knife become central to his life. Indeed Sarmiento believes that dictators like Rosas or Facundo brought the laws of the cattle ranch into the government of the republic and thus moved the country away from civilization.

Civilization and Barbarism

PHYSICAL ASPECT OF THE ARGENTINE REPUBLIC, AND THE FORMS OF CHARACTER, HABITS, AND IDEAS INDUCED BY IT

"The extent of the Pampas is so prodigious that they are bounded on the north by groves of palm-trees and on the south by eternal snows." —*Head.*

The continent of America ends at the south in a point, with the Strait of Magellan at its southern extremity. Upon the west, the Chilean Andes run parallel to the coast at a short distance from the Pacific. Between that range of mountains and the Atlantic is a country whose boundary follows the River Plata up the course of the Uruguay into the interior, which was formerly known as the United Provinces of the River Plata, but where blood is still shed to determine whether its name shall be the Argentine Republic or the Argentine Confederation. On the north lie Paraguay, the Gran Chaco, and Bolivia, its assumed boundaries.

The vast tract which occupies its extremities is altogether uninhabited, and possesses navigable rivers as yet unfurrowed even by a frail canoe. Its own extent is the evil from which the Argentine Republic suffers; the desert encompasses it on every side and penetrates its very heart; wastes containing no human dwelling are, generally speaking, the unmistakable boundaries between its several provinces. Immensity is the universal characteristic of the country: the plains, the woods, the rivers, are

---

From *Civilization and Barbarism*, chapter 1, "Physical Contents of the Argentine Republic, and the Forms of Character, Habits, and Ideas Induced by It," trans. Mary Mann (New York: Hafner Press, 1868), pp. 1–6, 9–10, 13, 20–23.

all immense; and the horizon is always undefined, always lost in haze and delicate vapors which forbid the eye to mark the point in the distant perspective, where the land ends and the sky begins. On the south and on the north are savages ever on the watch, who take advantage of the moonlight nights to fall like packs of hyenas upon the herds in their pastures, and upon the defenseless settlements When the solitary caravan of wagons, as it sluggishly traverses the pampas, halts for a short period of rest, the men in charge of it, grouped around their scanty fire, turn their eyes mechanically toward the south upon the faintest whisper of the wind among the dry grass, and gaze into the deep darkness of the night, in search of the sinister visages of the savage horde, which, at any moment, approaching unperceived, may surprise them. If no sound reaches their ears, if their sight fails to pierce the gloomy veil which covers the silent wilderness, they direct their eyes, before entirely dismissing their apprehensions, to the ears of any horse standing within the firelight, to see if they are pricked up or turned carelessly backward. Then they resume their interrupted conversation, or put into their mouths the half-scorched pieces of dried beef on which they subsist. When not fearful of the approach of the savage, the plainsman has equal cause to dread the keen eyes of the tiger, or the viper beneath his feet. This constant insecurity of life outside the towns, in my opinion, stamps upon the Argentine character a certain stoical resignation to death by violence, which is regarded as one of the inevitable probabilities of existence. Perhaps this is the reason why they inflict death or submit to it with so much indifference, and why such events make no deep or lasting impression upon the survivors.

The inhabited portion of this country—a country unusually favored by nature, and embracing all varieties of climates—may be divided into three sections possessing distinct characteristics, which cause differences of character among the inhabitants, growing out of the necessity of their adapting themselves to the physical conditions which surround them.

In the north, an extensive forest, reaching to the Chaco, covers with its impenetrable mass of boughs a space whose extent would seem incredible if there could be any marvel too great for the colossal types of Nature in America.

In the central zone, lying parallel to the former, the plain and the forest long contend with each other for the possession of the soil; the trees prevail for some distance, but gradually dwindle into stunted and thorny bushes, only reappearing in belts of forest along the banks of the streams, until finally in the south, the victory remains with the plain, which displays its smooth, velvet-like surface unbounded and unbroken. It is the image of the sea upon the land; the earth as it appears upon the map—the earth yet waiting for the command to bring forth every herb yielding seed after its kind. We may indicate, as a noteworthy feature in the configuration of this country, the aggregation of navigable rivers, which come together in the east, from all points of the horizon, to form the Plata by their union, and thus worthily to present their mighty tribute to the Ocean, which receives it, not without visible marks of disturbance and respect. But these immense canals, excavated by the careful hand of Nature, introduce no change into the national customs. The sons of the Spanish adventurers who colonized the country hate to travel by water, feeling themselves imprisoned when within the narrow limits of a boat or a pinnace. When their path is crossed by a great river, they strip themselves unconcernedly, prepare their horses for swimming, and plunging in, make for some island visible in the distance, where horse and horseman take breath, and by thus continuing their course from isle to isle, finally effect their crossing.

Thus is the greatest blessing which Providence bestows upon any people disdained by the Argentine gaucho, who regards it rather as an obstacle opposed to his movements, than as the most powerful means of facilitating them; thus the fountain of national growth, the origin of the early celebrity of Egypt, the cause of Holland's greatness, and of the rapid development of North America, the navigation of rivers, or the use of canals, remains a latent power, unappreciated by the inhabitants of the banks of the Bermejo, Pilcomayo, Parana, and Paraguay. A few small vessels, manned by Italians and adventurers, sail up stream from the Plata, but after ascending a few leagues, even this navigation entirely ceases. The instinct of the sailor, which the Saxon colonists of the north possess in so high a degree, was not bestowed upon the Spaniard. Another spirit is needed to stir these arteries in which a nation's life-blood now lies stagnant. Of all these rivers which should bear civilization, power, and wealth, to the most hidden recesses of the continent, and make of Santa Fé, Entre Rios, Corrientes, Cordova, Saltas, Tucuman, and Jujui, rich and populous states, the Plata alone, which at last unites them all, bestows its benefits upon the inhabitants of its banks. At its mouth stand two cities, Montevideo and Buenos Ayres, which at present reap alternately the advantages of their enviable position. Buenos Ayres is destined to be some day the most gigantic city of either America. Under a benignant climate, mistress of the navigation of a hundred rivers flowing past her feet, covering a vast area, and surrounded by inland provinces which know no other outlet for their products, she would ere now have become the Babylon of America, if the spirit of the Pampas had not breathed upon her, and left undeveloped the rich offerings which the rivers and provinces should unceasingly bring. She is the only city in the vast Argentine territory which is in communication with European nations; she alone can avail herself of the advantages of foreign commerce; she alone has power and revenue. Vainly have the provinces asked to receive through her, civilization, industry, and

European population; a senseless colonial policy made her deaf to these cries. But the provinces had their revenge when they sent to her in Rosas the climax of their own barbarism.

Heavily enough have those who uttered it, paid for the saying, "The Argentine Republic ends at the Arroyo del Medio." It now reaches from the Andes to the sea, while barbarism and violence have sunk Buenos Ayres below the level of the provinces. We ought not to complain of Buenos Ayres that she is great and will be greater, for this is her destiny. This would be to complain of Providence and call upon it to alter physical outlines. This being impossible, let us accept as well done what has been done by the Master's hand. Let us rather blame the ignorance of that brutal power which makes the gifts lavished by Nature upon an erring people of no avail for itself or for the provinces. Buenos Ayres, instead of sending to the interior, light, wealth, and prosperity, sends only chains, exterminating hordes, and petty subaltern tyrants. She, too, takes her revenge for the evil inflicted upon her by the provinces when they prepared for her a Rosas! . . .

From these characteristics arises in the life of the Argentine people the reign of brute force, the supremacy of the strongest, the absolute and irresponsible authority of rulers, the administration of justice without formalities or discussion. The caravan of wagons is provided, moreover, with one or two guns to each wagon, and sometimes the leading one has a small piece of artillery on a swivel. If the train is attacked by the savages, the wagons are tied together in a ring, and a successful resistance is almost always opposed to the blood-thirsty and rapacious plunder of the assailants. Defenseless droves of pack-mules often fall into the hands of these American Bedouins, and muleteers rarely escape with their lives. In these long journeys, the lower classes of the Argentine population acquire the habit of living far from society, of struggling single-handed with nature, of disregarding privation, and of depending for protection against the dangers ever imminent upon no other resources than personal strength and skill.

The people who inhabit these extensive districts belong to two different races, the Spanish and the native; the combinations of which form a series of imperceptible gradations. The pure Spanish race predominates in the rural districts of Cordova and San Luis, where it is common to meet young shepherdesses fair and rosy, and as beautiful as the belles of a capital could wish to be. In Santiago del Estero, the bulk of the rural population still speaks the Quichua dialect, which plainly shows its Indian origin. The country people of Corrientes use a very pretty Spanish dialect. "Dame, general, una chiripà," said his soldiers to Lavalle. The Andalusian soldier may still be recognized in the rural districts of Buenos Ayres; and in the city foreign surnames are the most numerous. The Negro race, by this time nearly extinct (except in Buenos Ayres), has left, in its zambos and mulattoes, a link which connects civilized man with the denizen of the woods. This race mostly inhabiting cities, has a tendency to become civilized, and possesses talent and the finest instincts of progress. . . .

The Argentine cities, like almost all the cities of South America, have an appearance of regularity. Their streets are laid out at right angles, and their population scattered over a wide surface, except in Cordova, which occupies a narrow and confined position, and presents all the appearance of a European city, the resemblance being increased by the multitude of towers and domes attached to its numerous and magnificent churches. All civilization, whether native, Spanish, or European, centers in the cities, where are to be found the manufactories, the shops, the schools and colleges, and other characteristics of civilized nations. Elegance of style, articles of luxury, dress-coats, and frock-coats, with other European garments, occupy their appropriate place in these towns. I mention these small matters designedly. It is sometimes the case that the only city of a pastoral province is its capital, and occasionally the land is uncultivated up to its very streets. The encircling desert besets such cities at a greater or less distance, and bears heavily upon them, and they are thus small oases of civilization surrounded by an untilled plain, hundreds of square miles in extent, the surface of which is but rarely interrupted by any settlement of consequence. . . .

In the absence of all the means of civilization and progress, which can only be developed among men collected into societies of many individuals, the educationof the country people is as follows: The women look after the house, get the meals ready, shear the sheep, milk the cows, make the cheese, and weave the coarse cloth used for garments. All domestic occupations are performed by women; on them rests the burden of all the labor, and it is an exceptional favor when some of the men undertake the cultivation of a little maize, bread not being in use as an ordinary article of diet. The boys exercise their strength and amuse themselves by gaining skill in the use of the lasso and the bolas, with which they constantly harass and pursue the calves and goats. When they can ride, which is as soon as they have learned to walk, they perform some small services on horseback. When they become stronger, they race over the country, falling off their horses and getting up again, tumbling on purpose into rabbit burrows, scrambling over precipices, and practicing feats of horsemanship. On reaching puberty, they take to breaking wild colts, and death is the least penalty that awaits them if their strength or courage fails them for a moment. With early manhood comes complete independence and idleness.

Now begins the public life of the gaucho, as I may say, since his education is by this time at an end. These men, Spaniards only in their language and in the confused religious notions preserved among them, must be seen, before a right estimate can be made of the indomitable and haughty character which grows out of this struggle of isolated man with untamed nature, of the rational being with the brute. It is necessary to see their visages bristling with beards, their countenances as grave and serious as those of the Arabs of Asia, to appreciate the pitying scorn with which they look upon the sedentary denizen of the city, who may have read many books, but who cannot overthrow and slay a fierce bull, who could not provide himself with a horse from the pampas, who has never met a tiger alone, and received him with a dagger in one hand and a poncho rolled up in the other, to be thrust into the animal's mouth, while he transfixes his heart with his dagger.

This habit of triumphing over resistance, of constantly showing a superiority to Nature, of defying and subduing her, prodigiously develops the consciousness of individual consequence and superior prowess. The Argentine people of every class, civilized and ignorant alike, have a high opinion of their national importance. All the other people of South America throw this vanity of theirs in their teeth, and take offense at their presumption and arrogance. I believe the charge not to be wholly unfounded, but I do not object to the trait. Alas, for the nation without faith in itself! Great things were not made for such a people. To what extent may not the independence of that part of America be due to the arrogance of these Argentine gauchos, who have never seen anything beneath the sun superior to themselves in wisdom or in power. The European is in their eyes the most contemptible of all men, for a horse gets the better of him in a couple of plunges.

If the origin of this national vanity among the lower classes is despicable, it has none the less on that account some noble results; as the water of a river is no less pure for the mire and pollution of its sources. Implacable is the hatred which these people feel for men of refinement, whose garments, manners, and customs they regard with invincible repugnance. Such is the material of the Argentine soldiery, and it may easily be imagined what valor and endurance in war are the consequences of the habits described above. We may add that these soldiers have been used to slaughtering cattle from their childhood, and that this act of necessary cruelty makes them familiar with bloodshed, and hardens their hearts against the groans of their victims.

Country life, then, has developed all the physical but none of the intellectual powers of the gaucho. His moral character is of the quality to be expected from his habit of triumphing over the obstacles and the forces of nature; it is strong, haughty, and energetic. Without instruction, and indeed without need of any, without means of support as without wants, he is happy in the midst of his poverty and privations, which are not such to one who never knew nor wished for greater pleasures than are his already. Thus if the disorganization of society among the gauchos deeply implants barbarism in their natures, through the impossibility and use-lessness of moral and intellectual education, it has, too, its attractive side to him. The gaucho does not labor; he finds his food and raiment ready to his hand. If he is a proprietor, his own flocks yield him both; if he possesses nothing himself, he finds them in the house of a patron or a relation. The necessary care of the herds is reduced to excursions and pleasure parties; the branding, which is like the harvesting of farmers, is a festival, the arrival of which is received with transports of joy, being the occasion of the assembling of all the men for twenty leagues around, and the opportunity for displaying incredible skill with the lasso. The gaucho arrives at the spot on his best steed, riding at a slow and measured pace; he halts at a little distance and puts his leg over his horse's neck to enjoy the sight leisurely. If enthusiasm seizes him, he slowly dismounts, uncoils his lasso, and flings it at some bull, passing like a flash of lightning forty paces from him; he catches him by one hoof, as he intended, and quietly coils his leather cord again.

José Martí
(1853–1895)

Born in Havana in 1853, José Martí's short life was devoted to ending Spanish colonial rule in Cuba. He was a great statesman, poet, and journalist, exerting great influence upon the intellectual landscape of Latin America.

In 1870, at the age of seventeen, he was jailed for his anticolonial political activity. His treatment in jail was brutal, leaving him in such a weak condition that he suffered health problems for the rest of his life. In 1871 he was deported to Spain, where he began to study law at the Universidad Central of Madrid. He finished his studies in law and philosophy at the University of Zaragoza in 1874. Martí then traveled throughout France and journeyed to Mexico in 1875, where he became active in the Worker's Movement. He spent some time in Guatemala from 1877 to 1878, where he was a professor of philosophy at the university. He returned to Cuba in 1878, yet after delivering a series of political speeches was promptly deported again to Spain.

His time in Mexico and Guatemala established his presence in those regions of Latin America. His long and significant stays in the United States began in 1880 when he arrived in New York City. He left just months later for Venezuela, where he founded the *Revista Venezolana*. In 1881 he returned to New York City, where he remained until 1895, writing and organizing independence efforts.

His first major publication came in 1882 with his *Ismaelillo*, a collection of poetry. In 1882 he also wrote *Versos libres*. During this time, he was actively involved with several newspapers, magazines, and journals in the United States and Latin America. Martí became known as a keen and informed observer of U.S. society—documenting both the strengths and weaknesses of the country and its culture. He was an important diplomat, the consul general in the United States representing Uruguay, Paraguay, and Argentina.

In 1891 Martí resigned from all of his diplomatic posts in order to devote himself full time to the cause of Cuban independence. In the same year, he published *Versos sencillos* and the essay *Nuestra América*. In 1892 Martí established the Cuban Revolutionary Party and the newspaper *Patria*, founded to further the cause of the revolution. In the next few years, Martí, who was not only a brilliant writer but also an engaging and passionate orator, traveled widely throughout the United States and the Caribbean speaking on behalf of the cause of Cuban independence. In 1895, after decades devoted to the organization that led to the Cuban war of independence, Martí returned to Cuba to join the fight, falling in one of the first battles of the war, the Battle of Dos Ríos, on May 19, 1895.

Nuestra América has been heralded by generations of Latin Americans as a mirror, both beautiful and accurate, of the Latin American circumstance. Given Martí's engaged struggle for independence, it should not come as a surprise that the great liberators of Latin America are chronicled in his work. A tribute to Simón Bolívar was delivered as an address to the Hispanic-American Literary Society in October 1893. Martí's concern for the freedom of Cuba came with a concern for freeing the island of any traces of racism as well—he insisted that a free Cuba be a just Cuba and that all races be treated equally. Indeed, Martí saw the struggle for independence as a necessary condition for the freedom of those groups traditionally oppressed under Spanish rule. He believed that the future must be free of racism, for "whoever foments and spreads antagonism and hate between the races, sins against humanity." For this reason, his short piece *My Race* (1893) is especially relevant for coming to an understanding of his social vision. Given recent interest in the problem of race and its philosophical significance, we are reminded that we still have much to learn from this great humanist.

Our America

The conceited villager believes the entire world to be his village. Provided that he can be mayor, or humiliate the rival who stole his sweetheart, or add to the savings in his strongbox, he considers the universal order good, unaware of those giants with seven-league boots who can crush him underfoot, or of the strife in the heavens between comets that streak through the drowsy air-devouring worlds. What remains of the village in America must rouse itself. These are not the times for sleeping in a nightcap, but with weapons for a pillow, like the warriors of Juan de Castellanos—weapons of the mind, which conquer all others. Barricades of ideas are worth more than barricades of stone.

There is no prow that can cut through a cloudbank of ideas. A powerful idea, waved before the world at the proper time, can stop a squadron of iron-clad ships, like the mystical flag of the Last Judgment. Nations that do not know one another should quickly become acquainted, as men who are to fight a common enemy. Those who shake their fists, like jealous brothers coveting the same tract of land, or like the modest cottager who envies the squire his mansion, should clasp hands and become one. Those who use the authority of a criminal tradition to lop off the lands of their defeated brother with a sword stained with his own blood, ought to return the lands to the brother already punished sufficiently, if they do not want the people to call them robbers. The honest man does not absolve himself of debts of honor with money, at so much a slap. We can no longer be a people of leaves living in the air, our foliage heavy with blooms and crackling or hum-

From *Our America by José Martí: Writings on Latin America and the Struggle for Cuban Independence*, trans. Elinor Randall and ed., with an introduction and notes, Philip S. Foner (New York: Monthly Review Press, 1977), pp. 84–94. Copyright © 1977 by MR Press. Reprinted by permission of Monthly Review Foundation.

ming at the whim of the sun's caress, or buffeted and tossed by the storms. The trees must form ranks to keep the giant with seven-league boots from passing! It is the time of mobilization, of marching together, and we must go forward in close order, like silver in the veins of the Andes.

Only those born prematurely are lacking in courage. Those without faith in their country are seven-month weaklings. Because they have no courage, they deny it to others. Their puny arms—arms with bracelets and hands with painted nails, arms of Paris or Madrid—can hardly reach the bottom limb, and they claim the tall tree to be unclimbable. The ships should be loaded with those harmful insects that gnaw at the bone of the country that nourishes them. If they are Parisians or from Madrid, let them go to the Prado under lamplight, or to Tortoni's for a sherbet. Those carpenters' sons who are ashamed that their fathers are carpenters! Those born in America who are ashamed of the mother who reared them, because she wears an Indian apron, and who disown their sick mother, the scoundrels, abandoning her on her sickbed! Then who is a real man? He who stays with his mother and nurses her in her illness, or he who puts her to work out of sight, and lives at her expense on decadent lands, sporting fancy neckties, cursing the womb that carried him, displaying the sign of the traitor on the back of his paper frockcoat? These sons of Our America, which will be saved by its Indians and is growing better; these deserters who take up arms in the armies of a North America that drowns its Indians in blood and is growing worse! These delicate creatures who are men but are unwilling to do men's work! The Washington who made this land for them, did he not go to live with the English, to live with the English at a time when he saw them fighting against his own country? These "iconoclasts" of honor who drag that honor over foreign soil, like their counterparts in the French Revolution with their dancing, their affectations, their drawling speech!

For in what lands can men take more pride than in our long-suffering American republics, raised up from among the silent Indian masses by the bleeding arms of a hundred apostles, to the sounds of battle between the book and the processional candle? Never in history have such advanced and united nations been forged in so short a time from such disorganized elements.

The presumptuous man feels that the earth was made to serve as his pedestal because he happens to have a facile pen or colorful speech, and he accuses his native land of being worthless and beyond redemption because its virgin jungles fail to provide him with a constant means of traveling over the world, driving Persian ponies and lavishing champagne like a tycoon. The incapacity does not lie with the emerging country in quest of suitable forms and a utilitarian greatness; it lies rather with those who attempt to rule nations of a unique and violent character by means of laws inherited from four centuries of freedom in the United States and nineteen centuries of monarchy in France. A decree by Hamilton does not halt the charge of the plainsman's horse. A phrase by Sieyès does nothing to quicken the stagnant blood of the Indian race. To govern well, one must see things as they are. And the able governor in America is not the one who knows how to govern the Germans or the French; he must know the elements that compose his own country, and how to bring them together, using methods and institutions originating within the country, to reach that desirable state where each man can attain self-realization and all may enjoy the abundance that Nature has bestowed on everyone in the nation to enrich with their toil and defend with their lives. The government must originate in the country. The spirit of the government must be that of the country. Its structure must conform to rules appropriate to the country. Good government is nothing more than the balance of the country's natural elements.

That is why the imported book has been conquered in America by the natural man. Natural men have conquered learned and artificial men. The native half-breed has conquered the exotic Creole. The struggle is not between civilization and barbarity, but between false erudition and Nature. The natural man is good, and he respects and rewards superior intelligence as long as his humility is not turned against him, or he is not offended by being disregarded—a thing the natural man never forgives, prepared as he is to forcibly regain the respect of whoever has wounded his pride or threatened his interests. It is by conforming with these disdained native elements that the tyrants of America have climbed to power, and have fallen as soon as they betrayed them. Republics have paid with oppression for their inability to recognize the true elements of their countries, to derive from them the right kind of government, and to govern accordingly. In a new nation a governor means a creator.

In nations composed of both cultured and uncultured elements, the uncultured will govern because it is their habit to attack and resolve doubts with their fists in cases where the cultured have failed in the art of governing. The uncultured masses are lazy and timid in the realm of intelligence, and they want to be governed well. But if the government hurts them, they shake it off and govern themselves. How can the universities produce governors if not a single university in America teaches the rudiments of the art of government, the analysis of elements peculiar to the peoples of America? The young go out into the world wearing Yankee or French spectacles, hoping to govern a people they do not know. In the political race entrance should be denied to those who are ignorant of the rudiments of politics. The prize in literary contests should not go for the best ode, but for the best study of the political factors of one's country.

Newspapers, universities, and schools should encourage the study of the country's pertinent components. To know them is sufficient, without mincing words; for whoever brushes aside even a part of the truth, whether through intention or oversight, is doomed to fall. The truth he lacks thrives on negligence, and brings down whatever is built without it. It is easier to resolve our problem knowing its components than to resolve it without knowing them. Along comes the natural man, strong and indignant, and he topples all the justice accumulated from books because he has not been governed in accordance with the obvious needs of the country. Knowing is what counts. To know one's country and govern it with that knowledge is the only way to free it from tyranny. The European university must bow to the American university. The history of America, from the Incas to the present, must be taught in clear detail and to the letter, even if the archons of Greece are overlooked. Our Greece must take priority over the Greece which is not ours. We need it more. Nationalist statesmen must replace foreign statesmen. Let the world be grafted onto our republics, but the trunk must be our own. And let the vanquished pedant hold his tongue, for there are no lands in which a man may take greater pride than in our long-suffering American republics.

With the rosary as our guide, our heads white and our bodies mottled, both Indian and Creole, we fearlessly entered the world of nations. We set out to conquer freedom under the banner of the virgin. A priest, a few lieutenants, and a woman raised the Republic of Mexico onto the shoulders of the Indians. A few heroic students, instructed in French liberty by a Spanish cleric, made Central America rise in revolt against Spain under a Spanish general. In monarchic garb emblazoned with the sun, the Venezuelans to the north and the Argentinians to the south began building nations. When the two heroes clashed and the continent was about to rock, one of them, and not the lesser, handed the reins to the other. And since heroism in times of peace is rare because it is not as glorious as in times of war, it is easier for a man to die with honor than to think with logic. It is easier to govern when feelings are exalted and united than after a battle, when divisive, arrogant, exotic, or ambitious thinking emerges. The forces routed in the epic struggle—with the feline cunning of the species, and using the weight of realities—were undermining the new structure which comprised both the rough-and-ready, unique regions of our half-breed America and the silk-stockinged and frock-coated people of Paris beneath the flag of freedom and reason borrowed from nations skilled in the arts of government. The hierarchical constitution of the colonies resisted the democratic organization of the republics. The cravated capitals left their country boots in the vestibule. The bookworm redeemers failed to realize that the revolution succeeded because it came from the soul of the nation; they had to govern with that soul and not without it or against it. America began to suffer, and still suffers, from the tiresome task of reconciling the hostile and discordant elements it inherited from a despotic and perverse colonizer, and the imported methods and ideas which have been retarding logical government because they are lacking in local realities. Thrown out of gear for three centuries by a power which denied men the right to use their reason, the continent disregarded or closed its ears to the unlettered throngs that helped bring it to redemption, and embarked on a government based on reason—a reason belonging to all for the common good, not the university brand of reason over the peasant brand. The problem of independence did not lie in a change of forms but in a change of spirit.

It was imperative to make common cause with the oppressed, in order to secure a new system opposed to the ambitions and governing habits of the oppressors. The tiger, frightened by gunfire, returns at night to his prey. He dies with his eyes shooting flames and his claws unsheathed. He cannot be heard coming because he approaches with velvet tread. When the prey awakens, the tiger is already upon it. The colony lives on in the republic, and Our America is saving itself from its enormous mistakes—the pride of its capital cities, the blind triumph of a scorned peasantry, the excessive influx of foreign ideas and formulas, the wicked and unpolitic disdain for the aboriginal race—because of the higher virtue, enriched with necessary blood, or a republic struggling against a colony. The tiger lurks behind every tree, lying in wait at every turn. He will die with his claws unsheathed and his eyes shooting flames.

But "these countries will be saved," as was announced by the Argentinian Rivadavia, whose only sin was being a gentleman in these rough-and-ready times. A man does not sheathe a machete in a silken scabbard, nor can he lay aside the short lance in a country won with the short lance merely because he is angered and stands at the door of Iturbide's Congress, "demanding that the fair-haired one be named Emperor." These countries will be saved because a genius for moderation, found in the serene harmony of Nature, seems to prevail on the continent of light, where there emerges a new realistic man schooled for these realistic times in the critical philosophy which in Europe has replaced the philosophy of guesswork and phalanstery that saturated the previous generation.

We were a phenomenon with the chest of an athlete, the hands of a dandy, and the brain of a child. We were a masquerader in English breeches, Parisian vest, North American jacket, and Spanish cap. The Indian hovered near us in silence, and went off to the hills to baptize his children. The Negro was seen pouring out the songs of his heart at night, alone and unrecognized among the rivers and wild animals. The peasant, the creator, turned in blind indignation against the disdainful city, against his own child. As for us, we were nothing but epaulets and professors' gowns in countries that came into the world wearing hemp sandals and headbands. It would have been the mark of genius to couple the headband and the professors' gown with the founding fathers' generosity and courage, to rescue the Indian, to make a place for the competent Negro, to fit liberty to the body of those who rebelled and conquered for it. We were left with the judge, the general, the scholar, and the sinecure. The angelic young, as if caught in the tentacles of an octopus, lunged heavenward, only to fall back, crowned with clouds, in sterile glory. The native, driven by instinct, swept away the golden staffs of office in blind triumph. Neither the European nor the Yankee could provide the key to the Spanish American riddle. Hate was attempted, and every year the countries amounted to less. Exhausted by the senseless struggle between the book and the lance, between reason and the processional candle, between the city and the country, weary of the impossible rule by rival urban cliques over the natural nation tempestuous or inert by turns, we begin almost unconsciously to try love. Nations stand up and greet one another. "What are we?" is the mutual question, and little by little they furnish answers. When a problem arises in Cojímar, they do not seek its solution in Danzig. The frockcoats are still French, but thought begins to be American. The youth of America are rolling up their sleeves, digging their hands in the dough, and making it rise with the sweat of their brows. They realize that there is too much imitation, and that creation holds the key to salvation. "Create" is the password of this generation. The wine is made from plantain, but even if it turns sour, it is our own wine! That a country's form of government must be in keeping with its natural elements is a foregone conclusion. Absolute ideas must take relative forms if they are not to fail because of an error in form. Freedom, to be viable, has to be sincere and complete. If a republic refuses to open its arms to all, and move ahead with all, it dies. The tiger within sneaks in through the crack; so does the tiger from without. The general holds back his cavalry to a pace that suits his infantry, for if the infantry is left behind, the cavalry will be surrounded by the enemy. Politics and strategy are one. Nations should live in an atmosphere of self-criticism because criticism is healthy, but always with one heart and one mind. Stoop to the unhappy, and lift them up in your arms! Thaw out frozen America with the fire of your hearts! Make the natural blood of the nations course vigorously through their veins. The new Americans are on their feet, saluting each other from nation to nation, the eyes of the laborers shining with joy. The natural statesman arises, schooled in the direct study of Nature. He reads to apply his knowledge, not to imitate. Economists study the problems at their point of origin. Speakers begin a policy of moderation. Playwrights bring native characters to the stage. Academies discuss practical subjects. Poetry shears off its romantic locks and hangs its red vest on the glorious tree. Selective and sparkling prose is filled with ideas. In the Indian republics, the governors are learning Indian.

America is escaping all its dangers. Some of the republics are still beneath the sleeping octopus, but others, under the law of averages, are draining their lands with a sublime and furious haste, as if to make up for centuries lost. Still others, forgetting that Juárez went about in a carriage drawn by mules, hitch their carriages to the wind, their coachmen soap bubbles. Poisonous luxury, the enemy of freedom, corrupts the frivolous and opens the door to the foreigner. In others, where independence is threatened, an epic spirit heightens their manhood. Still others spawn an army capable of devouring them in voracious wars. But perhaps Our America is running another risk that does not come from itself but from the difference in origins, methods, and interests between the two halves of the continent, and the time is near at hand when an enterprising and vigorous people who scorn or ignore Our America will even so approach it and demand a close relationship. And since strong nations, self-made by law and shotgun, love strong nations, and them alone; since the time of madness and ambition— from which North America may be freed by the predominance of the purest elements in its blood, or on which it may be launched by its vindictive and sordid masses, its tradition of expansion, or the ambitions of some powerful leader—is not so near at hand, even to the most timorous eye, that there is no time for the test of discreet and unwavering pride that could confront and dissuade it; since its good name as a republic in the eyes of the world's perceptive nations puts upon North America a restraint that cannot be taken away by childish provocations or pompous arrogance or parricidal discords among Our American nations—the pressing need of Our America is to show itself as it is, one in spirit and intent, swift conqueror of a suffocating past, stained only by the enriching blood drawn from hands that struggle to clear away the ruins, and from the scars left upon us by our masters. The scorn of our formidable neighbor who does not know us is Our America's greatest danger. And since the day of the visit is near, it is imperative that our neighbor know us, and soon, so that it will not scorn us. Through ignorance it might even come to lay hands on us. Once it does know us, it will remove its hands out of respect. One must have faith in the best in men and distrust the worst. One must allow the best to be shown so that it reveals and prevails over the worst. Nations should have a pillory for whoever stirs up useless hates, and another for whoever fails to tell them the truth in time.

There can be no racial animosity, because there are no races. The theorists and feeble thinkers string together and warm over the bookshelf races which the well-disposed observer and the fair-minded traveler vainly seek in the justice of Nature where man's universal identity springs forth from triumphant love and the turbulent hunger for life. The soul, equal and eternal, emanates from bodies of various shapes and colors. Whoever foments and spreads antagonism and hate between the races, sins against humanity. But as nations take shape among other different nations, there is a condensation of vital and individual characteristics of thought and habit, expansion and conquest, vanity and greed which could—from the latent state of national concern, and in a period of internal disorder, or the rapidity with which the country's character has been accumulating—be turned into a serious threat for the weak and isolated neighboring countries, declared by the strong country to be inferior and perishable. The thought is father to the deed. And one must not attribute, through a provincial antipathy, a fatal and inborn wickedness to the continent's fair-skinned nation simply because it does not speak our language, or see the world as we see it, or resemble us in its political defects, so different from ours, or favorably regard the excitable, dark-skinned people, or look charitably from its still uncertain eminence upon those less favored by history, who climb the road of republicanism by heroic stages. The self-evident facts of the problem should not be obscured, because the problem can be resolved, for the peace of centuries to come, by appropriate study, and by tacit and immediate unity in the continental spirit. With a single voice the hymn is already being sung. The present generation is carrying industrious America along the road enriched by their sublime fathers; from the Río Grande to the Straits of Magellan, the Great Semí, astride his condor, is showing the seed of the new America throughout the Latin nations of the continent and the sorrowful islands of the sea!

My Race

This word "racist" has taken on a confused meaning, and it must be clarified. A man has no particular rights because he happens to belong to one particular race; when one says "man," that should include all the rights. A Negro is neither inferior nor superior to another because he is black; the white man carries redundancy too far when he says "my race," and so does the Negro when he makes the same statement. Everything that divides men, everything that separates or herds men together in categories, is a sin against humanity. What sensible white man would think of taking pride in being white, and what must the Negro think of the white man who is proud of being white and feels he has special privileges as a result? What must the white man think of the Negro who takes pride in his color? Always to dwell on the divisions or differences between the races, in people who are sufficiently divided already, is to raise barriers to the attainment of both national and individual well-being, for these two goals are reached by bringing together as closely as possible the various components that form the nation. If the Negro is said to have no aboriginal guilt or virus that incapacitates him for fully developing his human soul, it is the truth and must be so stated and shown, because there is much injustice in this world, and much ignorance that passes for wisdom, and there are still people who believe quite honestly that the Negro is incapable of the courage and intelligence of the white man. And if this defense of Nature is called racism, so be it, because it is only natural and a voice from the heart crying out for the peace and welfare of his country.

From *Our America by José Martí: Writings on Latin America and the Struggle for Cuban Independence*, trans. Elinor Randall and ed., with an introduction and notes, Philip S. Foner (New York: Monthly Review Press, 1977), pp. 311–14. Copyright © 1977 by MR Press. Reprinted by permission of Monthly Review Foundation.

If it is claimed that the state of slavery in itself does not show inferiority in the enslaved races, since blue-eyed, blond-haired Gauls were sold as slaves in the Roman marketplace, that is a good form of racism because it stands for justice and helps to rid the ignorant white man of some of his prejudices. But a just racism ends with the Negro's right to maintain and prove that his color does not deprive him of any of the privileges and capabilities of the human species.

How can the white racist, who imagines that his race is the more privileged, complain of the Negro racist who regards his race as superior? And the Negro racist who looks upon his race as especially endowed, what right has he to complain of the white racist? The white man, who because of his race considers himself superior to the Negro, admits the idea of racial difference and provokes the Negro racist to take a similar stand. The Negro who proclaims his race, even if it may be his mistaken way of proclaiming the spiritual identity of all races, is justifying and provoking the white racist. Peace demands of Nature the recognition of human rights; discriminatory rights, which are opposed to Nature, are the enemies of peace. The white man who isolates himself isolates the Negro. The Negro who isolates himself provokes the white man to isolation.

In Cuba there is no fear whatever of racial conflict. A man is more than white, black, or mulatto. A Cuban is more than mulatto, black, or white. Dying for Cuba on the battlefield, the souls of both Negroes and white men have risen together. In the daily life of defense, loyalty, brotherhood, and shrewdness, there has always been a Negro standing beside every white man. Negroes as well as white men classify themselves according to their characteristics: bravery or timidity, selfishness or unselfishness. Political parties are aggregates of hopes, concerns, interests, and personal attributes. Essential resemblances in parties are sought and found beneath the superficial differences; the common purpose is the fusion of that which is basic in the analogous characters, even if these may hold differing opinions on incidentals. But all told, the similarities in men's natures are the decisive and dominant factors when forming parties, and they outweigh the inner frictions between men of varying color and the difficulties that at times result. Affinity of character is more powerful than affinity of color. The Negro, consigned to the unequal or hostile pursuits of the human spirit, could not, nor would he wish to, ally himself against the white man in like position. Negroes are too weary of slavery to voluntarily enter the slavery of color. Conceited and self-seeking men will go to one side, and generous and unselfish men will go to the other, regardless of their color. True men, black or white, will treat each other with loyalty and tenderness for the sake of merit alone, and in the pride of all that honors the land of their birth. The word "racist" will disappear from the lips of the Negroes who use it today in good faith, once they understand that it is the only apparently valid argument that sincere but timid men can offer for denying the Negro his full rights as a man. Negro racists and white racists must share the blame. But many white men have forgotten their color, and so have many Negroes. The two races are working together for the improvement of their minds, the propagation of virtue, and the triumph of creative labor and a spirit of charity.

There will never be a racial war in Cuba. The republic cannot move backward, and ever since that memorable day when the Negro won his redemption in Cuba, ever since the drafting of the first constitution of independence on April 10 in Guáimaro, the republic has not said one word about Negroes or white men. The civil rights conceded by the Spanish government for purely political reasons, and put into general practice before the island's independence came about, can no longer be denied, either by the Spaniard, who will as long as he breathes Cuban air continue dividing the Cuban Negro from the Cuban white man, or by independence for us, which could not deny in freedom the rights that the Spaniard conceded in slavery.

And as for the rest, each one will be free in the sanctity of his own household. Merit, the manifest and continuous evidence of culture, and the constant process of trade will eventually unite all men. There is a plentiful supply of greatness in Cuba, in Negroes and white men alike.

Patria (New York), April 16, 1893

José Carlos Mariátegui (1894–1930)

José Carlos Mariátegui was born in Moquegua, Peru, in 1894 to a lower-middle-class family. He was a sickly child, and due to the increasing poverty of his family was not able to study beyond the primary-education level. Despite his lack of an extensive formal education, he demonstrated a great talent for learning, becoming one of Peru's leading intellectual and political figures. In an all-too-brief life that spanned only thirty-five years, he helped to lead his country to a deeper exploration of art, politics, and Peruvian reality. He was a prolific writer who was deeply concerned with social justice. Some claim him as the father of Peruvian communism.

It is remarkable that he achieved all of this in spite of his poverty and endemic bad health—he was a self-made intellectual. His formation took place within the world of Peruvian journalism, and in the style of his writings one observes these journalistic roots. In 1909 he began to work for the Lima newspaper *La Prensa*. He started as an errand boy, became a proofreader, and eventually rose to become a writer for the paper, composing under the pen name Juan Coniquer. In 1914 he began to contribute to the journal *Mundo Limeño*, joining important writers of the period such as Abraham Valdelmoar and César Falcón. This group was more concerned with the literary dimensions of journalism than any political or social agenda that could be attained therewith.

In the years that followed, Mariátegui continued to write for various journals and helped to establish a circle of journalists. His activity was not limited to the press; he also made important contributions to the theater and to poetry.

In 1918, with the establishment of *Nuestra Epoca*, a magazine with clear socialist leanings, Mariátegui entered a new phase in his career, a

257

phase dominated by a concern for social and political issues rather than the aesthetic ones that had dominated his earlier work. He dropped his pen name and openly identified himself as the author of articles that contained scathing critiques of the Peruvian army and political establishment. For this reason, *Nuestra Epoca* was a short-lived publication. Another scandal concerning the opinions expressed in his publications led Mariátegui to choose a government-sponsored trip to Europe over jail. He traveled widely throughout Europe, and in Italy he met Ana Chiappe, who became his wife. In 1923 he returned to Lima with his wife and their son.

Upon returning to Lima, he continued to be an important critical voice. In 1924 he became the director of the Universidad Popular and editor of the journal *Claridad*. While his professional position became more secure, his health problems flared up. His one good leg was amputated. Although confined in terms of physical mobility, his mind remained as active as ever, perhaps more so. In 1925 he published *La escena contémporanea*, compiled in part of articles previously published. In 1926 he founded the journal *Amauta*, which had a distinctive interest in adapting European ideas to Peruvian reality, especially the indigenous population. In the pages of this journal, Mariátegui's Marxist leanings were subtly expressed. During this period, his political activity became more centered on labor issues; he founded the newspaper *Labor* in 1928, to serve workers. He was also involved in attempts to establish a socialist party in Peru. His Marxist views come to full fruition in *Seven Interpretative Essays on Peruvian Reality*, which was published in 1928.

In this last work, Mariátegui's broad knowledge is evident as he uses socialist theory, European literary trends, and Peru's indigenous legacy to analyze the social reality of his native country. In the essay included here, "The Problem of the Indian," Mariátegui argues that only after the Peruvians recognize that the roots of the social injustices faced by Indians are found in the feudal regime and its accompanying system of land tenure, can any progress toward resolving the socioeconomic problems which the indigenous groups suffer be made. He completely rejects the notion that the oppression of the Indians can only be resolved by mixing these groups with Europeans. He argues that the church cannot solve the problem of oppression, nor can education solve it, for until the underlying conditions of economic and social inequality are changed, no great changes can be expected to come through other means.

Mariátegui was not a systematic thinker. He was a committed intellectual who never developed a grand, unifying system, but who paved the way for the development of a strong Peruvian intellectual tradition. There is no doubt that he was influenced by European ideas, but as he worked with those ideas, adapting them to the Peruvian social reality, the ideas took on a new, original shape.

Seven Interpretive Essays on Peruvian Reality

THE PROBLEM OF THE INDIAN

Any treatment of the problem of the Indian—written or verbal—that fails or refuses to recognize it as a socioeconomic problem is but a sterile, theoretical exercise destined to be completely discredited. Good faith is no justification. Almost all such treatments have served merely to mask or distort the reality of the problem. The socialist critic exposes and defines the problem because he looks for its causes in the country's economy and not in its administrative, legal, or ecclesiastic machinery, its racial dualism or pluralism, or its cultural or moral conditions. The problem of the Indian is rooted in the land tenure system of our economy. Any attempt to solve it with administrative or police measures, through education or by a road-building program, is superficial and secondary, as long as the feudalism of the *gamonales* continues to exist.[1]

Gamonalismo necessarily invalidates any law or regulation for the protection of the Indian. The hacienda owner, the *latifundista*, is a feudal lord. The written law is powerless against his authority, which is supported by custom and habit. Unpaid labor is illegal, yet unpaid and even forced labor survive in the latifundium. The judge, the subprefect, the commissary, the teacher, the tax collector, all are in bondage to the landed estate. The law cannot prevail against the *gamonales*. Any official who insisted on applying it would be abandoned and sacrificed by the central government; here, the influences of *gamonalismo* are all-powerful, acting directly or through parliament with equal effectiveness.

A fresh approach to the problem of the Indian, therefore, ought to be much more concerned with the consequences of the land tenure system than with drawing up protective legislation. The new trend was started in 1918 by Dr. José A. Encinas in his *Contribución a una legislación tutelar indígena*, and it has steadily gained strength.[2] But by the very nature of his study, Dr. Encinas could not frame a socioeconomic program. Since his proposals were designed to protect Indian property, they had to be limited to legal objectives. Outlining an indigenous homestead act, Dr. Encinas recommended the distribution of state and church lands. Although he did not mention expropriating the land of the latifundium *gamonales*, he repeatedly and conclusively denounced the effects of the latifundium system[3] and, thereby, to some extent ushered in the present socioeconomic approach to the Indian question.

This approach rejects and disqualifies any thesis that confines the question to one or another of the following unilateral criteria: administrative, legal, ethnic, moral, educational, ecclesiastic.

The oldest and most obvious mistake is, unquestionably, that of reducing the protection of the Indian to an ordinary administrative matter. From the days of Spanish colonial legislation, wise and detailed ordinances, worked out after conscientious study, have been quite useless. The republic, since independence, has been prodigal in its decrees, laws, and provisions intended to protect the Indian against exaction and abuse. The *gamonal* of today, like the *encomendero* of yesterday, however, has little to fear from administrative theory; he knows that its practice is altogether different.

The individualistic character of the republic's legislation has favored the absorption of Indian property by the latifundium system. The situation of the Indian, in this respect, was viewed more realistically by Spanish legislation. But legal reform has no more practical value than administrative reform when confronted by feudalism intact within the economic structure. The appropriation of most communal and individual Indian property is an accomplished fact. The experience of all countries that have evolved from their feudal shows us, on the other hand, that liberal rights have not been able to operate without the dissolution of feudalism.

The assumption that the Indian problem is ethnic is sustained by the most outmoded repertory of imperialist ideas. The concept of inferior races was useful to the white man's West for purposes of expansion and conquest. To expect that the Indian will be emancipated through a steady crossing of the aboriginal race with white immigrants is an antisociological naïveté that could only occur to the primitive mentality of an importer of merino sheep. The people of Asia, who are in no way superior to the Indians, have not needed any transfusion of European blood in order to assimilate the most dynamic and creative aspects of Western culture. The degeneration of the Peruvian Indian is a cheap invention of sophists who serve feudal interests. The tendency to consider the Indian problem as a moral one embodies a liberal, humanitarian, enlightened nineteenth-century attitude that in the political sphere of the Western world inspires and motivates the "leagues of human rights." The antislavery conferences and societies in Europe that have denounced more or less futilely the crimes of the colonizing nations are born of this tendency, which always has trusted too much in its appeals to the conscience of civilization. González Prada was not immune to this hope when he wrote that "the condition of the Indian can improve in two ways: either the heart of the oppressor will be moved to take pity and recognize the rights of the oppressed, or the spirit of the oppressed will find the valor needed to turn on the oppressors."[4] The Pro-Indian Association (1900–1917) represented the same hope, although it owed its real effectiveness to the concrete and immediate measures taken by its directors in defense of the Indian. This policy was due in large measure to the practical, typically Saxon idealism of Dora Mayer,[5] and the work of the Association became well known in Peru and the rest of the world. Humanitarian teachings have not halted or hampered European imperialism, nor have they reformed its methods. The struggle against imperialism now relies only on the solidarity and strength of the liberation movement of the colonial masses. This concept governs anti-imperialist action in contemporary Europe, action that is supported by liberals like Albert Einstein and Romain Rolland and, therefore, cannot be considered exclusively Socialist.

On a moral and intellectual plane, the church took a more energetic or at least a more authoritative stand centuries ago. This crusade, however, achieved only very wise laws and provisions. The lot of the Indian remained substantially the same. González Prada, whose point of view, as we know, was not strictly Socialist, looked for the explanation of its failure in the economic essentials: "It could not have happened otherwise; exploitation was the official order; it was pretended that evils were humanely perpetrated and injustices committed equitably. To wipe out abuses, it would have been necessary to abolish land appropriation and forced labor, in brief, to change the entire colonial regime. Without the toil of the American Indian, the coffers of the Spanish treasury would have been emptied."[6] In any event, religious tenets were more likely to succeed than liberal tenets. The former appealed to a noble and active Spanish Catholicism, whereas the latter tried to make itself heard by a weak and formalist criollo liberalism.

But today a religious solution is unquestionably the most outdated and antihistoric of all. Its representatives—unlike their distant, how very distant, teachers—are not concerned with obtaining a new declaration of the rights of Indians, with adequate authority and ordinances; the missionary is merely assigned the role of mediator between the Indian and the *gamonal*.[7] If the church could not accomplish its task in a medieval era, when its spiritual and intellectual capacity could be measured by friars like Las Casas, how can it succeed with the elements it commands today? The Seventh-Day Adventists, in that respect, have taken the lead from the Catholic clergy, whose cloisters attract fewer and fewer evangelists.

The belief that the Indian problem is one of education does not seem to be supported by even a strictly and independently pedagogical criterion. Education is now more than ever aware of social and economic factors. The modern pedagogue knows perfectly well that education is not just a question of school and teaching methods. Economic and social circumstances necessarily condition the work of the teacher. *Gamonalismo* is fundamentally opposed to the education of the Indian; it has the same interest in keeping the Indian ignorant as it has in encouraging him to depend on alcohol.[8] The modern school—assuming that in the present situation it could be multiplied at the same rate as the rural school-age population—is incompatible with the feudal latifundium. The mechanics of the Indian's servitude would altogether cancel the action of the school if the latter, by a miracle that is inconceivable within social reality, should manage to preserve its pedagogical mission under feudal regime. The most efficient and grandiose teaching system could not perform these prodigies. School and teacher are doomed to be debased under the pressure of the feudal regime, which cannot be reconciled with the most elementary concept of progress and evolution. When this truth becomes partially understood, the saving formula is thought to be discovered in boarding schools for Indians. But the glaring inadequacy of this formula is self-evident in view of the tiny percentage of the indigenous school population that can be boarded in these schools.

The pedagogical solution, advocated by many in good faith, has been discarded officially. Educators, I repeat, can least afford to ignore economic and social reality. At present, it only exists as a vague and formless suggestion which no body or doctrine wants to adopt.

The new approach locates the problem of the Indian in the land tenure system.

NOTES

1. In my prologue to *Tempestad en los Andes* by Valcárcel, an impassioned and militant champion of the Indian, I have explained my point of view as follows: "Faith in the renaissance of the Indian is not pinned to the material process of 'Westernizing' the Quechua country. The soul of the Indian is not raised by the white man's civilization or alphabet but by the myth, the idea, of the Socialist rev-

olution. The hope of the Indian is absolutely revolutionary. That same myth, that same idea, are the decisive agents in the awakening of other ancient peoples or races in ruin: the Hindus, the Chinese, et cetera. Universal history today tends as never before to chart its course with a common quadrant. Why should the Inca people, who constructed the most highly developed and harmonious communistic system, be the only ones unmoved by this worldwide emotion? The consanguinity of the Indian movement with world revolutionary currents is too evident to need documentation. I have said already that I reached an understanding and appreciation of the Indian through socialism. The case of Valcárcel proves the validity of my personal experience. Valcárcel, a man with a different intellectual background, influenced by traditionalist tastes and oriented by another type of guidance and studies, politically resolved his concern for the Indian in socialism. In this book, he tells us that 'the Indian proletariat awaits its Lenin.' A Marxist would not state it differently.

"As long as the vindication of the Indian is kept on a philosophical and cultural plane, it lacks a concrete historical base. To acquire such a base—that is, to acquire physical reality—it must be converted into an economic and political vindication. Socialism has taught us how to present the problem of the Indian in new terms. We have ceased to consider it abstractly as an ethnic or moral problem and we now recognize it concretely as a social, economic, and political problem. And, for the first time, we have felt it to be clearly defined.

"Those who have not yet broken free of the limitations of a liberal bourgeois education take an abstractionist and literary position. They idly discuss the racial aspects of the problem, disguising its reality under a pseudo-idealistic language and forgetting that it is essentially dominated by politics and, therefore, by economics. They counter revolutionary dialectics with a confused critical jargon, according to which a political reform or event cannot solve the Indian problem because its immediate effects would not reach a multitude of complicated customs and vices that can only be changed through a long and normal evolutionary process.

"History, fortunately, dispels all doubts and clears up all ambiguities. The conquest was a political event. Although it abruptly interrupted the autonomous evolution of the Quechua nation, it did not involve a sudden substitution of the conquerors' law and customs for those of the natives. Nevertheless, this political event opened up a new period in every aspect of their spiritual and material existence. The change in regime altered the life of the Quechua people to its very foundations. Independence was another political event. It, too, did not bring about a radical transformation in the economic and social structure of Peru; but it initiated, notwithstanding, another period of our history. Although it did not noticeably improve the condition of the Indian, having hardly touched the colonial economic infrastructure, it did change his legal situation and clear the way for his political and social emancipation. If the republic did not continue along this road, the fault lies entirely with the class that profited from independence, which was potentially very rich in values and creative principles.

"The problem of the Indian must no longer be obscured and confused by the perpetual arguments of the throng of lawyers and writers who are consciously or unconsciously in league with the *latifundistas*. The moral and material misery of the

Indian is too clearly the result of the economic and social system that has oppressed him for centuries. This system, which succeeded colonial feudalism, is *gamonalismo*. While it rules supreme, there can be no question of redeeming the Indian.

"The term *gamonalismo* designates more than just a social and economic category: that of the *latifundistas* or large landowners. It signifies a whole phenomenon. *Gamonalismo* is represented not only by the *gamonales* but by a long hierarchy of officials, intermediaries, agents, parasites, et cetera. The literate Indian who enters the service of *gamonalismo* turns into an exploiter of his own race. The central factor of the phenomenon is the hegemony of the semifeudal landed estate in the policy and mechanism of the government. Therefore, it is this factor that should be acted upon if the evil is to be attacked at its roots and not merely observed in its temporary or subsidiary manifestations.

"*Gamonalismo* or feudalism could have been eliminated by the republic within its liberal and capitalist principles. But for reasons I have already indicated, those principles have not effectively and fully directed our historic process. They were sabotaged by the very class charged with applying them and for more than a century they have been powerless to rescue the Indian from a servitude that was an integral part of the feudal system. It cannot be hoped that today, when those principles are in crisis all over the world, they can suddenly acquire in Peru an unwonted creative vitality.

"Revolutionary and reformist thought can no longer be liberal; they must be Socialist. Socialism appears in our history not because of chance, imitation, or fashion, as some superficial minds would believe, but because it was historically inevitable. On the one hand, we who profess socialism struggle logically and consistently for the reorganization of our country on Socialist bases; proving that the economic and political regime that we oppose has turned into an instrument for colonizing the country on behalf of foreign imperialist capitalism, we declare that this is a moment in our history when it is impossible to be really nationalist and revolutionary without being Socialist. On the other hand, there does not exist and never has existed in Peru a progressive bourgeoisie, endowed with national feelings, that claims to be liberal and democratic and that derives its policy from the postulates of its doctrine."

2. González Prada had already said in one of his early speeches as an intellectual agitator that the real Peru was made up of the millions of Indians living in the Andean valleys. The most recent edition of *Horas de lucha* includes a chapter called "Nuestros indios" that shows him to be the forerunner of a new social conscience: "Nothing changes a man's psychology more swiftly and radically than the acquisition of property; once his viscera are purged of slavery, he grows by leaps and bounds. By simply owning something, a man climbs a few rungs in the social ladder, because classes are divided into groups classified by wealth. Contrary to the law of aerostatics, what weighs the most goes up the most. To those who say schools the reply is schools and bread. The Indian question is economic and social, rather than pedagogic."

3. "Improving the economic condition of the Indian," writes Encinas, "is the best way to raise his social condition. His economic strength and all his activity are found in the land. To take him away from the land is to alter profoundly and dangerously the ancestral tendency of his race. In no other place and in no other

way can he find a better source of wealth than in the land" (*Contribución a una legislación tutelar indígena*, p. 39). Encinas says elsewhere (p. 13): "Legal institutions related to property are derived from economic necessities. Our civil code is not in harmony with economic principles because it is individualistic. Unrestricted property rights have created the latifundium to the detriment of Indian property. Ownership of unproductive land has condemned a race to serfdom and misery."

4. González Prada, "Nuestros indios," in *Horas de lucha*, 2d ed.

5. Dora Mayer de Zulen summarizes the character of the Pro-Indian Association in this way: "In specific and practical terms, the Pro-Indian Association signifies for historians what Mariátegui assumes to be an experiment in the redemption of the backward and enslaved indigenous race through an outside protective body that without charge and by legal means has sought to serve it as a lawyer in its claims against the government." But, as appears in the same interesting review of the association's work, Dora Mayer believes that it tried above all to create a sense of responsibility. "One hundred years after the republican emancipation of Peru, the conscience of the governors, the *gamonales*, the clergy, and the educated and semi-educated public continued to disregard its responsibilities to a people who not only deserved philanthropic deliverance from inhuman treatment, but to whom Peruvian patriotism owed a debt of national honor, because the Inca race had lost the respect of its own and other countries." The best result of the Pro-Indian Association, however, was, according to Dora Mayer's faithful testimony, its influence in awakening the Indian. "What needed to happen was happening; the Indians themselves were learning to do without the protection of outsiders and to find ways to redress their grievances."

6. González Prada, *Horas de lucha*.

7. "Only the missionary," writes José León y Bueno, one of the leaders of Acción Social de la Juventud, "can redeem and make restitution to the Indian. Only he can return to Peru its unity, dignity, and strength by acting the tireless intermediary between the *gamonal* and the resident hacienda laborer and between the *latifundista* and the communal farmer; by preventing the arbitrary acts of the governor, who heeds solely the political interests of the criollo cacique; by explaining in simple terms the objective lessons of nature and interpreting life in its fatality and liberty; by condoning excesses during celebrations; by cutting off carnal appetites at their source; and by revealing to the Indian race its lofty mission." *Boletín de la A. S. J.*, May 1928.

8. It is well known that the production—and also the smuggling—of cane alcohol is a profitable business of the *hacendados* of the sierra. Even those on the coast exploit this market to some extent. The alcoholism of the peon and the resident laborer is indispensable to the prosperity of our great agricultural properties.

José Vasconcelos (1882–1959)

V asconcelos must undoubtedly be considered one of the most interesting and controversial figures in the history of Latin American philosophy. A committed philosopher, an excellent writer, a dedicated educator and political activist, he represents in his life and in his work a profound sense of Mexican destiny and of Latin American culture in general.

He was born in Oaxaca, Mexico, in 1882. In 1897 he moved to the capital, Mexico City, and remained there the rest of his life. He studied at the National College of Jurisprudence, graduating in 1905. His thesis, "La teoría dinámica del derecho," which was later published in *Revista positiva* (1907), reflects the positivist perspective that dominated his thought at the time. His sympathy for positivism was, however, transitory. A year later, in 1908, he, along with a group of like-minded young thinkers, founded the Ateneo de la Juventud, which became a center of artistic and philosophical productivity from which the Mexican national intellectual movement emerged. From that time on he was no longer identified with the ideological positivism that had dominated the Mexican intellectual environment throughout the dictatorship of Porfirio Díaz.

During the turmoil caused by the revolutionary years of 1910 and following, Vasconcelos actively participated in the national struggle. He was exiled on two occasions, in 1910 and again in 1913, and was obliged to remain in the United States for some time. In 1914 he returned to Mexico to assume the position of minister of public education. During the government of Venustiano Carranza, he left the country again. In 1919 he was appointed president of the National University and later minister of education for the second time. During this period he began the intensive activity involved in providing a foundation for the Mexican educational system. His unsuccessful bid for the national presidency in the elections of 1929 brought an end to his political ambitions. From 1939 onward, his public activity was limited in great part by the responsibilities associated with his post as director of the national library. He died in Mexico on June 30, 1959.

Parallel with his intense political activity and teaching responsibilities, Vasconcelos developed a philosophical system inspired by Bergson, Schopenhauer, Plotinus, and Pythagoras—a system he characterized as "aesthetic monism." Its development begins with *Pítagoras, una teoría del ritmo* (1916) and continues through many books and essays, among which the most important are *El monismo estético* (1918) and *Tratado de metafísica* (1929). *Todología* (1952) concludes the development of Vasconcelo's system and constitutes the most important synthesis of his thought. In it he provides the final statement of his philosophical system and attempts to integrate it with the principles of Christianity to which he had been converted shortly before. Within this system the human being is the highest expression of the principle that makes reality intelligible. Vasconcelos goes on to claim that human beings are the genuine albeit small reflections of the universe and that therefore they constitute true microcosms.

In a series of works that attained great popularity—*Estudios indostánicos* (1920), *La raza cósmica* (1925), *Indología* (1926)—Vasconcelos optimistically heralds a new dawn for Latin America. The passage included here is from *La raza cósmica*. In this short work, we find Vasconcelos's claim that the foundation of the bright and promising future of Latin America will be constituted by a cosmic race, a synthesis of the four basic races of the present world, that will emerge in the region of the Amazon and fulfill "the divine mission of America." In contrast to what he considered to be the ethnic egoism, materialism, and typical racism of the Anglo-Saxon people of Europe and North America, the new race will be characterized by a universal spirit based on love. Vasconcelos celebrates the mixing of races that has taken place in Ibero-American lands, contrasting this to the annihilation of the Indians in North America and the impenetrable boundaries drawn between blacks and whites in the Anglo-Saxon world. It is his view that the destiny of the races will be decided in the New World.

The Cosmic Race

MESTIZAJE

I

In the opinion of respectable geologists, the American continent includes some of the most ancient regions of the world. The Andes are, undoubtedly, as old as any other mountain range on earth. And while the land itself is ancient, the traces of life and human culture also go back in time beyond any calculations. The architectural ruins of legendary Mayans, Quechuas, and Toltecs are testimony of civilized life previous to the oldest foundations of towns in the Orient and Europe. As research advances, more support is found for the hypothesis of Atlantis as the cradle of a civilization that flourished millions of years ago in the vanished continent and in parts of what is today America. . . .

If we are, then, geologically ancient, as well as in respect to the tradition, how can we still continue to accept the fiction, invented by our European fathers, of the novelty of a continent that existed before the appearance of the land from where the discoverers and conquerors came?

The question has paramount importance to those who insist in looking for a plan in History. The confirmation of the great antiquity of our continent may seem idle to those who see nothing in the chain of events but a fateful repetition of meaningless patterns. With boredom we should regard the work of contemporary civilization, if the Toltec palaces

Vasconcelos, José. Afterword by Joseba Gabilondo. *The Cosmic Race/La raza cósmica*, trans. Didier T. Jaén (Baltimore, MD: Johns Hopkins University Press, 1997), pp. 7–9, 10–19, 32–33, 38–40. Copyright © 1997 José Vasconcelos. Reprinted with permission of The Johns Hopkins University Press.

269

would tell us nothing else but that civilizations pass away leaving no other fruit than a few carved stones piled upon each other or forming arched vaults or roofs of two planes intersecting at an angle. Why begin again, if within four or five thousand years other new immigrants will distract their leisure by pondering upon the remains of our trivial contemporary architecture? Scientific history becomes confused and leaves unanswered all these ruminations. Empirical history, suffering from myopia, loses itself in details, but it cannot determine a single antecedent for historical times. It flees from general conclusions, from transcendental hypotheses, to fall into the puerility of the description of utensils and cranial indices and so many other, merely external, minutiae that lack importance when seen apart from a vast and comprehensive theory.

Only a leap of the spirit, nourished with facts, can give us a vision that will lift us above the micro-ideology of the specialist. Then we can dive deeply into the mass of events in order to discover a direction, a rhythm, and a purpose. Precisely there, where the analyst discovers nothing, the synthesizer and the creator are enlightened. Let us, then, attempt explanations, not with the fantasy of the novelist, but with an intuition supported by the facts of history and science.

The race that we have agreed to call Atlantean prospered and declined in America. After its extraordinary flourishment, after having completed its cycle and fulfilled its particular mission, it entered the silence and went into decline until being reduced to the lesser Aztec and Inca empires, totally unworthy of the ancient and superior culture. With the decline of the Atlanteans, the intense civilization was transported to other sites and changed races: It dazzled in Egypt; it expanded in India and Greece, grafted onto new races. The Aryans mixed with the Dravidians to produce the Hindustani, and at the same time, by means of other mixtures, created Hellenic culture.

Greece laid the foundations of Western or European civilization; the white civilization that, upon expanding, reached the forgotten shores of the American continent in order to consummate the task of recivilization and repopulation. Thus we have the four stages and the four racial trunks: the Black, the Indian, the Mongol, and the White. The latter, after organizing itself in Europe, has become the invader of the world, and has considered itself destined to rule, as did each of the previous races during their time of power. It is clear that domination by the whites will also be temporary, but their mission is to serve as a bridge. The white race has brought the world to a state in which all human types and cultures will be able to fuse with each other. The civilization developed and organized in our times by the whites has set the moral and material basis for the union of all men into a fifth universal race, the fruit of all the previous ones and amelioration of everything past.

White culture is migratory, yet it was not Europe as a whole that was in charge of initiating the reintegration of the red world into the modality of preuniversal culture, which had been represented for many centuries by the white man. The transcendental mission fell upon the two most daring branches of the European family, the strongest and most different human types: the Spanish and the English. . . .

Our age became, and continues to be, a conflict of Latinism against Anglo-Saxonism; a conflict of institutions, aims, and ideals. It marks the climax of a secular fight that begins with the disaster of the Invincible Armada and gets worse with the defeat of Trafalgar. Since then, the location of the conflict began to change and was transferred to the new continent, where it still had fateful episodes. The defeats of Santiago de Cuba, Cavite, and Manila were distant but logical echoes of the catastrophes of the Invincible and Trafalgar. Now the conflict is set entirely in the New World. In History, centuries tend to be like days; thus it is not strange at all that we still cannot completely discard the impression of defeat. We are going through times of despair, we continue to lose not only sovereignty, but moral power. Far from feeling united in the face of disaster, our determination is dispersed in search of small and vain goals. Defeat has brought us the confusion of values and concepts; the victor's diplomacy deceives us after defeating us; commerce conquers us with its small advantages. Despoiled of our previous greatness, we boast of an exclusively national patriotism and we do not even see the dangers that threaten our race as a whole. We deny ourselves to each other. Defeat has debased us to the point that, without even being aware of it, we serve the ends of the enemy policy of defeating us one by one; of offering particular advantages to some of our brothers while the vital interests of the others are sacrificed. Not only were we defeated in combat; ideologically, the Anglos continue to conquer us. The greatest battle was lost on the day that each one of the Iberian republics went forth alone, to live her own life apart from her sisters, concerting treaties and receiving false benefits, without tending to the common interests of the race. The founders of our new nationalism were, without knowing it, the best allies of the Anglo-Saxons, our rivals in the possession of the continent. The unfurling of our twenty banners at the Pan American Union in Washington, should be seen as a joke played by skillful enemies. Yet, each of us takes pride in our humble rags, expression of a vain illusion, and we do not even blush at the fact of our discord in the face of the powerful North American union. We ignore the contrast presented by Anglo-Saxon unity in opposition to the anarchy and solitude of the Ibero American emblems. We keep ourselves jealously independent from each other, yet one way or another we submit to, or ally ourselves with, the Anglo-Saxon union. Not even the national unity of the five Central American states has been possible, because a stranger has not granted us his approval and because we lack the true patriotism to sacrifice the present for the future. A lack of creative thinking and an excess of critical zeal, which we have certainly borrowed from other cultures, takes us to fruitless discussions in which our common aspirations are denied as often as they are ascertained. Yet, we do not realize that, in times of action, and despite all the doubts of English thinkers, the English seek the alliance of their American or Australian brothers, and the Yankee feels as English as the Englishman from England. We shall not be great as long as the Spaniard from America does not feel as much a Spaniard as the sons of Spain. This does not preclude that we may differ whenever necessary, as long as we do not drift away from the higher common mission. This is the way we have to act, if we are to allow the Iberian culture to finish producing all its fruits; if we are going to keep Anglo-Saxon culture from remaining triumphant in America without opposition. It is futile to imagine other solutions. Civilization is neither improvised nor curtailed, nor can it grow out of the paper of a political constitution. It always derives from a long, secular preparation and purification of elements that are transmitted and combined from the beginning of History. For that reason, it is stupid to initiate our patriotism with Father Hidalgo's cry of independence, or the conspiration of Quito, or the feats of Bolívar, because if we do not root it in Cuauhtemoc and Atahualpa, it will have no support. At the same time, it is necessary to trace our patriotism back to our Hispanic fountainhead and educate it on the lessons we should derive from the defeats, which are also ours, of Trafalgar and the Invincible Armada. If our patriotism is not identified with the different stages of the old conflict between Latins and Anglo-Saxons, it shall never overcome a regionalism lacking in universal breadth. We shall fatefully see it degenerate into the narrowness and myopia of parochialism, or into the impotent inertia of a mollusk attached to its rock.

So that we shall not be forced to deny our own fatherland, it is necessary that we live according to the highest interests of the race, even though this may not be yet in the highest interest of humanity. . . .

The first stage of the profound conflict was decided in Europe and we lost. Afterward, when all the advantages were on our side in the New World, since Spain had conquered America, the Napoleonic stupidity gave Louisiana away to the Englishmen from this side of the ocean, to the Yankees; this decided the fate of the New World in favor of the Anglo-Saxons. The "genius of war" could see no farther than the miserable boundary disputes between puny European states, and did not realize that the cause of Latinism, which he claimed to represent, was defeated on the same day that the Empire was proclaimed, by the sole fact that the common destiny was placed in the hands of an incompetent. On the other hand, European prejudice hid the fact that, in America, the conflict that Napoleon could not comprehend in its full transcendence had already acquired universal dimensions. Napoleon, in his foolishness, was not able to surmise that the destiny of the European races was going to be decided in the New World. When, in the most thoughtless manner, he destroyed French power in America, he also weakened the Spaniards. He betrayed us and placed us at the mercy of the common enemy. Without Napoleon, the United States would not exist as a world empire, and Louisiana, still French, would have to be part of the Latin American Confederation. The defeat of Trafalgar, then, would have been irrelevant. None of these facts were even considered because the destiny of the race was in the hands of a fool, because caesarism is the scourge of the Latin race.

Napoleon's betrayal of the global destiny of France mortally wounded the Spanish empire in America at the moment of its greatest weakness. The English-speaking people took possession of Louisiana without combat, reserving their ammunitions for the now easy conquest of Texas and California. Without the base of the Mississippi, the English, who call themselves Yankees out of a simple richness of expression, would not have been able to take possession of the Pacific; they would not be the masters of the continent today; they would have remained in a sort of Netherlands transplanted to America, and the New World would be Spanish and French. Bonaparte made it Anglo-Saxon.

. . . Should one talk to the most exalted Indianist of the convenience of adapting ourselves to Latinism, he will raise no questions; but tell him that our culture is Spanish and he will immediately bring up counterarguments. The stain from the spilled blood still remains. It is an accursed stain that centuries have not erased, but which the common danger must annul. There is no other recourse. Even the pure Indians are Hispanized, they are Latinized, just as the environment itself is Latinized. Say what one may, the red men, the illustrious Atlanteans from whom Indians derive, went to sleep millions of years ago, never to awaken. There is no going back in History, for it is all transformation and novelty. No race returns. Each one states its mission, accomplishes it, and passes away. This truth rules in biblical times as well as in our times; all the ancient historians have formulated it. The days of the pure whites, the victors of today, are as numbered as were the days of their predecessors. Having fulfilled their destiny of mechanizing the world, they themselves have set, without knowing it, the basis for a new period: The period of the fusion and mixing of all peoples. The Indian has no other door to the future but the door of modern culture, nor any other road but the road already cleared by Latin civilization. The white man, as well, will have to depose his pride and look for progress and ulterior redemption in the souls of his brothers from other castes. He will have to diffuse and perfect himself in each of the superior varieties of the species, in each of the modalities that multiply revelation and make genius more powerful.

. . . It seems as if God Himself guided the steps of the Anglo-Saxon cause, while we kill each other on account of dogma or declare ourselves atheists. How those mighty empire builders must laugh at our groundless arrogance and Latin vanity! They do not clutter their mind with the Ciceronian weight of phraseology, nor have they in their blood the contradictory instincts of a mixture of dissimilar races, *but they committed the sin of destroying those races, while we assimilated them, and this gives us new rights and hopes for a mission without precedent in History.*

For this reason, adverse obstacles do not move us to surrender, for we vaguely feel that they will help us to discover our way. Precisely in our differences, we find the way. If we simply imitate, we lose. If we discover and create, we shall overcome. The advantage of our tradition is that it has greater facility of sympathy toward strangers. This implies that our civilization, with all defects, may be the chosen one to assimilate and to transform mankind into a new type; that within our civilization, the warp, the multiple and rich plasma of future humanity is thus being prepared. This mandate from History is first noticed in that abundance of love that allowed the Spaniard to create a new race with the Indian and the Black, profusely spreading white ancestry through the soldier who begat a native family, and Occidental culture through the doctrine and example of the missionaries who placed the Indians in condition to enter into the new stage, the stage of world One. Spanish colonization created mixed races, this signals its character, fixes its responsibility, and defines its future. The English kept on mixing only with the whites and annihilated the natives. Even today, they continue to annihilate them in a sordid and economic fight, more efficient yet than armed conquest. This proves their limitation and is indication of their decadence. The situation is equivalent, in a larger scale, to the incestuous marriages of the pharaohs which undermined the virtues of the race; and it contradicts the ulterior goals of History to attain the fusion of peoples and cultures. To build an English world and to exterminate the red man, so that Northern Europe could be renovated all over an America made up with pure whites, is no more than a repetition of the triumphant process of a conquering race. This was already attempted by the red man and by all strong and homogeneous races, but it does not solve the human problem. America was not kept in reserve for five thousand years for such a petty goal. The purpose of the new and ancient continent is much more important. Its predestination obeys the design of constituting the cradle of a fifth race into which all nations will fuse with each other to replace the four races that have been forging History apart from each other. The dispersion will come to an end on American soil; unity will be consummated there by the triumph of fecund love and the improvement of all the human races. In this fashion, the synthetic race that shall gather all the treasures of History in order to give expression to universal desire shall be created.

The so-called Latin peoples, because they have been more faithful to their divine mission in America, are the ones called upon to consummate this mission. Such fidelity to the occult design is the guarantee of our triumph.

Even during the chaotic period of independence, which deserves so much censure, one can notice, however, glimpses of that eagerness for universality which already announced the desire to fuse humanity into a universal and synthetic type. Needless to say, Bolívar, partly because he realized the danger into which we were falling by dividing ourselves into isolated nationalities, and partly because of his gift for prophecy, formulated the plan for an Ibero-American Federation which some fools still question today.

It is true that, in general, the other leaders of Latin American independence did not have a clear conception of the future. Carried away by a provincialism that today we call patriotism, or by a limitation that today is dubbed national sovereignty, every one of them was only concerned with the immediate fate of their own people. Yet, it is also surprising to observe that almost all of them felt animated by a humane and universal sentiment which coincides with the destiny that today we assign to the Latin American continent. Hidalgo, Morelos, Bolívar, Petion the Haitian, the Argentinians in Tucuman, Sucre, all were concerned with the liberation of the slaves, with the declaration of the equality of all men by natural right, and with the civil and social equality of Whites, Blacks, and Indians. In a moment of historical crisis, they formulated the transcendental mission assigned to that region of the globe: The mission of fusing all peoples ethnically and spiritually.

Thus, what no one even thought of doing on the Anglo-Saxon area of the continent was done on the Latin side. In the north, the contrary thesis continued to prevail: The confessed or tacit intention of cleaning the earth of Indians, Mongolians, or Blacks, for the greater glory and fortune of the Whites. In fact, since that time, the systems which, continuing to the present, have placed the two civilizations on opposing sociological fields were very well defined. The one wants exclusive dominion by the Whites, while the other is shaping a new race, a synthetic race that aspires to engulf and to express everything human in forms of constant improvement. If it were necessary to adduce proof, it would be sufficient to observe the increasing and spontaneous mixing which operates among all peoples in all of the Latin continent; in contrast with the inflexible line that separates the Blacks from the Whites in the United States, and the laws, each time more rigorous, for the exclusion of the Japanese and Chinese from California.

The so-called Latins insist on not taking the ethnic factor too much into account for their sexual relations, perhaps because from the beginning they are not, properly speaking, Latins but a conglomeration of different types and races. Whatever opinions one may express in this respect, and whatever repugnance caused by prejudice one may harbor, the truth is that the mixture of races has taken place and continues to be consummated. . . .

No contemporary race can present itself alone as the finished model that all the others should imitate. The mestizo, the Indian, and even the Black are superior to the White in a countless number of properly spiritual capacities. Neither in antiquity, nor in the present, have we a race capable of forging civilization by itself. The most illustrious epochs of humanity have been, precisely, those in which several different peoples have come into contact and mixed with each other. India, Greece, Alexandria, Rome are but examples that only a geographic and ethnic universality is capable of giving the fruits of civilization. In the contemporary period, while the pride of the present masters of the world asserts through the mouth of their scientists the ethnic and mental superiority of the Whites from the north, any teacher can corroborate that the children and youths descendant from Scandinavians, Dutch, and English found in North American universities, are much slower, and almost dull, compared with the mestizo children and youths from the south. Perhaps this advantage is explained as the result of a beneficial spiritual Mendelianism, caused by a combination of contrary elements. The truth is that vigor is renewed with graftings, and that the soul itself looks for diversity in order to enrich the monotony of its own contents. Only a long-lasting experience will be able to show the results of a mixture no longer accomplished by violence, nor by reason of necessity, but by the selection founded on the dazzling produced by beauty and confirmed by the *pathos* of love. . . .

We have, then, in the continent all the elements for the new Humanity: A law that will gradually select elements for the creation of predominant types; a law that will not operate according to a national criterion, as would be the case with a single conquering race, but according to a criterion of universality and beauty; and we also have the land and the natural resources. No people in Europe could replace the Ibero-American in this mission, no matter how gifted they might be, because all of them have their culture already made and a tradition that constitutes a burden for such enterprises. A conquering race could not substitute us, because it would fatefully impose its own characteristics, even if only out of the need to exert violence in order to maintain its conquest. This mission cannot be fulfilled either by the peoples of Asia, who are exhausted, or at least, lacking in the necessary boldness for new enterprises.

The people that Hispanic America is forming in a somewhat disorderly manner, yet free of spirit and with intense longings on account of the vast unexplored regions, can still repeat the feats of the Castilian and Portuguese conquerors. The Hispanic race, in general, still has ahead of it this mission of discovering new regions of the spirit, now that all lands have already been explored.

Only the Iberian part of the continent possesses the spiritual factors, the race, and the territory necessary for the great enterprise of initiating the new universal era of Humanity. All the races that are to provide their contribution are already there: The Nordic man, who is today the master of action but who had humble beginnings and seemed inferior in an epoch in which already great cultures had appeared and decayed; the black man, as a reservoir of potentialities that began in the remote days of Lemuria; the Indian, who saw Atlantis perish but still keeps a quiet mystery in the conscience. We have all the races and all the aptitudes. The only thing lacking is for true love to organize and set in march the law of History.

Many obstacles are opposed to the plan of the spirit, but they are obstacles common to all progress. Of course, some people may object, saying that how are the different races going to come to an accord, when not even the children of the same stock can live in peace and happiness within the economic and social regime that oppresses man today. But such a state of mind will have to change rapidly. All the tendencies of the future are intertwined in the present: Mendelianism in biology, socialism in government, growing sympathy among the souls, generalized progress, and the emergence of the fifth race that will fill the planet with the triumphs of the first truly universal, truly cosmic culture.

If we view the process panoramically, we shall find the three stages of the law of the three states of society, each one vivified with the contribution of the four fundamental races that accomplish their mission and, then, disappear in order to create a fifth superior ethnic specimen. This gives us five races and three stages, that is, the number eight which in the Pythagorean gnosis represents the ideal of the equality of all men. Such coincidences are surprising when discovered, although later they may seem trivial.

In order to express all these ideas that today I am trying to expound in a rapid synthesis, I tried, some years ago, when they were not yet well defined, to assign them symbols in the new Palace of Public Education in Mexico. Lacking sufficient elements to do exactly what I wished, I had to be satisfied with a Spanish renaissance building, with two courtyards, archways, and passages that give somewhat the impression of a bird's wing. On the panels at the four corners of the first patio, I had them carve allegories representing Spain, Mexico, Greece, and India, the four particular civilizations that have most to contribute to the formation of Latin America. Immediately below these four allegories, four stone statues should have been raised, representing the four great contemporary races: the white, the red, the black, and the yellow, to indicate that America is home to all and needs all of them. Finally, in the center, a monument should have been raised that in some way would symbolize the law of the three states: The material, the intellectual, and the aesthetic. All this was to indicate that through the exercise of the triple law, we in America shall arrive, before any other part of the world, at the creation of a new race fashioned out of the treasures of all the previous ones: The final race, the cosmic race.

Samuel Ramos
(1897–1959)

Ramos is the most outstanding Mexican philosopher in the generation that followed "the founders." He was born in Zitácuaro in 1897. He studied at the National High School at San Nicolás de Hidalgo and later in Mexico City under Antonio Caso. In 1920 he collaborated with Vasconcelos in the Ministry of Public Education. He lived for a time in France and Italy and later became a professor of philosophy at the National University in Mexico City. In particular, he held the chairs of aesthetics and history of philosophy and letters and later became a member of the Colegio Nacional, an institution that brought together the most important intellectuals of Mexico.

In his first work, *Hypothesis* (1928), he tells of the vicissitudes of his spiritual pilgrimage and of his debt to and his break with Caso. Ortega y Gasset, Scheler, Hartmann, and Adler also influenced his thought.

The perspectivism of Ortega helped to provide a foundation for his preoccupation with a national philosophy and to clarify the "Mexican nature." Ramos was attracted to two apparently contradictory impulses that he attempted to reconcile. He sought to remain true to the particularity of Mexican reality and yet he aspired to knowledge and values that are universal. He succeeded in avoiding both an abstract universalism and a false folkloric nationalism, maintaining that "'the norm of nationalism' must be to purify our own life without impairing it as it approaches the level of universal forms."

He analyzes these problems in his work *Perfil del hombre y la cultura en México* (1934). This was the first attempt by a philosopher to interpret Mexican culture. In applying the psychoanalytic theory of Adler, Ramos believed he had discovered that the fundamental characteristic of a Mexican, taken individually as well as collectively, is an inferiority complex.

This interpretation is continued later by Octavio Paz in his well-known book *El laberinto de la soledad* (1947).

The selection from Ramos included here illustrates his philosophical engagement with the "destiny of culture in Mexico," his concern for lifting the shadows of false Europeanism, and opening a path toward the development of an authentic and proud Mexican culture. Ultimately, Ramos believed that the spiritual renewal of his country would be achieved by a profound educational reform that would be based on a new theory of man. He developed these thoughts in one of his most important works, *Hacia un nuevo humanismo. Programa de una antropología filosófica* (1940), which had great influence on the authors included earlier in Part II. In 1943 he wrote the first history of philosophy in Mexico (*Historia de la filosofía en México*), which influenced Zea's turn toward Mexican philosophical traditions.

Profile of Man and Culture in Mexico

THE PROFILE OF MEXICAN CULTURE

In one of his observations on the New World, Bolívar wrote that we Americans are Europeans by heritage. In Mexico this heritage was abused for an entire century; there was excessive imitation of Europe, with no other guide than individual caprice. The original sin of Mexican Europeanism was its lack of a standard for selecting foreign seeds of culture which in our spiritual earth could have produced the appropriate remedies for particular needs. That standard should have been none other than reality itself, but reality was unknown, because all our attention and interest had turned to Europe. The fallacy of always attempting to imitate Europe was possibly derived from an erroneous concept of culture which by extravagant idealization separated it from life, as if warmth and energy were not indispensable to the spirit's survival.

The prevailing culture—present or future—is necessarily that which determines vocation of the race and its historical destiny. We shall try to draw the profile of a culture that conceivably could exist in Mexico, given certain organic circumstances of society and man as the results of a particular history.

We must not continue to practice a false Europeanism; but it is just as urgent to avoid another dangerous illusion, cherished by an equally false type of Mexicanism. Enlivened by a resentment against everything foreign, this Mexicanism seeks to rebuild our national life on other bases than those which it has had up to now—as if it were possible to undo in one moment our entire history. There is an attempt to isolate Mexico from all contact with the outside world so as to free its native qualities from all extraneous elements. Just as "Europeanism" was founded on the ideal of a culture which could exist apart from life, "nationalism" was founded on the belief that Mexico was already complete in itself, with a definitive national physiognomy, and that its only need was to be drawn out into the light of day, like an unearthed idol. Such a belief is supported by an inclination to the picturesque—mountain scenes, dotted with Indian figures in their typical white cotton suits and with cactus plants. Recent art has undertaken an amplification—as in a resounding box—of the "picturesque" dimensions that have found wide acceptance, especially among Yankee tourists. But this Mexico of the *charro* (Mexican horseman) and the Mexico of the *china poblana* (colorful style of women's regional dress), as well as the Mexico of the legendary savage (whose novelty and attraction for Europeans I cannot understand; there is proof of their own savagery in what has transpired since 1914), constitute a Mexico for export which is just as false as the romantic Spain of the tambourine.

But if we can rid our nationalistic spirit of all its resentment against things foreign (the kind of resentment which is typical in those suffering from an inferiority complex), there will undoubtedly remain a moral substance of absolute value for Mexico. This will be the voice of our most authentic being, which now finally makes itself heard after so many years in which the Mexican turned a deaf ear to his destiny. It is almost impossible to believe that this is a novelty; but it is. Mexicans have not lived naturally; their history has always lacked candor. That is why they now should quickly heed that voice, which demands a life of sincerity. We must have the courage to be ourselves and the humility to accept the life that fate bestowed upon us without being ashamed of its poverty. All the ills that have outlived us are due to our failure to practice these simple rules of austerity; we have chosen to feign a situation which is very superior to that in which we actually live. Many of the sufferings which now afflict us will disappear the day we cure ourselves of our vanity. As a consequence of living outside the reality of our being, we are lost in a chaotic world, in the midst of which we walk blindly and aimlessly, buffeted about by the four winds. For times of radical confusion there is no better remedy than to withdraw into ourselves, to return to the native soil. There is no doubt that after periods of muddled thinking and debilitation men and even entire peoples have revived. In our particular case, a figurative return to our own land will give us the physical and moral health necessary for recovering confidence in the future. It is a consolation to note that for some years the Mexican conscience has steadfastly sought true national introspection. But unfortunately the examination of our conscience has not been undertaken with the rigor, depth, and objectivity that the case requires. How can people be impartial judges in questions which affect their personal interests and partisan passions? Human experience shows that an interest or a passion cannot be defeated except by a greater interest or a greater passion. Therefore, we shall be incapable of knowing ourselves as individuals or as a people until we can overcome our little passions with the great passion for truth. This is one of the ways of disinterested love for persons and things, whether real or ideal. Love of knowledge was best symbolized by the *eros* of Plato. In order to develop, this love of knowledge must become a fundamental concern of Mexican education.

The man who has this passion for truth will have also the indispensable moral strength to carry out a merciless analysis of himself, overcoming the weaknesses that might prevent a clear and objective view of his interior world. But the achievement of his high mental vantage point, from which we can look at things not as if we were extraterrestrial beings, but merely intelligent spectators, would not suffice to probe the inner recesses of reality. To this moral discipline an intellectual discipline must be added. It would be senseless to insist on this point if there were not a trend of opinion obviously favorable to scientific learning as the absolute prerequisite for an investigation of Mexican problems. A false concept of science seems to support this dangerous error.

Indeed, it is an exceedingly vulgar concept, the result of ignorance of superficiality, in which one can hear the distant echo of positivism; it is the fallacy that knowledge is acquired simply by opening up the five senses to reality. In this way of thinking, the intellectual function becomes subservient to the scientific process, to the extent that experience by its own virtue has the magic capacity of converting itself into ideas. Scientific research is reduced to a matter of accumulating facts, as if gathering them up to a certain amount were sufficient to cause scientific knowledge to burst into light. The chauvinistic mentality supposes, since science is European, that all intellectual preparation must constitute a bias in the scholar's mind, and accordingly blinds him to its native originality.

Therefore it is not surprising that such a theory of science should encourage the notion of creating a "Mexican science" which would admit no debt to the principles of universal science.

This is why in Mexico the true theory of science must be assimilated, because the popularized image that we have just described is no more than its caricature. Scientific research is impracticable if it does not confront reality with a prejudgment. Prejudgment is what guides the attention toward a given phenomenon; to prejudgment we owe our discovery of the relationship among different facts and perceive the continuity of a single process in events of diverse appearance. In a word, prejudgment is what within the medium of experience leads us to the scientific idea. But one cannot acquire these prejudgments without learning, before the actual investigation, the principles of the science in question.

To believe that we can develop in Mexico an original culture unrelated to the rest of the world constitutes a total misunderstanding of what culture is. The commonest notion is that culture is pure *knowledge*. One fails to recognize the truth that it is rather a function of the spirit destined to humanize reality. But it is clear that this function is not spontaneous. Education, then, develops in the mind of each individual the wealth of culture already accumulated. Once that education is properly oriented, it should not simply work toward an increase in knowledge, but toward the transformation of the latter into a spiritual capacity to comprehend and elaborate the substance of every meaningful experience. Only by extracting from traditional culture its most subtle essence and making it a basic element of our spirit, can we speak of an "assimilation of culture."

Each spirit needs for its development the support and stimulus of a universal culture. It is therefore evident that the good intention of examining Mexican conscience may come to naught if we isolate it from the outside world, closing our doors to every possible foreign influence, for then we shall be left in the dark. The two extreme options in educational method are equally injurious to the future of national culture. One is to ignore Mexican reality altogether, which is what happened during the past century, so as to obtain a European culture at the possible cost of destroying our own ideas. The other is to deny categorically the significance of European culture, in the utopian hope of creating a Mexican culture which of course could not grow out of nothing. We shall never be able to decipher the mysteries of our being unless we can illuminate its depths with a guiding ideal that can come only from Europe.

When we reach some understanding of the idiosyncrasies of our national soul, we will have a standard to guide us through the complexities of European culture—which contains many important elements that are of no interest to us. Only by scientific knowledge of the Mexican mind will we have a basis for a systematic exploration of the maze of European culture and a separation of those elements which can be assimilated to our environment. Up to now, fashion has been the only arbiter for evaluating the heterogeneous products of spiritual life in the Old World. Lacking precise data on the nature of our soul, we have also lacked reference points for acquiring a Mexican perspective of European phenomena. The idea of selecting conscientiously and methodically the forms of European culture potentially adaptable to our own environment has never occurred to us. There is no doubt that such a system is possible, on the basis of choosing certain instinctive affinities that persuade our race to prefer certain cultural aspects over others. The hard thing is to distinguish between genuine congenialities and certain misguided interests which have nevertheless drawn our attention to culture. With the exception of an insignificant minority, Mexicans up to now have not cared about getting to the bottom of culture; instead, they have been content to stand aside, dazzled by its brilliant outward effects.

In the future Mexico must have a Mexican culture, but we have no illusions about its being original or unique. By Mexican culture we mean universal culture made over into *our own*, the kind that can coexist with us and appropriately express our spirit. Curiously enough, the only way open to us—in order to shape this Mexican culture—is to continue learning about European culture. Our race is a branch of a European race. Our history has unfolded in a European manner. But we have not succeeded in forming our own culture, because we have separated culture and life. We no longer want an artificial culture that lives like a hothouse flower; we do not want a false Europeanism.

It is therefore essential to approach our problem in that modern spirit which by reiteration has become trite: to relate culture to life. As far as scientific knowledge is concerned, it is necessary to correlate continually the study of universal scientific principles with a specific analysis of our own reality. One reason for the hostility toward culture is the Mexican's individualistic character, resistant to all authority and to every standard. Accordingly, to accept the idea of radical "nationalism" would be tantamount to perpetuating the spiritual crisis; it would mean taking the path of least resistance, so as to continue facile achievements, superficial observations, and fragmentary studies devoid of scientific rigor. To give substance to our spiritual work of the future, it will be necessary to prepare our young people in schools and universities by means of an austere program basically oriented toward discipline of the will and intelligence. Concrete knowledge is what should least concern us with regard to culture. The critically important thing for Mexico now is to glean from culture as much as it can of intellectual and moral discipline. When this is achieved it will be possible to show that even those who reach the highest pinnacles of spiritual life need not, in their haughtiness, succumb to the error of rejecting native values. On the contrary, their enlightenment will permit them to comprehend and judge Mexican life more effectively.

Jorge J. E. Gracia
(b. 1942)

Jorge Gracia was born in Camagüey, Cuba, and immigrated to the United States in 1960, studying philosophy at Wheaton College, where he received a BA, and then pursuing advanced study at the University of Chicago, where in 1966 he received his master's degree in philosophy. Given his interest in medieval philosophy, he then attended the Pontifical Institute of Mediaeval Studies in Toronto, Canada, where he received an MSL in 1970. In 1971 he received his doctorate in philosophy at the University of Toronto. During this period he also studied at the Institut d'Estudis Catalans in Barcelona, Spain.

Apart from numerous articles in professional journals in Latin America, Europe, and the United States, Gracia has published many books ranging in topics from technical issues of medieval philosophy (*Introduction to the Problem of Individuation in the Early Middle Ages*, 1984), to hermeneutics (*A Theory of Textuality: the Logic and Epistemology*, 1995 and *Texts: Ontological Status, Identity, Author, Audience*, 1996), the relation between history and philosophy (*Philosophy and Its History: Issues in Philosophical Historiography*, 1992), and metaphysics (*Metaphysics and Its Task: The Search for the Categorial Foundation of Knowledge*, 1999). His work *Individuality: An Essay on the Foundations of Metaphysics* (1988) was awarded the Findley Prize in Metaphysics by the Metaphysical Society of America.

Gracia is active not only in publishing but in serving the philosophical communitythrough his work on editorial boards (among others, *Revista Latinoamericana de Filosofia* and *Cuadernos de Ética*) and the committees of various professional associations (for example, the American Philosophical Association's Committee for Hispanics, of which he was the founding chair from 1991 to 1995). He currently holds the Samuel P. Capen Chair in the Department of Philosophy at the State University of New York, Buffalo.

His devotion to Latin American philosophy is demonstrated by many articles and edited collections and special journal issues. He collaborated with Argentine philosopher Risieri Frondizi to produce a representative anthology of Latin American philosophy *El hombre y los valores en la filosofía latinoamericana del siglo XX: Antología* (1975) of which the current anthology is an expanded and translated version. With Iván Jaksić, Gracia published another anthology, *Filosofía e identidad cultural en América Latina* (1988). With Eduardo Rabossi (Argentina), Enrique Villanueva (Mexico), and Marcelo Dascal (Brazil/Israel), he edited *Philosophical Analysis in Latin America* (1984). This collection showed that the tradition of philosophical analysis associated with Anglo-American philosophy has strong roots in Latin America as well. One of the most characteristic contributions of Gracia's philosophical activity is the way in which it serves as a crucial bridge between the Anglo and Latin American philosophical worlds. His work has served to open the field of Latin American philosophy to scholars in the United States.

His most recent publications deal with the philosophical dimensions of the problems facing Hispanics/Latinos in the United States. With Pablo De Greiff, he edited the collection *Hispanics/Latinos in the United States: Ethnicity, Race, and Rights* (2000). The selection included here is from his recent book *Hispanic Identity: A Philosophical Perspective* (2001).

In this selection, Gracia argues that the terms "Latin American" and "Latin America" are problematic and so is the term "Latino/a." He argues in favor of the use of the term "Hispanic" to reveal a social and historical identity. According to Gracia, the term "Hispanic" captures an important historical reality and allows us to speak of a common identity among all Hispanics "without imposing a homogenous conception of who or what we are." Moreover, it permits multiplicity and development, recognizes diversity, respects differences, acknowledges a common past, and "prevents totalizing, homogenizing attitudes that could be used to oppress and dominate." Gracia uses a conceptual and historical analysis to argue for the position that the concept of Hispanic identity arises not from common properties or political needs but rather from a historical reality "which is founded on diversity and *mestizaje.*" He argues that the conception of Hispanic identity he proposes is not hegemonic in that "it does not rule out other identities," but gives rise to a view of identity that is open and pluralistic.

What Makes Hispanics/Latinos Who We Are? The Key to Our Unity in Diversity

Four different types of objections [are frequently] raised against the use of ethnic names for Hispanics/Latinos, but their general thrust [is] the same: ethnic names are inaccurate and dangerous. One way to answer these objections, then, albeit indirectly, is to show that at least one of these names is neither inaccurate nor dangerous. This seems to be an effective and economical way to proceed, and I have adopted it [here]. The features which make the use of ethnic names inaccurate and dangerous are that they supposedly homogenize what is not homogeneous and imply common characteristics when there are none. The view I present here avoids both homogenization and the false identification of common characteristics. This in turn should help avoid the dangers of oppression, domination, discrimination, marginalization, and the inequitable distribution of resources.

This way of proceeding is quite specific insofar as it deals with particular objections and proposes a way to understand the notion of Hispanic. There are also general considerations which argue in favor of the adoption of ethnic names by those named by them. Insofar as they tell us something about those they name, ethnic names both identify them and have the power to mold attitudes toward them. Epistemologically, they convey information about those they name; ontologically, they help establish their identity. These can be harmful to the degree that ethnic names are used to stereotype, objectify, and disempower. But they can also be beneficial when ethnic names are the source of knowledge and empowerment.

From Jorge J. E. Gracia, *Hispanic/Latino Identity: A Philosophical Perspective*, chap. 3, "What Makes Us Who We Are? The Key to Our Unity in Diversity" (Oxford: Blackwell, 2000), pp. 45–69. Reprinted by permission of the author.

Whether the use of ethnic names is harmful or beneficial depends to a large extent on at least three factors: (1) those who do the naming and set the concomitantly required conditions; (2) the positive or negative character of those conditions; and (3) the breadth and rigidity with which the conditions are understood. Let us look at these in more detail.

The first factor is important because it is one thing to adopt a name to identify ourselves, and quite another to be named and have our identity defined by someone else. Note that I say "define" rather than "establish" or "discover." I do this because, for present purposes, I want to stay away from the controversy between social constructivists and nonconstructivists. The first argue that identities are the result of social construction; the latter, that they are the result of events outside the power of societies and, therefore, discovered rather than constructed. By using "define" I intend to separate myself from either one of these extreme positions. Indeed, my view is that group and ethnic identities are the result of both social construction and factors outside the power of societies. Now, leaving aside this issue, the point that needs to be emphasized is that to adopt a name and define one's identity is both a sign of power and an act of empowerment. It is a sign of power because those without power do not even have the prerogative of doing it; others establish how they are to be called and who they are. In this, those without power are at the mercy of those who establish what is important or pertinent in them. This has serious consequences, for social perceptions change social realities. How one is perceived determines how one is treated, and this in turn eventually affects who one is. Social perception is a factor in social change. Our individual or group identity depends on others.

To adopt a name and define one's identity is, moreover, an act of empowerment because it limits the power of others to name and identify us. It tells others: Look, I am who I am, and not who you think or want me to be. I tell you who I am, and you have to honor this; you have no power to tell me who I am, only I have such power. Indeed, it is not surprising that Yahweh ("I am who I am") is the name God chose for himself in the Bible.

The second important factor in the adoption of ethnic names is the positive or negative character of the name and the conditions associated with the identity it defines. Obviously, a name whose connotations are negative can do much harm, whereas one with positive connotations can do much good. But keep in mind that the adoption or reassertion of names with bad connotations by groups who have suffered discrimination can be a sign of defiance and an act of empowerment when accompanied with an appropriate understanding of the name. This is, for example, what has happened with "Jew." Thirty years ago, this term carried with it all sorts of bad connotations among non-Jews, and for these reasons it was avoided by those opposed to anti-Semitism, whether Jewish or not. Today, however, the use of the term has become a sign of power and pride.

The third important factor in the adoption of ethnic names is the rigidity and breadth with which the identity conditions they define are understood. Part of the reason that the adoption of an ethnic name is empowering is that it liberates those who adopt it from a relation of dependence with those who do, or may, impose other names on them. Naming ourselves and defining our identity may also imply liberation insofar as it makes explicit prejudices that may hinder us from acting in various ways, opening the way to discard those prejudices and change the way we act. Knowing who we are can change not only the way others think about us, and even how we think about ourselves, but also the course of our actions in the future. But there is also a danger: A name and the identity conditions it implies can function as limiting factors and as sources of conflict if they are conceived too narrowly and restrictively. To be something may be taken as making it impossible to be something else. Recall the ancient Parmenidean conundrum: What is is, and what is not is not. If a group is conceived as having certain abilities and limitations, this may be used to close avenues of development and growth. For this reason, the value of an ethnic name and the conditions of identity it implies will depend on the breadth of those conditions and the rigidity with which they are understood.

In short, then, the use of ethnic names and the definition of the conditions of group identity can in principle be beneficial for the groups in question. It is generally beneficial if three conditions are met: if the naming and defining is done by the group; if the conditions used in the definition are positive; and if the conditions are neither narrow nor rigid. To this extent, the use of ethnic names and the corresponding self-identification are important insofar as they help establish self-meaning and direction. Otherwise, the use of ethnic names and the definition of the conditions of the group's identity can do more harm than good. It is my claim [here] that the name I propose for Hispanics/Latinos and the way I conceive our identity are beneficial if measured by the requirements noted.

THE ARGUMENT FOR HISPANIC IDENTITY

In order to support my thesis, I need to [bring out into the open] an assumption that [is] behind the discussion of [identity]. According to this assumption, the effective use of a common name requires the identification of an essence, that is, a property or set of properties which characterizes the things called by the name. If there is no essence that can be identified, the name is meaningless, merely a sound without substance, and therefore must be abandoned lest it should cause confusion.

Joined to this is another assumption frequently made by those who discuss identity. This is that a proper identity corresponding to a name should involve both consistency and purity. To have an identity requires properties which constitute a coherent whole and are themselves unmixed.

The view that the effective use of names requires a property, or a set of properties, that can be identified has been effectively challenged in contemporary philosophy. This does not mean that there are no names whose use is justified by an essence. It means only that not all names are of the same sort and, therefore, their use need not be justified in this way. Some names are such that they can be effectively used even when there is no property, or set of properties, they connote. Wittgenstein gave the example of "game." This term is effectively used in English and yet, when we try to identify even one common property to all games that also distinguishes them from other things, we can never find it. Some games use balls, some do not; some games give pleasure, some do not; some games take a long time, some do not; some games require concentration, some do not; some games involve physical effort, some do not; and so on.

We can grant, then, that there are no common properties to all those people whom we wish to call Hispanics, and yet that does not mean that the use of the term is unjustified or meaningless. In general, my point is that there is a way to understand the concept of Hispanic that allows us to speak meaningfully of, and refer effectively to, Hispanics, even when the people named by it do not share any property in common at all times and places. More particularly, my thesis is that the concept of Hispanic should be understood historically, that is, as a concept that involves historical relations. Hispanics are the group of people comprised by the inhabitants of the countries of the Iberian peninsula after 1492 and what were to become the colonies of those countries after the encounter between Iberia and America took place, and by descendants of these people who live in other countries (e.g., the United States) but preserve some link to those people. It excludes the population of other countries in the world and the inhabitants of Iberia and Latin America before 1492 because, beginning in the year of the encounter, the Iberian countries and their colonies in America developed a web of historical connections which continues to this day and which separates these people from others.

This group of people must be understood as forming a unit which goes beyond political, territorial, linguistic, cultural, racial, or genetic frontiers. It is not even necessary that the members of the group name themselves in any particular way or have a consciousness of their identity. Some of them may in fact consider themselves Hispanic and even have a consciousness of their identity as a group, but it is not necessary that all of them do. Knowledge does not determine being. What ties them together, and separates them from others, is history and the particular events of that history rather than the consciousness of that history; a unique web of changing historical relations supplies their unity.

Obviously, historical relations tend to generate common properties, but such properties might not go beyond certain periods, regions, or subgroups of people. There can be unity without community. A may follow B, and B may follow C, and C may follow D, implying a connection between A and D even when A has nothing in common with D. Let me explain this further. Consider the case of A, B, C, and D. A has a relation (*aRb*) with B; B has a relation (*bRc*) with C; and C has a relation (*cRd*) with D. But there are no direct relations between A and C or D, or between B and D. (In order to simplify matters I assume that the relation between A and B is the same as the relation between B and A, and so on with the others.) Now, the mentioned relations allow us to group A, B, C, and D even though there is no property common to all of them, not even a relation that unites them directly. There is, however, a relation between A and B, another between B and C, and another between C and D. At the same time, these relations allow us to separate the group ABCD from other groups, say MNOP, because none of the members of ABCD has relations with the members of MNOP, or because the relations between A, B, C, and D are different from the relations between M, N, O, and P. To group implies to unite and separate, and to unite and separate are made easy when it is done in terms of properties common to all the members of a group, but it is not necessary that it be done on the basis of such properties. It can be done on the basis of properties or relations that are not common to all the members of the group as long as there are relations or properties that tie each member of the group with at least one other member of the group.

This is the kind of unity that I submit justifies the notion of Hispanic. We are speaking here of a group of people who have no common elements considered as a whole. Their unity is not a unity of commonality; it is a historical unity founded on relations. King John II of Portugal has nothing in common with me, but both of us are tied by a series of events that relate us and separate us from Queen Elizabeth II and Martin Luther King. There is no need to find properties common to all Hispanics in order to classify them as Hispanics. What ties us is the same kind of thing that ties the members of a family, as Wittgenstein would say. There may not be any common properties to all of us, but nonetheless we belong to the same group because we are historically related, as a father is to a daughter, an aunt to a nephew, and grandparents to grandchildren. Wittgenstein's metaphor of family resemblance is particularly appropriate in this case, for the history of Hispanics is a history of a group of people, a community united by historical events. But the metaphor of the family must be taken broadly to avoid any understanding of it as requiring genetic ties. One does not need to be tied genetically to the other members of a family to be a member of the family. Indeed, the very foundation of a family, marriage, takes place between people who are added to a family through contract, not genesis. And in-laws become members of families indirectly, again not through genesis. This means that the very notion of resemblance used by Wittgenstein is misleading insofar as it appears to require a genetic connection which in fact is not required at all. It also means that any requirements of coherence and purity do not apply. Families are not coherent wholes composed of pure elements. They include contradictory elements and involve mixing. Indeed, contradiction and mixing seem to be of the essence, for a living unity is impossible without contradiction and heterogeneity. We are related clusters of persons with different, and sometimes incompatible, characteristics, and purity of any kind is not one of our necessary conditions. This is why families are in a constant process of change and adaptation. My claim is that this is how we should understand ourselves as Hispanics.

Now, families are formed by marriages. So we are entitled to ask: Is there a point in history where our Hispanic family came to be? Since our community includes not only the inhabitants of the Iberian peninsula, but also those of the parts of America appropriated by Iberian countries, we must find a point in history when we came together, and this, I propose, is the encounter of Iberia and America. It makes no sense to speak of Hispanics before the encounter in 1492. Our family first came into being precisely because of the events which the encounter unleashed.

In spite of all that has been said, one can still question the need or advantage of using the category "Hispanic." If there are no common properties to all Hispanics, what can we get out of an account of Hispanics that is not already present in accounts of the countries and the peoples that are gathered under this category? In short, by using this term can we get to know anything that we do not already know through the study of, say, the Spanish, Catalan, Mexican, Argentinian, and Hispanic American peoples? My answer to this question is that in this way we understand better a historical reality which otherwise would escape us.

The study of people involves the study of their relations, how they influence each other. In particular, a historical account must pay careful attention to the events and figures that played important roles in history, avoiding artificial divisions in the account. Keeping this in mind, I submit that the notion of Hispanic represents, better than any other, the people of the Iberian nations and of Latin American countries that were former Iberian colonies, as well as the descendants of these people who live elsewhere but maintain close ties to them, because it emphasizes the fact that there is a historical reality that unites us. To divide Hispanics in terms of political, territorial, racial, linguistic, ethnic, genetic, or cultural criteria results in the loss of many dimensions of this historical reality.

The concept of Hispanic allows us to see aspects of our reality that would otherwise be missed. They would be missed to a great extent because the conceptual frameworks used would be either too broad or too narrow to allow us to see them. Earlier I pointed out that concepts are windows to reality. The concept of Hispanic is indeed a window to the history of a chapter in universal human history, our history. In the vast panorama of humankind, it introduces a frame that directs the attention of the observer toward something that, under different conditions, would be given little attention, or missed altogether, because of the vastness of the view. Thanks to it, we see more of less. "Hispanic" opens for us a window to ourselves which yields knowledge we would otherwise not have. At the same time, it allows us to notice things which we would miss if we used narrower concepts such as Mexican, Argentinian, Spanish, and so on. These are also windows, but like any window, they reveal something by excluding something else. By using these narrower categories, we would be losing a larger view. The use of "Hispanics," then, reveals something unique by narrowing and widening our view at the same time.

This does not mean that the use of the term should be exclusionary. To speak and think about Hispanics should not prevent us from speaking and thinking in other ways as well, that is, from using other principles of organization, and therefore from including the consideration of other unities. For these other organizations and unities will surely explain, emphasize, and reveal other facts which, under different arrangements, would go unnoticed. We need not look out only through one window. My point is that the perspective based on the notion I have proposed explains, emphasizes, and reveals aspects of our reality which would otherwise be neglected. I do not mean to exclude other arrangements. Indeed, there are many other enlightening ways of thinking about the reality comprised under the term "Hispanic." We could think in regional terms, such as Latin American, Iberian, Central American, and South American; in linguistic terms, such as Quechua, Castilian, and Basque; in political terms, such as Brazilian or Mexican; and so on. And all these would, if the notions are historically warranted, reveal to us aspects of the Hispanic reality which, under different conceptions, would be overlooked.

In short, my proposal is to adopt "Hispanic" to refer to us: the people of Iberia, Latin America, and some segments of the population in the United States, after 1492, and to the descendants of these peoples anywhere in the world as long as they preserve close ties to them. Moreover, I have argued that the use of this term does not imply that there are any properties common to all of us throughout history. Its use is justified rather by a web of concrete historical relations that ties us together, and simultaneously separates us from other peoples.

Note, moreover, that the use of "Hispanic" is not intended to reflect just that some persons choose to call themselves Hispanics. Applying a contemporary name theory to ethnic names, it is sometimes argued that self-naming (or self-identification, as it is often put) is both a necessary and sufficient condition of the appropriate use of an ethnic name. If I choose to call myself Hispanic, others should call me so. But, in fact, self-naming is neither necessary nor sufficient in this way. It is not sufficient because the use of a name calls for a rationale of its use. There must be a reason why I choose to call myself Hispanic. And it is not necessary because, even if I do not choose to call myself Hispanic, it may be appropriate to call me so. Indeed, there are names we reject even though we deserve them. Not many criminals, for example, would be willing to call themselves criminals even though the epithet may be appropriate. The theory I have proposed does not face these objections for, although it does not accept that there are common properties to all Hispanics at all times and in all places, it allows for common properties at certain times and places arising from particular historical relations. My view, then, does not suffer from emptiness or circularity.

Now we must go back to the question of identity and see the implications of what has been said concerning the use and understanding of "Hispanic" for this question. . . . [I]dentity and identification [have] to do with sets of necessary and sufficient conditions which could be understood achronically, synchronically, or diachronically. Achronically, the set of conditions in question would make explicit why something is whatever it is irrespective of time; synchronically, the set of conditions would reveal why something is whatever it is at a particular time; and diachronically, the set of conditions would specify what makes something whatever it is at two or more different times. The achronic identity of Hispanics, then, involves the properties which make Hispanics who we are, apart from any consideration of time; synchronic identity involves such properties at a particular time; and diachronic identity has to do with such properties at two (or more) different times.

The question is: Are there such conditions? Does it make sense to talk about an achronic Hispanic identity, a synchronic Hispanic identity, or a diachronic Hispanic identity? It should be clear that, achronically and strictly, it makes no sense to speak of any set of necessary and sufficient conditions which apply to all Hispanics, for as I have argued, Hispanics do not share any properties in common which they must have and which distinguish them from others. Nonetheless, it does make sense to speak of an achronic Hispanic identity in the sense mentioned earlier, based on historical, familial relations, rather than on relations of commonality.

Synchronically, again, the issue is not simple. There is no reason why, in principle, all Hispanics could not have some properties in common which tie them together and distinguish them from others at some particular time. But the reality appears different. For Hispanic ties, even at a particular time, tend to be familial and historical rather than across the board. Every Hispanic group is tied to some other Hispanic group, but no Hispanic group is tied to all other Hispanic groups in the same way.

Finally, diachronically, a similar phenomenon occurs. There are easily discernible resemblances among those we count as Hispanics at different times, but those resemblances tend to be historical and familial, rather than based on common properties. Throughout our history, Hispanics display the kind of unity characteristic of families rather than the unity characteristic of sets or classes based on shared properties.

In this, Hispanics appear to be different from Asians and Asian Americans, Africans and African Americans, and Amerindians and Native Americans. Asians are, like Hispanics, divided into many subgroups—Koreans, Chinese, Japanese, Malaysians, and so on—but unlike Hispanics, these groups do not easily form a historical family in the way Hispanics do. Indeed, rather than one family, they appear to be clusters of families only occasionally related to each other. And the same can be said about Africans and Amerindians. Apart from superficial and controversial unifying factors, such as territory and race, Africans and Amerindians seem to constitute clusters of largely independent groups.

The situation of Hispanics is also different from the situation of Asian Americans, African Americans, and Native Americans. Asian Americans generally reflect the diversity of their origins and cultures without a strong historical tie to unite them. In this case, then, a common name is particularly artificial. The situation with African Americans is just the reverse. The Africans who were brought into the United States were as diverse as the Asians; they came from different parts of Africa, from different nations, and from different cultures. But here they were forced to homogenize. Culturally, they were beaten into a pulp to such an extent that some of their most idiosyncratic characteristics were obliterated, or nearly obliterated: their language, values, religion, and so on. The case of Native Americans resembles that of Asians, for this group is composed of subgroups which have very little to do with each other except in a remote origin. What do Seminoles, Mohicans, Apaches, and Pueblos have to do with each other? The lumping together of all these under the label "Native Americans" is just as artificial as the lumping of Vietnamese, Chinese, Koreans, and other groups who live in the United States, under the label "Asian Americans."

In contrast with Asian Americans and Native Americans, Hispanics have a historical tie that unites them and, in contrast with African Americans, they lack the homogenization that characterizes them to a large extent. History ties Hispanics together in a way that is missing in the cases of Asians, Asian Americans, Africans, Amerindians, and Native Americans. There is a sense in which Hispanics all over the world belong together that does not apply to Asians, Africans, and Amerindians. There are perhaps stronger physical ties between all Africans, including African Americans, and between all Asians, including Asian Americans, and between all Amerindians, including Native Americans, than between Hispanics, including Hispanic Americans. But there is a historical and familial element which is absent in Asians, Africans, and Amerindians which is strongly evident among all Hispanics.

TWO INITIAL OBJECTIONS

There are at least two serious objections to the view I have proposed that I must take up. The first attacks my view by arguing that it does not do justice to the fact that Hispanics are, indeed, different from other groups, and that this difference cannot be explained merely in terms of historical connections. Hispanics are different from the Chinese, the French, and certainly Anglo-Saxon Americans, so the argument goes. We can tell who is and who is not Hispanic and we are quite aware of the differences that separate us from other groups. A good explanation of these differences must refer to deep ways of thinking and acting. It will not do to argue, as I have done, that there are actually no properties that Hispanics have in common, for if this were the case, then it would not be possible, as it in fact is, to tell us apart from others. Of course, uncovering such common properties might be difficult, or even factually impossible at times, but that does not entail that such properties do not exist. That those which have been suggested thus far do not work does not entail that the task is logically impossible.

The answer to this objection is that I do not claim that there are no common properties to Hispanics and, therefore, that we can never in fact tell Hispanics apart from other groups. Rather, I have argued that there are no properties common to all Hispanics at all times and in all places that are discernible. This view does not prevent one from holding that there are properties common to some Hispanics at all times and in all places, at all times and in some places, or at some times and in all places; or properties common to all Hispanics at all times and in some places, or at some times and in all places. Nor can my position be construed as implying even that there are no common properties to Hispanics at all times and places. My point is only that there are no properties which can be shown to be common to all Hispanics at all times and in all places. Indeed, I believe there are properties common to Hispanics at some times and in some places and it is precisely such properties that serve to identify us at those times and in those places. At every time and in every period, some Hispanics have properties that tie them among themselves and distinguish them from other groups, but these properties do not necessarily extend beyond those times and places and, indeed, they do not need to extend beyond them to account for our identity and distinction from other groups.

At any particular time and place, there are familial relations that Hispanics share and which both distinguish us from non-Hispanics and are the source of properties which also can be used to distinguish us from non-Hispanics. Particular physical characteristics, cultural traits, language, and so on, can serve to distinguish Hispanics in certain contexts, although they cannot function as criteria of distinction and identification everywhere and at all times. In a place where all and only Hispanics speak Spanish, for example, the language can function as a sufficient criterion of Hispanic identification even if, in other places, it does not. Likewise, in a society or region where all and only Hispanics have a certain skin color, or a certain religion, and so on, these properties can be used to pick out Hispanics, even if elsewhere there are Hispanics who do not share these properties. Even though Hispanics do not constitute a homogeneous group, then, particular properties can be used to determine who counts as Hispanic in particular contexts. Hispanic identity does not entail a set of common properties which constitutes an essence, but this does not stand in the way of identification. We can determine who counts as Hispanic in context. Just as we generally and easily can tell a game from something that is not a game, we can tell a Hispanic from a non-Hispanic in most instances. But there will be, as with games, borderline cases and cases which overlap.

In the case of Hispanics in the United States in particular, there are added reasons that facilitate an answer to the question, Who counts as Hispanic? Two of these may be considered. First, we are treated as a homogeneous group by European Americans and African Americans; and second, even though Hispanics do not constitute a homogeneous group, we are easily contrasted with European and African Americans because we do not share many of the features commonly associated with these groups. Our identification in the United States, then, is not just possible, but relatively unproblematic.

This clarification of my position serves also to answer the second objection mentioned earlier. This objection argues that the criterion for Hispanic identity I have proposed is too weak because it could describe a situation in which only a single property is shared by any two individuals, and that would not be enough to set the group apart from other groups. Consider two groups of, say, six individuals each which we wish to distinguish from each other: Group 1 is composed of members A, B, C, D, E, and F. And group 2 is composed of members G, H, I, J, K, and L. Now, according to the view I have proposed, there would be nothing wrong with a situation in which each of the members of each group had only two properties. For the first group the properties would be as follows (in parentheses): A(a, b), B(b, c), C(c, d), D(d, e), E(e, f), and F(f, g). For the second group the properties would be as follows: G(g, h), H(h, i), I(i, j), J(j, k), K(k, l), and L(l, m). Now, the point to note is that the last member of the first group has one property in common with the first member of the second group. The significance of this fact is that this makes the break between the two groups arbitrary. That is, there is no more reason to end the first group with F and to begin the second group with G than to end the first group with B and begin the second group with C. True, the set of properties of the first group (a, b, c, d, e, f, and g) is different from the set of properties (g, h, i, j, k, and l) of the second. But the fact that there is at least one common property (g) between the first and the second group makes the break into the two groups arbitrary, for we could say that the first group, rather than being composed of A, B, C, D, E, and F, is composed of A, B, C, D, and E; and the second group, rather than being composed of G, H, I, J, K, and L, is composed of F, G, H, I, J, K, and L. And, of course, other combinations and breakdowns would also be possible.

The situation is even more serious when one considers that in reality the members of any group, and certainly the members of a group such as Hispanics, share not one, but more than one property with members of other groups that presumably we want to distinguish, as groups, from the group of Hispanics. In short, the view I have presented, so the objection goes, is too weak.

One way to answer this second objection is to modify the view I have proposed as follows. Instead of speaking of members of a group, each of which shares at least one property with at least one other member of the group, propose a set of properties several of which are shared by each member of the group. We could call this position the Common-Bundle View. Say that we identify a group with six members: A, B, C, D, E, and F. And let us propose a set of six properties also: a, b, c, d, e, and f. According to this view each member of the group would have several of these properties as, for instance: A (a, b), B(a, b, e, f), C(c, d, f), D(b, c, d, e, f), E(a, e), and F(b, e, f). The advantages of this answer should be obvious. Here we have a stronger position and one that can solve the weaknesses pointed out earlier. Clearly, now we have a tighter bond between the members of the group we want to distinguish, and we can also easily set the group apart from other groups by simply showing how individuals who are not members of the group do not have any, or a sufficient number, of the set of properties used to define the group.

Now let us apply the Common-Bundle View to Hispanics and say that there is a set of twelve properties several of which all Hispanics have (the selection presented here is purely arbitrary and should be given no significance): speaker of Iberian language, Iberian descent, born in Iberia, born in Latin America, Amerindian descent, African descent, citizen of Iberian country, citizen of Latin American country, resident in Iberian country, resident in Latin American country, Iberian surname, lover of Latin American music. Using this criterion, Juan de los Palostes qualifies as Hispanic because he is of Iberian descent, was born in Latin America, and speaks Spanish. His daughters also qualify because they speak Spanish, are of Iberian descent, have Spanish surnames, and love Latin music, although they were not born and do not reside in an Iberian or a Latin American country. And some children from Anglo-American fathers and Latin American mothers who do not speak Spanish and were born in the United States can also be considered Hispanic because of their partial Latin American descent and their love of Latin American music. At the same time we can distinguish this group from those who might have one of these properties, say that they speak an Iberian language or were born in Latin America, but do not have any other. Moreover, it would exclude, for example, children of Anglo-Saxon missionaries in Latin America and African Americans who have learned Portuguese in school.

Clearly, adopting the Common-Bundle View is a promising way of answering the objection against my original position, the Historical-Family View. And there is in fact no reason why it cannot be integrated into my view, except that, upon further reflection, there are problems with it. I see three difficulties in particular that make me hesitate. First, there is the problem of determining the particular set of properties we should identify as pertinent. How and on what bases do we decide on the set of properties which Hispanics share? Indeed, even in the rather innocuous list I provided as an illustration, there are some properties that are bound to create difficulties. For example, why should the child of Anglo-Saxon American missionaries who was born in Colombia, holds Colombian citizenship, and speaks some Spanish, not be considered Hispanic? And we might keep in mind the problems raised earlier concerning political, territorial, cultural, racial, and other such properties.

A second problem with this way of answering the objection that should also be obvious from the example is that, even if we were able to settle on a satisfactory list of properties some of which all Hispanics share, we have no easy way of determining the number of these properties required for someone to qualify as Hispanic. Two? Three? Four? Twenty? And does it make a difference which properties are involved? In the earlier example, does it make a difference whether we include love of Latin American music and Amerindian descent or not? Indeed, are two of some kinds of properties sufficient (e.g., lover of Latin American music and Amerindian descent), whereas of other kinds three or four are needed? Obviously, this complicates matters tremendously, and it is not clear on what basis a decision can be reached.

The third problem is still more vexing. It has to do with the fact that, even if we were able to settle on a set of properties and on the number that need to be shared, this could turn out to be of use only for the past and the present and not the future. We do not know what properties will be pertinent for Hispanic identity in the future. The set of properties which Hispanics share could change, and so could the proportion of properties necessary for qualification. After all, we are speaking of a historical reality, and historical realities are in a constant process of change. Our identity is flexible and subject to evolution and transformation. We can easily illustrate this point with a reference to language. Suffice it to say that the English spoken in the Middle Ages would be unintelligible to an American today, and yet we still consider it to be English. So, whatever we think pertinent for Hispanic identity in the past and present could in time change. If tigers can be bred to lose their stripes, there is no reason why Hispanics could not become quite different than they are today or were in the past.

In short, the view we have been discussing as an answer to the second objection is simply too unhistorical and inflexible. There cannot be a fixed list of properties in which Hispanics share. There can be, of course, a list at any time, but the list must always remain open-ended. This is why it is still better to think in terms of history and family ties rather than in terms of a list of properties. Hispanics are part of a historical reality and, therefore, the criteria to identify them must take cognizance of that fact. Note that I began by allowing the possibility that in principle there could be such a list of properties even if we cannot identify it. Now, however, it should be clear that I am not willing to allow the possibility of such a list even in principle. This does not mean, however, that Hispanics cannot be identified as such in particular contexts. Even though there are no essential properties, there can be criteria in context. Consider, for example, that knowing how to swim is not an indication of being human. But in a place where only humans know how to swim and all humans know how to swim, knowing how to swim can function effectively as a criterion of being human.

ANSWERS TO [OTHER] OBJECTIONS

The view I have presented here takes care, I believe, of [many commonly voiced] objections against the use of "Hispanic" . . . but it does not answer all the objections [that have been] raised. Indeed, it does not deal with [one of] the most serious objections that [has been] presented against it: "Hispanic" is repugnant because of what Iberians, and particularly Spaniards, did to Amerindian populations, and it is particularly repugnant to Hispanic Americans from the southwest of the United States because it is the term used by an ethnocentric and racist group to distinguish itself from *mestizos* and Mexican Americans; "Hispanic" unfairly privileges Spanish, Iberian, and European elements to the detriment of Amerindian and African ones; "Hispanic" perpetuates or tends to perpetuate the submission of America to Europe, and particularly of Latin America to Spain; and, finally, "Hispanic" is a deprecatory term whose use serves only to degrade us in the eyes of others and to put obstacles in the way of our social acceptance and development.

These objections, although appearing very powerful prima facie, when examined more carefully reveal that they are based in part on misinformation, prejudice, and ignorance. Moreover, they result in the same sort of bias and discrimination they are aimed to prevent, although those who suffer such bias and discrimination are not the same people. Indeed, these objections presuppose the same totalizing and exclusionary principles against which they are formulated.

Consider, for example, that these objections reject "Hispanic" because they identify everything that is Hispanic with racial purity, Eurocentrism, exploitation, and oppression. But Hispania has been from the very beginning a place where Europe and other parts of the world meet. The Iberian peninsula is eminently *mestiza*, both racially and culturally. From its earliest history this piece of European land has been the place where Africa, Europe, and the Middle East have met and mingled in every possible way. Indeed, some have gone so far as to say that Spain is a part of Africa rather than Europe. It is a misconception to think of anything Hispanic as exclusively European or exclusively Caucasian, even if "Hispanic" is restricted to what is Iberian. A short trip through certain parts of Spain and Portugal should quickly disabuse anyone, who has eyes to see, from this prejudice. So much then for the connotation of racial purity or Eurocentrism. After 1492, it makes little sense to speak of Iberian purity, a culture separate and distinct from that of Latin America.

As far as the identification of "Hispanic" with oppression and exploitation, again this charge is partly based on both ignorance and prejudice. Mind you, I do not agree with the fallacious argument that we should not blame the conquistadors for the atrocities they committed because others did it too. This kind of reasoning is not only fallacious, but pernicious, even though it seems to carry quite a bit of weight in some quarters. My argument is rather that to blame all Iberians for the crimes of a few is as unjustified as saying that all Mexicans are lazy because a few are, that all Colombians are drug traffickers because a few are, or that no Cuban is serious because there are some who are not. These generalizations are false, and not only that, they are malicious and nefarious. But just as malicious and nefarious is the one that lumps all Iberians together into one group of monsters. Atrocities were committed in the encounter, but many of these atrocities were denounced from the very beginning by Iberians themselves. Indeed, the great names of Bartolomé de Las Casas, Juan de Zumárraga, and Vasco de Quiroga should be sufficient to show that not all Iberians were monsters and that many prominent ones took up the cause of the natives and the oppressed. Nor can it be said with impunity that even the Iberian governments were completely biased and generally silenced dissenters. The famous disputation between Las Casas and Sepúlveda shows that there was concern among some members of the Spanish government to do the right thing, or at least to provide a forum for dissenters. Indeed, at a time when the world in general had little awareness of the rights of conquered and oppressed peoples, some laws were enacted in Spain and Portugal for the protection of Amerindians and of African slaves, indicating that at least some Iberians were concerned about their welfare. Moreover, philosophers like Vitoria and Suárez openly and unambiguously tried to think through all the issues that the encounter with America brought up without considerations of profit or power.

So, no, not all Iberians are to be blamed and regarded as evil. Therefore, "Hispanics" need not denote only bad guys and connote only what was evil about some Iberians. Indeed, the selfless sacrifices of many who tried to mitigate the effects of what was, without a doubt, a tragic catastrophe of epic proportions, cannot, because of that, be ignored or disregarded. Most identities have been forged in blood, but it is not the blood alone that counts. Besides, there are countless cases, both in Latin America and the United States, where Iberians have been key players in the advancement of non-Iberian Hispanics. It makes no sense to demonize all Iberians because of the sins of some of them.

But this is not all, for what are we going to do with the many residents of the Iberian peninsula who had nothing to do with the conquest of America? What about the farmers, the members of the small bourgeoisie, the maids and servants? What about the Catalans, who, because of an agreement between Isabella and Ferdinand, were largely kept out of America? And what about the descendants of those people who now live in Spain or Portugal and never had anything to do with the conquest and colonization of America? Are they also to be rejected, repelled, and blamed? They are as Hispanic as the conquistadors and yet they have nothing to do with the atrocities committed by them. So why should "Hispanic" be rejected simply because of what some Iberians did between 1500 and 1900? We certainly do not change our last name every time a member of our family does something reprehensible. And few, if any, Americans today would reject the term "American" merely because some Americans committed atrocities against some segments of the American population at some point in the history of the United States. There is something drastically wrong with judgments based on faulty logic, and the faulty logic in this case is the understanding of the connotation of a term based on properties which apply only to some of the members of the set the term names.

Moreover, why should "Hispanic" be associated only with Iberia, or even more narrowly, Spain or Castile? That Castilians appropriated the name for themselves because of their aggressive and imperialistic behavior should not force others to surrender their rights to bear the name. I refuse to give up what is mine by right, even if others can be easily convinced to do so. I am Hispanic, but not Castilian or Spanish. I speak Castilian, not Spanish, but with a Cuban accent. And in being Hispanic I share with Catalans, Basques, Galicians, Portuguese, Andalucians, Mayans, Aztecs, Argentinians, Brazilians, and some Africans, among many others, a history which ties us together in a plurality of ways.

That certain ethnocentric and racist groups in the southwest of the United States appropriated the term "Hispanics" and used it to distance themselves from *mestizos* and Mexican Americans, out of racist concerns, and that other groups elsewhere also do so for similar reasons, should not be sufficient reason for us to acquiesce. First of all, ethnic and racial purity is a myth when it comes to Hispanics of any kind. We are not pure in any meaningful sense of the word. So it makes very little sense to use "Hispanic," or any other term for that matter, to indicate the purity of any of our groups. Second, if not absolute purity, but merely Spanish purity is involved, namely, pure unmixed Spanish ancestry, then "Hispanic" is the wrong term to use. The right term is "Spanish" or "of Spanish descent." "Hispanic" connotes mixture and derivation, as we saw in one of the other objections voiced earlier. "Hispanic" in this sense is like "Hellenistic," not like "Greek." Third, although there is considerable racism among Latin Americans, Iberians, and Hispanic Americans, this has never reached the levels it reached among Anglo-Saxons in the United States. After all, it was after and because of the annexation of the Mexican southwest by the United States, and the immigration of Anglo Americans into the newly acquired territories, that an attempt was made by certain groups to distinguish themselves from *mestizos* and Mexicans, precisely because Anglo Americans made Mexican Americans feel inferior.

As I said, there is considerable racism in Latin America. Generally, the darker one is, the worse one is. But there is not a great deal of favoritism toward Iberians either. Spaniards in particular are often regarded as uncouth, ignorant, provincial, and inflexible by Latin Americans. To be

Spanish or Iberian is not a status symbol, but quite the contrary. Whiteness that comes from English, German, and French origins is more coveted, however. So we find the common custom of tacking some English, German, or French name from a distant ancestor to the Spanish last name in order to emphasize the non-Iberian, European connection. To have English, German, or French blood really counts.

Even more significant is that there is no distinction between Hispanics and *mestizos* in Latin America. Latin Americans have made distinctions between whites, blacks, Indians, *mestizos*, *castizos*, mulattos, *criollos*, and various other labels at various times in history, but some of these terms are more cultural than racial, and to my knowledge the term *hispano* has never been used to distinguish upper-class pure descendants of Spaniards from *mestizos*, Indians, blacks, or mulattos. This phenomenon is American, and a result of Anglo-American racism.

My thesis can also be used to answer the third objection, namely, that the use of "Hispanic" should help perpetuate a sense of cultural subservience in America toward Europe in general and Spain in particular. If the notion of Hispanic does not connote a particular set of properties, it cannot be argued that it necessarily connotes anything European or Spanish. True, some may understand it so, but this is inaccurate, and should not deter us from using a name which can otherwise be useful and whose justification is rooted in history. African Americans should not cease to call themselves so because some, or even many, think "African" means racially or culturally inferior; Jews should not cease to call themselves so because some, or even many, associate that term with negative qualities; and we should not surrender "Hispanic" because some, or even many, mistakenly think it means Spanish.

This leads me to the last objection, that the use of "Hispanics" is counterproductive because it is associated with negative traits. Again, that some people put the wrong spin on certain terms should not make us avoid them if those terms reflect something historically important about us. Indeed, I am not sure that name changes are a good thing. Are we going to change our name every time someone decides to use it negatively? And is not something important lost every time a name is changed? Doesn't a name change often create unnecessary division and dissension in the community whose name is being changed? Should we not rather concentrate on defending the historical bases of the term? A term like "Hispanics," which makes historical sense, should be kept even if some people choose to interpret it negatively. Rather than dropping it, we should wear it with a certain defiance and assertion; this will eventually do more for our image than a change of name. We need to change people's attitudes toward us rather than acquiesce to the rules of a game they impose on us; and a name can be an effective tool in this task.

This does not mean that the community to which I refer as Hispanics is here to stay forever, or that it is a closed community which allows no one to leave or enter it. We cannot deny the past. If we have been part of that community, we will always have been part of it—this should not need to be stated—but to be part of it, or to have been part of it, does not entail continuing being part of it in the future. And not to have been part of it in the past does not preclude the possibility of joining it in the future. Communities are fluid, open, forever changing; members come and go, enter and leave, as they forge new relations with others. I am no historicist. We are not trapped in our history, albeit history cannot be denied. Nor am I proposing a kind of neo-essentialism. There is no essence here; there is only a complex historical reality. Only a misguided sense of identity, based on notions of coherence and purity, leads to essentialistic conceptions of ethnicity.

CONCLUSION

In conclusion, the category "Hispanic" is useful to describe and understand ourselves. It also serves to describe much of what we produce and do, for this product and these actions are precisely the results of who we are, and we are in turn the result of our history. "Hispanic" is a term that serves a purpose today, and will continue to serve a purpose in the study of our past. It is possible, however, that at some future time it could cease to be useful for the description of a reality current at the time. The term is justified now because of a historical reality, that is, the relations among us; if those relations should diminish considerably or cease altogether, then the term could become obsolete. The extension of the term should not be understood to be hard and fast, for human relations are anything but that. There is constant regrouping, and our understanding of these relations requires the constant realignment of our conceptual framework. For the moment, however, there is use for "Hispanic."

The strength of the position I have presented here lies precisely in that it allows us to speak of a common identity to all Hispanic/Latinos without imposing a homogeneous conception of who or what we are. It is an open-ended, historically based conception of our identity which permits multiplicity and development. It recognizes our diversity; it respects our differences; it acknowledges our past; and it prevents totalizing, homogenizing attitudes that could be used to oppress and dominate all or some of us. It is meant to provide understanding in the recognition of both the strength and weakness of our ties.

Part of my task has been to do a bit of conceptual analysis to clear the way for a more precise understanding of a notion that I think can be used to refer to all of us. Moreover, I have tried to show how there are historical grounds for accepting my conclusions. My argument has been in fact, contrary to what some believe, that the use of "Hispanic," as I have understood it here, does not strip us of our historical identity, reduce us to imputed common traits, or imply our false homogenization. Indeed, I have argued just the reverse, for it is my position that the use of "Hispanic," rightly understood, helps us respect diversity, is faithful to our historical reality, and leaves the doors open to development in many directions. Moreover, the lack of a homogeneous conception should be sufficient to preclude oppressive and discriminatory uses of "Hispanic." My most powerful answer to the objection against the use of "Hispanic," or any other ethnic name, to refer to us, is that "Hispanic" works by helping us understand the bases for the identity of our ethnic family.

Note also that I have stayed away from the political argument some use in support of a single name for all Hispanics in the American context. According to this argument, Hispanic Americans need a common name to strengthen our political clout. A large group has more muscle than a small one. The overarching notion of Hispanic (or Latino, for that matter) should make the rest of the United States take us seriously.

This is, indeed, a strong argument that has been routinely voiced by those who favor a single name for Hispanic Americans. The problem with it is that it does not properly take into account the diverse character and needs of the various groups which are covered by the name. Politically, the name does not produce the right results and may in fact be counterproductive. Puerto Ricans do not have the same needs as Chicanos, or Argentinians as Venezuelans, for example. Whether we speak of international or national politics, the use of one name need not be a good thing if the proper emphasis on the diversity among Hispanic groups is not maintained. The justification for one name should not be based on politics, but on historical fact, and should recognize that a common name for all Hispanics does not arise from common properties or political needs, but from a historical reality which is founded on diversity and *mestizaje*. This leads us directly to the consideration of the origins of our identity. . . .

Note that the objections [often] raised against the use of "Hispanic" work also against some labels proposed by those who oppose it. Terms such as "Latin American" and "Latin America" are very problematic, and if this is the case, so is "Latino/a." Indeed, even more restrictive terms based on national origins, favored by some groups opposed to "Hispanic," are questionable. For the countries of Latin America, like other countries of the world, are to a large extent artificially created. Even a brief trip through the territories of various Latin American countries should convince anyone who is not ideologically blind that in terms of identity other than political identity, these nations do not have much to do with many of the peoples who are considered part of them. This means that the use of terms based on national origins for Hispanic groups in the United States is even more artificial, for most of these Americans are not politically related to these countries today. The case of recent immigrants is different, of course, but that does not change the situation for others. Keep in mind also that, historically, the territorial integrity of many of these countries has more to do with how Spain and Portugal divided and governed their empires in America than with the identity of the current or past inhabitants of those countries. This makes the use of terms of national origin for Hispanic Americans, by those who want to avoid anything Spanish or Iberian, particularly paradoxical.

Of course, the reason why some Hispanic Americans want to emphasize their ties to particular countries of Latin America is quite understandable. After all, repeated attempts have been made to strip them of their values, dignity, culture, language, political power, and social status. Naturally, they need to fight these attempts, and the idea of a country of origin, with a great past and potential for the future, appears to be just the right tool to counteract ethnic discrimination and racism. Just as African Americans find a source of strength in Africa, so Hispanics find it in Mexico, Brazil, or Peru. All this is very well, as long as it is based on a realistic understanding of the situation and is not used to encourage misguided nationalism, ethnic strife, and unrealistic expectations. . . .

Finally, let me point out two major positive advantages of the use of "Hispanic" and the conception of Hispanic identity I have proposed. First, they allow us to participate fully in the cultural diversity of Hispanics without losing our more particular identities. The diversity, variety, and mixture which characterize Hispanics are enormous. It is probably not an overstatement to say that Hispanics are more diverse and varied than any other group in the world. Think of African Hispanics, Catalans, Tarahumaras, and so many others who are part of our historical family. Indeed, think of Sephardic Jews, who, after centuries living outside Hispanic territories, are still closely tied in many ways to the rest of us. Conceiving our identity in the terms I have outlined helps us understand this phenomenon, and allows us to share in each other's cultural riches: Paraca cloth, Maya architecture, African rhythms, Spanish literature, and Portuguese pottery, to name a few examples.

The second major advantage of the conception of Hispanic identity I have proposed is that it is not hegemonic; it does not rule out other identities, for it does not conceive Hispanics as sharing a set of properties which actually conflict, or can potentially conflict, with other properties shared by members of Hispanic subgroups. This conception of who we are is open and pluralistic, allowing the coexistence of other, multiple, and variegated identities. Its social and political implications are substantial then, for this way of conceiving Hispanic identity undermines intolerance and any totalizing and hegemonic attempts at imposing on others narrow conceptions of who we are.

Linda Martín Alcoff
(b. 19——)

L inda Martín Alcoff was born in Panama to a Panamanian father of
 Spanish, Indian, and African descent and a white, Anglo-Irish
mother from the United States. She describes her family as "postcolonial
and postmodernist," with "an open-ended set of indeterminate national,
cultural, racial, and even linguistic allegiances." Her firsthand experience
with the issues of mixed identity has informed some of her recent work in
race theory and the problem of Latina/o identity in the United States.

Alcoff was raised in central Florida and studied philosophy at Georgia
State University, receiving her BA in 1980 and her MA in 1983. She was
awarded a PhD from Brown University in 1987 under the supervision of
Ernest Sosa and Martha Nussbaum.

Alcoff has held teaching positions at Kalamazoo College, Florida
Atlantic University, and Brown University. She is currently a professor of
philosophy at Syracuse University, where she has worked since 1988. Her
main areas of research and publication are in continental philosophy, epistemology, feminist theory, and race theory. In her work she combines
these areas to open new paths in the field of philosophy. Her innovative
work has been acclaimed. *Feminist Epistemologies* (1993), a volume that
Alcoff coedited, was named a Critic's Choice Book by the American Educational Studies Association. Two other volumes on epistemology, *Real
Knowing: New Versions of Coherence Epistemology* (1996) and *Epistemology: The Big Questions* (1998), as well as numerous articles in this area
have made her a leading figure in the field of epistemology.

Alcoff's recent work has been directed to race theory and the problem
of identity. She has coedited two volumes on these topics: *Thinking from
the Underside of History: Enrique Dussel's Philosophy of Liberation* (2000)
and *Identities: Race, Class, Gender, and Nationality* (2003). She has con-

tributed to many journals, including *Philosophy Today*, *Hypatia*, and the *Philosophical Forum*, among others, both as guest editor and as author. Two articles representative of her contributions to the field of Latin American philosophy are "Mestizo Identity" and "Latina/o Identity Politics."

In the article included here, Alcoff explores the problem of Latina/o identity within the context of the current political and social realities of the United States. She begins by pointing to the limitations of the conventional categories of race in the United States, claiming that these "racialized identities have long connoted homogeneity, easily visible identifying features and biographical heredity." The *mestizo* identity of many Latinas/os defies the notion that racial identity is a straightforward matter, bound up with presumptions of purity as having intrinsic value. Within the context of the United States, the highly heterogeneous Latina/o population complicates the discussion of identity understood in terms of race. This leads Alcoff into an investigation of Latina/o identity as a problem of social ontology: that is, to the question of whether Latina/o is an ethnic category, a racial category, neither, or both.

Alcoff analyzes various political and metaphysical arguments that have been given in favor of abandoning an understanding of Latina/o identity in terms of race, and of accepting in its stead an understanding of identity in terms of ethnicity. The move to dislodge race and understand Latina/o identity in terms of ethnicity faces many difficulties and so Alcoff favors instead a move toward shifting the meaning of race and understanding identity in terms of both race and ethnicity (ethnorace). Alcoff concludes with a reminder that even within the context of an ethnorace understanding of identity, race must be de-essentialized, that is, it must be understood as a function of history, social location, and forms of cultural expression.

Is Latina/o Identity a Racial Identity?

I s Latina/o identity a racial identity? Given the social basis of racializing categories and the dynamic nature of identities, there is no decontextual, final, or essential answer to this question. However, I would describe my concern in this paper as being in the realm of social ontology in the sense that I seek the truth about how Latina/o identity is configured as well as lived in the context of North America today. The question then can be formulated in the following way: What is the best, or most apt, account of Latina/o identity that makes the most sense of the current political and social realities within which we must negotiate our social environment? Although I am interested here in the politics of identity, that is, the political effects of various accounts of identity in and on popular consciousness, both among Latinas/os and among Anglos, my principal concern is at the level of experience, ideology, and meaning rather than the attendant political rights that may be associated with identity.

As will be seen, much of the debates over Latinas/os and race weave together strategic considerations (a concern with political effects) and metaphysical considerations (a concern with the most apt description). It is not clear to me that these concerns can, in fact, be disentangled. There are two reasons for this. One is that strategic proposals for the way a community should represent itself cannot work if there is no connection whatsoever to lived experience or to the common meanings that are prominent in the relevant discourses and practices. Thus, the strategic efficacy of political proposals are dependent on correct assessments of metaphysical realities. But, second, the question of what is the most apt description of those metaphysical realities is not as clear-cut as some philosophers might suppose. And this is because the concepts of "race," "Latina/o," and even "identity" admit of different meanings and have complicated histories, such that it is not possible to simply say, "This is *the* meaning." Thus, we must make a judgment about meaning, a judgment that will be underdetermined by usage, history, science, or phenomenological description of experience. And in making these judgments, we must look to the future and not just the past. In other words, given that we are participating in the *construction* of meanings in making such judgments, we must take responsibility for our actions, which will require carefully considering their likely real-world effects.

The question of Latina/o identity's relationship to the conventional categories of race that have been historically dominant in the United States is a particularly vexing one. To put it straightforwardly, we simply don't fit. Racialized identities in the United States have long connoted homogeneity, easily visible identifying features, and biological heredity, but none of these characteristics apply to Latinas/os in the United States, nor even to any one national subset, such as Cuban Americans or Puerto Ricans. We are not homogeneous by "race," we are often not identifiable by visible features or even by names, and such issues as disease heredity that are often cited as the biologically relevant sign of race are inapplicable to such a heterogeneous group.

Moreover, the corresponding practices of racialization in the United States—such as racial border control, legal sanctions on cross-racial marriage, and the multitudinous demands for racial self-identification on nearly every application form from day care to college admissions—are also relatively unfamiliar south of the border. Angel R. Oquendo recounts that before he could even take the SAT in Puerto Rico he was asked to identify himself racially. "I was caught off guard," he says. "I had never thought of myself in terms of race."[1] Fortunately, the SAT included "Puerto Rican" among the choices of "race" and Oquendo was spared what he called a "profound existential dilemma." Even while many Latinas/os consider color a relevant factor for marriage, and antiblack racism persists in Latin America along with a condescension toward indigenous peoples, the institutional and ideological forms that racism has taken in Latin America are generally not analogous to those in the North. And these differences are why many of us find our identity as well as our social status changing as we step off the plane or cross the river: race suddenly becomes an all-important aspect of our identity, and sometimes our racial identity dramatically changes in ways over which it feels as if we have no control.

In the face of this transcontinental experiential dissonance, there are at least three general options possible as a way of characterizing the relationship between Latina/o identity and race. One option is to refuse a racialized designation and use the concept of "ethnicity" instead. This would avoid the problem of racial diversity within Latina/o communities and yet recognize the cultural links among Latinas/os in the North. The concept of ethnicity builds on cultural practices, customs, language, sometimes religion, and so on. One might also be motivated toward this option as a way of resisting the imposition of a pan-Latina/o ethnicity, in order to insist that the only meaningful identities for Latinas/os are Cuban American, Puerto Rican, Mexican American, and so on.[2]

A second option would resist the ethnic paradigm on the grounds that, whatever the historical basis of Latina/o identity, living in the context of North America means that we have become a racialized population and need a self-understanding that will accurately assess our portrayal here. A third option, adopted by many neoconservatives, is to attempt to assimilate to the individualist ideology of the United States both in body and in mind, and reject the salience of group identities a priori.

None of these responses seems fully adequate, though some have more problems than others. It is hard to see how the diversity among Latinas/os could be fairly represented in any concept of race. And it is doubtful that many Latinas/os, especially those who are darker-skinned, will be able to succeed in presenting themselves as simply individuals: they will still be seen by many as instantiations of a group whose characteristics are considered both universally shared within the group and largely inferior, even if they do not see themselves this way. On the face of it, the first option—an account of Latina/o identity as an ethnic identity—seems to make the most sense, for a variety of reasons that I will explore in this paper. This option could recognize the salience of social identity, allow for more internal heterogeneity, and resist the racializing that so often mischaracterizes our own sense of self. However, I will ultimately argue that the "ethnic option" is not fully adequate to the contemporary social realities we face, and may inhibit the development of useful political strategies for our diverse communities. My argument in this paper primarily will take the form of a negative: that the ethnic option is not adequate. Developing a fully adequate alternative is beyond my scope or ambitions here, but the very failure of the ethnic option will establish some of the necessary criteria for such an alternative.

My argument will take the following steps. First, I will explain briefly the context of these debates over identity, which will go some way toward refuting the individualist option. Next, I will go over some of the relevant facts about our populations to provide the necessary cultural context. Then I will zero in on the ethnicity argument, assess its advantages and disadvantages, and conclude by posing the outline of an alternative.

WHY CARE ABOUT IDENTITY?

If I may be permitted a gross overgeneralization, European Americans are afraid of strongly felt ethnic and racial identities. Not all, to be sure. The Irish and Italian communities, as well as some other European American nationalities, have organized cultural events on the basis of their identities at least since the 1960s, with the cooperation of police and city councils across the country. The genealogy of this movement among the Irish and the Italians has been precisely motivated by their discrimination and vilification in U.S. history, a vilification that has sometimes taken racialized forms.

But there is a different attitude among whites in general toward "white ethnic" celebrations of identity and toward those of others, that is, those of nonwhites. And this is, I suspect, because it is one thing to say to the dominant culture, "You have been unfairly prejudiced against me," as southern European ethnicities might say, and quite another to say, "You have stolen my lands and enslaved my people and through these means created the wealth of your country," as African Americans, Latinas/os, and Native Americans might say. The latter message is harder to hear; it challenges the basic legitimizing narratives of this country's formation and global status, and it understandably elicits the worry, "What will be the full extent of their demands?" Of course, all of the cultural programs that celebrate African, indigenous, or Latina/o heritage do not make these explicit claims. But in a sense, the claims do not need to be explicit: any reference to slavery, indigenous peoples, or Chicano or Puerto Rican history implies challenges to the legitimizing narrative of the United States, and any expression of solidarity among such groups consciously or unconsciously elicits concern about the political and economic demands such groups may eventually make, even if they are not made now.

This is surely part of what is going on when European Americans express puzzlement about the importance attached to identity by non–European Americans, when young whites complain about African Americans sitting together in the cafeteria, or when both leftist and liberal political theorists, such as Todd Gitlin and Arthur Schlesinger, jump to the conclusion that a strong sense of group solidarity and its resultant "identity politics" among people of color in this country will fracture the body politic and disable our democracy.[3]

A prominent explanation given for these attachments to identity, attachments that are considered otherwise inexplicable, is that there is opportunism at work, among leaders if not among the rank and file, to secure government handouts and claim special rights. However, the demand for cultural recognition does not entail a demand for special political rights. The assumption in so much of contemporary political philosophy that a politics of recognition—or identity-based political movements—leads automatically to demands for special rights is grounded, I suspect, in the mystification some feel in regard to the politics of cultural identity in the first place. Given this mystification and feeling of amorphous threat, assumptions of opportunism and strategic reasoning become plausible.

Assumptions about the opportunism behind identity politics seem to work on the basis of the following understanding of the recent historical past: in the 1960s, some groups began to clamor for the recognition of their identities, began to resist and critique the cultural assimilationism of liberal politics, and argued that state institutions should give these identities public recognition. Thus, on this scenario, first we had identity politics asserting the political importance of these identities, and then we had (coerced) state recognition of them. But denigrated identity designations, particularly racial ones, have *originated* with and been enforced by the state in U.S. history, not vice versa. Obviously, it is the U.S. state and U.S. courts that initially insisted on the overwhelming salience of some racial and ethnic identities, to the exclusion of rights to suffrage, education, property, marrying whomever one wanted, and so on. Denigrated groups are trying to reverse this process; they are not the initiators of it. It seems to me that they have two aims: (1) to valorize previously derided identities, and (2) to have their own hand at constructing the representations of identities.

The U.S. pan-Latina/o identity is perhaps the newest and most important identity that has emerged in the recent period. The concept of a pan-Latina/o identity is not new in Latin America: Simón Bolívar called for it nearly two hundred years ago as a strategy for anticolonialism, but also because it provided a name for the "new peoples" that had emerged from the conquest. And influential leaders such as José Martí and Che Guevara also promoted Latin American solidarity. It is important to note that populations "on the ground" have not often resonated with these grand visions, and that national political and economic leaders continue to obstruct regional accords and trade agreements that might enhance solidarity. But the point remains that the invocation of a pan-Latina/o identity does not actually originate in the North.

Only much more recently is it the case that some Latina/o political groups in the North have organized on a pan-Latina/o basis, although most Latina/o politics here has been organized along national lines, for example, as Puerto Ricans or Chicanos. But what is especially new, and what is being largely foisted on us from the outside, is the representation of a pan-Latina/o identity in the dominant North American media, and it is this representation we want to have a hand in shaping. Marketing agen-

318   Part IV: The Search for Identity–A. *The Nation and the People*

cies have discovered/created a marketing niche for the "generic" Latina/o. And Latina/o-owned marketing agencies and advertising agencies are working on the construction of this identity as much as anyone, though of course in ways dominated by strategic interests or what Habermas calls purposive rationality. There are also more and more cultural representations of Latinas/os in the dominant media and in government productions such as the census. Thus, the concern that U.S. Latinas/os have with our identity is not spontaneous or originating entirely or even mostly from within our communities; neither is the ongoing representation of our identity something we can easily just ignore.[4]

WHAT WE ARE DEPENDS ON *WHERE* WE ARE

Social identities, whether racial or ethnic, are dynamic. In Omi and Winant's study of what they call "racial formations" in the United States between the 1960s and the 1980s, they argued, "Racial categories and the meanings of race are given concrete expression by the specific social relations and historical context in which they are embedded."[5] Moreover, these categories are constantly facing forms of resistance and contestation that transform both their impact and their effective meaning. Clearly this is the case with ethnic as well as racial identities. As social constructions imposed on variable experiential facts, they exist with no stable referent or essential, nonnegotiable core. And because such identities are often also the site of conflict over political power and economic resources, they are especially volatile. Any analysis of Latina/o identity, then, must chart historical trends and contextual influences, which themselves will vary across different parts of the country.

Since the passage of the 1965 immigration law that ended the quotas on immigration from South and Central America and the Caribbean, millions of Latinas/os have entered the United States from various countries, causing a great diversification of the previously dominant Chicano, Puerto Rican, and Cuban communities. Thus today, Dominicans are vying with Puerto Ricans in New York City to be the largest Latina/o population, and even Cubans no longer outnumber other Latinas/os in Miami. As the immigrant communities settle in, younger generations develop different identities than their parents, adapting to their cultural surroundings. Young people also tend to experience similar problems across the national divisions, such as Dominican and Puerto Rican, and this promotes a sense of common identity. So in one sense diversity has increased as new immigrations continue and new generations of younger Latinos depart from some aspects of their parents' cultural identity, such as being Spanish-dominant or being practicing Catholics, while in another sense diversity has decreased as Latinas/os experience common forms of discrimination and chauvinism in the United States and an increasingly common cultural interpellation.

In the 1960s, U.S. state agencies began to disseminate the ethnic label "Hispanic" as the proper term for identifying all people of Latin American and even Spanish descent.[6] So today we have a population of thirty million or so "Hispanics" in the United States. The mass media, entertainment, and advertising industries have increasingly addressed this large population as if it were a coherent community.[7] As Suzanne Oboler's study reveals, this generic identity category feels especially socially constructed to many of the people named by it, given that it is not how they self-identified previously.[8] Oboler asks, somewhat rhetorically:

> Are marketers merely taking advantage of an existing "group" as a potentially lucrative target population? Or are their advertising strategies in fact helping to "design" the group, "invent" its traditions, and hence "create" this homogeneous ethnic group?[9]

One might well be concerned that adapting to any such pan-Latina/o identity as constructed by dominant institutions—whether economic or political ones—represents a capitulation or is simply the inevitable effect of what Foucault might call governmentality.

However, much of the debate over this interpellation among those named by it does not so much critique the fact of its social construction or even the fact that its genesis lies in government and marketing agencies, but focuses instead on its political implications and its coherence with lived experience, for example, the way in which it disallows multiplicity or the way in which it erases national allegiance. In this way, the debate shifts to a more productive set of concerns, it seems to me. I witnessed an interesting exchange on some of these points at the "Hispanics: Cultural Locations" conference held at the University of San Francisco, in 1997. Ofelia Schutte, a leading Latina philosopher, presented a paper arguing that a pan-U.S. Latina/o identity may be a means to disaffiliate us from our nations of birth or ancestry, nations that have been invaded or otherwise harmed by the U.S. government. Thus, thinking of ourselves primarily as U.S. Latinas/os rather than, say, Panamanians or Salvadorans may work to dislodge or weaken feelings of loyalty to countries outside the U.S. borders. In the discussion period after her paper, one member of the audience argued strongly that as a half-Spanish, half–Puerto Rican woman who grew up among Chicanos in California, she had found the emergence of a pan-Latina/o identity a welcome relief. Although she recognized the dangers that Schutte was describing, identifying herself simply as Latina allowed her to avoid having to make complicated choices between the various aspects of her identity, and it helpfully named her experience of connection with a multiplicity of Latina/o communities.[10]

Another political concern I have heard voiced against overhomogenizing Latina/o identities is that it could allow those members of the group who are themselves less disadvantaged to reap the benefits of affirmative action and other forms of economic redress that have mainly been created for (and often mainly fought for by) Chicanos and Puerto Ricans, that is, the more disadvantaged members. We are already seeing this happen because of the label "Hispanic." It is unclear how to effectively police this problem other than to rely on people's own moral conscience (which is not terribly effective). In some cases, targeted groups are designated with specificity as Mexican Americans or Puerto Ricans in order to avoid, for example, giving scholarships to Argentinians of recent European extraction. However, the problem here is that one cannot assume that no Argentinians in the United States have suffered discrimination, given their particular racialized identity, skin tone, the way their accent may be mediated by their class background, and so forth. Given the racial heterogeneity of every Latin American and Caribbean country, one cannot exclude an entire country from measures aimed at redressing discrimination without excluding many who are racially marked as inferior north of the border.

The resistance to a pan-Latina/o identity is most likely a losing battle, moreover, as both government and marketing agencies are increasingly winning hegemony in their public interpellations. Moreover, as both Arlene Davila and Daniel Mato have argued in separate studies, the marketing and advertising agencies are not simply forcing us to use labels that have no real purchase on our lives, but participating in a new subject construction that affects how Latinas/os think about and experience our identity and our interrelatedness to other Latinas/os with whom we may have felt little kinship before.[11] Mato points out that the television corporation Univisión, which is jointly owned by U.S. and Latin American companies, is exposing its viewers to a wide array of programming such that viewers are becoming familiar with a diversity of communities, in both the South and the North, and in this way "Univisión is participating in the social construction of an imagined community."[12] To say that an identity is socially constructed is to say not that it does not refer to anything in reality, but that what it refers to is a contingent product of social negotiations rather than a natural kind. And the exchange I described above at the "Hispanics: Cultural Locations" conference indicates that the pan-Latina/o identity does in fact correspond at least to some contemporary Latina/os' lived experience.

Latin America itself is probably the most diverse area in the world, producing extreme racial and ethnic diversity *within* Latina/o communities. By U.S. categories, there are black, brown, white, Asian, and Native American Latinas/os. There are many Latinas/os from the Southern Cone whose families are of recent European origin, a large number of Latinas/os from the western coastal areas whose families came from Asia, and of course a large number of Latinas/os whose lineage is entirely indigenous to the Americas or entirely African. The majority of Latinas/os in North and South America are no doubt the product of a mix of two or more of these groups. And being mixed is true, as Jorge Gracia reminds us, even of the so-called Hispanics who are direct descendants of Spain and Portugal. And it is true as well of many or most of the people identified as black or *moreno*, as is the case in the United States. Latin Americans are thus generally categorized "racially" in the following way: white (which often involves a double deceit: a claim to pure Spanish descent, very rare, and a claim that pure Spanish descent is purely white or European, also very rare); black (meaning wholly or mostly of African descent, usually sub-Saharan); Indian (meaning being some or mostly of pre-Columbian or Amerindian descent); and mixed (which is sometimes divided into subcategories, mestizo, mulatto, *cholito*, and so on), with the mixed category always enjoying a majority. Asians are often entirely left off the list, even though their numbers in several countries are significant.

Different countries vary these main racial designations, however. During a recent weekend festival for Latino Heritage Month in Syracuse, Latinas/os of different nationalities provided information about their countries for passersby, information that included statistics, culled from government sources, on what in every case was called the country's "ethnic makeup." Racial categories of identity were given *within* this larger rubric of ethnic makeup, suggesting an equation between ethnicity and race. For example, in the Dominican Republic the ethnic makeup is said to consist of 73 percent "mixed people," 16 percent "white," 11 percent "black." In Ecuador the categories are listed as "mestizo," "Indian," "Spanish," and "black." In Chile there is a single category called "European and mestizo," which makes up 95 percent of the population. In Cuba we get categories of "mulatto," which is 51 percent of the population, and we also get categories of "white," "black," and "Chinese." In Bolivia the breakdown is between "Quechua," "Aymara," "mestizo," and "white."

One is reminded of the encyclopedia invented by Borges, which divides dogs into such categories as "(a) belonging to the Emperor. . . (b) tame . . . (c) drawn with a very fine camel hair brush . . . and (d) having just broken the water pitcher."[13] There is no internally consistent or coherent theory of ethnic or racial identity underlying the diversity of categorizations. Under the rubric of ethnicity are included a mix of cultural, national, and racial groups, from Spanish to Quechua to white. The sole point that seems to be consistent throughout is that the category "black" is the only one that is invariably racialized, that is, presented as black or mulatto and never presented as "West Indian" or "African." Interestingly, the category "white" is also often racialized, though it is sometimes replaced with "European" or "Spanish." I would suggest that there is a strong relationship between these two facts. That is, it becomes important to use the category "white," and to self-identify as "white," when the category "black" is present, in order to establish one's clear demarcation, and out of concern that a category such as "mestizo" might be allowed to include black people. "White" is also used to distinguish oneself from "Indian," a category that bears racialized meanings in Latin America and negative associations similar to the associations with African Americans in the United States.

Blackness does, of course, signify differently in Latin America; thus it is not likely that a typical white American landing in Santo Domingo would look around and think only 11 percent of the population is black. However, it seems clear that the striking use of the category "black" for all people of African descent, rather than cultural and national markers, is an indication of antiblack racism. The people so designated are reduced to skin color as if this were their primary characteristic rather than some self-created marker such as nationality, language, or culture. One may have been born into a culture and language not of one's own choosing, but these are still more indicative of human agency than is any classification by phenotype. From this, one might argue that replacing "black" with another ethnicity category, such as "West Indian" or "African," might help equalize and dignify the identities.

The category "Indian," however, even though it might initially look to be more of an ethnicity than a race (since it is not merely the name of a color), has primarily a racial meaning, given that the term does not say anything about language, mode of life, religion, or specific origin. Also, in nonindigenous communities of discourse, the term often carries associations as negative as "black" does. Here one might argue that disaggregating the category "Indian" would be helpful. If the main meaning of "Indian" is a kind of racial meaning, then the use of "Quechua," "Aymara," and so on reduces the significance of the racialized connotations of the identity, subordinating those to the specificity of linguistic and cultural markers.

Despite all this variety and heterogeneity, when Latinas/os enter the United States, we are often homogenized into one overarching "Hispanic" identity. This generic Hispanicity is not, as Jorge Gracia reminds us, actually homogeneous. That is, in European American eyes, "Hispanic" identity does not carry the same connotations in every part of the United States. Gracia explains:

In Miami it means Cuban; in New York City it means Puerto Rican; and in the southwest it means Mexican. So in California I am supposed to have as my native food tacos, in New York City, *arroz con gandules*, and in Miami, *arroz con frijoles negros!*[14]

I, too, cannot even count the times it has been assumed that I must naturally like hot and spicy food, even though the typical food in Panama is extremely mild.

Still, there is one feature at least that persists across this variety of "generic" Hispanic identities, and that is that our identity in the United States, whether or not it is homogenized, is quite often presented as a racial identity. In a recent report in the *Chronicle of Higher Education*, just to give one example, differences in average SAT scores were reported in the following way:

The average verbal scores *by race* were: white, 526; black, 434; Asian American, 498; American Indian, 480; Mexican American, 453; Puerto Rican, 452; and other Hispanic students, 461.[15]

So again, like Angel Oquendo, we find that "Puerto Rican" is a racial identity, and a different one at that from the "race" of Mexican Americans. Whereas in the categorizations I just analyzed from Latin America, racial categories are subsumed within an overall account of "ethnic makeup," in this example from the United States, ethnic categories are subsumed within an overall account of racial difference. But in both cases, race and ethnicity are all but equated.

THE ETHNICITY PARADIGM

Latinas/os in the United States have responded to racialization in a variety of ways. One response, still ongoing, has been to deny vigorously any racial interpellation as other-than-white. Thus some Latinos have literally campaigned to be called white, apparently thinking that if they are going to have to be racialized, whiteness is the one they want. Anita Allen reported in 1994 that the largest petitioning group that had thus far requested changes to the year 2000 U.S. census was the Association of White Hispanics, who were agitating for that designation to be on the census form.[16] In the self-interested scramble for social status, this group perceived correctly where the advantages lay.

Another response, especially among groups of young people, has been to use the discourse of racialization as it exists in the United States to self-identify, but in positive rather than derogatory ways. Thus Chicanos in the

August Twenty-Ninth Movement and in Mecha, as well as the primarily Puertorriqueno Young Lords in the Northeast, at times adopted and adapted the concept of a brown racial identity, such as the "Brown Berets," as if Latinas/os in these communities shared a visible phenotype. One relevant causal factor for this among Puerto Ricans may be their long experiential history of U.S. colonization, which imposed racialization even before they ever entered the United States. Latinas/os from countries without this experience of intensive colonization are more surprised by being racially designated when they come here.[17]

But neither "white" nor "brown" works for a pan-Latina/o identity (or even for the specific nationalities they want to represent). What better unites Latinas/os both across and even within our specific national cultures is not race or phenotype but precisely those features associated with culture: language, religious traditions, cultural values, characteristics of comportment. Thus, another response to forced racialization that has existed for a long time among some Latina/o communities and which has enjoyed a recent resurgence is to deny that race applies in any way to Latinas/os and to argue for, and self-identify as, an ethnic group that encompasses different nationalities and races within it.[18] The U.S. census has adopted this approach at times, in having no Latina/o identity listed under possible racial categories and including it only under the list of ethnic categories. Let us look at the main arguments in favor of this approach, both the political as well as the metaphysical arguments.

1. There is powerful sentiment among Latinas/os toward resisting the imposition of U.S. racializations and U.S. categories of identity. It is not as if the system of racial classification here has benefited anyone except the white majority. As Jorge Klor de Alva provocatively put it to Cornel West in a conversation in *Harper's*, "What advantage has it been, Cornel, for blacks to identify as blacks?"[19] Oquendo argues against the use of such racial terms as "Black Hispanics" and "White Hispanics" on the grounds that these categories "project onto the Latino/a community a divisive racial dualism that, much as it may pervade U.S. society, is alien to that community."[20] Our identity is about culture and nationality, not race: for example, as Clara Rodriguez has shown, Puerto Ricans of all colors self-identify first as Puerto Rican.[21]

But in the United States, cultural, national, ethnic, religious, and other forms of identification are constantly subordinated to race. So Afro-Cubans, English-speaking West Indians, and Afro-Brazilians are grouped as "black," in ways that often counter people's own felt sense of identity or primary group alliances. Race trumps culture, and culture is sometimes even seen as a simple outgrowth of race. Shouldn't this ridiculous biological essentialism be opposed and the use of race as an identity or as an all-important category of identity be diminished?

2. Within the United States itself, many African Americans have been opting out of racial categories ever since Jesse Jackson started pushing for the use of the term "African American" in the late 1980s. This was a self-conscious strategy to encourage analogies between African Americans and other hyphenated ethnic groups—to, in a sense, normalize African American identity by no longer having it set apart from everyone else. Shouldn't Latinas/os unite with and support this trend?

3. The strategy of using ethnic terms rather than racial ones will have the effect of reducing racism or prejudice generally. This was clearly Jackson's thinking. A representation by ethnic terms rather than racial ones confers agency on a people; it invokes historical experience as well as cultural and linguistic practices, all of which are associations with human subjectivity, not objectivity. In contrast, race is often said to be something one has no control over, something one "can't help." This surely perpetuates the association between denigrated racial categories and victimhood, animal-driven natures, inherent inferiority and superiority, and so on. For whites, racial essentialism confers superiority whether or not they've done anything to deserve it; superior intelligence is just in their genes. These beliefs may be more unconscious than conscious, but given the historically sedimented and persistent layers of the ideology of race as an essential determinant, no matter what one intends by use of a word, its historical meanings will be brought into play when it is in use. Naomi Zack, Anthony Appiah, Klor de Alva, and many others today argue that any use of racial terms will be inevitably embedded with biological essentialism and historically persistent hierarchies of moral and cognitive competence.[22] Luis Angel Toro calls on us to "abandon the outdated racial ideology embodied in [the Office of Management and Budget's Statistical] Directive no. 15 and replace it with questions designed to determine an individual's membership in a socially constructed, cultural subgroup."[23] The goal here, of course, is not only to change whites' assumptions about racialized groups, but also to help alter the self-image of people in those groups themselves toward a more affirming identity, an identity in which one can take justifiable pride.

Some also point to the relative success of Jamaican immigrants in the United States as an example here. Grosfoguel and Georas write, "The Jamaican's community's strategy was to emphasize ethnic over racial identity. The fact that Jamaicans were not subsumed under the categorization 'African American' avoided offsetting the positive impact of their skilled background. Thus Jamaicans were successfully incorporated into the host labor market in well-paid public and private service jobs . . . [and] are currently portrayed by the white establishment in New York as a model minority."[24]

These are strong arguments. To summarize them, the political arguments are that (1) the use of ethnicity will reduce racism because it refers to self-created features rather than merely physiological ones, and (2) this will also resist the imposition of U.S. forms of identifying people, thus disabusing North Americans of their tendency to naturalize and universalize the predominant categories used here in the United States. The metaphysical arguments are that (3) ethnicity more accurately identifies what really holds groups together and how they self-identify, and (4) ethnicity is simply closer to the truth of Latina/o identity, given its racial heterogeneity. All of these arguments are, in my view, good ones. But the problem is that there are other considerations, and once they are put on the table, the picture unfortunately becomes more complicated.

RACIAL REALITIES

Let us look at the case of Cuban Americans. By all measures, they have fared very well in this country in terms of both economic success and political power. They have largely run both politics and the press in Miami for some time, and presidential candidates neglect Cuban issues at their peril. Of course, one cannot argue, as some do in the case of Jamaicans, that Cubans' strong ethnic identification is the main reason for their success; most important has been their ability to play an ideological (and at times military) role for the United States in the cold war. The enormous government assistance provided to the Cubans who fled the Cuban revolution was simply unprecedented in U.S. immigration history: they received language training, educational and business loans, job placement assistance, and housing allocations, and their professional degrees from Cuban institutions were legally recognized to an extent other Third World immigrants still envy. In 1965, when President Johnson began his Great Society programs, the amount of assistance they received from the government actually increased.[25]

But one may legitimately wonder whether the Cubans' status as refugees from Communism was all that was at work here, or even the overriding factor. The Cubans who came in the 1960s were overwhelmingly white or light-skinned. They were generally from the top strata of Cuban society. It is an interesting question whether Haitians would ever have been treated the same way. The Cubans who left Cuba after 1980, known as the Marielitos, were from lower strata of Cuban society, and a large number were Afro-Cubans and mulattos.[26] These Cubans found a decidedly colder welcome. They were left penned in refugee camps for months on end, and those who were not sent back to Cuba were released into U.S. society with little or no assistance, joining the labor ranks at the level of Puerto Ricans and Dominicans.

There are no doubt many factors at work in these disparate experiences of Cuban immigration, having to do, for example, with the geopolitical climate. But surely one of these important factors is race, or racialized identity. Perceived racial identity often *does* trump ethnic or cultural identity.

Look again at the passage about Jamaicans quoted earlier from Grosfoguel and Georas, with certain words emphasized: "The Jamaican community's strategy was to emphasize *ethnic* over *racial* identity. The fact that *Jamaicans* were not subsumed under the categorization 'African American' avoided offsetting the positive impact of their skilled background." Grosfoguel and Georas contrast the *ethnic* Jamaican identity with what they revealingly take to be a *racial* African American identity, even though the term "African American" was Jackson's attempt to replace race with ethnicity. This again suggests that the racialization of black Americans will overpower any ethnic or cultural marker. It may also be the case that the category "African" is overly inclusive, since under its umbrella huge cultural and linguistic differences would be subsumed, and thus it is incapable of signifying a unified ethnic identity. But that may be assuming more knowledge about Africa among white Americans or even among Latinas/os than one reasonably should. More likely is the fact that "African American" is still understood primarily as a racial designation, in a way that terms such as "German American" or "Irish American" never are. Thus it is questionable whether the strategy of using an ethnic term for a currently racialized group will have the effect of reducing racism if it continues to simply signify race.

And after all, the first meaning given for the word *ethnic* in *Webster's Unabridged Dictionary* is "heathen, pagan." The concept of ethnicity is closely associated with the concept of race, emerging at the same moment in global history, as this meaning indicates. The common usage of the category "white ethnic" indicates that unless otherwise identified, "ethnics" are assumed to be nonwhite and thus they are racialized. For many people in the United States, "ethnic" connotes not only nonwhite but also the typical negative associations of nonwhite racial identity. Meanings given for the word *heathen* in the same dictionary include "rude, illiterate, barbarous, and irreligious." In this list, it is striking that "irreligious" comes last.

Like "African American," the fact is that in the United States the category "Latina/o" often operates as a racialized category. Grosfoguel and Georas themselves argue that "no matter how 'blonde or blue-eyed' a person may be, and no matter how successfully he can 'pass' as white, the moment a person self-identifies as Puerto Rican, he enters the labyrinth of racial Otherness."[27] Virginia Dominguez even makes this case in regard not only to ethnicity but to cultural identity as well. She suggests that case

[handwritten marginal note: ex: lighten mexicans tend to be favored more]

studies from Canada to Brazil reveal that "people may speak culture but continue to think race. Whether in the form of cultural pluralism or of the current idiom of multiculturalism, the concept of culture is used in ways that naturalize and essentialize difference."[28]

My suspicion is that this works for some Latina/o identities, such as Puerto Rican, Dominican, and Mexican, but not always for others, such as Chilean or Argentinian or perhaps South Americans in general, depending on their features. And as mentioned earlier, some of these groups—Puerto Ricans and Mexicans in particular—have a long history of seeing their identities interpellated through dominant U.S. schemas. In terms of the pan-Latina/o identity, this would mean that when Mexicans or Puerto Ricans are called "Latina/o," the latter category will connote racial meanings, whereas Argentinians who are called "Latina/o" in the North may escape these connotations. Identity terms, as Omi and Winant argue, gain their meaning from their context. Just as Gracia said "Latino" means tacos in California and *arroz con gandules* in New York, it will mean race in California, Texas, New York, and Florida, and perhaps ethnicity only in a few locations. Thus, moving from race to ethnicity is not necessarily moving away from race.

Surely, an optimist might want to interject here, the persistence of racial connotations evoked by ethnic categories is not insurmountable. After all, the Irish *did* transform in wide popular consciousness from a race to an ethnicity, and Jews are making the same transition, at least in the United States. Is it truly the case that only light-skinned people can enjoy this transformation, and that darker-skinned people will *never* be able to?

In order to answer this question, we need to ask another one: What *are* the obstacles to deracializing people of color in general?[29] Is it really the mere fact of skin tone?

I would make two suggestions. First, race, unlike ethnicity, has historically worked through visible markers on the body that trump dress, speech, and cultural practices. In Mississippi, a Jamaican is generally still a black person, no matter how skilled. Race demarcates groups visually, which is why racist institutions have been so upset about nonvisible members of "races" and why they have taken such trouble in these cases to enforce racial identifications. What I am suggesting is that in popular consciousness—in the implicit perceptual practices we use in everyday life to discern how to relate to each other—ethnicity does not "replace" race. When ethnic identities are used instead of racial ones, the perceptual practices of visual demarcation by which we slot people into racial categories continue to operate because ethnic categories offer no substituting perceptual practice. In other words, the fact that race and ethnicity do not map onto the same kinds of identifying practices will make race harder to dislodge. This was not the case for the Irish or for at least some Jewish people, who could blend into the European American melting pot without noticeable distinctiveness. For them, ethnicity could replace race, because their racial identity as Irish and Jewish did not operate exclusively or primarily through visible markers on the body so much as through contextual factors such as neighborhood and accent. So their identity could shift to white race plus Jewish or Irish ethnicity without troubling the dominant perceptual practices of racial identification. However, for those who are visibly identified by such dominant practices as nonwhite, as "raced," the shift to a primary ethnic identity would require eradicating these practices. It is unlikely that the use of new terms alone will have that effect. At best, for people of color, ethnic identities will operate alongside racial ones in everyday interactions. At worst, ethnic identities, perhaps like "African American," will operate simply as a racial identity.

Although this is a fact about the visible features of the body, it is not an immutable fact: the meanings of the visible are of course subject to change. However, the phenomenology of perception is such that change will be neither quick nor easy, and that word usage will be nowhere near sufficient to make this change.[30] The transformation of perceptual habits will require a more active and a more practical intervention.

The second obstacle to the deracialization of (at least most) people of color has nothing to with perception or bodily features. This obstacle refers back to a claim I made at the beginning, that assertions of group solidarity among African Americans, Native Americans, and Latinas/os in the United States provoke resistance among many whites because they invoke the history of colonialism, slavery, and genocide. Thus, their acceptance as full players within U.S. society comes at much greater cost than the acceptance of previously vilified groups such as the Irish and Jews—groups that suffered terrible discrimination and violence including genocide but whose history is not a thorn in the side of "pilgrim's progress," "manifest destiny," "leader of the free world," and other such mythic narratives that legitimize U.S. world dominance and provide white Americans with a strong sense of pride. The Irish and Jews were (are) colonized peoples in Europe, and there they are reminders of colonization and genocide. But they do not play this role in the legitimizing narratives of the U.S. state. Thus, the line between European ethnicities and people of color is not merely or perhaps even primarily about skin tone but about history and power and the narratives by which currently existing power arrangements are justified.

So what are we to do? If the move from race to ethnicity is not as easy as some have thought, what is a more realistic strategy, one that will also resist being fatalistic about racialization? How can we avoid both fatalism and naïveté? Are we to accept, then, that Latina/o identity is a racial identity, despite all the facts I have reviewed about our heterogeneity and different methods of self-identification, and all the pernicious effects of racialized identity? In conclusion, I can only sketch the outlines of an answer.

Although racial ideology and practices of racialization seem to always carry within them some commitment to biological essentialism, perhaps the *meaning* of race is transformable. If race is going to be with us for some time to come, it might still be the case that race itself will alter in meaning, even before the perceptual practices of racialization can be done away with. It seems to me that this change in meaning is exactly what Paul Gilroy is attempting to chart, as well as to promote, in *The Black Atlantic*, as well as what some other African American theorists are doing, such as Robert Gooding-Williams, bell hooks, Lewis Gordon, and Patricia Willlliams.[31] You will notice in their works an intentional use of the term *black* rather than *African American*; I think this is meant as a way to "be real" about the social reality we live in, and also as a way to suggest a linked fate between all black people across nationalities, at least in the diaspora. But in their works, blackness has been decidedly de-essentialized and given a meaning that consists of historical experience, collective memory, and forms of cultural expression. For Gilroy, there is a "blackness" that transcends and survives the differences of UK, Caribbean, and U.S. nationalities, a blackness that can be seen in culture and narrative focus. Blackness is social location, shared history, and a shared perception about the world. For Gooding-Williams, black identity requires a certain self-consciousness about creating the meaning of blackness. It requires, in other words, not only that one is treated as a black person, or that one is "objectively" black, but that one is "subjectively" black as well, and thus that one exercises some agency in regard to their identity. His argument is not simply that this is how we should begin to use the term *black*, but it is how the term is actually used in common parlance, as in "Is Clarence Thomas really black?"

Whether such an approach can be used for Latinas/os, I am not sure. There is probably even greater diversity among Latinas/os in relation to history, social location, and forms of cultural expression than there is among black people across the diaspora. And the question of where black Latinas/os "fit" is still unresolved, even when we make racial identity a matter of self-creation. This is a serious weakness in Gilroy's broad conceptualization of a "black Atlantic": Brazil, as large a country as it is, is nowhere to be found.

But I believe that we can take an important lesson from this body of work because it suggests that, even while we must remember the persistent power of racialization and the inability of ethnicity to easily take its place, the meanings of race are subject to some movement. Only a semantic essentialist could argue that race can mean nothing but biological essentialism; in reality, this is not the way meaning works. Let me be clear about my position here: I don't believe, à la some postmodernists, that signifiers are slippery items whose meanings and associations can be easily transformed. Like Michelle Moody-Adams, I would argue that some *can* be (as in "black is beautiful") and some *cannot* be (as in "spic").[32] Meaning works through iterability, that is, the invocation of prior meanings. When those prior meanings are centuries old and globally spread, they are going to be hard to dislodge. On the other hand, words do not simply pick out things that exist prior to their being picked out, and thus reference is mutable.

So the first point I am making is this: despite our hopes that the influx of Latinas/os on the North American continent, in all of our beautiful diversity, would transform and annihilate the binaries and purist racial ideologies prevalent in the United States, this is not likely, at least not very soon. Existing systems of meaning will absorb and transform our own self-identifying terms in ways that may not be immediately obvious but which we need to become aware of. However, although we may be stuck with racial categories for longer than some of us would wish, it may be easier to help "race" slowly evolve than to try to do away with it as a first step.

Latinas/os in the United States have without a doubt been racialized. And I would argue that the history, and even the contemporary socioeconomic situation, of Latinas/os in the United States simply cannot be understood using ethnicity categories alone; we have been shut out of the melting pot because we have been seen as racial and not merely cultural "others."

However, this has not been true to the same degree for all of us. It has been true of Mexicans, Puerto Ricans, and Dominicans most of all, much less so of some others. So what are we to do in the face of this diversity of historical experience and social location? Is race perhaps a way to understand some Latina/o identities but not all? For a pan-Latina/o moniker, shouldn't we refer to ethnicity?

My argument has been that given the way in which our ethnicity has been racialized, this is a doubtful solution. Moreover, we are in almost all cases racially different from Anglos, in the commonly used sense of race. That is—even for Spaniards, as Jorge Gracia is arguing—we are not "purely European," claims of white Hispanicity notwithstanding. In the very name of antiracism and solidarity with other racialized people of color, shouldn't we acknowledge this, and not go the route of those who would seek to better their social status by differentiating themselves from the vilified racial others? Perhaps we can help lift the meaning of race out of its status as an insult by uniting with the efforts of those such as Gilroy and Gooding-Williams, who seek to give it a cultural meaning.

people go off of race & not ones ethnicity!!

binary-2

Of course, it does not make sense to say simply that Latinas/os constitute a "race," either by the commonsense meaning or by more nuanced references to historical narrative and cultural production. I (still) believe that if the concept of "mestizo" enters into U.S. culture, it can have some good effects against the presumption of purity as having an intrinsic value. Still, the concept of mestizo when applied to Latinas/os in general, as if all Latinas/os or the essence of being Latina/o is to be mestizo, has the effect of subordinating all Latinas/os, both North and South, whose descendants are entirely African, Indian, or Asian. Mestizos then become the cornerstone of the culture, with others pushed off to the side. This is clearly intolerable.

A concept that might be helpful here has been coined by David Theo Goldberg: ethnorace. Unlike race, ethnorace does not imply a common descent, which is precisely what tends to embroil race in notions of biological determinism and natural and heritable characteristics. Ethnorace might have the advantage of bringing into play the elements of both human agency and subjectivity involved in ethnicity—that is, an identity that is the product of self-creation—at the same time that it acknowledges the uncontrolled racializing aspects associated with the visible body. And the term would remind us that there are at least two concepts, rather than one, that are vitally necessary to the understanding of Latina/o identity in the United States: ethnicity and race. Using only ethnicity belies the reality of most Latinas/os' everyday experiences, as well as obscures our own awareness about how ethnic identifications often do the work of race while seeming to be theoretically correct and politically advanced. Race dogs our steps; let us not run from it lest we cause it to increase its determination.

NOTES

Jorge Gracia gave me substantive help with this paper at all stages, for which I am extremely grateful. I am also very grateful to Pablo De Greiff, Eduardo Mendieta, Paula Moya, Angelo Corlett, and an anonymous reviewer for their helpful comments.

1. See Angel R. Oquendo, "Re-imagining the Latino/a Race," in *The Latino/a Condition: A Critical Reader*, ed. Richard Delgado and Jean Stefancic (New York: New York University Press, 1998), p. 61.

2. I do not mean to imply here that the recent marketing construction of a pan-Latina/o U.S. identity is the first or only time such an identity has been imagined. I will discuss this further on.

3. See Todd Gitlin, *The Twilight of Common Dreams: Why America Is Wracked by Culture Wars* (New York: Henry Holt, 1995), and Arthur M. Schlesinger Jr., *The Disuniting of America: Reflections on a Multicultural Society*

(New York: W. W. Norton, 1992). Also see Jennifer L. Hochschild, *Facing Up to the American Dream* (Princeton: Princeton University Press, 1996), and Jean Bethke Elshtain, *Democracy on Trial* (New York: HarperCollins, 1997).

4. See Daniel Mato, "Problems in the Making of Representations of All-Encompassing U.S. Latina/o—'Latin' American Transitional Identities," *Latino Review of Books* 3, nos. 1–2 (1997): 2–7; Arlene Davila, "Advertising and Latino Cultural Fictions," in *Mambo Montage: The Latinization of New York,* ed. Arlene Davila and Agustín Lao-Montes (New York: Columbia University Press, 2001); Juan Flores and George Yudice, "Buscando América: Languages of Latino Self-Formation," *Social Text* 24 (1990): 57–84.

5. Michael Omi and Howard Winant, *Racial Formations in the United States: From the 1960s to the 1980s* (New York: Routledge, 1986), p. 60.

6. Suzanne Oboler, *Ethnic Labels, Latino Lives: Identity and the Politics of (Re)Presentation in the United States* (Minneapolis: University of Minnesota Press, 1995), p. xiii.

7. Mato, "Problems in the Making of Representations," p. 2.

8. Oboler, *Ethnic Labels, Latino Lives,* see esp. chap. 1.

9. Ibid., p. 13.

10. As a Panamanian American who vividly remembers the 1989 U.S. invasion but who has lived most of my life in the United States, growing up especially around Cubans, I found both arguments persuasive.

11. See Davila, "Advertising and Latino Cultural Fictions"; Mato, "Problems in the Making of Representations."

12. Mato, "Problems in the Making of Representations," p. 2.

13. Cited in Michel Foucault, *The Order of Things: An Archaeology of the Human Sciences* (New York: Random House, 1970), p. xv.

14. Jorge Gracia, personal communication, December 1998.

15. "Disparities Grow in SAT Scores of Ethnic and Racial Groups," *Chronicle of Higher Education,* September 11, 1998, p. A42. Emphasis added.

16. Anita Allen, "Recent Racial Constructions in the U.S. Census," paper presented at the "Race: Its Meaning and Significance" conference, Rutgers University, November 1994.

17. Ramón Grosfoguel and Chloe S. Georas, "The Racialization of Latino Caribbean Migrants in the New York Metropolitan Area," *CENTRO Journal of the Center for Puerto Rican Studies* 8, nos. 1–2 (1996): 199.

18. See, for example, Jorge Klor de Alva's arguments (against Cornel West) on this point in "Our Next Race Question: The Uneasiness between Blacks and Latinos," *Harper's,* April 1996, pp. 55–63.

19. Klor de Alva, "Our Next Race Question," p. 56.

20. Oquendo, "Re-imaging the Latino/a Race," p. 60.

21. Clara E. Rodríguez, *Puerto Ricans Born in the U.S.A.* (Boston: Unwin Hyman, 1989).

22. Anthony Appiah, *In My Father's House: Africa in the Philosophy of Culture* (New York: Oxford University Press, 1992); Naomi Zack, *Race and Mixed Race* (Philadelphia: Temple University Press, 1993).

23. Luis Angel Toro, "Race, Identity, and 'Box Checking': The Hispanic Classification in OMB Directive No. 15," in *The Latino/a Condition,* ed. Richard Del-

gado and Jean Stefanic (New York: New York University Press, 1998), p. 58. Emphasis in original.

24. Grosfoguel and Georas, "The Racialization of Latino Caribbean Migrants," p. 197.

25. Ibid., p. 198.

26. Ibid., p. 199.

27. Ibid., p. 195.

28. Virginia Domínguez, "Editor's Foreword: The Dialectics of Race and Culture," *Identities: Global Studies in Culture and Power* 1, no. 4 (1998): 297–300.

29. I am very aware of the paradoxical way this question is raised (since in a project of deracialization one shouldn't refer to people by their color), and of other paradoxes with the categories I've used at times in this paper (e.g., the use of the category "black" when I have argued that it is oppressive). It is impossible to avoid all such paradoxes while maintaining clarity about which groups one is trying to pick out. All I can hope to have done is to problematize all such categories, and increase our self-reflectiveness about them.

30. I make these arguments in more depth in my paper "The Phenomenology ofRacial Embodiment," *Radical Philosophy* 95 (May/June 1999): 15–26.

31. See Paul Gilroy, *The Black Atlantic: Modernity and Double Consciousness* (Cambridge: Harvard University Press, 1993); Robert Gooding-Williams, "Race, Multiculturalism, and Justice," *Constellations* 5, no. 1 (1998): 18–41; Patricia Williams, *Seeing a Color Blind Future: The Paradox of Race* (New York: Farrar, Straus, and Giroux, 1997); Lewis Gordon, *Bad Faith and Antiblack Racism* (Atlantic Highlands, NJ: Humanities Press, 1995).

32. Michele Moody-Adams, "Excitable Speech: A Politics of the Performative," *Women's Review of Books* 15, no. 1 (October 1997): 13–14. And I would suggest that even John Leguizamo's brilliant comic use of terms like "Spic-o-rama" plays off the negative connotations of the term rather than transforming it into a positive term.

Ofelia Schutte
(b. 1945)

O felia Schutte is a native of Havana, Cuba. In 1960 she immigrated to the United States, along with her parents. She received her BA in English literature from Barry College in Miami, Florida. Schutte then devoted herself to philosophy and received her MA in philosophy from Miami University of Ohio. She earned her PhD in philosophy from Yale University in 1978, with a thesis on Nietzsche. A leading Nietzsche scholar, Schutte is the author of *Beyond Nihilism: Nietzsche without Masks* (1984), which offers a feminist reading of Nietzsche, as well as several articles on other aspects of Nietzsche's thought.

In addition to her work on Nietzsche, Schutte has published widely on contemporary Latin American philosophy, with a special emphasis on the problem of cultural identity and feminism in Latin America. In her book *Cultural Identity and Social Liberation in Latin American Thought* (1993), Schutte critically assesses many of the thinkers included in Part IV of this anthology (e.g., Mariátegui, Ramos, Vasconcelos, Dussel, and Zea). She was one of the first philosophers in the United States to treat Latin American philosophy in a serious and systematic way. Her path-breaking book brought together a decade of her work in the field, building on seminal articles such as "Toward an Understanding of Latin American Philosophy: Reflection on the Formation of Cultural Identity" (1987) and "Philosophy and Feminism in Latin America: Perspectives on Gender Identity and Culture" (1989).

Schutte spent a considerable part of her teaching career as a professor of philosophy at the University of Florida, Gainesville. She is currently a professor of women's studies and philosophy at the University of South Florida at Tampa. She has been the recipient of several prestigious awards, including a Fulbright scholarship for research at the Universidad Nacional

Autónoma de México (1985–86) and a Mary Ingraham Bunting Institute Fellowship at the Radcliffe Research and Study Center in Cambridge, Massachusetts (1993).

The article included here analyzes the problem of cultural identity within a feminist perspective. Schutte discusses the various aspects of Latina identities and their construction by referencing her own experience as a Cuban Latina in the multicultural United States, discussing the limitations and freedoms associated with membership in each of these groups and the resulting hybrid identities that form. She then turns to a discussion of how individuals, while bound to certain identities not "primarily directed by [them]," are free to negotiate certain aspects of these group identities and so are not bound to them in an oppressive way.

Considering the problem of group rights from an aesthetic-political standpoint, Schutte "tend[s] to look at group differences as products of a vital way of affirming the plurality of cultures, rather than as a conservative apparatus used to demarcate, discipline, and police the boundaries and identities of groups." Schutte shows that checking a box marked "Hispanic" need not condemn one to a static identity formed of stereotypical images. The category "Hispanic" ties one to a shared cultural history, which one can negotiate in individual ways. Schutte's meditation on how Latina identity is negotiated is guided by autobiographical reflections and rich references to both Gloria Anzaldúa's innovative work in exploring Chicana identity and José Martí's vision of Cuban culture. Schutte argues against giving in to collective identities "already predefined for us and where we are thought to belong by virtue of our race, gender, ethnicity, class, nation, or religion," while "retaining our commitment to the defense of our cultural history."

Negotiating Latina Identities

This [essay] first calls attention to the problem of representing individuals as members of groups, taking the construction of Latino identities as a social process not primarily directed by individuals themselves, and therefore making them respond to larger interests. In the second part and as a way of contrast, the individual as agent in the definition of her own identifications is highlighted, and the analysis moves to the subjective question of negotiating Latina identities in a complexly constructed multicultural world.[1]

THE INDIVIDUAL AND THE GROUP

If we look at individuals from the standpoint of social relations, one could say that the "I" is always already a part of a "we." Even in cases of a type of socialization that leads to the exclusion of persons from the group, the excluded may be seen in relation to the group or groups that exclude them. Broadly speaking, the identification of individuals as members of a group may be self-derived or imposed by others, and the qualities associated with group membership may be either positive or negative. One question that emerges in the consideration of group rights is the metastructure providing an umbrella for understanding the activity of multiple groups and the interactions among them. For a normative model of the healthy interaction among groups one would probably need to turn to social psychology, ethics, or a theory of justice. This is not the aim of my [essay].

What concerns me is the dynamic between the individual and the group (or groups), the role of groups in the definition of personal identity, and the subjection of individuals to prejudice and discrimination due to their inclusion in some groups or exclusion from others.

The civil rights movement and the struggle against racism have shown the difference between being excluded from a group *as an individual* and being excluded *as a member of a specific group*. The Martinican writer Frantz Fanon conceptualized the difference well when he noted that racism did not mean that he was disliked by one of his relatives or by a couple of neighbors across the street—situations that approximate the concept of individual rejection—but that the rejection is *group-derived:* "Look, a Negro!" anyone would say as he walked by.[2] The rejection had nothing to do with his individual characteristics, that is, with traits pertaining to his individual person; it had everything to do with his being identified as a member of the black race. Group membership, in normal conditions, is something that brings people social recognition—such as to be a member of a guild, of a profession, of a civic group. For this reason it is important that group membership does not turn into a condition of adversity for some and privilege for others. This is why, at the level of policymaking, our society needs to be concerned with the balance of group representation, and to make sure that leadership positions in civil society and the state are not only open to, but also filled by, members of "underrepresented groups."

Racial discrimination and prejudice, just like ethnic discrimination and prejudice, are group-related forms of discrimination. Individuals caught in the web of group discrimination have at least three ways to fight it: (1) try to disassociate as much as possible from the discriminated group, by adopting the values and norms of the dominant group, sometimes (though not necessarily) by marrying a member of the dominant group, or by assimilating "upward" into the dominant power; the cost of this option could be the separation from relatives and friends who remain trapped in the discriminated group, or the rejection of qualities in oneself that "mark" one as a member of the discriminated group; (2) migrate (translocate) to a more congenial environment, which could signify a more positive and less alienated form of assimilation; again, this is not always a possible option, and there may not be environments sufficiently free from prejudice to which one may migrate successfully; (3) work to change the group status and to reconstitute group rights along a model of fairness aimed at transforming the dominant society. The first two constitute individual solutions; the third involves a social solution.

The work of Hispanic intellectuals engaged in Latino/Latin American studies may constitute an intersection of (2) and (3). That is, we have become sufficiently assimilated to work in the U.S. academy and do so successfully. At the same time, we use our position, at least in part, to help sustain the recognition of Hispanic studies and, insofar as possible, support the inclusion of marginalized groups in various spheres of citizenship activities, including higher education. This is tricky conceptually, because even as we may refer to group rights or to the need for inclusion of members of underrepresented groups in higher education, for example, what we are actually doing is promoting conditions for the assimilation of members of the underrepresented groups into the mainstream. The main difference between today and yesteryear, however, is that in the past the conceptual framework marking the assimilation referred to persons gaining inclusion in terms of their individual merits, whereas today the framework is given, more often than not, by identifying persons as members of a group deserving special attention.

If I am not mistaken, we seem to be living in an era whose cultural-political profile is the assimilation of groups into one national and, ultimately, global agenda. The inclusion of multiple perspectives one hopes to promote by extending leadership positions to persons of differently constituted groups (by sex, race, or ethnicity) remains subordinate to the goals of an impersonal "system" whose task is continually to increase its performance through the incorporation of differences and the delivery of new products for ever more extensive markets of consumption. In other words, group segregation is giving way to group assimilation as capitalism expands throughout the world without opposition, while in the United States a percentage of individuals from economically marginalized minorities joins the middle class. What we may be learning, however, from the current global crisis in capitalist markets is that where assimilation fails, the phenomenon that describes the position of the nonassimilated is more one of "dropping off" than one of outright exclusion. Whole nations, we are told, will simply drop off the global network of investments if they cannot adjust to the requirements and constraints established by the International Monetary Fund. Charity toward the needy is being ruled out. I suspect that somehow, in an analogous vein, the extension of entitlements to minority populations is predicated on the assumption that these populations (or influential parts of them) will become a highly productive part of the current socioeconomic system and will indeed extend the market value of the system and its products to "developing" regions and populations.

Seen in this context, affirmative action initiatives are fundamentally strategies of economic and cultural integration wherein previously marginalized or alienated populations (or segments thereof) are brought into the mainstream of socioeconomic mores, work habits, and productive activities. Affirmative action should be neither romanticized as the happy path to fame and fortune for women and minorities, nor vilified as the tool of special interests. One might look at it as a process of adjustment and balancing for stimulating a nation's economic indicators, much like what happens when the Federal Reserve raises or lowers interest rates by a fraction of a percent. Affirmative action involves the bet that the individuals recruited by the system—a fraction of its minority populations—will stimulate its growth and act as catalysts for the stability of the system. It is a process that accommodates some cultural and political interests that may otherwise be excluded and marginalized, in exchange for the revitalization and increased efficacy of an excessively homogeneous system dominated by whites, males, and the upper class. Of course, one has to believe one wants a diversified cultural elite (by gender, race, economic background, and ethnicity) in order for affirmative action programs to work. In a racist and masculine-dominant environment, affirmative action will not be taken seriously, and the leaders chosen will all look, think, and dress more or less alike.

If we follow the logic that the goal of affirmative action is the integration of the marginalized into the mainstream, then looking further into the future, it may be posited that in the long run this may lead to an indifference toward the preservation of diversity as constituted by ethnic or racial group membership. This is due to the fact that as groups become more assimilated into the global system, what will become more valued is the mobility of members across groups rather than their permanence or settlement within them. This is why territorial enclaves with a large predominance of (homogeneously defined) group members, who form part of a nation's racial and ethnic minorities, are vulnerable to being targeted for disfavor by the dominant economic establishment. The displacement of community populations from old-time neighborhoods, for example, shows that even the social structures of old barrios can be disbanded as upwardly mobile property owners move in, rezone a neighborhood, and expel the previous occupants toward ever more marginalized urban peripheries.

In the transitional phase in which we are living, a challenge for Hispanics is how to negotiate the tensions in our identities, taking into account our drive to succeed in the midst of adverse conditions, our interest in maintaining a meaningful degree of identification and solidarity with other Hispanics and with Hispanic communities even as we are assimilated into positions previously unoccupied by members of our ethnic group, and the knowledge that full assimilation calls for the erasure, abolition, and/or further marginalization and displacement of our groups. For example, in much popular (antidiversity) political rhetoric today, it is argued that it is *against* (not *for*) the benefit of Latino children to have Spanish taught in the schools, or that it is *against* (not *for*) the interest of minorities to have programs of affirmative action. In other words, one sees the trend today, except in enclaves where ethnic or racial minority status is politically and economically quite strong, as in south

Florida, toward the erosion of minority group rights in the name of national unity and global citizenship.

My view is that, contrary to these indicators, it is in the best interest of Hispanics to retain our ethnic/cultural identifications and insist on some form of political representation based on group classifications. I say this, however, with some important reservations, for, like technology, which can either heal or kill, group classifications may be used for the good, but also for great evil—as in holocausts, genocides, ethnic cleansing, and massive discrimination. The classification of individuals into groups for purposes of social policy control is subject to a number of significant objections, including the fact that group identifications are vulnerable to manipulation, are subject to easy stereotyping, and in fact can do violence to individuals who differ substantially from the mainstream members of their groups. A different kind of objection with which I sympathize is that if one classifies people according to their membership in groups, in a racist society this will result in dividing people racially. There may be nothing more abusive than to classify individuals according to their racial features, especially if such features have had a long history of being used to privilege some and oppress others.

In view of these qualifications and objections, I think the argument for group rights should be derived from a broader principle of social justice, and not from an appeal to the intrinsic property of groups. I say this tentatively. But clearly, my tendency is to fortify not the concept of group properties as such, but a different and broader principle that looks at cultures in a broad scope, and then defends the concept of having a substrate of differentiating elements in cultures, such as the plurality of languages, the affirmation of historical-cultural precedents for individuals' current identifications, the extension of leadership positions to new constituencies that challenge the narrow-mindedness of patterns of behavior inherited from the past, and so on. In other words, the argument for "group rights" would not be derived (at least principally) from (1) the existence of groups or (2) the duty to preserve them (as, say, conservationists defend the preservation of endangered species—an approach that, in the case of biological groups, or species rights, I take to be fully justified). Rather, the argument would be derived from a conception guided by the principles of a culturally pluralist, democratic society. Such a conception recognizes that to deprive human beings of favorable conditions by which they can be recognized for their specific linguistic and historical-cultural achievements and contributions is to inflict a degree of violence on them. From an aesthetic-political standpoint, I tend to look at group differences as products of a vital way of affirming the plurality of cultures, rather than as a conservative apparatus used to demarcate, discipline, and police the boundaries and identities of groups. This is an important distinction, some of whose constitutive elements will be illustrated in the remaining part of this [essay].

FROM BICULTURALITY TO HYBRID IDENTITIES

When my family moved to this country over thirty-five years ago, the term used to refer to the successful integration of immigrants into U.S. society was *bicultural*. Times have changed. The speed at which the mobility across and the interaction among cultures, so as to reach multiple sites of intersection among them, is taking place today has led to a paradigm change from the concept of biculturality to that of hybrid identities. The objective is no longer to master one, two, or more cultures as wholes, or totalities, that one must integrate or else juxtapose to each other in a neat, symmetrical fashion. The model is no longer to become a specimen of a cultural kind, which is conceived as an integral whole, but rather to "shop around" and become individuated by selecting from various aspects of cultural practices and options we can participate in, as citizens of a dynamic and changing multicultural society. This paradigm change from a bicultural identity to a hybrid one, however, may not be universally applicable to the experiences of each and every Hispanic because of the vast differences in the U.S. Latino population. This population includes, among others, recently arrived immigrants, older immigrants (now U.S. citizens), U.S.-born children of immigrants, descendants of residents of Hispanic territories occupied by the United States in the Southwest/Pacific area and Puerto Rico, children of unions between Latinos and other Americans of various races and ethnicities, and so on. The U.S. Latino today is situated in a cultural space apt for the negotiation of identities. These identities, as I classify them initially and somewhat freely, are: the assimilationist identity, the culture-of-origin identity (whether applied to the primary site of Hispanic identification within the United States—such as Miami or New Jersey for Cuban Americans—or to the country of origin), and the Latino identity. Clearly, it could be argued that at this point in history the Latino identity might function as a mediator of the other two. This is its power but also its weakness, since the Latino identity is doubly marginal: in one respect, it is marginal vis-à-vis the community/country/culture of origin, be it Cuba or "Little Havana" in Miami, for example; nevertheless, it is also marginal vis-à-vis the mainstream identity of the Anglo-American U.S. citizen.

   The construction of identity is so problematic that even as one attempts to articulate and defend something one cares deeply about, one is simultaneously "written," or scripted, as something one is not—in the sense of the limits and borders placed on identities, the media representations that codify and distribute such identities, the consumer/marketing demands that reproduce and expand them in the economic sector, and the political platforms and interest groups organized to "represent" them. The result is the construction of blocks of political and economic interests that are no longer defined by individuals, but that rather define and limit the identities the "Latino" may represent.

For this reason some Hispanics are genuinely skeptical that the promotion of Hispanic "identity" does them any good, given the vulnerability these "identities" have to being manipulated by big business, politicians, and the corporate media. They see the commercialization of the term *Hispanic* in the same way I might see the commercialization of the term *woman*, realizing that under this label the markets are trying to sell me something—a hairdo, an outfit, a way of life—that does not necessarily fit my personal taste. I understand what this view is pointing to, which is definitely a part of our reality in the contemporary world. But the fact that the words *woman* and *Hispanic* may be politicized or commercialized well beyond my taste, and even contrary to it, does not lead me to stop describing myself with these terms. It does not lead me to reject these categories even though I know that their stereotypes can offend me or that I can feel very differently from what poses as the norm for each. What it leads me to do is to adopt the principle of *recognizing the internal differences* among women, Hispanics, Cuban Americans, or what have you. This principle allows one to identify as a member of a group without being coerced into compliance with the group's image of its normative type. For example, in some sectors of Hispanic culture one is expected to approve of bullfights and cockfights, to enjoy eating the entrails of animals, or not to use birth control. I deplore bullfights and cockfights, I follow a semivegetarian diet, and as a feminist, I believe a woman has a right to the full control of her body in sexual and reproductive matters. Do my views make me less of a Hispanic? I don't think so. I share a cultural history with many other Hispanic people, even if we may disagree about some particular opinions. It is the sharing of the cultural history and my investment in continuing the narrative of that cultural history, adding my own modifications to it, that makes me a Hispanic. And yet I agree that since the first time I filled out a form and marked the little box saying "Hispanic," and even prior to checking that box, the signifier "Hispanic" and its mainstream representations have been marking me, no doubt. Where this leaves me politically is with the awareness that with respect to ethnicity, as with respect to gender or national origin, I must constantly negotiate my identifications (my identity) in relation to the representation and the political forces that mark me. In the concluding part of the [essay] I offer a description of some of the tensions this negotiation entails.

IDENTITIES IN TENSION

In her now-classic work *Borderlands/La Frontera*, Gloria Anzaldúa provides an illustration of the multifaceted identity of a Chicana feminist.
Anzaldúa reflects on growing up in south Texas, where the legacies of different cultures intersect. She mentions how easy it is to be torn apart by
the variable and sometimes conflicting demands of a multicultural background composed of Indian, Mexican, and North American elements.
"Like all people," she says, "we perceive the version of reality that our culture communicates. Like others having or living in more than one culture,
we get multiple, even opposing messages."[3] There is, above all, the pain
of realizing that some of these elements have been oppressors of others:
the Mexican has oppressed the Indian, and the North American has
oppressed the other two. It is important for her to overcome the anger and
the resentment that can build up when she sees the ways Chicanos are
discriminated against. Anzaldúa realizes one must be strong to fight and
overcome the effects of discrimination on one's people and on one's self.
In her own self, however, she has to bring together her complex identifications, and not let one or more of them exploit another. She has to create
a healing relationship between the Indian, the Chicana, and the North
American aspects of her self. I think that, apart from her psychological
attitude of inclusiveness and respect for all the different elements that
make up her self, she succeeds in creating this balance through the use of
language, alternating between English and Spanish in much of her prose,
from time to time using indigenous imagery to ground her thoughts. In
other words, in her writing and choice of how to define the topics she
writes about, she is able to bring together creatively the different elements
of her self. "The possibilities are numerous," she writes, "once we decide
to act and not to react."[4] Yet she adds a warning in a mixed tongue: "*Pero
es difícil* differentiating between *lo heredado, lo adquirido, lo impuesto*"
(yet it is difficult to differentiate between what is inherited, what is
acquired, and what is imposed).[5]

   Anzaldúa's example shows one creative way to approach the heterogeneity and mixture of elements in a person's multicultural background.
In fact, she describes her consciousness as one that speaks up for "la
nueva mestiza" (the new mestiza), where the word *mestiza* already indicates the concept of mixture. In referring to her position as that of "la
nueva mestiza" (emphasis added), a new cultural horizon is opened—one
that allows us to move to a larger category than "Chicana/Tejana." The
concept of "mestiza" is transferable to the category "Latina," which, like
"mestiza," encompasses far more than a reference to Chicana feminists.
Since the 1980s "Latina" has been used increasingly to describe women of

all Hispanic American backgrounds residing in the United States. It allows Hispanic American women the use of a common designator, surpassing the more specific designators of "Chicana," "puertoriqueña," "Cubana-Americana," and so on. One question I raise regarding this new identity category in terms of which we are often asked to speak and write as members of the designated group is: What are we gaining and losing with the use of the ethnic terms? What difference does it make, for example, if I speak as a Cuban American or as a Latina in various contexts?

The answer to this question is not a simple one. To start the discussion, let me raise another question: Is it the case that "Latina" references our identity in terms of a minority population in the United States (that is, taking the United States as a national entity), whereas a category such as "Chicana," "puertoriqueña," or "Cubana-Americana" references us in terms of our home region or homeland (whether inside or outside the official United States)? For example, is it the case that "puertoriqueña" would reference one with respect to the island culture or its diaspora, whereas "Latina," used to refer to the same person, would mark her as a minority of Latin origin in the United States? And what are the connotations of meaning taken by these signifiers of difference (since both signify a difference vis-à-vis the Anglo Americans in the United States)? What are the social expectations accompanying one term or another? In my own case, as a Cuban American, I ask: Is it the case that "Latina" functions as a mark of difference with respect to the dominant sectors of North American society, whereas "cubana" functions as something that gives me historical roots and the mark of a freedom-loving people? As these terms apply to my life, "Latina" is a signifier of the demand for inclusion; "cubana" is a signifier of the demand for freedom. As the representation of these two ethnic identities intersect in my life, sometimes they are in agreement, yet they can also be in conflict, for it is easy to see that the demand for inclusion could lead to a loss of freedom, and the demand for freedom to a loss of inclusion. In this context, one may note that both the socialist and the anti-Communist Cubans (despite their disparate objectives) have preferred to take the consequences of exclusion rather than accept inclusion into a dominant order where they do not feel free. Cubans in the island and those "in exile" have responded, however differently, to the political heritage of José Martí, whose vision of culture was essentially linked to the exercise of freedom.[6] Martí believed that a people should be educated for the practice of freedom. One could push this thought to the limit, raising this question: If the order of representation into which one is likely to be included does not permit one's freedom (or one's freedom as grounded in citizen participation in a sovereign nation, as Martí believed), what sense does it make to demand inclusion in it?

The conflict or tension between one's homeland heritage and one's "minority" condition in the translocated environment does not end here for Hispanic women. As in the case of all women living in masculine-dominant societies, whether these be of Hispanic or some other cultural heritage, the body of woman is overdetermined by a masculine orientation in social symbolism. For example, the *cubana*'s body is free but it is also a symbol of service to the *patria*, the fatherland. When subordinated to North American values, in contrast, the *Latina*'s body is represented as undergoing liberation through assimilation in North American culture and its more individualistic values, yet it is also represented as a racialized (nonwhite) body, as an exotically sexual body, or as an impoverished, health-risk body in need of special assistance from the public health services. As Latina women, we have to negotiate our identity constantly in the midst of a complex of stereotypes that include masculine-dominant expectations (both Hispanic and non-Hispanic) as to what a woman should do with her body, in addition to undertaking another whole set of negotiations with respect to what a woman will do with her mind and how she will apply her intelligence.

In the imagined and existential horizons of Latino as well as Anglo-American moral expectations, ethical concepts such as freedom and justice can easily acquire one standard meaning for males, another for females. The moral virtues, such as prudence, love, and fairness, are engendered in their social codification, just as their social meaning also reflects a class stratification. Patriarchal gender ideology has understood sexual difference primarily through the symbolism of gender complementarity. The masculine and the feminine are viewed essentially as complementary, just as the feminine is essentially tied to the maternal. These views reinforce the view that heterosexuality and the woman's body as destined for motherhood are necessary requirements for a woman to be in good standing before the cultural community. It isn't until a culture provides alternative ways of constructing personal identity and gender identities—usually by introducing another principle of legitimization women can appeal to in order to justify new gender behaviors—that the old-fashioned gender requirements begin to get broken. This means that alternative gender cultures must be built and established that will break the hegemony, at the national or local level, of the body of woman serving to illustrate the unspoken myths of the nation or the community.[7] The body of woman needs to be disconnected from its instrumental role in the pursuit of national or ethnic objectives and given back to the women themselves. Thus the positions of reproductive choice, the right to pursue a person's sexual orientation, the rights to divorce, remarriage, and so on, constitute important developments in democratic culture, for a free person cannot exist without the right to regulate freely the affairs of her own sexuality and her own body. The traditionalists' appeal to culture in order to counter a woman's right to these freedoms is just as inappropriate as the appeal to culture to limit a subaltern race from receiving rights to full personhood.

LATINAS AND RACE

With respect to the body of the Latina, some feminist writers have reported a racialized objectification of their bodies and persons.[8] As a partial answer to this problem, feminists in the United States have set forth the category "women of color" as a positive, empowering term to designate women whose backgrounds are Asian, African, Indo-American, and Hispanic.

The degree to which the category "women of color" has been embraced by a large number of Latinas in the United States appears to indicate that this category works well for many people. Still, for Latinas who are white, this category may represent a problem, at least initially. Much more clarification and discussion are needed to determine what meaning those of us who are directly affected by the use of these terms want to give this category. Here I address two concerns. The first is to recommend that the category "women of color" be used critically. It should not rest on a binary opposition between white and nonwhite, wherein it is assumed that unless a woman is white, she is a woman of color. To maintain this binary, where white is also hierarchized over nonwhite, is to reproduce the ideology that white is the norm and brown, yellow, red, black, and mixed race are the marks of difference. This way of thinking, which reproduces the vestiges of racism, limits the Latina's voice to the repeated demand for inclusion in an order of representation marking her as "other." Instead, the meaning of "women of color" needs to assume a political significance, as it generally does in feminist theory, with respect to the agency of women in racially and ethnically marginalized groups who actively oppose racism, sexism, cultural imperialism, heterosexism, and so on.[9]

The second concern is addressed to the tendency to reduce "women of color" to "nonwhite women," the result of which is to identify Latinas as nonwhite. Unless it is stipulated by definition that all Latinas are nonwhite, it will be observed that some Latinas are white. Why is this so? "Latina," which signifies one's cultural heritage, refers to people of a great many racial configurations and mixtures. The caution here would be not to collapse all ethnic or cultural categories into racial categories (as when a cultural category, "Latina," is collapsed into the racial category "nonwhite"). Moreover, it is important to keep in mind that features associated with groups are not necessarily distributed evenly among individuals pertaining to such groups. This principle applies when making generalizations about culture, race, and geography. For instance, just as it would be inappropriate to say that New Yorkers (as individuals) are not white because the group "New Yorkers" contains people of many different races, so it is inappropriate to say that Latin Americans (as individuals) are not white, because the group "Latin Americans" is multiracial. We need to be cautious about generalizations that fail to take into account the internal differences within groups, just as we need to be watchful regarding how various groups in different parts of the world exercise and reproduce their own forms of racism against vulnerable populations.

But what if "Latina" (in the United States) should come to be understood only in the sense of "woman of color"? Could "color" refer to a certain way of relating to people and to a culture, without a direct correlation to the "color" of one's skin? Should white Latinas in the United States be excluded from the category "Latina"? I do not think so, because we come from a mestizo culture, and this culture is profoundly infectious (in the positive sense), that is, it is deep in our psyches. At least those of us who are committed to celebrating the inclusion of indigenous, Afro-Latin, and mestizo elements of Latino cultures will continue speaking from the Latina position. In my case, I cannot pretend to speak as a nonwhite person because I have not suffered in my body the kind of racialized discrimination routinely affecting many other Hispanics. Still, I know what it is to feel ethnic discrimination in terms of my cultural differences and particularly as an immigrant. There is a part of me that would like to say I am nonwhite in solidarity with all the Hispanics—as well as women, men, and children of other ethnic, national, and racial groups—who have definitely suffered the profound effects of racial discrimination. Yet I stop myself from going so far because I write from my own lived experience, and with respect to race I have a relative privilege many others have not enjoyed. Each one of us has a different history of assimilation and discrimination. If we follow the recognition of internal differences I mentioned earlier, this principle will allow us to speak as Latinas and Latinos, though not all our experiences are identical. The differences among us are important in the degree to which they make us strong. The consciousness of the differences in the way we have been discriminated against—by class, color, gender, sexual orientation, accent, migration status, national origin, and so on—make us stronger as a collective when it comes to denouncing injustice than if we limited the Latino identity only to those who were most down-and-out, primarily the poverty-stricken, non-English-speaking population. In fact, it is a strategy of hegemonic power to try to limit the acceptable categories of what counts as discrimination to the minimum of instances and to the most extreme and dire cases of need, precisely so that the multiple forms of discrimination currently existing in our daily lives, and not fitting the extreme category of the supra-oppressed, remain unredressed and invisible.

RECONCILING DIFFERENCES

Finally, and speaking about the heterogeneity of Latino voices, as a Cuban-American individual I confess I have spent a good part of the last fifteen years of my life simply negotiating the meaning of this small hyphen that stands between my Cuban and U.S. identities. I have often thought of the political/ideological relation between these two terms (Cuba and the United States) as the greatest binary, something constructed as a hard political opposition where a person must choose one or the other but not both. In the eyes of the self-identified "exile," even a family visit to a relative in Cuba or a visit to the island for personal reasons may qualify as collaboration with "Communism" and the island's political regime. This interpretation of Cuban Americans' reality, however, denies the differences existing both within the Cuban-American population and within the population of Cubans living in Cuba.[10] It represents a construct projecting an inflexible reading on the meaning of individuals' variously motivated activities and desires, including the desire to travel to hard-to-reach places and see things firsthand, in terms of one's on-site, concrete, embodied experience.[11] These activities and desires have a personal meaning for each individual and cannot be legislated for individuals by a political group.

My views on Cuba resemble the mainstream views of Canadians, Mexicans, and Europeans (to choose only some examples). It should be up to individuals themselves whether or not they choose to travel to Cuba, including how often they want to travel. The control of information on Cuba for propaganda purposes is much more likely to take place when travel is restricted than when travel is open and free. I want to have a normal relationship to my country of birth and to the people who live there, which also includes some family members. One of the hardest elements in the negotiation of my Latina identity was getting my relatives in Miami to accept the fact that I was going to travel to Cuba, visit relatives, revisit the sites of my childhood, and participate in international conferences there (all acceptable though not necessarily recommended activities as far as the U.S. government is concerned). In this context, I have found the Hispanic-Latina identity very comforting, because it allows me to speak as a Latina in terms of a broader group whose political views are not homogeneous and whose conception of culture recognizes the diversity of Latino/a experiences.[12] The Latina identification encourages me to recover my early childhood roots in my culture of origin, without forcing me, as a Cuban American, to split my cultural legacy, in terms of national origin, into two irreconcilable political halves. In this case, the Latina identity has provided me with a freedom and an opportunity that the political pressures on the expression of my Cuban-American identity made very difficult, if not impossible.

CONCLUSION

The concept of negotiating identities is one that feminists have employed in discussions of the politics of location. Insofar as movements such as identity politics have become part of the political discourse in the United States, so have feminists' efforts to maintain a healthy distance from what I could call "essentialized locations." We have learned to look at identities through the lenses of historical, cultural, economic, and other characteristics. Thanks to women of different sexual orientations, to women of different racial and ethnic backgrounds, to young and aging women, we have learned to look at the differences within groups and not just at the external differences among groups. If identities are products of history and culture and if one is not born with an essential identity written up in heaven and destined to be carried out for the term of one's life, then, given the right historical circumstances, a person can negotiate her way through the different pressures, conflicts, and tensions that bear on her concept of self as well as on her ongoing understanding of her social and political identity. Opportunities for transformative experiences where one fights one's way through the many trappings of ideology are needed if there is to be personal growth. In particular, I have tried to argue that it is important to resist the pressure to fit into collective identities already predefined for us and where we are thought to belong by virtue of our race, gender, ethnicity, class, nation, or religion. Without losing sight of the role of these variables and, in the case of Hispanics, while retaining our commitment to the defense of our cultural history and the continued relevance of the Spanish language in a multicultural, multiethnic, and multiracial society, the critique of essentialism has taught us to be suspicious of orthodoxy and to consider the full political implications—as well as opportunities for personal fulfillment—associated with the identities-in-the-making we ascribe to ourselves.

NOTES

1. In this essay, *Latino* and *Hispanic* have been used interchangeably. Throughout the paper, I am taking *identity* in the sense of the specificity of a person's self-image and values, rather than in a metaphysical sense of a oneness that exists in the midst of change and variations. The types of identities that are the focus of this paper are in fact identities in tension, unresolved identities. It is

only because a human being occupies multiple social roles and because there can be an imperfect fit between these roles or between the individual and the roles she is forced to occupy that the question arises, how do I negotiate my way through these different expectations? Moreover, how does one establish priorities among potentially conflicting expectations and roles?

2. Frantz Fanon, *Black Skin, White Masks* (New York: Grove, 1967), pp. 111–14.

3. Gloria Anzaldúa, *Borderlands/La Frontera* (San Francisco: Aunt Lute, 1987), p. 78.

4. Ibid., p. 79.

5. Ibid., p. 82.

6. Martí's political speeches and articles were often very pedagogical, insofar as he held that if others, including and especially North Americans, learned about the Cuban people's love of freedom, they would support and respect the Cubans'struggle against colonialism. For example, see the letter to the *New York Herald* dated May 2, 1895, signed by José Martí and Máximo Gómez, in their respective roles as the delegate of the Cuban Revolutionary Party and the chief of the Liberatory Army in the Cuban war of independence against Spain. José Martí, *Política de Nuestra América* (Mexico: Siglo XXI, 1979), pp. 284–92.

7. Compare Norma Alarcón, "Traddutora, Traditora: A Paradigmatic Figure of Chicana Feminism," in *Scattered Hegemonies*, ed. Inderpal Grewal and Caren Kaplan (Minneapolis: University of Minnesota Press, 1994), pp. 110–33.

8. See particularly María Lugones and Elizabeth V. Spelman, "Have We Got a Theory for You! Feminist Theory, Cultural Imperialism and the Demand for 'the Woman's Voice,'" *Women's Studies International Forum* 6, no. 6 (1983): 573–81; María Lugones, "Playfulness, 'World-Travelling,' and Loving Perception," *Hypatia: A Journal of Feminist Philosophy* 2, no. 2 (1987): 3–19.

9. The oppositional sense is used by Lugones in the article coauthored with Spelman. But note that even here the Hispana's chief or primary concern is the "complaint of exclusion" (Lugones and Spelman, "Have We Got a Theory for You!" p. 575). Thus the Latina voice comes to symbolize what I note both here and above as the demand for inclusion (with recognition of specific differences). The oppositional sense of "woman of color" can also be extended further to signify opposition to a racist "heteropatriarchy." This latter meaning can elicit the cooperation of politically progressive people across racial categories and sexual orientations. Nevertheless, it may alienate members of minority groups who do not identify primarily as feminist, queer, gay, or lesbian.

10. For an example of the diversification of points of view among Cubans and Cuban Americans, see Ruth Behar, ed., *Bridges to Cuba/Puentes a Cuba* (Ann Arbor: University of Michigan Press, 1995).

11. It is insufficient to relate to a place of origin relying only on personal memories, photographs, videos and movies, radio reports, newsprint, or narratives of others who recently have lived in that place, though this is not to say that the former are not helpful. As long as human beings are embodied beings, full contact with a geographical site involves the ability to visit it at least on occasion.

12. There are in fact many internal differences among Cuban Americans, though on the issue of U.S. policy toward Cuba the predominant view is conservative.

B.
The Thought
and Philosophy

Leopoldo Zea
(b. 1912)

Leopoldo Zea was born in Mexico City, where he studied with Antonio Caso, Samuel Ramos, and later with the Spanish exile José Gaos. He is currently a professor at the Universidad Nacional Autónoma de Mexico. In 2000 he was awarded the Belisario Domínguez medal from the Mexican government. He has also received honorary degrees from the Universidad de Santiago (Chile), the Universidad de la Habana (Cuba), and the National University of Athens (Greece), as well as recognition from the Venezuelan government for his contributions to Latin American thought.

These awards come at the end of a life devoted to the cultivation of intellectual life in Mexico and beyond. Zea was the organizer of the philosophical group Hiperión, which had as its aim the establishment of a philosophy based on the examination of the Mexican man and his characteristics. Among the thinkers who took part in this group and who followed Zea's direction are Emilio Uranda, Ricardo Guerra, Joaquín McGregor, Jorge Portilla, Luis Villoro, and Fausto Vega.

The first of Zea's important works was *El positivismo en Mexico* (1943), which was his master's thesis. In the next year, his doctoral thesis, *Apogeo y decadencia del positivismo en México* (1944), appeared. He wrote this under the supervision of the Spanish *transterrado*, José Gaos. Through Gaos, the work of the Spanish philosopher José Ortega y Gasset had a strong influence on the development of Zea's views. One of Ortega's most important insights was that in order to understand ourselves, we must understand our circumstance. Zea developed this view while studying the history of Mexican philosophy and reflecting upon the specific historical circumstances from which it emerged.

Among Zea's most important books are *En torno a una filosofia Amer-*

icana (1945), *La filosofia como compromiso y otros ensayos* (1952), *Conciencia y posibilidad del mexicano* (1952), *América como conciencia* (1953), *La filosofia en Mexico* (1955), *La filosofia sin más* (1969), *Latinoamérica: Tercer Mundo* (1977), *Discurso desde la marginación y la barbarie* (1988), and *Descubrimiento e identidad latinoamericana* (1990). Many of his works have been translated into English, and he published several articles early in his career in North American philosophical journals.

His thought focuses upon a very particular conception of philosophy. Philosophy for him is not a system of abstract and theoretical propositions, but the product of "men of flesh and bones struggling in their own circumstances." Every philosophy, according to Zea, emerges from specific historical situations; this is why one must reflect upon such circumstances in order to understand reality.

Zea was one of the first Latin American thinkers explicitly concerned with the search for the identity of Latin American thought. The first of the two articles by him included here is one of the earliest he published on the subject of the search for identity. It was groundbreaking. His position, based on a culturalist point of view, categorically affirms the existence of a Latin American philosophy. Zea argues that every form of thought emerging in Latin America is Latin American philosophy. The reason is that Latin American thought arises from specifically historical Latin American circumstances and addresses those circumstances.

The second article addresses specific moments in the history of Latin American countries; the colonization and the fight for independence from colonial powers, and the struggle to assert a cultural identity and to free the countries of Latin America from dependence upon other powers. In this article, Zea discusses a topic that is central to his thought, *mestizaje*. The term *mestizaje* points to Zea's interest in issues related to race and culture, and Zea uses the term to open a philosophical discussion concerning the identity of a person who is of both Spanish and indigenous heritage. As issues of race have recently become more central in philosophy, Zea's contributions are more relevant than ever.

The Actual Function of
Philosophy in Latin America

1

Some years ago, a young Mexican teacher published a book that caused much sensation. This young teacher was Samuel Ramos and the book was *El perfil del hombre y la cultura en México*. This book was the first attempt at interpreting Mexican culture. In it Mexican culture became the subject of philosophical interpretation. Philosophy came down from the world of ideal entities to a world of concrete entities like Mexico, a symbol of men who live and die in their cities and farms. This daring attempt was derogatorily termed *literature*. Philosophy could not be anything other than a clever game of words taken from an alien culture. These words of course lacked meaning: the meaning they had for that alien culture.

Years later another teacher, this time the Argentinian Francisco Romero, emphasized Ibero-America's need to begin thinking about its own issues, and the need to delve into the history of its culture in order to take from it the issues needed for the development of a new type of philosophical concern. This time, however, Romero's call was based on a series of cultural phenomena that he identified in an essay entitled "Sobre la filosofía en Iberoamerica." In this article he showed how the interest in philosophical issues in Latin America was increasing on a daily basis. The public at large now follows and asks with interest for works of a philosophical character and nature. This has resulted in numerous publications—books, journals, newspaper articles, etc.—and also in the creation of institutes and centers for philosophical studies where philosophy is

From Leopoldo Zea, *Ensayos sobre filosofía en la historia* (Mexico City: Stylo, 1948), pp. 165–77. Originally published in *Cuadernos Americanos* (1942). Reprinted by permission of the author.

practiced. This interest in philosophy stands in sharp contrast with periods when such an activity was confined to a few misunderstood men. Their activity did not transcend literary or academic circles. Today, we have reached the level that Romero calls "the period of philosophical normalcy," that is, a period in which the practice of philosophy is seen as a function of culture just as is the case with any other activity of a cultural nature. The philosopher ceases to be an eccentric whom nobody cares to understand and becomes a member of his country's culture. There is what one may call a "philosophical environment," that is, a public opinion that judges philosophical production, thus forcing it to address the issues that concern those who are part of this so-called public opinion.

Now, there is one particular issue that concerns not only a few men in our continent, but the Latin American man in general. This issue concerns the possibility or impossibility of Latin American culture, and, as an aspect of the same issue, the possibility or impossibility of Latin American philosophy. Latin American philosophy can exist if there is a Latin American culture from which this philosophy may take its issues. The existence of Latin American philosophy depends on whether or not there is Latin American culture. However, the formulation and attempt to solve this problem, apart from the affirmative or negative character of the answer, are already Latin American philosophy, since they are an attempt to answer affirmatively or negatively a Latin American question. Hence, the works of Ramos, Romero, and others on this issue, whatever their conclusions, are already Latin American philosophy.

The issue involved in the possibility of Latin American culture is one demanded by our time and the historical circumstances in which we find ourselves. The Latin American man had not thought much about this issue before because it did not worry him. A Latin American culture, a culture proper to the Latin American man, was considered to be an irrelevant issue; Latin America lived comfortably under the shadow of European culture. However, the latter culture has been shaken (or is in crisis) today, and it seems to have disappeared from the entire European continent. The Latin American man who had lived so comfortably found that the culture that supported him fails him, that he has no future, and that the ideas in which he believed have become useless artifacts, without sense, lacking value even for their own authors. The man who had lived with so much confidence under a tree he had not planted now finds himself in the open when the planter cuts down the tree and throws it into the fire as useless. The man now has to plant his own cultural tree, create his own ideas. But a culture does not emerge miraculously; the seed of that culture must be taken from somewhere, it must belong to someone. Now—and this is the issue that concerns the Latin American man—where is he going to find that seed? That is, what ideas is he going to develop? To what ideas is he going to give his faith? Will he continue to believe and develop the ideas inherited from Europe? Or is there a group of ideas and issues to be developed that are proper to the Latin American circumstance? Or rather, will he have to invent those ideas? In a word, the problem of the existence, or lack of existence, of ideas that are proper to America, as well as the problem of the acceptance or rejection of ideas belonging to European culture that is now in crisis, comes to the fore. Specifically, the problem of the relationship between Latin America and European culture, and the problem of the possibility for a genuinely Latin American ideology.

2

In light of what has been said it is clear that one of the primary issues involved in Latin American philosophy concerns the relations between Latin America and European culture. Now, the first thing that needs to be asked has to do with the type of relations that Latin America has with that culture. There are some who have compared this relationship to that between Asia and European culture. It is said that Latin America, just as Asia, has assimilated only technology from Europe. But if this is so, what would belong to Latin American culture? For the Asian man, what he has adopted from European culture is regarded as something superimposed that he has had to assimilate owing to the change in his own circumstance caused in turn by European intervention. However, what he has adopted from European culture is not properly the culture, that is, a lifestyle, a worldview, but only its instruments, its technology. Asians know that they have inherited an age-old culture that has been transmitted from generation to generation; they know that they have their own culture. Their view of the world is practically the opposite of the European. From Europeans they have only adopted their technology, and only because they have been forced to do so by the intervention of Europeans and their technology in a circumstance that is properly Asian. Our present day shows what Asians can do with their own worldview while using European technology. Asians have little concern for the future of European culture, and they will try to destroy it if they feel that it gets in their way or continues to intervene in what they regard as their own culture. Now, can we Latin Americans think in a similar way about European culture? To think so is to believe that we have our own culture, but that this culture has not perhaps reached full expression yet because Europe has prevented it. In light of this, one could think that this is a good time to achieve cultural liberation. If that were the case, the crisis of European culture would not concern us. More than a problem, such a crisis would be a solution. But this is not the case: we are deeply concerned about the crisis of European culture; we experience it as our own crisis.

This is due to the fact that our relationship with European culture as Latin Americans is different from that of the Asians. We do not feel, as Asians do, the heirs of our own autochthonous culture. There was, yes, an indigenous culture—Aztec, Maya, Inca, etc.—but this culture does not represent, for us contemporary Latin Americans, the same thing that ancient Oriental culture represents for contemporary Asians. While Asians continue to view the world as their ancestors did, we Latin Americans do not view the world as the Aztecs or the Mayans did. If we did, we would have the same devotion for pre-Columbian temples and divinities that an Oriental has for his very ancient gods and temples. A Mayan temple is as alien and meaningless to us as a Hindu temple.

What belongs to us, what is properly Latin American, is not to be found in pre-Columbian culture. Is it to be found in European culture? Now, something strange happens to us in relation to European culture: we use it but we do not consider it ours; we feel *imitators* of it. Our way of thinking, our worldview, is similar to the European. European culture has a meaning for us that we do not find in pre-Columbian culture. Still, we do not feel it to be our own. We feel as bastards who profit from goods to which they have no right. We feel as if we were wearing someone else's clothes: they are too big for our size. We assimilate their ideas but cannot live up to them. We feel that we should realize the ideals of European culture, but we also feel incapable of carrying out the task: we are content with admiring them and thinking that they are not made for us. This is the knot of our problem: we do not feel heirs of an autochthonous culture, because that culture has no meaning for us; and that which has meaning for us, like the European, does not feel as our own. There is something that makes us lean toward European culture while at the same time resists becoming part of that culture. Our view of the world is European but we perceive the achievements of that culture as alien. And when we try to realize its ideals in Latin America we feel as imitators.

What is properly ours, what is Latin American, makes us lean toward Europe and at the same time resists being Europe. Latin America leans toward Europe as a son to his father, but at the same time it resists becoming like his own father. This resistance is noticeable in that, despite leaning toward European culture, Latin America still feels like an imitator when it seeks to achieve what that culture does. It does not feel that it is realizing what is proper to it but only what Europe alone can achieve. That is why we feel inhibited by and inferior to Europeans. The malaise resides in that we perceive what is Latin American, that is, what is ours, as something inferior. The Latin American man's resistance to being like a European is felt as an incapacity. We think as Europeans, but we do not feel that this is enough; we also want to achieve the same things that Europe achieves. The malaise is that we want to adjust the Latin American circumstance to a conception of the world inherited from Europe, rather than adjusting that conception of the world to the Latin American circumstance. Hence the divorce between ideas and reality. We need the ideas of European culture, but when we bring them into our circumstance we find them to be too big because we do not dare to fit them to this circumstance. We find them big and are afraid to cut them down; we prefer to endure the ridicule of wearing an oversize suit. Indeed, until recently the Latin American man wanted to forget what he is for the sake of becoming another European. This is similar to the case of a son who wants to forget being a son in order to be his own father: the result has to be a gross imitation. This is what the Latin American man feels: that he has tried to imitate rather than to realize his own personality.

Alfonso Reyes portrays the Latin American man's resistance to being Latin American with great humor. The Latin American man felt "in addition to the misfortune of being human and modern, the very specific misfortune of being Latin American; that is, having been born and having roots in a land that was not the center of civilization, but rather a branch of it."[1] To be a Latin American was until very recently a great misfortune, because this did not allow us to be European. Today it is just the opposite: the inability to become European, in spite of our great efforts, allows us to have a personality; it allows us to learn, in this moment of crisis for European culture, that there is something of our own that can give us support. What this something is should be one of the issues that a Latin American philosophy must investigate.

3

Latin America is the daughter of European culture; it is the product of one of its major crises. The discovery of America[2] was not a matter of chance, but rather the product of necessity. Europe needed America: in every European mind there was the idea of America, the idea of a promised land. A land where the European man could place his ideas, since he could no longer continue to place them in the highest places. He could no longer place them in the heavens. Owing to the emergence of a new physics, the heavens were no longer the home of ideals but rather became something unlimited, a mechanical and therefore dead infinity. The idea of an ideal world came down from heaven and landed in America. Hence the European man came out in search of the land and he found it.

The European needed to rid himself of a worldview of which he was tired. He needed to get rid of his past and begin a new life. He needed to build a new history, one that would be well planned and calculated, without excess or wanting. What the European was afraid of openly proposing in his own land, he took for granted in this land called America. America became the pretext for criticizing Europe. What he wanted Europe to be became imaginarily fulfilled in America. Fantastic cities and governments that corresponded to the ideals of the modern man were imagined in America. America was presented as the idea of what Europe should be. America became Europe's utopia. It became the ideal world that the old Western world was to follow to rebuild itself. In a word, America was the ideal creation of Europe.

America was born to history as a land of projects, as a land of the future, but of projects and a future that were not its own. Such projects and such future were Europe's. The European man who put his feet in this America—becoming part of the Latin American circumstance and giving rise to the Latin American man—has been unable to see what is properly American. He has only seen what Europe wanted America to be. When he did not find what European imagination had placed in the American continent, he was disappointed, and this produced the uprooting of the Latin American man from his own circumstance. The Latin American man feels European by origin, but he feels inferior to the European man by reason of his circumstance. He feels inadequate because he regards himself as superior to his circumstance, but inferior to the culture he comes from. He feels contempt for things Latin American, and resentment toward Europe.

Rather than attempting to achieve what is proper to Latin America, the Latin American man labors to achieve the European utopia and thus stumbles, as it could be expected, into a Latin American reality that resists being anything other than what it is: Latin America. This gives rise to the feeling of inferiority about which we already have spoken. The Latin American man considers his reality to be inferior to what he believes to be his destiny. In Anglo-Saxon America this feeling expresses itself in the desire to achieve what Europe has achieved in order to satisfy its own needs. North America has strived to become a second Europe, a magnified copy of it. Original creation does not matter, what matters is to achieve the European models in a big way and with the greatest perfection. Everything is reduced to numbers: so many dollars or so many meters. In the end, the only thing that is sought with this is to hide a feeling of inferiority. The North American tries to show that he is as capable as the European. And the way to show it is by doing the same things that Europeans have done, on a bigger scale and with greater technical perfection. But this only demonstrates technical, not cultural ability, because cultural ability is demonstrated in the solution one gives to the problems of man's existence, and not in the technical imitation of solutions that other men found for their own problems.

The Latin American man, however, feels inferior not only to the European, but also to the North American man. Not only does he no longer try to hide his feeling of inferiority, but he also exhibits it through self-denigration. The only thing that he has tried to do so far is to live comfortably under the shadow of ideas he knows are not his own. To him, ideas do not matter as much as the way to benefit from them. That is why our politics have turned into bureaucracy. Politics is no longer an end but an instrument to get a job in the bureaucracy. Banners and ideals do not matter anymore; what matters is how these banners and ideals can help us get the job we want. Hence the miraculous and quick change of banners; whence also that we always plan and project but we never achieve definitive results. We are continually experimenting and projecting with always-changing ideologies. There is no single national plan because there is no sense of nation. And there is no sense of nation for the same reason that there is no sense of what is Latin American. He who feels inferior as Latin American also feels inferior as a national, that is, as a member of one of the Latin American nations. This is not to say that the fanatic nationalist who talks about a Mexican, Argentinian, Chilean, or any other Latin American nation's culture, to the exclusion of anything that smacks of foreign, has any better sense of what a nation is. No, in the end he would only try to eliminate what makes him feel inferior. This is the case of those who say that this is the appropriate time to eliminate everything European from our culture.

This position is wrong because, whether we want it or not, we are the children of European culture. From Europe we have received our cultural framework, what could be called our structure: language, religion, customs; in a word, our conception of life and world is European. To become disengaged from it would be to become disengaged from the heart of our personality. We can no more deny that culture than we can deny our parents. And just as we have a personality that makes us distinct from our parents without having to deny them, we should also be able to have a cultural personality without having to deny the culture of which we are children. To be aware of our true relations with European culture eliminates our sense of inferiority and gives us instead a *sense of responsibility*. This is the feeling that animates the Latin American man today. He feels that he has "come of age," and, as any other man who reaches maturity, he acknowledges that he has a past that he does not need to deny, just as no one is ashamed of having had a childhood. The Latin American man knows himself to be the heir of Western culture and now demands a place in it. The place that he demands is that of collaborator. As a son of that culture he no longer wants to live off it but to work for it. Alfonso Reyes, speaking on behalf of a Latin America that feels responsible, demanded from Europe "the right of universal citizenship that we have already conquered," because already "we have come of age."[3] Latin America is at a point in its history when it must realize its cultural mission. To determine this mission constitutes another issue that what we have called Latin American philosophy has to develop.

4

Once we know our cultural relations with Europe, another task for this possible Latin American philosophy would be to continue to develop the philosophical issues of that culture, but most especially the issues that European philosophy regards as universal. That is, issues whose level of abstraction allows them to be valid at any time and at any place. Among such issues are those of being, knowledge, space, time, God, life, death, etc. A Latin American philosophy can collaborate with Western culture by attempting to resolve the problems posed by the issues that European philosophy has not been able to resolve, or to which it has failed to find a satisfactory solution. Now, it could be said—particularly by those who are interested in building up a philosophy with a Latin American character— that this cannot be of interest to a philosophy concerned with what is properly Latin American. This is not true, however, because both the issues that we have called universal and the issues that are peculiar to the Latin American circumstance are very closely linked. When we discuss the former we need also to discuss the latter. The abstract issues will have to be seen from the Latin American man's own circumstance. Each man will see in such issues what is closest to his own circumstance. He will look at these issues from the standpoint of his own interests, and those interests will be determined by his way of life, his abilities and inabilities, in a word, by his own circumstance. In the case of Latin America, his contribution to the philosophy of such issues will be permeated by the Latin American circumstance. Hence, when we address abstract issues, we shall formulate them as issues of our own. Even though being, God, etc., are issues appropriate for every man, the solution to them will be given from a Latin American standpoint. We may not say what these issues mean for every man, but we can say what they mean for us Latin Americans. Being, God, death, etc., would be what these abstractions mean for us.

It should not be forgotten that all European philosophy has worked on these issues on the assumption that their solutions would be universal. However, the product has been an aggregate of philosophies very different from each other. Despite their universalistic goals, the product has been a Greek philosophy, a Christian philosophy, a French philosophy, a British philosophy, and a German philosophy. Likewise, independently of our attempts to realize a Latin American philosophy and despite our efforts to provide universal solutions, our solutions will bear the mark of our own circumstance.

Another type of issue to be addressed by our possible Latin American philosophy is related to our own circumstance. That is, our possible philosophy must try to resolve the problems posed by our circumstance. This point of view is as legitimate and valid a philosophical issue as the one we have just discussed. As Latin Americans we have a series of problems that arise only in the context of our circumstance and that therefore only we can resolve. The posing of such problems does in no way diminish the philosophical character of our philosophy, because philosophy attempts to solve the problems that man encounters during his existence. Hence the problems encountered by the Latin American man are the problems of the circumstance in which he lives.

Among such issues is that of our history. History is part of man's circumstance: it gives him a configuration and a profile, thus making him capable of some endeavors and incapable of others. Hence we must take our history into account, because it is there that we can find the source of our abilities and inabilities. We cannot continue to ignore our past and our experiences, because without knowing them we cannot claim to be mature. Maturity, age, is experience. He who ignores his history lacks experience, and he who lacks experience cannot be a mature, responsible man.

With respect to the history of our philosophy, one might think that nothing could be found in it other than bad copies of European philosophical systems. In effect, that is what one will find if one is looking for Latin American philosophical systems that have the same value as European ones. But this is a shortsighted attempt: we must approach the history of our philosophy from a different standpoint. This standpoint is provided by our denials, our inability to do much besides bad copies of European models. It is pertinent to ask the reason why we do not have our own philosophy: perhaps the very answer will be a Latin American philosophy. This may show us a way of thinking that is our own and that perhaps has not needed to express itself through the formulae used by European philosophy.

It is also pertinent to ask why our philosophy is a *bad copy* of European philosophy. Because being a bad copy may very well be part of our Latin American philosophy. To be a bad copy does not necessarily mean to be bad, but simply different. Perhaps our feeling of inferiority has made us consider bad anything that is our own just because it is not like, or equal, to its model. To acknowledge that we cannot create the same European philosophical systems is not to acknowledge that we are inferior to the authors of those philosophies, but simply that we are different. On the basis of this assumption we will not view our philosophers' production as an aggregate of bad copies of European philosophy, but as Latin American interpretations of that philosophy. The Latin American element will be present in spite of our philosophers' attempts at objectivity. It will be present despite our thinkers' attempt to depersonalize it.

5

Philosophy in its universal character has been concerned with one of the problems that has agitated men the most at all times: the problem of the relations between man and society. This problem has been posed as political, asking about the forms of organization of these relations, that is, the organization of human interaction. Since the institution in charge of such relations is the State, philosophy has asked by whom it should be established and who should govern. The State must take care to maintain the balance between individual and society; it must take care to avoid both anarchy and totalitarianism. Now, in order to achieve this balance a moral justification is necessary. Philosophy attempts to offer such a justification. Hence, every metaphysical abstraction ultimately leads to ethics and politics. Every metaphysical idea provides the foundation for a concrete fact, the justification for any proposed type of political organization.

There is a multitude of philosophical examples in which metaphysical abstractions have provided the basis for a political construct. One example is found in Plato's philosophy, whose theory of ideas provides the basis and the justification for *The Republic*. In Saint Augustine's *The City of God* we find another example: the Christian community, the Church, is supported by a metaphysical being that in this case is God. The *Utopias* of the Renaissance constitute yet other examples where rationalism justifies the forms of government that have given birth to our present democracy. One thinker has said that the French Revolution finds its justification in Descartes's *Discourse on Method*. The Marxist revision of Hegel's dialectics has given way to such forms of government as communism. Even totalitarianism has sought metaphysical justification in the ideas of Nietzsche, Sorel, and Pareto. Many other examples from the history of philosophy can be cited where metaphysical abstraction provides the basis for social and political practices.

What we have just discussed underlines how theory and practice must go together. It is necessary that man's material acts be justified by ideas, because this is what makes him different from animals. But our times are characterized by a schism between ideas and reality. European culture is in crisis because of this schism. Man is now lacking a moral theory to justify his acts and hence has been unable to resolve the problems of human interaction. All that he has achieved is the fall into the extremes of anarchy and totalitarianism.

The various crises of Western culture have been produced by a lack of ideas to justify human acts, man's existence. When some ideas have no longer justified this existence, it has been necessary to search for other sets of ideas. The history of Western culture is the history of the crises that man has endured when the harmony that should exist between ideas and reality has been broken. Western culture has gone from crisis to crisis, finding salvation sometimes in ideas, sometimes in God, other times in reason, up to the present time when it no longer has ideas, God, or reason. Culture is now asking for new foundations of support. But this is, from our point of view, practically impossible. However, this point of view belongs to men who are in a situation of crisis, and this could not be otherwise, since we would not be in a situation of crisis if the problem seemed to us to have an easy solution. The fact that we are in a crisis, and that we do not have the much-wanted solution, still does not mean that the solution does not exist. Men who like us have been in situations of crisis before have had a similar pessimism; however, a solution has always been found. We do not know which values will replace those that we see sinking, but what we do know for certain is that such values will emerge, and it is our task as Latin Americans to contribute to this process.

From this we can infer yet another goal for a possible Latin American philosophy. The Western culture of which we are children and heirs needs new values on which to rest. These new values will have to be derived from new human experiences, that is, from the experiences that result from men being in the new circumstances of today. Because of its particular situation, Latin America can contribute to culture with the novelty of untapped experiences. That is why it is necessary that it tell its truth to the world. But it must be a truth without pretensions, a sincere truth. Latin America should not pretend to be the director of Western culture; what it must aspire to do is to produce culture purely and simply. And that can be accomplished by attempting to resolve the problems that are posed to the Latin American man by his own Latin American perspective.

Latin America and Europe will find themselves in a similar situation after the crisis. Both will have to resolve the same problem: what will be the new way of life that they will have to adopt to deal with the new circumstances? Both will have to continue ahead with the interrupted task of universal culture. But the difference is that Latin America will no longer be under the shadow of Europe's accomplishments, because there is neither a shadow nor a place of support at this point. On the contrary, Latin America finds itself at a vantage point in time—which may not last long—but that must be used to initiate the task that belongs to it as an adult member of Western culture.

A Latin American philosophy must begin the task of searching for the values that will provide the basis for a future type of culture. And this task will be carried out with the purpose of safekeeping the human essence: that which makes a man a man. Now, man is essentially an individual who is at the same time engaged in interaction with others, and hence it is necessary to maintain a balance between these two components of his essence. This is the balance that has been upset to the point of leading man to extremes: individualism to the point of anarchy, and social existence to the point of massification. Hence it is imperative to find values that make social interaction possible without detriment to individuality.

This task, which is universal and not simply Latin American, will be the supreme goal of our possible philosophy. This philosophy of ours cannot be limited to purely Latin American problems, that is, the problems of Latin America's circumstance. It must be concerned with the larger circumstance called humanity, of which we are also a part. It is not enough to attempt to reach a Latin American truth, but we must also attempt to reach a truth that is valid for all men, even if this truth may not in fact be accomplished. What is Latin American cannot be regarded as an end in itself, but as a boundary of a larger goal. Hence the reason why every attempt to make a Latin American philosophy, guided by the sole purpose of being Latin American, is destined to fail. One must attempt to do purely and simply philosophy, because what is Latin American will arise by itself. Simply by being Latin American, philosophers will create a Latin American philosophy in spite of their own efforts at depersonalization. Any attempt to the contrary will be anything but philosophy.

When we attempt to resolve the problems of man in any spatiotemporal situation whatever, we will necessarily have to start with ourselves because we are men; we will have to start with our own circumstances, our limitations, and our being Latin Americans, just as the Greeks started with their own circumstance called Greece. But, just like them, we cannot limit ourselves to stay in our own circumstances. If we do that it will be in spite of ourselves, and we will produce Latin American philosophy, just as the Greeks produced Greek philosophy in spite of themselves.

It is only on the basis of these assumptions that we will accomplish our mission within universal culture, and collaborate with it fully aware of our abilities, and be aware also of our capacities as members of the cultural community called humanity, as well as of our limits as children of a circumstance that is our own and to which we owe our personality: Latin America.

NOTES

1. Alfonso Reyes, "Notas sobre la inteligencia americana," *Sur*, no. 24 (September 1936).

2. Zea consistently uses "America" and "Americanos" to refer to Latin America and its inhabitants. I use "Latin America" and "Latin Americans" respectively to render these terms throughout the [essay], except in the present case, because here Zea is referring to the period of discovery, when there was no distinction between Anglo-Saxon and Latin America.—TRANS.

3. Reyes, "Notas."

Identity: A Latin American Philosophical Problem

1. *Philosophy, in the Strict Sense, and Ideology:* In the history of philosophy, strictly speaking, there seems to be no room for problems about identity, as raised by Latin American philosophy—more so when they also fall within areas that seem not to be strictly philosophical, like the political and the social. Apparently, philosophy raises only problems considered universal, and because they are universal and abstract, they are beyond what is everyday to man, his world, and his society. Philosophy is concerned with problems that are general, universal, and because they are universal, about the motley world of the concretely human. The philosophy of values, fashionable in the recent past, is rooted in the phenomenological method. As such, it exemplifies the detachment of the ideal from the real, of what is considered strictly philosophical from what is considered ideological, and thus alien to a genuine philosophy. Above the ever-changing human world are the values that give it meaning, realized or not, for they are situated in an abode unaffected by the ordinary. Equally philosophical are the tools of knowledge that allow man to perceive his reality and change it, yet at the same time, construe change as alien to a philosophizing whose goal is only knowledge in the strict sense.

Within this philosophizing, problems like the ones Latin American philosophy raises about its identity seem to be only parochial, that is, regional, and because of that, limited to a relative point of view proper to a concrete man, and thus, alien to what is truly universal. The demand for a specific identity seems to be something limited in relation to what is considered the questioning par excellence, a questioning about the whole. This question about Being was what philosophy was asking from its

From the *Philosophical Forum* 20, nos. 1–2 (fall–winter 1988–89). Copyright © 1988 by the Philosophical Forum, Inc.

beginnings in Greece, so we are told, about Being in general, not this or that concrete being. It was a questioning about the whole.

But, the whole of what?—paradoxically, the whole of what the concrete man, the philosopher, pretended to encompass with his question; a whole, whether one likes it or not, limited by the concrete capacity of vision of the one who asks. Aware of this limitation, the Greeks used to say that only God has eyes that see all, ears that hear all, and a reason that knows all. From then on, philosophers, though never attaining it, desired to be godlike, "the useless desire to be God," as Jean Paul Sartre used to say not long ago. In the past few years, philosophy has stressed the limitations of philosophizing construed strictly. Historicism, perspectivism, pragmatism, existentialism, and others, turning inward, have reflected on the limitations of philosophical contributions, philosophy's circumstantiality and, concomitantly, the plurality of its expressions. Many other interpretations, diverse in what they construe as strict, are only expressions of the new conception of universality.

In this new conception of philosophy, great and trivial expressions of a multifaceted philosophizing parade against a background that resembles a gigantic mosaic in which its myriad pieces have to be fitted. In an essay, *The Dream*, about Raphael's "The Academy," Wilhelm Dilthey showed the oppositional philosophical world that tears apart whoever persists in opting for this or that philosophical figure in the painting. Nowadays, many distinguished philosophers, like Hans-Georg Gadamer and Karl-Otto Apel, attest to a philosophical plurality and its unavoidable assumptions, and try to reconcile philosophy in a strict sense with ideological philosophizing. Apel, recalling his youth, tells us that he had to face even then the problem of the relation between theory and praxis: Do honest thinkers and radicals have to arrive at the conclusion, he asked, of the necessity of changing an impotent and illusory community of philosophers for the real community, truly united in the political compromise? But doesn't this imply an abandoning of theoretical discourse? At stake here is not a choice but a reconstruction of problems that are inescapably linked among themselves because they have an origin in man. The philosopher does not have to give up being a philosopher to face the many problems of a reality different from theory. Without ceasing to be a philosopher he can philosophically, rationally, confront man's daily problems and seek possible solutions. Philosophy does not have to choose between a strict knowledge of reality and one that allows actions to change that reality. For that reason, contemporary European philosophy has seen in philosophical labor the tool of knowledge capable of reconciling theory and practice, formal knowledge and knowledge for action. Philosophy is considered an attitude proper to man, and tries to solve many of the problems that ail him, problems proper to his reality, including those of the community to which he belongs and the many men that originate it. This has been the way of philosophy throughout its long history. Philosophy has not emerged in enclaves of prosperity and freedom but in situations of social inequality. Lack of freedom presents problems that philosophers had been obliged to face in order to solve them. It has been so since Plato, through Augustine, Aquinas, Descartes, Kant, Hegel, Marx, and up to the present.

2. *The Question of Being:* The first question that philosophy raised in the remote days of classical Greece referred to the problem of Being. What is Being? Being in general? This question was asked by the only concrete entity capable of answering it—man—man as philosopher. Concrete man, of flesh and bone, faces an ever-changing reality that drags and destroys the limited expression of Being, that is man—man who refuses to be anni-hilated, "nihilized," annulled by a changing nature or manipulated by his peers. Because of this, the philosopher undertakes a search for the princi-ples that rule the natural order, and through these principles, the ones that rule the social order. Whoever has knowledge of the order of the cosmos also has knowledge of the order of the *polis.* Thus Plato's words about the necessity of philosophers being kings or kings philosophers, or Aristotle's saying that it was just for the wiser to rule over the less wise.

The question of Being in general, of its principles of order, is an onto-logical question asked by the concrete entity that is the questioner, man, in relation to himself. The concrete entity that is man, tries to take a posi-tion, define himself within nature and in relation to his peers. This man refuses to be the blind expression of nature or an instrument of others. He wants to manipulate nature, not be its simple expression. But he also resists being manipulated, as part of nature, by his peers. He is not a part of nature that is to be manipulated. Man tries to manipulate other men, not recognizing in them fellow men but useful or useless objects.

Such is the problem, an ancient problem for man and his philosophy, raised as crucial by Latin American philosophy—the question of the con-crete Being of men occupying a vast region of Earth and subjected to the manipulations of others. They are the victims of a gigantic cover-up over identity begun on October 12, 1492, whose importance and consequences must be studied. A study of the Latin Americans who form part of this region will unveil an identity that defines them as equal to the rest of mankind. The British philosopher of history, Arnold Toynbee, spoke of this cover-up of identity when he referred to the expansion of the so-called Western over the rest of the world, and stumbled with other entities that could not be regarded as fellow men but as a part of nature that had to be used. "When we Westerners speak of 'Natives,'" wrote Toynbee, "we implicitly take the cultural color out of our perception of them. We see them as trees walking, or as wild animals infesting the country in which we happen to come across them. In fact, we see them as part of the local flora and fauna and not as men of like passions with ourselves; and seeing them thus as something suprahuman, we feel entitled to treat them as though they did not possess ordinary human rights.[1] According to this vision, it is the "native" who, starting from his own and concrete experience, has to prove his own humanity before this judge. The Indian, the native, as any native in any region of the earth beyond the centers of culture and civilization par excellence, is outside what is considered the only expression of humanity. Native will be called in America anyone who is born there, the Indian as much as the creole or the *mestizo.*

3. *Bargaining and Assertion of Identity:* The problem of the identity of the men of this region, with a special emphasis on that America which will be called Latin, was raised by its *conquistadores* and colonizers. Christopher Columbus, who, by sailing westward, expected to arrive more quickly in the distant lands of the Great Khan, began to wonder about these strange and docile entities, manlike but very different from the warlike Mongols of which Marco Polo spoke and from the ferocious inhabitants of Cipango. They were good people, naked and cowardly, and also easily deceived, and thus, easy to dominate, the opposite of the ferocious subjects of the powerful lord of the Chinese and the Tartars with whom he had hoped to meet. "These people," Columbus writes, "are very gentle and fearful, naked, as I have said, without weapons or laws. These lands are very fertile."[2] There are fertile lands and much gold, but in the hands of people for whom it lacked the value it had for the Europeans. On his First Voyage, Columbus already had realized that these people were very different from the ones he was searching for and with whom he had expected to negotiate in the name of his lords, the Catholic Kings of Spain—people, he gathered, easy to conquer and own, who did not seem to be the subjects of the Great Khan, and thus, awaited other lords. Hence, Columbus's negotiating mission was transformed into the first mission of conquest for Spain and the Europe that was afterward to follow and challenge the new dominions. Columbus went on taking possession of lands, riches, and men in the name of his lords. At the end of the First Voyage, he advised his lords not to allow any strangers into those lands already under dominion, except for Catholic ones, for, as he believed, this was, in the end, the royal purpose of the voyage—to increase and glorify the Christian religion. Incorporated into Christianity would be men, peoples, and lands left out because of the devil, as the first missionaries who came to these strange lands proposed. These were people of good understanding and could, for that reason, become good Christians, but they had to be subdued first. These were kinds of people inferior to their discoverers, people over whose supposed humanity there were doubts. That was the position, almost from the beginning of the conquest, concerning the identity of the men found in this region—the humanity or bestiality of the

Indians, as shown in the polemics between Sepúlveda and Las Casas. This identity the men of the "New World" was to be put on trial and judged by the jury of its conquerors. So it was to be the dominators who ultimately decided this supposed humanity.

To this haggling over humanity were subjected not only the Indians, but anyone born in this land, making their own and concrete identity the main concern of the men of the region. On this identity, on this knowledge of what one is, hinged all claims against the metropolis for any treatment other than that of manipulation to which they were subjected—a preoccupation that was important to the Americas under Saxon domination, but in an America under Iberian domination, reached even greater dimensions. This dimension was the result of the degree of *mestizaje* that colonization reached in the so-called Latin America. As a consequence, not only was one inferior by virtue of being born into the region, but even more, because of a mixture of races of a purported inferior quality, one was inferior culturally and racially; a depreciation, not only cultural as represented by Spain's dominance, but also natural as represented by the idea of a civilization that spoke of superior and inferior races. The racial *mestizaje* that did not bother the Iberian conquerors and colonizers was to disturb greatly the creators of the new empires of America, Asia, and Africa. Christianity blessed the unity of men and cultures regardless of race, more a function of their ability to be Christian. But modern civilization stressed racial purity, the having or lacking of particular habits and customs proper to a specific type of racial and cultural humanity. This was the concern that deeply worried the men of Latin America upon breaking with the old dominator and preparing to participate in the world order created by European civilization. The question of Being, of being concretely, of the men of this region will be more dramatic. Who am I? What is my identity?

4. *The Question of Identity*: The concern over the identity of men and peoples of the region was palpable in two thinkers and men of action from an America that was breaking with Iberian colonialism: the Venezuelan Simón Bolívar and the Argentinian Domingo Faustino Sarmiento. The first raised it at the outset of the struggle against Iberian colonialism; the second asked himself about the future of an American region that had just attained its freedom from the colonialism imposed by Iberia. Who are we? asks the Liberator, Simón Bolívar: " . . . we are not Europeans, we are not Indians, but a species in between the aborigines and the Spaniards. Americans by birth and Europeans by right, we find ourselves in the difficult position of challenging the natives for title of possession, and of upholding the country that saw us born against the opposition of the invaders. Thus, our case is all the more extraordinary and complicated."[3] Further on he adds: "We must bear in mind that our own country is not Europe nor the

America of the North, it is more a composite of Africa and America, an emanation from Europe, since even Spain stops being European because of its African blood, its institutions, and its character. It is impossible to identify correctly to what human family we belong. Most of the Indians have been annihilated, Europeans have mixed with Americans and Africans, and the result has mixed with Indians and Europeans. Born all of the same mother, our fathers, different in origin and blood, are aliens and all show it in their skins. This dissimilarity implies an obligation of the greatest transcendence." Years later, Domingo F. Sarmiento was to ask himself, "What are we? Europeans? So many copper faces contradict us! Indigenous? The disdainful smiles of our blond ladies perhaps answer us. *Mestizos?* No one wants to be that and there are thousands that would not want to be called American or Argentinian. Nation? A nation without a blending of accumulated materials, without agreements or bases?"[4]

Paradoxically, the conflicting and opposing expression of the identity that Latin Americans find, is to be considered the denial of any possible and authentic identity—a conflict that Sarmiento and his generation formulated in the disjunction "Civilization or Barbarism." For them, civilization is everything that one has to be but is not; barbarism everything one is but does not want to be. The disjunction between what one is and what one wants to be, the terrible and useless desire of the men of this region to be something else, is an identity conflict that lasted throughout the nineteenth century. Let us be Europe, let us be like France, England, or the United States! Let us be the United States of South America! Let us be the Yankees of South America! demanded both the Mexican Justo Sierra and the Argentinian Juan Bautista Alberdi. Out of this conflict arose, during the second half of the nineteenth century, the civilizing and positivist project that became widespread in an America that had broken the Iberian yoke. This conflict was to be resolved more or less harshly with either brainwashing, and the adoption of philosophies that supposedly caused the greatness of western Europe and the United States, or through the extraordinary blood-washing of an immigration policy adopted by the southern part of the continent, where the density of Indian population did not reach the volume of the altiplanos. There must be a break with the colonial past; a break with the fruit of that colonization; a repeal of the racial crossbreeding with inferior forms and of cultures already outside the history expressed by Iberia.

5. *Assertion of Identity:* At the end of the nineteenth century, an event shook the conscience of the men who began to call themselves Latin Americans: the 1898 war between the United States and Spain. This was to show Iberoamericans the impossibility of being something other than what they were—the impossibility of making of this region another United States or another Europe. The triumph of the United States over Spain

began the expansion of a new empire over the old empires, like the Spanish. The United States began its move to fill the "power vacuum" that old European empires had left—a project that extended the one begun with the war against Mexico, in 1847, and the presence in Central America, in 1856, of the American pirate William Walker. A new colonialism threatened the identity of the region. One cannot be anything but what one is, and the problem of identity was reformulated with greater strength. The Uruguayan José Enrique Rodó wrote his *Ariel*, assuming Latinity as an expression of the identity of the region. The United States, says Rodó, is "carrying out among ourselves a kind of moral conquest. Admiration for its greatness and its strength is a feeling that is making great strides in the spirit of our leaders . . . and we can pass through a transition from admiring to imitating them."[5] And imitation leads, in turn, to dependency, but a dependency freely accepted now. "It is, thus," he continues, "how the vision of a *de-Latinized* America, by its own free will, without the inconvenience of a conquest, and regenerated later on in the image and likeness of the Northern archetype, appears in the dreams of many sincere people interested in our future." This new subordination must be avoided and our own and ineluctable identity must be regained. "We have our *nordomanía*. It is necessary to draw the boundaries that reason and the sentiments clearly show." With Rodó, there is the voice of the Cuban José Martí, who died fighting against Spanish colonialism, yet warned Latin Americans of a new colonialism. A particular identity of which Bolívar had already spoken must be assumed—an identity that must be strengthened, possessed, and not rejected. Made out of Latinity (which has nothing to do with the project of Napoleon III), it is the expression of the search for identity. Through this Latinity, we will regain Spain, not the imperial Spain, but the Spain that with its blood and culture has made this a *mestizo* America, and because of this, a Spain open to all of man's expressions. America is Latin because of *mestizaje,* as *mestizo* was the Latinity with which Rome united the peoples who, like Spain, emerged from her. This America made possible the identity of that particular type of human being with which Bolívar would answer his questions about the region's identity—a particular type of human being, open to every expression of man, a humanity open and plural. Of this conception of the human being, Bolívar would say, "In the march of the centuries, only one nation will be found covering the universe." Like Bolívar, Andrés Bello struggled to join what should not be separated; there are also the Colombian José María Torres Caicedo and the Chilean Francisco Bilbao, who already spoke of a Latin as opposed to the Saxon America that had wrestled from Mexico half of its territory, and sent the pirate William Walker to dominate Central America.

With the twentieth century, the region's intelligentsia, who had adopted the adjective "Latin," raised the question of their own identity. A constellation of intellectuals, among whom shine the Mexicans José Vasconcelos, Alfonso Reyes, and Antonio Caso; the Dominican Pedro Henríquez Ureña; the Peruvian Manuel González Prada; the Argentinian Manual Ugarte; and the Venezuelan Césàr Zumeta, made their own the concern over the Latin American identity question that stemmed from Bolívar, Bello, Bilbao, Torres Caicedo, Rodó, and Martí. That concern, already raised during the nineteenth century over the existence and possibility of a Latin American literature and culture, is reformulated and given other answers. The response comes from an intelligentsia that assumed with assuredness its own peculiar identity as the source of a horizontal relation of identity and not of a vertical one of dependency. No more are there greater or lesser men; there are concrete men, and because they are concrete, they are different among themselves. Equals, precisely because they are different, that is, particular, concrete; but not so different and particular as to make some more or less men than others. And no longer is there any doubt about the identity of the men of the region that has adopted the adjective "Latin." This is the region proper to a group of men that are different from other men and regions, but without this difference lessening their concrete humanity. Affirmed of the man of region is the unarguable identity, which was doubted from the moment they entered into the history of its discoverers, conquerors, and colonizers. Affirmed is the identity, over and again, fraudulently hidden by the discoverers, conquerors, and colonizers, an identity that is raised as the central concern of a Latin American philosophy. This is the same concern we already found in the history of philosophy, a questioning about Being in general in order to assert one's own and concrete Being; the same metaphysical question about God in order to save one's own weak existence in Him; the question about reason made by a few men, for whom God is no longer on the horizon; the anguishing question of present-day man to assert an identity alienated by his own creations.

6. *History of Ideas, Philosophy of History, and Ontology:* The concern of Latin American thought over the identity of the region and its men crystallized in the twentieth century as a strictly philosophical concern, a concern that Euro-western philosophy was clarifying from a broader and more plural conception of reality. Latin American philosophy, moved by this concern, was to raise the problems of identity in a series of steps. The first was expressed in what has been called the *history of ideas,* a history that would allow the delimitation between the supposed imitation of other philosophies *and* the ways in which these would be received by or adapted to that reality object of its adoption. Of extraordinary importance in this first step was the presence of some distinguished Spanish philosophers who had come to Mexico, and elsewhere in Latin America, as a con-

sequence of the Spanish Civil War, begun in 1936. One of these men was José Gaos, who was to call himself *transterrado*, and who would stimulate this study among his many students.

What would these studies show? Hegel, in his *Philosophy of History*, said that America had been up to then but "echo and shadow" of Europe and its culture. America, especially Spanish America, had originated nothing but bad copies of the emulated culture. In philosophy, one could speak only of Thomism, Enlightenment, Positivism, and relativism in Latin America. The presence of these currents was odd and barely represented "bad copies," caricatures, false formulations of the adopted models. The history of ideas—that is, the history of how, why, and for what purposes these philosophies had been adapted and the ways in which this adoption had been represented—showed something different from what had been asserted. Even though it was not their intention, those who adopted these philosophies transformed them according to the reality and problems for which they had been adopted. They were barbarized; that is, they were made to say something that was not the intention of their creators. The Latin American, upon adopting specific philosophizings and philosophies to face the problems raised by his reality, gave to what was adopted a different meaning from the one it had for its creators. Even in imitation, there was creation and re-creation. The philosophizing adopted took thus another sense which, compared to the models, resulted in "bad copies of the originals" but were originals with respect to the problems that they tried to solve, thus resulting in different philosophical utterances than those of the adopted models. In this adoption, adaptation, and utterances, a peculiar mode of expression would be evident in those who had used philosophies alien to their experiences.

This history of ideas would show an interpretation of history different from that philosophy of history so masterfully expressed by Hegel. José Gaos, on reviewing one of the studies that had been made about the history of Latin American ideas, would speak of its peculiar interpretation of history. The secular position of the region's dependency and its consciousness raising, would originate a conception of history which, far from seeking the assimilation or assumption of history—the Hegelian *Aufhebung*—juxtaposes over and again its experiences. Spain tried to juxtapose its own Christian culture over the indigenous one it had stumbled on and considered demoniacal. Liberalism and positivism, in turn, tried to erase the imposed colonial past, superimposing on what was inherited the fruits of another culture alien to their experiences, and from then on continued to juxtapose expressions of cultures alien to their own. This fact is revealed by the history of ideas of the region. All of this is manifest in the peculiar philosophy of Latin American history, different from the philosophy of history of Europe and of the world called Western: juxtaposing instead of assimilating, trying to be something else in the most useless way. "The effort to break with the past and rebuild according to an alien present," Gaos said, "cannot be believed precisely because it is an effort no less utopian than any other. Because if the rebuilding according to an alien present seems possible, the ridding of one's own past, instead, isn't." This is what the history of ideas of the region showed, and in doing so, it also showed the need for another philosophizing proper to the history of the region, of Latin America. "Rather than getting rid of the past," Gaos said, "one should try an *Aufhebung* with it . . . and rather than rebuild according to an alien present, rebuild according to a past and present more like ours and with an eye to a future more like ours." Assimilate our history and experience, no matter how negative they might seem, and departing from this assimilation or assumption, project our own unique future.

From this expression we would pass on to a third and final one of this philosophizing, the one referring strictly to the concrete identity of the being who asks about himself, about his own and peculiar identity. This question about Being is an ontological stage, like that of philosophy in a strict sense at its inception. It is about a being which, in fact, is the one that asks and can answer, man—not man the abstract but man the concrete, of flesh and bone, with his own particular problems, yet not particular that they do not cease being proper to man. Through these particular problems, and precisely because they are particular, other men can be acknowledged as peers, an acknowledgment and respect for what is acknowledged in a search for a horizontal relation of solidarity of peers among peers and not the vertical one of dependency which had originated that unique problem of philosophy in Latin America.

NOTES

1. Arnold Toynbee, *A Study of History* (Oxford: Oxford University Press, 1934), 1:152.
2. Columbus, *Letters*, First Voyage.
3. Simón Bolívar, "Cartas de Jamaica."
4. Ibid.
5. J. E. Rodó, *Ariel*, trans. F. J. Stimson (Boston, 1922).

Augusto Salazar Bondy (1927–1974)

Salazar Bondy was born and educated in Lima, Peru. At the time of his death he was full professor at the Universidad Nacional Mayor de San Marcos and director of the Biblioteca Filosófica, a publication series of the mentioned university. Salazar Bondy was a prolific and active philosopher who traveled extensively throughout the American continent, giving lectures in Latin American and North American universities and attending many congresses of philosophy. The impact of his thought was strongly felt in Peru and in several other Latin American countries.

Among his many works we may mention: *La filosofía en el Perú* (1954), *Irrealidad e idealidad* (1958), *Tendencias contemporáneas de la filosofía moral británica* (1962), *Historia de las ideas en el Perú contemporáneo* (1965), *Breve antología filosófica* (1967), *Existe una filosofía de nuestra América?* (1968), *Sentido y problema del pensamiento filosófico hispanoamericano* (1969), and *Para una filosofía del valor* (1971).

Salazar Bondy began his philosophical career from a phenomenological perspective inspired by Hartmann and Heidegger. Later he became interested in some Marxist ideas and in the last few years of his life adopted a more analytic approach, particularly with respect to value theory. This lack of rigid ideology was a direct result of his view of philosophy as a broad and integrating discipline.

As is clear from the titles of the works cited above, from the very beginning of his philosophical career this author was interested in the philosophy of his country and later in the philosophy of Latin America in general. His knowledge of Latin American philosophy and his contributions as critic and historian of it led him to an examination of the problem of philosophical identity in Latin America. The position he adopted is critical. According to him, the type of philosophy practiced in Latin America

379

has been the product of the efforts of intellectual elites that, having no originality of their own, imitated the different philosophical currents fashionable in Europe. The result has been a nonauthentic philosophy, divorced from Latin American society and its needs; Latin American philosophy is a direct product of the alienation of Latin American society.

The Meaning and Problem of Hispanic American Philosophic Thought

I

This [essay] assumes that Hispanic American philosophical thought began with the discovery of America and the Spanish Conquest; and that it is now possible to trace its development, to classify its distinctive epochs, and to define its characteristic traits. The assumption arbitrarily casts aside the rich pre-Columbian cultural past for a variety of reasons. First, there are no data sufficiently precise and trustworthy concerning the thought of the indigenous peoples. Second, there was no integration, nor even sufficient sociopolitical and cultural interaction among the pre-Conquest peoples. The historic community which we customarily call Hispanic America did not exist before the sixteenth century, and it is only beginning with this century that we can find cultural products that are definitely philosophical. These considerations explain, at least methodologically, the point of departure and the thematic focus and limitation of my presentation.

The process of Hispanic American philosophical thought begins with the introduction of the dominant Spanish currents of the period within the framework of the official political and ecclesiastical system of education. The principal goal was to form the subjects of the New World according to the ideas and values sanctioned by the Spanish State and Church. Those doctrines harmonious with the political and spiritual domination pursued by the temporal and religious organs of Spain were brought to America and propagated in our countries. In this way, Hispanic Americans

From Augusto Salazar Bondy, *The Meaning and Problem of Hispanic American Thought*, ed. John P. Augelli (Lawrence: Center of Latin American Studies of the University of Kansas, 1969). Reprinted by permission.

learned as a first philosophy or mode of thought, a system of ideas that responded to the motivations of men of the Old World.

Except for the sporadic and, at times, heroic appearance of philosophies with a greater critical edge and fewer ideological-political compromises with the established power (such as renaissance platonism and erasmist humanism), the doctrine officially disseminated and protected is the scholastic in its late Spanish version. Although it certainly was not lacking in some high points, such as Suárez, it was following paths very different from those of the modern spirit. Thus, besides being official and centered on European interests, the first Hispanic American philosophy was conservative and antimodern in thought.

American themes did not, however, fail to make themselves felt as a new element in the theoretical concern. There is a wealth of philosophic-theological meditations on the humanity of the Indian, on the right to make war on the aborigines, and on the justification to dominate America, which constitutes the most valuable thought of the sixteenth and seventeenth centuries. Because of it, scholasticism momentarily achieved a live and creative tone, precisely when it touched on the problems of existence in this area which had been recently conquered and was in the process of colonization. But, apart from those few outstanding Hispanic American teachers and disseminators of philosophy in this period, much of the philosophical theorizing, including that which dealt with specifically American themes, was done from the Spanish perspective. There was not, and perhaps could not have been, at least at the beginning of the Spanish period, anything like an original American approach to a doctrine that would respond to the motivations of men of this continent.

The predominance of scholasticism lasted until the eighteenth century. Then, America began to feel the impact of ideas and currents that were contrary to scholasticism and very representative of the new direction that European thought took beginning with the Renaissance. This was due in part to factors operating in Spain itself, such as the liberalizing policy of the ministers of Charles III and the work of writers of a reform spirit, like Father Feijoo. It was also due to such factors as travelers and scientific expeditions that were operating within the territories under Spanish domination. Descartes, Leibniz, Locke, and Hugo Grotino, as well as Galileo and Newton, were among the first authors who had a revolutionary effect among us, even though the phenomenon, measured against European chronology, is clearly late.

The number of foreign books and magazines and of commentaries and readers of modern taste increased hurriedly as the eighteenth century advanced, and resounding names of powerful progressive influence appeared on the intellectual horizon of the Hispanic Americans. Some of the principal ones are Condillac, Rousseau, Adam Smith, and Benjamin

Constant. At the same time, educational and cultural institutions were renovated in those cities that served as viceregal capitals or seats of the *audiencia*; the so-called Caroline colleges and the "Friends of the Country" societies appeared; and cultural reviews of unquestionable value were published. An awakening of critical awareness and a first hint of national and American consciousness are perceptible in the period. This cultural atmosphere is equivalent, at least on the exterior, to what is known in Europe as the period of the Enlightenment. And the doctrinary link is clear, for the enlightened Hispanic American ideology is nothing other than the transplantation of the philosophy of the European, especially the French, Enlightenment. Like France, this epoch in Hispanic America was also a period of important political changes, which was garbed in modern philosophical thought: the changes of the emancipating revolution which by 1824 was to cancel out Spanish power in the majority of our countries.

The new political plateau achieved with political independence in Hispanic America was paralleled in philosophic thought. Subsequently, this thought developed freely, without the hindrance of monarchical censorship. On the other hand, it had to develop within the precariousness imposed by the sociopolitical crisis confronted by nearly all the brand-new republics in this part of the hemisphere during the nineteenth century. Let us consider briefly this later development.

There is an initial, well-defined period of evolution that extends from the revolution of independence until approximately 1870. Because it coincides with Romanticism, it is customarily designated as romantic. It was dominated successively by the so-called philosophy of ideology—that is, the last form of French sensualism—, the doctrines of the Scottish school of common sense, and finally, the eclectic spiritualism of French derivation and the Krausist version of German idealism. These doctrines constituted the philosophic sustenance not only of academicians, but also of publicists and the politicians of the time. The latter generally adhered to two principal parties, one of a liberal tendency, and the other conservative. Their bitter disputes were often concerned more with pragmatic and political differences than with the ultimate philosophical bases of their thought. They were not always opposed, for example, in metaphysics and esthetics, and it is not unusual to find the same European philosophers accepted as doctrinary mentors by both liberal and conservative writers. Perhaps it would be more exact to say that the same philosophies were selectively accepted by both groups and applied according to their own orientation. Also in this period Hispanic America felt, albeit weakly, the influence of utopic socialism and anarchism.

In the final decades of the century the tendency of the Hispanic American intelligentsia was to turn toward another doctrine, or complex of doctrines, formed by the positivism of Auguste Comte in France, and various other contemporary currents of thought, such as Naturalism, Materialism, Experimentalism, and Evolutionism. From all these ideological elements was gleaned the so-called positivist creed that the intellectual sectors of practically all Hispanic American countries, in varying intensity and amplitude, adopted and defended for nearly four decades, until the early years of this century.

In this period, the popularity of Comte was equaled, if not exceeded, by that of Spencer. Through his teachings, evolution was imposed as a universal explanatory principle, applied to realms of both physical nature and society. In the latter case, it was used equally to justify the predominance of the bourgeoisie and the claims of the proletariat. Nevertheless, Positivism was fundamentally a philosophical doctrine adopted by the upper classes of Hispanic America in the period of establishment and consolidation of international capitalism in our countries.

In the midst of the Positivist movement itself, there arose surpassing tendencies which, when amplified and strengthened, were to mark a new stage in Hispanic American thought. This phenomenon was, above all, a reflection of the changes in European philosophic conscience, but it must also be explained in part by the movement's doctrinary heterogeneity, in which the most laic and even irreligious convictions were tolerated alongside the most frank professions of Christian faith. Some individuals characterized as representatives of the Positivist philosophy were, indeed, the first to criticize their earlier convictions. They were convinced not only of the necessity of rectifying the errors and raising the barriers of Positivist thought, but they also felt that there already were figures and systems in the philosophic market of the period capable of replacing the old doctrine advantageously.

Added to these impulses of self-criticism was the decisive action of a group of dynamic university professors. At the time they were dedicating their best efforts both to disposing Positivist philosophy and to the development of a serious university philosophical movement. For this reason they have been called the *founders*. Outstanding among them were the Argentine Alejandro Korn, the Uruguayan Carlos Vaz Ferreira, the Chilean Enrique Molina, the Peruvian Alejandro Deustua, and the Mexicans José Vasconcelos and Antonio Caso. They are certainly not the only ones, but are indeed the principal ones in the strictly academic dominion of philosophy. They acted in harmony with other intellectual figures dedicated to giving a new meaning and a profounder and more authentic basis to the culture of our countries. Of the latter, Pedro Henríquez Ureña and Alfonso Reyes are representative. (Let us add parenthetically that it is not by chance that until now we have not felt obliged to mention a single Hispanic American philosopher while tracing the history of our thought. As we shall see, there is reason for it. There were figures worthy of mention as teachers of valuable work, comparable to that of the *founders*, although generally possessed of less critical conscience and historical maturity than the latter. The

Mexican Antonio Rubio, the Peruvian Diego de Avendaño, the Venezuelan Agustín de Quevedo y Villegas, and the Chilean Alfonso de Briceño are scholastics of importance. The Mexican Benito Días de Gamarra is a very representative and distinguished, enlightened thinker. José de la Luz y Caballero, in Cuba, Andrés Bello, from Venezuela, José Vitoriano Lastarria of Chile, and the Argentine hero Juan Bautista Alberdi stand out in the first period of the nineteenth century. Some notable names of the Positivist movement are González Prada of Peru, the Mexican Justo Sierra, Eugenio María de Hostos from Puerto Rico, the Cuban Enrique José Varona, and the Argentine José Ingenieros. Let us content ourselves with this brief list, because we do not propose to depict in detail the development of our philosophical ideas, but rather to understand its character and meaning.)

The *founders*, whose work covers the first decades of this century, coincided not only in the rejection of Positivism, but also in the type of orientation that they wished to give philosophical thought and the Western mentors that they sought for this undertaking. They were fundamentally antinaturalists, with marked idealistic or vitalistic sympathies (positions which are not always easily distinguished one from the other). They had a preference for dynamic concepts and intuitive thought that was not rigidly logical and consequently, they acquiesced generally with metaphysical speculation. Hence, their admiration for such authors as Boutroux, Croce, James, and above all, Bergson. The last became for the intellectuals the oracle that Spencer had once been. Bergsonism, with its concept of duration, of concrete and qualitative becoming, was consulted for all explanations, and was embraced and exalted not only by conservative sectors, but also by liberals. It was even accepted by the Marxists, who at this time were beginning to represent a definite current of thought in Hispanic America.

With Marxism and other orientations of social thought related or opposed to it, we reach the contemporary stage of Hispanic American philosophy, which extends approximately from the third decade of this century to the present. In the consideration of contemporary currents, it must be said of Marxism that, although it has had important political repercussions in recent years (such as the establishment of the socialist regime in Cuba) it is not the most influential philosophy in the universities, nor even among wide sectors of writers and intellectuals. It is, however, along with Catholic philosophy, the one that has received the greatest effort toward popularization.

In addition to Catholic philosophy, especially the neo-Thomist, favored by the Church in Hispanic America and generally concentrated in the confessional universities, other currents should be mentioned, for their impact on the university movement has been greater. These are, in the first place, phenomenology, both in Husserl's original form and in its ethical, esthetic, and ontological derivations developed by such thinkers as Max Scheler, Moritz Geiger, Alexander Pfaender, and Nicolai Hartmann.

The phenomenological current is related to the existentialism of Heidegger (who was associated initially with Husserl), the Christian existential thought of Jaspers, and the atheistic existentialism of Sartre.

The diffusion of these and like philosophies, such as those of Eucken, Klages, and Keiserling, took place mainly from the end of the twenties until the Second World War. Viewed from a complementary perspective, this represents the influence of Germanic thought in Hispanic America, contemporary with the political and economic expansion of Germany that concluded with the slaughter of the war. Symptomatically, in the latter part of the forties, French philosophy began to penetrate and achieve great diffusion. In the main, it was the new existentialist trend represented by Sartre, as well as Camus, Marcel, and Merleau-Ponty. Sartrian penetration was facilitated by the use of literature as a means of expressing ideas, which made the themes and problems of contemporary philosophy accessible to a wider public than the strictly academic. The literary works of Camus have had an analogous effect. On the other hand, French existentialism is a thought directly connected with social and political problems, through doctrinary principles and the personal vocation of its creators. The committed intellectual (*éngagé*) according to this philosophy, is the paradigm of the man of thought and letters. Hence, in spite of its technical complexities as a philosophy, it is welcomed among political spirits and the socially committed. This does not mean that French existentialism, especially that of Sartre, has not likewise penetrated Hispanic American academic circles. There, however, Sartre shares the favor of the professional public with Merleau-Ponty, and frequently with Heidegger, who continues to be considered the greatest theorist of the philosophy of existence.

Other themes and problems solicit the attention of those who have a serious philosophic concern, above all in centers of higher education. Logic, epistemology, and the investigation of language find ever-increasing numbers of cultivators. By the nature of their theoretical interest, they are prone to a more rigorous and objective—more technical, if you will—focus on the content of knowledge, and receive different influences from others mentioned above. One might insert here the influence of currents such as logical positivism, the analytic and linguistic school, or the Zurich school, associated with the names of Bertrand Russell, Rudolf Carnap, Gaston Bachelard, Ferdinand Gonseth, G. E. Moore, and Ludwig Wittgenstein. This type of philosophy has become noticeably more important in Hispanic America during recent years as a consequence of the worldwide development of science and technology, and also the predominance of Anglo-American culture.

In the course of the process outlined here, philosophy has achieved in Hispanic America a level of acceptance and considerable expansion. University departments and professorships, societies and associations of specialists, periodicals, books, and international connections are found today in practically all nations of Hispanic America. All of these factors, according to the most common critics of our time, are manifestations of a normal philosophical activity, and determine in large part the character and orientation of contemporary philosophical development. What used to be a sporadic exercise and an ephemeral product of very limited repercussions, is today a stable activity that can count on the necessary social means to assure its survival and progress, and increase its penetration in the life of the community.

But precisely to the degree that this regularization of philosophic practice (or *normalization*, as Francisco Romero called it) has been achieved, a profound interest has been aroused in the evolution of our ideas, and in the meaning and scope of our thought. Systematic studies of the history of ideas, reviews and organized schemes of philosophy in Hispanic America, supported by a proven scientific methodology, have sprung up, and have been disseminated and increased in the most recent decades. Likewise, a very serious and profound discussion has begun concerning the character and potential of philosophy in Hispanic America. This means that, as a result of all previous history, about which we know much more today than in the past, we are conscious (perhaps for the first time fully conscious) of the problems that affect our thought, or, better said, the radical problem of the authenticity and justification for our philosophizing.

II

Following this direction of current Hispanic American thought, let us inquire about the quality and scope of the intellectual products of the philosophizing whose four-hundred-year evolution we have briefly reviewed. Our balance cannot fail to be negative, as has been that of practically all historians and interpreters of ideas in Hispanic America. In fact, it is impossible to extract clearly from this process an articulation of ideas, a well-structured dialectic of reflections and expositions, and of concepts and solutions nurtured by its historical and cultural circumstance. On the contrary, what we find in all our countries is a succession of imported doctrines, a procession of systems which follows European, or, in general, foreign unrest. It is almost a succession of intellectual fashions without roots in our spiritual life and, for this very reason, lacking the virtue of fertility. Just as scholastic colonial thought, as we saw, was imposed by the interests of the mother country, so also the systems that replaced it responded to [a] historical logic that was foreign to the conscience of our peoples. For this reason these systems were abandoned as quickly and easily as they were embraced, having been chosen by the upper class and the intellectual sectors of Hispanic Americans according to their immediate preferences and momentary affinities. To review the process of Hispanic American philosophy is to relate the passing of Western philosophy *through* our countries, or to narrate European philosophy *in* Hispanic America. It is not to tell the history of a natural philosophy *of* Hispanic America. In our historical process there are Cartesians, Krausists, Spencerians, Bergsonians, and other European "*isms.*" But this is all; there are no creative figures to found and nurture their own peculiar tradition, nor native philosophic "*isms.*" We search for the original contributions of our countries in answer to the Western challenge—or to that of other cultures—and we do not find it. At least we find nothing substantial, worthy of a positive historical appraisal. No one, I believe, can give testimony to its existence if he is moderately strict in his judgment.

The characteristics which, according to this balance, stand out in boldest relief in Hispanic American thought are the following:

1. *Imitative sense of thought.* Thinking is done according to theoretical molds already shaped in the pattern of Western thought—mainly European—, imported in the form of currents, schools, and systems totally defined in their content and orientation. To philosophize is to adopt a preexistent foreign "*ism,*" to incorporate into one's thought theses adopted during the process of reading, and to repeat more or less faithfully the works of the most resounding figures of the period.

2. *Universal receptivity.* An indiscriminate disposition to accept all manner of theoretical product coming from the most diverse schools and national traditions, with extremely varied styles and spiritual purposes. This, of course, always providing that they will have obtained a certain reputation, a perceptible ascendancy in some important country of Europe. This receptivity, which betrays a lack of substance in ideas and convictions, has often been taken for [a] Hispanic American virtue.

3. *Absence of a characteristic, definitive tendency,* and of an ideological, conceptual proclivity capable of founding a tradition of thought, of sketching a profile in an intellectual manner. Notice the "empiricist" seal that Britannic thought has, perceptible even in the work of its speculative idealists. There is no solid basis upon which to define a similar style in Hispanic American philosophy. At times one speaks of a practical inclination in the Hispanic American, at others, of a speculative vein. Apart from the fact that these two traits are contradictory, their manifestations—weak and confusing—have disappeared rapidly and almost completely each time that contrary influences have prevailed. The only alternative is to count as a distinctive character precisely the absence of definition and the nebulous state of conceptions, which is merely to confirm the thesis.

4. *Correlative absence of original contributions,* capable of being incorporated into the tradition of world thought. There is no philosophic system of Hispanic American roots, or doctrine with meaning in the

entirety of universal thought. Neither are there polemic reactions to the affirmations of our thinkers, nor sequels and doctrinary effects of them in other philosophies. All of this is an additional proof of the inexistence of our own ideas and theses. The most relevant philosophical figures of Hispanic America have been commentators or professors, but, no matter how fruitful their action in this field may have been for the educational process of our countries, it has not had an effect beyond our own cultural circle.

5. *Existence of a strong sense of intellectual frustration* among cultivators of philosophy. It is symptomatic that, throughout the history of our culture, its most lucid interpreters have planted time and again the question of the existence of their own philosophic thought. Responding to it, as we said, almost unanimously with a complete negation, they have formulated projects for the future construction of such thought. Significantly, this unrest and reflection are not found, or are rarely found, among those nations that have made fundamental contributions to the development of philosophy. They are, so to speak, well installed in the territory of philosophic theory and move within it as in their own dominion. Hispanic Americans, on the other hand, have always, in this regard, felt themselves to be in alien territory, as one who makes furtive and clandestine incursions, for they have had a vivid consciousness of their lack of speculative originality.

6. *There has existed permanently in Hispanic America a great distance between those who practice philosophy and the whole of the community.* There is no way to consider our philosophies as national thought, with a differential seal, as one speaks of a German, French, English, or Greek philosophy. It is also impossible for the community to recognize itself in these philosophies, precisely because we are dealing with transplanted thought, the spiritual products of other men and other cultures, which a refined minority makes an effort to understand and to share. We do not deny that there is a universal factor in philosophy, nor do we think that philosophy has to be popular. However, when an elaborate intellectual creation is genuine, it reflects the conscience of a community finding in it profound resonance especially through its ethical and political derivations.

7. *The same scheme of historic development and the same constellation of traits–although negative–are suitable to the activity unfolded during more than four centuries by the men dedicated to philosophy in a plurality of countries*, often far removed physically and socially from each other as is the case of Hispanic America. Not only does it permit a general judgment of Hispanic American thought—without ignoring the existence of special cases and regional variants resulting from divergent influences within the common framework—it also demonstrates that in order to comprehend the thought of our countries it is necessary to define the basic cultural-historical reality that links them beneath their nearly always artificial confrontations and political separations.

III

In his *Lectures on the History of Philosophy*, Hegel wrote: "Philosophy is the philosophy of its time, a link in the great chain of universal evolution; from whence it derives that it can only satisfy the peculiar interests of its time." In another place, confronted with the existence of systems that pretend to reproduce doctrines of the past, that is, to make a kind of transfer from one mode of thinking to another, he formulated this bitter disqualification: "These attempts are simple translations, not original creations; and the spirit only finds satisfaction in the knowledge of its own and genuine originality." With this the great master of the history of philosophy underscored a very important fact in the dominion of thought. To wit, philosophy as such expresses the life of the community, but it can fail in this function, and, instead of manifesting its uniqueness, it can detract from it or conceal it. Accordingly, an unauthentic philosophy, or a mystified thought may develop.

To what extent a philosophy can be unauthentic will be made clear in an attempt to specify the purpose and meaning of philosophic thought. As we understand it, a philosophy is many things, but among them it cannot fail to be the manifestation of the rational conscience of a community. It is the conception that expresses the mode in which the community reacts before the whole of reality and the course of existence, and its peculiar manner of illuminating and interpreting the being in which it finds itself installed. Because it comprises the whole of reality, it deals with that which is essential to man, with his vital commitment. In this respect it differs from science which does not commit the whole man. On the other hand, to the extent that philosophy is a rational conscience, an attempt to make the world and life intelligible, it is not confused with religious faith which operates through feeling and suggestion. Thus, philosophy deals with the total truth of a rationally clarified existence, that appeals to the totality of the personal human being and its full lucidity. The latter are the two means of referring to that which is most unique in each man.

But philosophy can be unauthentic, as we have seen. How does this happen? Man constructs his self image as an individual and as a social entity; he is, in the words of Ortega, the novelist of himself. But he may be that as an original writer or as a plagiarist; as someone who portrays himself, outlining his genuine idea, or as someone who is self-deluding, "getting ideas" about himself, and takes another's as his own image. And so, thinking that he knows himself, he remains ignorant. A philosophy can be this illusory image of itself, the mystified representation of a community, through which the community "gets ideas"—real ideas—about itself and loses itself as a truthful conscience. This happens when philosophy is constructed as an imitated thought, as a superficial and episodic transference of ideas and principles motivated by the existential projects of other men, by attitudes toward the world that cannot be repeated or shared. At times they may even be contrary to the values of other communities. He who assumes this imitated thought thinks he sees himself expressed in it and in fact makes an effort to live it as his own, but he almost never finds himself in it. The illusion and unauthenticity that prevail in this case are paid for with sterility, and sterility, which betrays a vital defect, is always a risk for collective and individual life.

This anthropological illusion has, nevertheless, a truthful side. The man of mystified conscience expresses through this conscience his own defects and deficiencies. If a community adopts foreign ideas and values, if it cannot give them life and empower them, but instead imitates them in their foreign character, it is because alienating and deficient elements prevail in its being. An illusory self-concept is only possible to the degree that there is no self-fulfillment, at least in certain very important sectors of historical existence. On this point it is, then, inexact—although not false—to deny the veracity of unauthentic philosophies. It is more exact to say that they lie about the being that assumes them, but by lying they reveal their defective existence. They fail in not offering a proper image of reality as it ought to be, but they succeed, unwittingly, as an expression of the lack of a complete and original being.

Because of scientific demands of precision and objectivity, when one speaks of culture in social science, one usually means by the term a unique and neutral concept. Although this use has permitted the empirical manipulation of social life and the generalization of explanations, it is, nevertheless, insufficient. I believe that this science is now in a position to consider as positive data and to elaborate theoretically the facts concerning the unauthenticity and alienation of society and culture. Marxism and psychoanalysis, empirically controlled, can make very valuable suggestions in this respect. I say this because to me it seems impossible to comprehend human life without distinguishing historical deficiencies and plenitudes, the accomplishments and alienations of communities and the individuals that constitute them, all of which obliges us to diversity concepts. In this respect, I think that it behooves us to wield a strong and unique concept of *culture* as the organic articulation of the original and differentiating manifestations of a community—susceptible to serving as a guide to contrast the historic work of peoples—. We reserve other meanings and other concepts, such as those of mode of working, mode of proceedings, or manner of reacting to other parallel phenomena. These concepts, unlike that of culture, would be applicable to any social group, even if such a group did not achieve cultural originality and maturity in the strict sense of the word. It then is necessary to include in anthropological terminology, at the social and cultural level, the concepts of frustration, alienation, authenticity, and mystification, without which the multiple variety of historical existence cannot be comprehended, as we are proving in the case of Hispanic American philosophy.

IV

In Hispanic America a defect of culture may be observed. Hispanic American philosophic thought—and all other thought of similar explanatory purposes—offers that stamp of negativity to which we have been referring in speaking of philosophies as illusory self-conscience. Because of its imitative nature across the centuries, until today it has been an alienated and alienating conscience that has given a superficial image of the world and life to man in our national communities. It has not truly responded to motivations felt by this man, but rather has responded to the goals and vital interests of other men. It has been a plagiarized novel and not the truthful chronicle of our human adventure.

As we have indicated earlier, there is a consensus among the interpreters of Hispanic American thought and culture regarding the existence of a problem that affects its meaning and function. The demonstration of this problematic situation in its applicability to philosophy has suggested various attempts at explanation that should be recalled and examined, even if it is only by way of a very brief résumé.

1. A first reaction is to evaluate Hispanic American thought, such as it is, positively, while disregarding its negative aspects or interpreting them by a kind of sublimation as original forms, different from ordinary philosophic thought, but valuable in themselves as spiritual creations. One may exalt, for example, the universalism of our thought, which is the optimistic reverse of the limitless receptivity that we mentioned earlier, or the disguise that conceals a weakness of theoretical reflection. A kind of autochthonism joins hands here with a conformist conscience in order to see in deficiency or weakness an original mode of philosophizing. It forgets that our thought has proved that it cannot live without external sustenance, and that it is incapable of making its personality felt, for example, by provoking polemic reactions or determining influences that might prolong and enrich it, in the course of world thought.

2. Although close to the preceding, a second attitude has a rather negative cast. Those who adopt it recognize that there is no vigorous and creative philosophy in Hispanic America, and they explain this fact appealing generally to ethnic causes. It is said, for example, that this situation is the effect of our mentality, that our race does not have a philosophic disposition. It is held that philosophy does not harmonize with the genius of our people, which is better endowed for other spiritual creations. The thesis generally

presupposes the existence of a vigorous body of values and genuine cultural products different from the philosophic, of which there is, of course, no proof. This opinion cannot long resist the confrontation with well-known facts that demonstrate that deficiencies and unauthenticity reach other very important fields, and even cover the entire gambit of culture.

3. A third explanation appeals to the historical cultural youth of our peoples. It is thought that four hundred years of evolution, without counting the process of previous civilizations, are not sufficient to acclimate philosophy, and that one should reasonably expect a perceptible change in this aspect when the Hispanic American community achieves the maturity that it is lacking today. It is forgotten in this context that other "younger" peoples with a less-aged intellectual tradition, as is patently the case with the United States, have indeed managed to create a philosophic thought of their own.

4. Another explanation approaches a position of greater historical realism, although in my opinion it does not touch the most decisive factors. It appeals to the precariousness of institutional conditions and of the necessary social means for the development and advance of genuine theoretical thought. In this case we are considering mainly the coordinated professional and academic organization that encourages the cultivation of philosophy as a university specialty, along with the varied professional activities of Hispanic American thinkers. This allows for the hope of a favorable evolution in view of the fact that in our time a normality has been achieved in the academic status of philosophic studies. At the base of this explanation there is a very limited and partial idea of the conditions in which philosophy prospers. The latter is regarded as a standardized activity and it is taken for granted that the university atmosphere is rather the natural abode of thought. Aside from the fact that such an idea risks confusing creative philosophers with mere professors of philosophy, it passes over the very significant fact that many of the greatest thinkers did not enjoy the facilities mentioned, nor were they—and more than once they did not wish to be—university professors. Take for example Descartes, Locke, Spinoza, Leibniz, Hume, to mention only a few famous names who were dedicated to activities very distinct from that of teaching.

If the explanations that I have reviewed are insufficient or erroneous, as it seems to me that they are, it is necessary to turn to another type of explanatory causes and factors. Broader and more profound, they operate in that sphere of fundamental realities that, in spite of disconnections and separations, lead to a coincidence in their characters and a common evolution of philosophic thought in Hispanic American nations. One must recognize the necessity of seeking in the mode of living of our nations, as social organisms and historical-cultural entities, the causes of the problem that concerns us. A defective and illusory philosophic conscience causes one to suspect the existence of a defective and unauthentic social being, the lack of a culture in the strong and proper sense of the term as previously defined. This is the case in Hispanic America.

V

Commenting on a book of mine about the history of contemporary ideas in Peru, the young French historian Jean Piel asked, in a paraphrase of Montesquieu's famous sentence, "How can one be Peruvian?" The question is equally applicable to all of Hispanic America, because there is a problem of authenticity in man in this part of the world. Certainly, on the level of simple, natural facts, the question offers no difficulty, and perhaps it is not worth posing. One can be anything from the moment that one is. But when one takes into account all that a historical being as such entails, all that it implies by way of aspirations, plans, norms, and values, besides natural realities, then the question acquires full meaning. It is equivalent to asking about the potential and destiny of an unauthentic existence. Because the truth is that Hispanic Americans live behind a feigned being.

Hence it is that in our communities mystification and fiction prevail. Many institutions have a different design from what they declare, while the majority of ideas acquire a sense that is different from and, as often as not, opposite from the original meaning that they officially possessed. The most varied forms of conduct and interpersonal relationships coincide in functioning and being motivated in a manner contrary to what supposedly corresponds to them. Reflect, for example, on Hispanic American democracy or free enterprise, justice, religion, the University, morality, and it will be seen to what an inversion of being my considerations point. In the last analysis, we live on the conscious level according to models of culture that have no roots in our condition of existence. In the raw material of this historical reality, imitative conduct yields a deformed product which passes itself off as the original model. This model operates as a myth that impedes our recognizing our situation and laying the bases for a genuine building of ourselves. The same kind of mystified awareness leads us, for example, to define ourselves as Westerners, Latins, moderns, democrats, or Catholics. We imply in each one of these cases—through the work of the disguising myths that enjoy free rein in our collective conscience—something different from what in truth exists.

This use of foreign and inadequate patterns, ideas, and values that do not jibe with reality, and reflect a partial or falsified image of our mode of being is what, in the last analysis, Hispanic American philosophy sanctions. Because of the ambivalence of our existence, it sanctions it in a double sense: (a) as the conscious assumption of concepts and norms without roots in our historical-existential concern; (b) as an imitation of foreign thought, with neither originality nor force. Hispanic American philosophy sanctions unauthenticity in our culture by presenting itself in its ideas and values—whose purpose is to illuminate life—as a product that ignores reality and alienates the spirit.

It is not strange that a community which is disintegrated and lacking in potential should produce a mystified philosophic awareness. Philosophy, which in an integral culture is the highest form of consciousness, cannot help but be an artificial and insubstantial expression in a defective culture. It cannot help but be a thought alien to the living body of history, foreign and alienating in principle to the destiny of the men in whose community it is nourished.

VI

Where is the cause, the determining complex of this condition of Hispanic America as an entity and also of each of its constituent nations? If we are aware that this condition is not peculiar to Hispanic American countries, but is largely similar to that of other communities and regional groups of nations, belonging to what today is called the Third World, then it is clear that, to explain it, we must utilize the concept of underdevelopment, with the correlative concept of domination. In fact, underdeveloped countries present an aggregate of basically negative characteristics which, one way or the other, are related to dependent bonds with other centers of economic and political power. These centers of power—which direct the activities of the dependent countries according to their own interests—are situated in the developed nations, in the mother countries, or in great industrial powers. And these negative characteristics correspond to factors which easily explain the phenomena of a culture like that of Hispanic America. It was not by accident that our countries were first subject to Spanish power and that they evolved from this situation as Spanish political colonies to that of factories and supply centers or markets of the British Empire, subject to their economic control. The United States inherited this empire, with a closer and more effective network of power. As dependents of Spain, England, or the United States, we have been and continue to be underdeveloped—if I may use the expression—*under* these powers, and, consequently, countries with a *culture of domination*.

I am giving here the broader traits of the conditions and global references to the phenomenon of the underdevelopment and domination of Hispanic America. I prefer to remain on this level so as better to call attention to the basic fact of our culture. One could object, no doubt, to the simplicity of the explanation. I believe that it could be shaded considerably without varying the substance of the thesis: but I fear that the trees of the shading might not permit us to see the forest of the basic cause; I fear that the refined pluralism of the explanation might distract us from the original comprehension. Therefore, I insist that the decisive factor in our Hispanic American case is underdevelopment, the dependency and bonds of domination, with the peculiar qualities that allow us to define it as [a] historical phenomenon.

The sociocultural effect of this state of things is that misshapen society and defective culture that philosophy reveals. Let us remember that our philosophy was originally a thought imposed by the European conqueror in accord with the interests of the Spanish Crown and Church. It has since been a thought of the upper class or of a refined oligarchical elite, when it has not corresponded openly to waves of foreign economic and political influence. In all these cases underdevelopment and domination are influential. On the other hand, the qualities that we indicated in describing our thought not only fail to contradict this explanation through underdevelopment, but instead harmonize fully with it. The dominated countries live with a view to the outside, depending in their existence upon the decisions of the dominant powers, that cover all fields. This trait is not alien to the receptivity and the imitative character of the philosophy—and not only the philosophy—that is typical of Hispanic America. Likewise, these countries lack vigor and dynamism because of their depressed economy and because of the lack of cohesion in their society that underdevelopment creates. Thus, there is no distinctive cast of thought that could neutralize this receptivity and this tendency toward imitation. Nor can the entirety of spiritual products achieve the necessary vigor to inject themselves as original contributions in the worldwide advance of civilization. The distance between those who practice philosophy and the community at large is in this case—unlike the normal relationship between the specialist and the public—the abyss between the enlightened elite who live according to a foreign model, and the illiterate, poverty-stricken masses, trapped in the framework of remote and sclerotic traditions. And the frustration is rooted in the impossibility of living according to foreign cultural patterns, while experiencing the simultaneous incapacity to make the life of the community fruitful in thought. As we have seen, this situation is common to Hispanic America in the same measure that underdevelopment is common, and with it, dependence and domination.

VII

Our thought is defective and unauthentic owing to our society and our culture. Must it necessarily remain so? Is there no alternative to this prospect? That is to say, is there no way of giving it originality and authenticity? Indeed there is, because man, in certain circumstances rises above his present condition, and transcends in reality toward new forms of life, toward unheard-of manifestations. These will endure or will bear fruit to the degree that the initiated movement can expand and provoke a general dialectic and totalization of development. In the sociopolitical field this is what constitutes revolutions. This means that that part of man which rises above his circumstances cannot do so fruitfully and in a lasting manner unless the movement is capable of articulating itself with the rest of reality and provoking in it an overall change. If this is valid for society and culture in general, it is also true of philosophy, for the latter, being the focus of man's total awareness, could, better than other spiritual creations, be that part of humanity that rises above itself, and overcomes the negativity of the present as it moves toward new and superior forms of reality. But, to achieve this, it must possess certain valences capable of turning theory into live reality. It must operate in such a way that, through an effective and prudent utilization of historical resources, it will produce the most fruitful dialectical reactions in the proper areas of social life. Hegel said that the owl of Minerva took flight at dusk, thus giving philosophy the character of a theory that elucidates the meaning of facts already accomplished. It is not always so. Contrary to what Hegel thought, we feel that philosophy can be, and on more than one historic occasion has had to be, the messenger of the dawn, the beginning of historic change through a radical awareness of existence projected toward the future.

Philosophy in Hispanic America has a possibility of being authentic in the midst of the unauthenticity that surrounds and consumes it, and to convert itself into the lucid awareness of this condition and into the thought capable of unleashing the process to overcome it. It must be a meditation *about* our anthropological status and *from* our own negative status, with a view to its cancellation. Consequently, Hispanic American philosophy has before it—as a possibility of its own recuperation—a destructive task that, in the long run, will be destructive to its current form. It must be an awareness that cancels prejudice, myths, idols; an awareness that will awaken us to our subjection as peoples and our depression as men. In consequence, it must be an awareness that liberates us from the obstacles that impede our anthropological expansion, which is also the anthropological expansion of the world. It must be, in addition, a critical and analytical awareness of the potentialities and demands of our affirmation as humanity. All of which requires a thought that from the beginning will cast aside every deceptive illusion and, delving into the historical substance of our community, will search for the qualities and values that could express it positively. These qualities and values must be precisely those capable of finding resonance in the entirety of Hispanic

America, and, along with other convergent forces, unleashing a progressive movement that will eliminate underdevelopment and domination.

I believe it necessary to call attention to the fact that I am not postulating the necessity of *practical*, *applied*, or *sociological* philosophy, as has been proposed more than once as a model of Hispanic American thought. It has been suggested, even by outstanding figures of our culture, that in the distribution of philosophical tasks, theory should belong to Europe and application to Hispanic America. I am convinced also, however, that the strict theoretical character, which is the highest contemplative requirement indispensable to all fruitful philosophy, is merely another way of condemning ourselves to dependency and subjection. In philosophy, as in science, only he who has the key to theory can appropriate the advances and powers of civilization. Our philosophy should be, then, both theory and application, conceived and executed in our own fashion, according to our own standards and qualities. Just as science, which in spite of its declared objectivity, tolerates, particularly in the social disciplines, an ingredient of interpretation and ideology, so too should philosophy be elaborated by us as theory according to our own standards and applied in accord with our own ends.

Consequently, those who heed the call of reflexive thought in Hispanic America cannot dispense with the acquisition of the techniques developed by philosophy in its long history, nor can they cast aside all those concepts capable of serving as support for a rigorous theory. At the cost of laborious efforts they must appropriate all these products, all the more difficult to acquire without the support of a solid national cultural base. But all the while they must keep in mind their provisional and instrumental character, and not take them as models and contents to be imitated and repeated as if they were absolute. Rather, they must be taken as tools to be utilized as long as there are no others more effective and more adequate to the discovery and expression of our anthropological essence.

This is the task that we have ahead of us. In some cases it would be impossible to fulfill its goals completely, but we must aim toward them with the awareness that the difficulty increases daily through the dynamics of world history. In the great field of international competition, the differences between the underdeveloped and developed countries, the proletarian and industrialized countries, are ever more pronounced. The subjection of the former to the latter is, therefore, increasingly stronger and more permanent. Likewise, the alienation of being becomes more serious in the dominated nations, among which the Hispanic American countries must be counted. But there is still the possibility of liberation. While this is so, we are obligated to choose a line of action that will materialize this possibility. Philosophy also has this option.

Arturo Andrés Roig
(b. 1922)

Roig was born in Mendoza, Argentina. Having graduated from the Universidad Nacional de Cuyo (1949), he did postgraduate work in the history of ancient philosophy, under the direction of Pierre-Maxime Schuhl, at the Sorbonne (France) between 1953 and 1954. Before his politically motivated discharge from the post he held at the Universidad Nacional de Cuyo in 1974, he had taught there for thirty years. In 1984 he was allowed to return to his former position, from which he has recently retired. In addition he has had visiting appointments in France, Mexico, and Ecuador.

He has published numerous articles in professional journals in Latin America, Europe, and the United States, as well as many books. Among the representative book titles are: *La filosofía de las luces en la ciudad agrícola* (1968), *Los krausistas argentinos* (1969), *Platón o la filosofía como libertad y expectativa* (1972), *El espiritualismo argentino entre 1850 y 1900* (1972), *Esquemas para una historia de la filosofía ecuatoriana* (1977 and 1982), *Filosofía, universidad y filósofos en América Latina* (1981), *Andrés Bello y los orígenes de la semiótica en América Latina* (1982), *El humanismo ecuatoriano de la segunda mitad del siglo XVIII* (1984), *Bolivarismo y filosofía latinoamericana* (1984), *Rostro y filosofía de América Latina* (1993), *El pensamiento latinoamericano y su aventura* (1994). Recently, Roig has published books on pedagogy and the university in Latin America. He has also edited important collections, such as *Proceso civilizatorio y ejercicio utópico en nuestra América* (1995).

As the titles of his books and articles indicate, Roig has specialized in the study of classical Greek as well as Latin American thought. In addition he has attempted to develop a philosophical position that could be characterized as a "historical empiricism." This view is rooted in an ontology based on the description of the human being. This philosophy, which is also described as a "philosophy of liberation," aims to supersede the various dichotomies which have traditionally prevailed in Western philosophy, such as subject and object, body and soul, barbaric and civilized. For Roig, it is most important to return philosophy to a study of the relation of humans and society, with a clear understanding that humans have a unique capacity to create new spaces within society and to lift the restraints that keep certain groups oppressed.

Essays on Philosophy
in History

THE ACTUAL FUNCTION OF PHILOSOPHY IN LATIN AMERICA

[A PHILOSOPHY OF LIBERATION]

Our present time is characterized by an attitude of commitment that is strongly felt by great nuclei of intellectuals throughout our continent. We could say that that commitment has a twofold aspect: on the one hand it is a commitment to knowledge itself in a strict sense, and on the other it is clearly a commitment to knowledge *qua* social function.

The second aspect is possibly the one that more strongly characterizes our human attitude. Its existence presupposes a form of positioning with respect to the very concrete reality of our peoples. If we had to identify the most obvious feature of that taking of a position we would say that it is connoted by the conviction that social structures, considered in themselves, are unjust insofar as they are based on the dominating-dominated relationship—a fact that becomes more acute because of our dependent cultural state. From this origin, the task that arises from this commitment has been characterized throughout the continent as a *social and national* liberation, and insofar as the liberating action required a cojoined realization of all the social groups who suffered dependency, it has been postulated with the character of *integration* as well.

Within this framework philosophy keeps alive some of the principles that guide contemporary European idealism, but most assuredly with a

From Arturo Andrés Roig, "Función de la filosofía en América Latina," in *La filosofía actual en América Latina* (Mexico City: Grijalbo, 1976), pp. 135–54.

401

new sense of direction. We demand that philosophical thought move "toward things-in-themselves" and we also demand that the knowledge of those things be a "knowledge without presuppositions"; but between this idealism of the essences and us has intervened the existential crisis that has the virtue of rendering bankrupt every form of Platonism, in the pejorative sense of that term, and has opened us toward the search for an ontology in whose field the foundation of our thinking is today disputed. At bottom, we live the bankruptcy of every philosophy of conscience on whose foundation Western rationalism has been founded during the nineteenth and twentieth centuries. The philosophies of what we might call denunciation, among which are principally Marxism and Freudianism, have provided the bases of assumptions, elements without which that commitment to knowledge *qua* social function would again run the risk of remaining behind the masked attitudes that would, finally, reduce the task of the philosopher to what it generally was among our "founders."

It is obvious, moreover, that the social function of knowledge and, parallel to it, the philosopher's mission, have for us a new meaning. The social, national, and continental liberation, as well as the integration of the Latin American peoples, is not the exclusive work of the intelligentsia, even if the latter may propose a change in mental attitude. Philosophy must become conscious of its task within the framework of the system of connections of its times, and it must be discussed whether if, within it, it will be added to those processes that move toward what is historically new or if, in the maturity of times, it will play a mere role of justification. This issue necessarily takes us to the reformulation of ontological knowledge within which the theme of the historicity of the [Latin] American man is fundamental, as it also takes us to a reformulation of our history of philosophy.

From the postulation of the forms and modes of *integration*, understood as condition of *liberation*, depends likewise the whole of philosophy. Every philosophy begins with the assumption that it is a mode of universal knowledge and because of that integrating, but the history of that claim has demonstrated and still demonstrates how integration has implied and still implies forms of rupture and marginalization. This fact, presented succinctly, takes them to the issue of the value, as much of conscience, as of the concept *qua* proper instrument of philosophical thought. It is appropriate that we ask ourselves how the philosophy of liberation must be organized in order not to fall into a new philosophy of dependence. Without exception, all of our "founders" spoke of "freedom" and their philosophy could be characterized for the whole continent as a "theory of freedom." Korn, Deústua, and Caso posit freedom as a basic category of their thought, but this message has turned out to be ambiguous and, if at some point present Latin American philosophy must supersede all ambiguity, it is purely in this regard. Integration requires, then, the elaboration of a doctrine that may provide us with adequate conceptual tools with which thinking man could, without treason, join the cause that is the cause of the people.

We know the epistemological difficulties that control our present-day philosophy in Latin America. Rationalism imposed the requirement of arriving at a strict philosophy from the point of departure of immediate and apodictic evidence. Our modern impulse for philosophizing is also immediate, but assertoric; it has to do with factual, not necessary truths that are inscribed in existence itself. Could we say that our beginning is given by *facticity*? We necessarily have to say it, but only as long as we do not understand by it a brute fact or a pure facticity, for there is no facticity except insofar as it is inscribed in an understanding and evaluation. Perhaps it might be necessary to say that it has to do with an enveloping facticity within which are given simultaneously the thinking subject and the object of thought. In other words, it has to do with an existential situation grasped with what we could call, along with Michel Foucault, a certain *historical a priori*, in spite of the risks it implies, and while pointing out that for us that concept ought to be redefined insofar as what is *a priori* is not so with regard to what is historical, as something that determines what is temporal from the outside, but that it is likewise historical. It is a determinate and determining historical structure in which social conscience plays, in our judgment, a preponderant causality and where *a priori*-ness is posited in a nonnecessary way beginning in experience and is, for that reason, also an *a posteriori*-ness in respect to its origin in the moments of formation of an epoch or of a generation. From what has been said, moreover, the *historical a priori* is not only constituted by intellectual categories, but also by states of mind that give sense as much to the discourse in which knowledge is expressed as it does to the conduct of those who develop that knowledge in relation to the medium in which they perform.

Neither does philosophy as we understand it fit in with the old classical category of contemplative and disinterested knowledge, or with the notion of objectivity that accompanied it and pretends to fulfill a social function from a critical consciousness with a new direction. At the same time, this philosophy claims to develop its discourse rigorously, but the requirement of rigor departs as well from the modalities with which it was understood within the vast ranges of modern and contemporary rationalism.

The "founders" also started off from a certain *historical a priori* from which they gave their own philosophical answers to their own facticity. The theory of objects and the theory of values—common themes to almost all of them—constitute an answer to a certain unconscious order proper to a cultural state on the basis of which they developed the classifications and on which experiences were judged. From that *a priori* that functions in them as a condition of the possibility of the hierarchical forms of entities and values, they were placed in a discourse from which they understood that they fulfilled, in their own fashion, the double requirement of rigorous knowledge and commitment. This fact permits the consideration of the "normalization" of the philosophical task in Latin America that began precisely with them, from the ideological point of view. The typically conservative discourse with which that was begun caused the Brazilian philosopher Luis Washington Vita to denounce as reactionary the philosophy of Bergsonian inspiration with which it expressed itself. The ideology of "normalization," inherited in our time by ontologists, phenomenologists, logical positivists, and structuralists, undoubtedly constituted a very special way of understanding the requirement of philosophical rigor.

Hence, that notion of "philosophy as such" has acquired for us a new meaning—for Risieri Frondizi it meant to do philosophy and immunize it against nonphilosophical activities (and politics in particular), since, as this author tells us, European thought had lost philosophical character in Latin America. Philosophy, Leopoldo Zea has said, does not only have to pay attention to "how it is done," but also to "for what it is done"; in other words, it must be something more than rigorous science, i.e., it must certainly also be consciously adopted ideology.

"Philosophy as such" cannot avoid substance and take refuge, as happens in some cases, in the mere sign or in mere structures, developing a formalist discourse that ignores the historical process. The strong influence of linguistic doctrines has precisely cut through the philosophical task and fractured it down to its very core. The requirement of rigor proper to "normalization" has dangerously led the way within the field of structuralist epistemology to an attempt at the analysis of the pure form of philosophical discourse, emptying it of its contents while earlier having eliminated the referential function of language, which is what ties it to the historically concrete. Having emptied the discourse of its substantial content, and therefore the human project it embraces, it has degenerated into a totalization of concepts through which the will to power is easily developed. In this way the rigor of academic philosophy has not only been content in some cases with the reduction of philosophical subject matter to essences, based on the teachings of Husserl, but by advancing further toward that requirement it has ended up altogether avoiding consciousness as a subject.

We have stated that "philosophy as such" cannot avoid substance, but neither can it lapse into another form of evasion of thought, the same one into which ontologism lapses. The assertion that being as well as the tendency to inquiry about being is lived or livable within the immediate experience of consciousness, is the essential characteristic of ontologism in our opinion. Consciousness ends up being understood as the place where what is real is revealed, whether as a result of eidetic intuition or as the fruit of the existential frame of mind that found an opening to being, and parallel to it, the task of man is to give himself to an alienating inquiry urged by the need to give an explanation to "entity," breaks asunder every dignity and ends up by nullifying man as the builder of his own world. As Agoglia has appropriately stated with regard to existentialism, its proposed substitution of the question of entity for the question of being is an evasion of philosophy at the ontological level, for what gives philosophical authenticity to the question concerning being is not an assumed or implied relation of being to man, but rather an inquiry about being in terms of man. Ontologism asserts, moreover, on the basis of the foundation of the claimed revelatory power of immediate consciousness, a permanent distinction between *doxa* and *episteme* from which it would be possible only to arrive at rigorous knowledge. [This is the dilemma into] which one falls with the condemnation of thought *qua* thought of the world, understanding [by] this the infinite web of entities and entitative relationships within which we move and have our being, such as is assumed in the realism of the common man and expressed in everyday speech. The need to erect the foundations of an ontology that does not fall into ontologism, therefore, implies the acknowledgement that consciousness is object before it is subject; that it is a social entity before it is an individual reality; that there is no transparent consciousness, which, for this reason, not every *episteme* need be developed on the basis of a criticism alone, but necessarily also on the basis of a self-criticism; that intuition does not take the place of the concept and that this concept is a representation; that the preeminence of being and of man as such is the inescapable point of departure and the terminus of every question about being; and, finally, that an ontology is also necessarily an anthropology.

Formalism and ontologism in all their diverse forms overlook two aspects that have significant importance if we give heed to the attitude of commitment that we referred to at the outset: the historicity of man and the relationship of man to technology. At bottom one sees in many instances the position evident within the aestheticism of our "founders," which was a predominant characteristic of nearly all of them, that in addition it included an ontologism and on its foundations an axiology in which what is economic, confused with what is crudely utilitarian, was presented as a pseudo-value. The case of Alejandro Deústua is typical in that sense. The line that proceeds from Bergsonian influence to Heideggerianism, as philosophy of consciousness and as intuition, has been a prime example of the uprooting and the alienation in Latin American thought denounced so vehemently by Augusto Salazar Bondy.

This fact is even more serious in our own time given the ignorance of the American man's historicity hidden beneath a profusion of investigation of that same historicity. The concrete case [of this profuse investigation] is found in the philosophy of "existential disposition" and in particular in one of its formulations developed by the Venezuelan philosopher Mayz Vallenilla, for whom the "disposition" that characterizes the Latin American man would be "expectation," which, as such, is subjected "to the most absolute contingency in relation to the content of what comes near and is convenient." This would be the reason why technology appears to us as something alien and as coming from the outside. It is in this manner that our dependency comes to be justified ontologically at the same time that the possibility of our man making himself in the act of his labor is denied.

We have already pointed to the close relationship that exists between the aestheticism of our "founders" and the ontologism of the present. But there is yet another fact that cuts negatively through to the historicity of our man: the continuation of a certain kind of ethicism expounded by Alejandro Korn and Antonio Caso. Undoubtedly, this ethicism is watered down nowadays and in some cases even apparently lost completely beneath the development of formalist philosophy; it is not for that reason less present. Ethicism is a consubstantial attitude with the mental structure imposed by liberalism on the whole continent, and it can only be explained within the framework of the "order" that arises out of the *historical a priori* within the scope we have assigned to this concept—this *a priori* serves as a substratum for all of our intellectuals, and makes their thought an expression of a determinate social class. Ethicism is a response that tries to maintain the *integrating* formula imposed by an age on a given society, resorting to a hierarchy of values that is above doubt, but is reinforced and even ontologically founded insofar as every social problem is reducible, on this view, to a moral program. Also, in its own way, ethicism reinforces the ahistorical view of our man insofar as the moral formulae of integration assert the roles of dominating and dominated groups, preventing in this way the rise of proper historicity, of the proper self-making that man, as such, deserves since it proposes no change of social structures and with them no new integrating formulae.

We face, in addition, the problem concerning the discourse in which we ought to locate ourselves, in other words, in what way ought we to act with respect to that *a priori* from which every discourse tends to develop. The single fact of denouncing its existence presupposes for Latin American philosophy a new and innovative attitude and leads, among other things, to the need to analyze its structure in those that preceded us. Thus arises once more the need to reexamine the thought of our "founders" from our present perspective and with our current methodological principles.

It is appropriate that we ask ourselves about the meaning of the fact in which they placed themselves with an almost generational sense within the framework of Bergsonian discourse and would continue to elaborate Rodó's discourse again. The symbol of Ariel and philosophy of the spirit appropriate to immediate consciousness were not incompatible. But we could say, moreover, that Arielism continued and was reinforced under the generalized influence of Bergsonian thought in that stage after the 1900s, and Ariel continued being the symbol of a task that those intellectuals from whom we are descended imposed upon themselves. To these influences must be added, without any doubt, the authority exerted by Ortguian philosophy, also a thought of enlightened elites. Though Rodó's spiritualism developed as an answer to the question concerning what our thought *qua* Hispanic American should be, and as a consequence of Ortega y Gasset's circumstantialism, there was an attempt to adopt the facticity that we spoke of at the beginning. With these tools our "founders" undoubtedly gave an answer to the pressing problem of cultural dependency, and they forcefully pointed out—and particularly in the case of Rodó—the presence of imperialism as one of the negative factors that integrated the facticity from which they, and we, begin. This was possible to the degree that the discourse of the "founders"—especially some of them such as José Vasconcelos—continued being, in spite of its ambiguity, a response to the problems of liberation and integration and for that very reason had not become emptied of content.

But this message requires that it be taken from a new beginning of our philosophy and the symbols in which it felt itself to be incarnated required a decodification, and to the degree that the symbol has an inner force that goes beyond a mere intellectual posturing of what is symbolized, our age needs, as Abelardo Villegas has indicated while commenting on Roberto Fernández Retamar, a new symbolism for Latin American culture. Let us not forget that "the old and reserved teacher, who was usually called Prospero, in reference to the wise teacher of Shakespeare's *The Tempest*," according to the initial words of Ariel, ends up in Roberto Arlt's short story by hanging himself in an outhouse. This hard and cruel image represents the end of the presuppositions from which those very elites developed their philosophical discourse.

The categories with which spiritualism tried to fulfill an integrating function undoubtedly find themselves in a crisis. Caliban, who is not an abject being, is our most direct symbol in the same way that we stopped believing in the "Civilization" that the liberal bourgeoisie in the nineteenth century placed in opposition to the "barbarism," which is the name Caliban is given in Sarmiento's framework. And in the same way we have lost our horror of the "masses," the sociological pseudoconcept with which Ortega y Gasset crippled his own circumstantialism and with which he in turn pointed out the presence of Caliban.

The mission of current Latin American philosophy essentially lies, then, in the search for new integrating concepts, whether or not they are expressed in new symbols. And because of that we feel the need of an ontology that may separate us from every formalism and may not fall, in turn, into a new ontologism: In other words, [we require] an ontology that insures the preeminence of the object with respect to consciousness, that may not flow into new forms of Platonism, and that may lay bare the historicity of man as a given reality in everyday experience, but beginning not with a singular and unique experience understood under a pretense as revealing the historicity of the privileged consciousness of the philosopher.

Philosophy is concerned with entity and being, but whether it is erected as an ontology of entity or an ontology of being, in the sense that it is beyond entity, or as an attempt at the dialectical integration of both, the inescapable point of departure is always given in entity. Man has no other access to being except through the way it is given to us *qua* entity, and it is realized in our own ontic nature. For this reason we may say with Miguel Angel Virasoro, that for us being does not speak with its own voice nor does it have its own sense and that its sense is built in entities so that being for man is primarily a pure availability that threshes itself out in the infinite world of entities and their relations. Now, although in any way that we may construe philosophy, there is always the risk of its being developed as a system of the oppression of life as exercised from the objective totality of the concept and orchestrated by the will to power, in other words, of falling into a Platonism such as the one Nietzsche denounced in his own times, something that appears to us unquestionable is only beginning from a strong preeminence of entity, captured in its otherness and in its novelty, we will be able to develop an open dialectical thought.

The fact that what is truly in an act is given for men in entity and for entity opens up to us the sense of his own historicity and his task as creator and transformer of his world. The struggle for the unmasking of the objective, oppressive totalities and the elaboration of the integrating categories that may not detract from his historical presence, but rather allow him to reintegrate himself with himself, is undoubtedly the principal undertaking of a philosophy of liberation. And every eschatological answer to the problem of being, that ignores this real and crude insertion of man within entity, cannot be but negative.

That facticity from which we begin is not, as we had said, a pure facticity without signification, for when man is found placed within his world he receives a "from where" and a "to where" that prescribe his destiny and from which he does not escape by denouncing everydayness as a form of alienation and by trying to separate himself from it by a singular and unique abstract experience, but rather it is within that very everydayness and in terms of it that he must assume his origin and his destiny.

In that same sense it is undoubtedly highly valuable to point out the affective relation to the world, conditioned by our social consciousness and on whose foundation we are disposed with respect to entities. An analysis of the *historical a priori* undoubtedly cannot avoid the existence of those states of mind that do not constitute a mythical opening with respect to an ontological reality, but a very concrete way that directs our evaluating activities in our relational life and is later projected in philosophical discourse.

If we had to mention the state of mind from which many of our intellectuals have opened up to their world, we would venture to say that it is one of fear. This affective attitude is the one that most obviously regulates and conditions behavior in a society in which the figures of master and slave, oppressor and oppressed, continue to exist. Dread runs through our continent in the face of the "revolt of the masses," "social revolution," "loss of order and hierarchies," "social decomposition," "changes of structures," "doctrines foreign to national interest," or "forgetfulness of our most treasured traditions." Oppressive political discourse offers, in this sense, a clear reading and a state of mind that conditions and has conditioned the theories of even those who believed themselves saved from the very facticity in which they began, and on which they confer an inevitably ideological content.

The "theory of freedom" that fills the discourse of our "founders" must, no doubt, be replaced by the "theory of liberation" that should have as its fundamental task the elaboration of new integrating categories beginning with a redemption of the historical sense of man. History, the occurrence, Carlos Astrada has stated, has to derive its meaning from existing man, whose fundamental ontological structure is already historicity. Meaning is not to be extracted from history as if man were an ahistorical subject that depends on it, as integrating categorical foundation alien to him, as hypostatic reality. History is history of man's realization in accordance with a historical repertoire of ends. The assuming of one's own ends presupposes a self-making, a self-happening, as act of freedom. As Oward Ferrari has said, "Finality means an ongoing task of man, it implies a *Geschehen*, a self-begetting, a self-making, because of which the thought of man's will leads directly to the *Geschichtlichkeit.*"

Because of that, history is an ontological vocation of man that is to be fulfilled and is fulfilled completely when the improper modes of self-making or self-begetting are denounced, modes that generally claim to make of history a tautology, a repetition of the same. In this was the self-making or the self-begetting that in history is developed theoretically over a justifying dialectic, that closes the doors to the rushing in of the other or that at least ignores it. But that self-begetting or self-making presupposes, as a constitutive note of man's being, an other-ness that, by its single presence, breaks the successive dialectic totalities with which the attempt was made to put a brake on the historical process of man's liberation.

The oppressed, the man who suffers pain, poverty, hunger, torture, persecution, and death, is the one who presents himself to us as the "other" with respect to our "self-ness" and of the integrating categories with which we attempt to support that self-ness, and it is the one that takes charge of the humanizing mission of imposing otherness as an essential condition of man. Undoubtedly, Caliban is the symbol of the latent or explicit force that begets what is new within the historical process. It is the Indian, the black, the mestizo face-to-face with the white, the humble man from the fields and the proletariat from the cities face-to-face with the oligarchies and diverse power groups; the old gaucho and the contemporary black head, in short, the man who came to be called anonymous and whose anonymity was consummated from the claimed integrating categories called "Civilization" or "Spirit" or "Christian Western World" and so many other similar types.

In relation to the self-begetting and self-making, an answer to the problem of technology must be given. Without a doubt our contemporary world has led to a loss of man that has given form to the vast theme of alienation. But technology, leaving aside whether man can attain or lose happiness through it, cannot be thought of as something alien to human nature, since it constitutes a fundamental part of self-begetting and self-making, which is precisely where freedom is gambled. For that reason, the problem of technology will find its adequate answer when the relation between man and production is formulated correctly, in other words, when labor is a function in which and through which man is able to make his humanity by himself.

Labor and technology, then, are two issues that must be understood on the basis of an ontology that affirms in a conclusive way the historicity on the basis of which is developed the self-realization or the self-destruction of man. It is certainly necessary to be on guard in order not to fall into ontologism insofar as this is a risk incurred in every type of answer. Abelardo Villegas has shown how it is present in the economic formulation of alienation, which in some cases would repeat, with modifications, the doctrine of the "natural state" to which we would have to return in order to be saved from the alienating situation. This supposedly natural man that originally was to be one with the products of his activity, turns out to be in this way an ahistorical being. Faced with this formulation one cannot but assert, as Villegas does, that there is no original ontological structure undone later by events that would turn out to be foreign to it, but that man is a developing being, immersed in social and historical conditions within which ab initio his possibilities of realization or frustration have been given.

The need that man reach his own humanity in his own self-making, through nonalienated labor, undoubtedly displaces the metaphysical need to inquire after being, and above all inhibits that inquiry to the degree that through it one runs the risk of deteriorating the liberating imperative. The problem of transcendence must be recognized from the perspective of that imperative. In that sense, the assumption of the "death of God" within theological thought, and particularly within our Latin American liberation theology, is an answer to the problem of the determination of new integrating categories, and has the heavy burden of finding the way to assume, for the believing man, the historicity of the self-making and the self-begetting, joining with this the vast liberating movement of peoples.

The great revolution of our age consists in the discovery of historicity, which is the fundamental key to every task concerned with decoding oppressive discourse. This one, we knew, has been essentially characterized by having interpreted as natural the relations among men, that is to say, as foreign to self-happening and self-making and the force with which dialectical totalities have been imposed over this base is directly related to fear and the will to power. In this sense the history of philosophies and the history of ideologies can be subjected to the same type of question and are not, in fact, two histories, but one: the history of thought and its multiple expressions. Undoubtedly, our times are not satisfied with a history of philosophy concerned exclusively with academic knowledge or knowledge expressed formally as philosophical discourse, but rather to the degree that that discourse has an epistemological status in terms of which we can declare it to be within the category of the particular discourse of the social sciences, or simply the spontaneous political discourse declared by the common man.

On the basis of everything that has been said there is no doubt that the function to be fulfilled by the historian of thought in Latin America requires him to redirect his task in a new orientation. The discovery that between a "philosophical discourse" and a "political discourse" it is possible to determine a common epistemological structure through which both can be understood as oppressive or liberating discourses—in other words, that it is possible to analyze them from common ideological points of view in close relationship to the *historical a priori* from which both arise—opens the door for an extension of the field of research. Methodologically what we propose is simply to accept a truth that has been enunciated many times, but that has not always been possible to incorporate into the historian's task, which is to assert the necessary relation that there is between philosophical discourse and the system of connections of a given age. If philosophy is the expression of a determined culture it is because it is integrated in it and what has to be looked for is how in its very root that relation is given. One of the unfocusings has been perhaps to think that within that system of connections "philosophical discourse" played a directing role from a level claimed to be purely theoretical, and the presence of factors that place that discourse at the same level as others has been neglected, causing the philosopher's metalanguage, once its presuppositions have been indicated to have ontologically neither more nor less value than the language of the common man. This is then part of the task: to reduce in that sense the metalanguages of language. For the construction of a philosophy of liberation there is nothing more important than to recognize that many times what is new, what truly shows man's historicity and his struggle to make his otherness explicit in its context, is not to be found in academic philosophies, but in the "political discourse" of marginal and exploited elements and that through it proceeds precisely a thought that would have had to have been adopted in the formally philosophical task. Thus we are far from the historiographic categories that were imposed as a consequence of the requirement of "normalization" and of "rigor" that have ruled to this day. Our "rigor" has as a goal to discover truly if a "philosophical discourse" is properly philosophy, above all, if we still harbor the belief that philosophical knowledge points to truth and in that sense to an unconcealment to the degree that we exercise the function of hiding, consciously or unconsciously, from a bad conscience. Certainly we do not wish with this to reduce philosophical historiography to the investigation of ideological presuppositions, for we know that philosophy, although containing what is ideological, also transcends it. There is a reason why philosophy claims to establish itself as critical and self-critical knowledge, located not beyond what is ideological, but rather adopting it openly and within the categories of a liberating thought. Because of what we have been saying, a historiography of Latin American philosophy could not be accomplished without undertaking the study of the development and the modes of social consciousness with all the thematic ramifications involved in this problem.

In order to finish, we should say a few words concerning the so-called "ontologies of the national being" and also something about what is utopian within the liberating discourse.

The horizon from which we intend to give an answer to the ontological question claims to consider the problems of the historicity of man *qua* man. This is to say that, properly speaking, there is neither an "ontology of the [Latin] American man" nor an "ontology of the national being" as it has been postulated, in some cases resulting in the bankruptcy of both rationality and universality. Precisely this requirement is among those listed by Leopoldo Zea in his meditation concerning our philosophy of history.

In that sense we do not accept the presupposition in which "populism" is founded, to the degree that within this doctrine the integrating categories of "people" and of "national being" deny, in our case, otherness, or deform it when they interpret it as an absolute cultural specificity. The notion of "people" is used to hide a real heterogeneity, on the basis of a claimed homogeneity, unreal, within which is disguised the class struggle, and social liberation is postponed with the pretext that it must be preceded by national liberation. The notion of "national being," in turn, is thus founded on an unreal heterogeneity. And that unreal heterogeneity, in its turn, hides a real homogeneity, that is to say, where national differences are emphasized until irrationality is reached. In this way "people" and "national being" appear as typical categories of "integration" proper to contemporary oppressing discourse. An ontology that claims to serve as basis for a philosophy of liberation should then neither ignore the presence of the diverse modes of otherness, nor deform it obscuring entity's rationality, something that makes impossible its understanding in relation to other beings before which it is "other." Without a doubt, "populism" has Caliban as its symbol, but it is a Caliban newly shackled and bound.

The problem of utopia is the problem of the regulating power of ideas. The issue concerns the question as to which is its function within the liberating discourse and whether its presence as a creative force is to be rejected. We understand that what is utopian is a natural ingredient of this discourse, just as the antiutopian attitude is proper to oppressive discourse, above all if we do not understand by utopian the return to the past, but to be open to the future as the place for what is new. This last is and will always be an answer given as a result of the preeminence of entity, without whose acknowledgment a philosophy of liberation is not possible. Our own discourse in which we have decided to situate ourselves cannot ignore the risks and benefits of what is utopian. A praxis that does not belong to the philosopher, but upon which philosophy must be developed, is giving the superseding formulae of the dialectical road that moves between the will to reality and reality itself.

4

Enrique Dussel
(b. 1934)

Born in La Paz, a small village in Argentina, in 1934, Enrique D. Dussel became part of the Catholic Action Movement at a young age. The son of a doctor, Dussel also became active in student politics at the Universidad Nacional de Cuyo in Mendoza, Argentina. In 1957 Dussel completed a licentiate thesis on the treatment of the common good from the pre-Socratics to Aristotle.

Dussel pursued his study of philosophy in Spain, where he wrote a doctoral dissertation on the common good in authors Charles de Konick and Jacques Maritain. In Spain, Dussel was influenced by the Madrid School of philosophy, that is, by thinkers such as Xavier Zubiri and José Ortega y Gasset. After successfully defending his dissertation, Dussel moved to Israel to live on a kibbutz from 1959 to 1961. There, Dussel explored Jewish and Christian religious traditions and learned Hebrew. He also began work on his first books, *Semitic Humanism* (1961), *Hellenic Humanism* (1963), and *Dualism in Anthropology of Christendom* (1968). Upon his return to Europe in 1964, Dussel wrote *Hypotheses of the Church in Latin America,* a work which marked his role as a leader in the field of liberation theology and his ensuing dedication to Latin American problems.

In 1967 Dussel returned to Argentina and became a member of the faculty of the Universidad Nacional de Cuyo as a professor of philosophical anthropology and ethics. He became familiar with the debates in Latin America concerning dependency theories, and also kept up with the most contemporary work by Continental European philosophers such as Emmanuel Levinas and Karl Otto Apel. In Argentina, Dussel, together with Arturo Andrés Roig, Osvaldo Ardiles, Horacio Cerutti-Guldberg, and others, developed the principles for a philosophy (rather than a theology) of liberation. This was intended as a tool of social change and was intrin-

415

sically tied to the political and social reality. The political climate of Argentina in the 1960s and 1970s did not prove to be hospitable for these views. Even after the death of Juan Perón in 1974, right-wing politics determined the political climate of Argentina, and the military worked with the government to rid universities of voices of dissent. Dussel was one of many intellectuals forced to leave Argentina in 1975. He sought exile in Mexico, where he remains to this day.

In Mexico, Dussel became a professor at the Universidad Nacional Autónoma de México. He published *Philosophy of Liberation* in 1975. This work is arguably the most detailed and systematic treatment of the basic tenets of his theories. Dussel's other works in English include: *Ethics and Theology of Liberation* (1964), *History of the Church in Latin America* (1972), *History and the Theology of Liberation* (1975), and *Ethics of Liberation* (1998). He is the author of many books and articles in Spanish which concentrate on the past and present role of the Catholic Church in Latin America as well as on dependency and liberation. Dussel's contributions continue to be important to current thinking in liberation theology, both in Latin America and abroad.

Philosophy of Liberation

HISTORY

The following . . . chapter serves simply as an example of how one essential phase of a philosophy of liberation can be developed. A philosophy of liberation must always begin by presenting the historico-ideological genesis of what it attempts to think through, giving priority to its spatial, worldly setting.

1.1 Geopolitics and Philosophy

1.1.1 Status Questionis

1.1.1.1 From Heraclitus to Karl von Clausewitz and Henry Kissinger, "war is the origin of everything," if by "everything" one understands the order or system that world dominators control by their power and armies. We are at war—a cold war for those who wage it, a hot war for those who suffer it, a peaceful coexistence for those who manufacture arms, a bloody existence for those obliged to buy and use them.

Space as a battlefield, as a geography studied to destroy an enemy, as a territory with fixed frontiers, is very different from the abstract idealization of empty space of Newton's physics or the existential space of phenomenology. Abstract spaces are naive, nonconflictual unrealities. The space of a world within the ontological horizon is the space of a world center, of the organic, self-conscious state that brooks no contradictions—

From *Philosophy of Liberation*, trans. Aquilina Martinez and Christine Morkovsky (Maryknoll, NY: Orbis Books, 1985), pp. 1–15. Reprint of English translation by permission of Orbis Books.

because it is an imperialist state. I am not speaking of the space of the claustrophobic or the agoraphobic. I am speaking of political space, which includes all existentially real spaces within the parameters of an economic system in which power is exercised in tandem with military control.

Unnoticed, philosophy was born in this political space. In more creative periods, it was born in peripheral spaces. But little by little it gravitated toward the center in its classic periods, in the great ontologies, until it degenerated into the "bad conscience" of moral—or rather, moralistic—times.

1.1.1.2   I am trying, then, to take space, geopolitical space, seriously. To be born at the North Pole or in Chiapas is not the same thing as to be born in New York City.

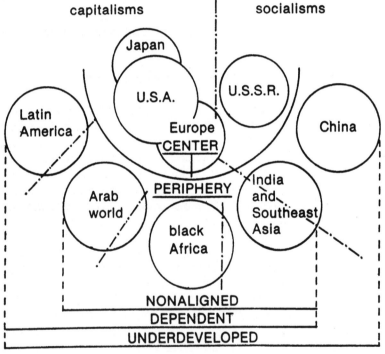

1.1.2 Oppression of the Colonial and Neocolonial Periphery

1.1.2.1   The claim that philosophy of liberation is postmodern is grounded in the following thesis: modern European philosophy, even before the *ego cogito* but certainly from then on, situated all men and all cultures—and with them their women and children—within its own boundaries as manipulable tools, instruments. Ontology understood them as interpretable beings, as known ideas, as mediations or internal possibilities within the horizon of the comprehension of Being.

Spatially central, the *ego cogito* constituted the periphery and asked itself, along with Fernández de Oviedo, "Are the Amerindians human beings?" that is, Are they Europeans, and therefore rational animals? The theoretical response was of little importance. We are still suffering from the practical response. The Amerindians were suited to forced labor; if not irrational, then at least they were brutish, wild, underdeveloped, uncultured—because they did not have the culture of the center.

1.1.2.2 That ontology did not come from nowhere. It arose from a previous experience of domination over other persons, of cultural oppression over other worlds. Before the *ego cogito* there is an *ego conquiro*; "I conquer" is the practical foundation of "I think." The center has imposed itself on the periphery for more than five centuries. But for how much longer? Will the geopolitical preponderance of the center come to an end? Can we glimpse a process of liberation growing from the peoples of the periphery?

1.1.3 Geopolitical Space and the History of Philosophy

1.1.3.1 Philosophy, when it is really philosophy and not sophistry or ideology, does not ponder philosophy. It does not ponder philosophical texts, except as a pedagogical propaedeutic to provide itself with interpretive categories. Philosophy ponders the nonphilosophical; the reality. But because it involves reflection on its own reality, it sets out from what already is, from its own world, its own system, its own space. The philosophy that has emerged from a periphery has always done so in response to a need to situate itself with regard to a center—in total exteriority.

1.1.3.2 Pre-Socratic thought appeared not in Greece but in Turkey and southern Italy, from a political periphery (they were dominated), from an economic periphery (they were colonies), and from a geopolitical periphery (they were threatened by the armies of the center). Medieval thought emerged from the frontiers of the empire; the Greek fathers were peripheral, as were the Latin fathers. Even in the Carolingian renaissance, renewal came from the peripheral Ireland. From peripheral France arose a Descartes, and Kant burst in from distant Königsberg.

Distant thinkers, those who had a perspective of the center from the periphery, those who had to define themselves in the presence of an already established image of the human person and in the presence of uncivilized fellow humans, the newcomers, the ones who hope because they are always outside, these are the ones who have a clear mind for pondering reality. They have nothing to hide. How could they hide domination if they undergo it? How would their philosophy be an ideological ontology if their praxis is one of liberation from the center they are opposing? Philosophical intelligence is never so truthful, clean, and precise as when it starts from oppression and does not have to defend any privileges, because it has none.

1.1.4 The Center, Classic Ontology, and the System

1.1.4.1   Critical thought that arises from the periphery—including the social periphery, the oppressed classes, the *lumpen*—always ends by directing itself toward the center. It is its death as critical philosophy; it is its birth as an ontology and ideology. Thought that takes refuge in the center ends by thinking it to be the only reality. Outside its frontiers is nonbeing, nothing, barbarity, non-sense. Being* is the very foundation of the system, the totality of the sense of a culture, the macho world of the man of the center.

1.1.4.2   For Aristotle, the great philosopher of the classical period, reared to accept slavery and pursue self-centeredness, the Greek was human. The European barbarians were not human, because they were unskilled; nor were Asians human, because they lacked strength and character; slaves were not human either; women were halfway human and children were only potentially human. The human being par excellence is the free man of the *polis* of Hellas. For Thomas Aquinas the feudal lord exercised his *jus dominativum* over the servant of his fiefdom, and the man did the same over the woman (Eve, even though she had sinned, could not transmit original sin, because the mother only supplies the matter, but the man gives Being to the child). For Hegel the state that bears the Spirit is the "dominator of the world," before which all other states are "devoid of rights (*rechtlos*)." For this reason Europe appointed itself "the missionary of civilization" to the world.

1.1.4.3   Ontology, the thinking that expresses Being—the Being of the reigning and central system—is the ideology of ideologies, the foundation of the ideologies of the empires, of the center. Classic philosophy of all ages is the theoretical consummation of the practical oppression of peripheries.

1.1.4.4   Thus philosophy of domination, at the center of the ideological hegemony of the dominant classes, plays an essential role in European history. Nonetheless, one could trace throughout all that history a critical thinking that is in some way a philosophy of liberation insofar as it articulates the ideological formation of dominated classes.

---

*I differentiate between Being (Latin, *esse*; German, *Sein*) and being(s) (Latin, *ens*, *entia*; German, *das Seiende*).

1.1.5 Greek Philosophy

1.1.5.1 Parmenides, from the periphery of Magna Graecia, proclaimed the radical beginning of philosophy as ontology: "Being is; non-Being is not." What is Being if not the foundation of the world, the horizon that encompasses the totality within which we live, the frontier that our armies control? Being coincides with the world; it is like the light (*phos*) that illumines an area but is not itself seen. Being is not seen; what it illuminates is seen—things (*onta*), tools, instruments (*pragmata*).

Being is that which is Greek, the light of Greek culture. Being extends as far as the frontiers of Hellenism. Over the horizon is non-Being, uncivilization, Europe and Asia. This sense of ontology is found in the political thought of Plato, Aristotle, Epicurus, and the Stoics.

1.1.5.2 From the poor colonist who like Heraclitus experienced Being as the *logos* that walls the city (defending it from barbarians), to the Alexandrine or Roman cosmopolitan who confused the city with the cosmos, the Greco-Roman city was divinized and identified with nature itself. Thus did ontology end up affirming that Being, the divine, the political, and the eternal are "one and the same thing." Power, domination, and the center are identical, above the colonies with other cultures, above slaves of other skin colors. The center is; the periphery is not. Where Being reigns, there reign and control the armies of Caesar, the emperor. Being is; beings are what are seen and controlled.

1.1.5.3 Classic Greco-Roman philosophies, with some exceptions, in fact articulated the interests of the dominant proslavery classes and justified their domination from the horizon of Being itself. It is easy to understand Aristotle's "The slave is a slave by nature" or the inclination of Stoics and Epicureans to extend deliverance to all the citizens of the empire, so as to ensure a "good conscience" in all its members, on the one hand, and to sanctify the empire, finite manifestation of the gods of cosmopolitanism, on the other.

1.1.6 Mediterranean Thought between Ancient and Modern Times

1.1.6.1 The peripheral humans of this transition were the poor Bedouin of the Arabian desert, not the Indo-Europeans who, crossing the Eurasian steppes with their horses, one day invaded Greece, Rome, and India. The Bedouin and shepherds of the desert did not experience Being as light but as proximity, face-to-face encounter with a brother or sister of the same ethnos or a stranger to whom hospitality was offered. One day the Bedouin comprised the kingdoms of Akkad, Assyria, and Babylonia; they will depart in exile to Egypt. They will be liberated with Moses. They will be the origin of the vision of the world that Maimonides will be able to define centuries later as "the philosophy of creation," a theoretical metaphysics that justifies the practico-political revolution of slaves and the oppressed (3.4.4).

1.1.6.2 From the periphery, the Being that strikes the ear of the attentive listener as freedom will also triumph in its classic epochs: in Constantinople after the fourth century, in Rome after the sixth century, in Baghdad after the ninth century, in Córdoba after the tenth century, in Paris after the thirteenth century. The Semitic world (Christian, Muslim, and Jewish) will also have its ontology, its expressed fundamental ideology. After having begun by stating "Blessed are the poor," and after having understood that Abel never built his city as Augustine prescribed in the *City of God*, they ended by again identifying Being with the ruling system, the earthly city (of the medievals or of the caliphs) with the city of God. Creation—which permitted the understanding of things, profits, systems, and kingdoms as contingent and possible (not necessary) and therefore changeable (3.4.5.2)—came to justify the medieval Mediterranean system: God wanted things *this way*. The ideologizing of the subversive and political metaphysics of creation was the beginning of its end, of its fossilization, of the modern centro-European revolution.

1.1.6.3 In the same way methodical Semitic-Christian thought, first articulated by the nomadic and austere tribes of the desert, ended by justifying the dominating class, the world of medieval feudalism. Critics of the mode of feudal production and the structure of prescribed tribute were not lacking, but they frequently ended up in the hands of the Holy Office, the Inquisition.

1.1.7 Modern European Philosophy

1.1.7.1 The modern age began when the Mediterranean millennium crumbled. For Cretans and Phoenicians as well as Arabs and Venetians, the Mediterranean was the central sea (*medi-terra*), the center of world history. Nevertheless, Germano-Latin Europe enclosed by the Turko-Arabic world (which extended, after the fall of Constantinople, from Andalusia in southern Spain to the gates of Vienna) could not expand into the wider world. The medieval Crusades were the first European expansionist attempts, but the Arabs were sufficiently powerful to return the frontiers to their former positions. Beginning with the fourteenth century, the Portuguese and then the Spanish began to control the North Atlantic (which from the end of the fifteenth century until today will be the center of history). Spain and Portugal opened Europe to the west; Russia will do it to the east. In the sixteenth century Spain discovered the Pacific to the west and Russia did the same to the east. Now the Arab world is enclosed and loses the centrality it had exercised for almost a thousand years. Later

Spain and Portugal will give way to the British empire. Now Europe is the center. From the experience of this centrality gained by the sword and by power, Europe begins to consider itself the archetypal foundational "I."

1.1.7.2 From the "I conquer" applied to the Aztec and Inca world and all America, from the "I enslave" applied to Africans sold for the gold and silver acquired at the cost of the death of Amerindians working in the depths of the earth, from the "I vanquish" of the wars of India and China to the shameful "opium war"—from this "I" appears the Cartesian *ego cogito*. This ego will be the unique substance, divine in Spinoza. In Hegel the *ich denke* of Kant will recover perfect divinity in the *absolutes Wissen*, absolute knowledge, which is the very act of totality as such: God on earth. If faith, the perfect cult of absolute religion in Hegel's *Philosophy of Religion*, is the certitude that the representation of the understanding is the absolute Idea, such certitude is that which world dominators have: they are the manifestation on earth of the divinity. The empires of the center—England and France as colonial powers, Nazi Germany, and later the United States with its Central Intelligence Agency (CIA)—thus once more possess an ontology that justifies them, a subtle ideology that gives them a "good conscience."

What is Nietzsche if not an apology for the human conqueror and warrior? What are phenomenology and existentialism if not the description of an "I" or a *Dasein* from which opens a world, always one's own? What are all the critical schools, or even those that launch themselves in search of a utopia, but the affirmation of the center as the future possibility of "the same"? What is structuralism but the affirmation of totality—though not leading to a politico-economic resolution in real liberation?

1.1.7.3 "God is dead"—that is to say, Europe is dead because it deified itself. At least the fetish has died for us and with it the United States as its quantitative extension. The death of the fetish is important, for just as "all criticism begins with the critique of (fetishist) religion," so liberation is possible only when one has the courage to be atheistic vis-à-vis an empire of the center, thus incurring the risk of suffering from its power, its economic boycotts, its armies, and its agents who are experts at corruption, violence, and assassination.

1.1.7.4 *Homo homini lupus* is the real—that is, political—definition of the *ego cogito* and of modern and contemporary European philosophy. It is the ontological expression of the ideology of the bourgeois class, triumphant in the British revolution, which will dominate the capitalist world. Philosophy again becomes the center of the ideological hegemony of the dominating class.

1.2 Philosophy of Liberation of the Periphery

1.2.1 Critique of the Conquest

1.2.1.1 Philosophy of liberation is recent. Nevertheless, its antecedents are older than modern European philosophy. Bartolomé de Las Casas (1484–1566) wrote that "they have used two ways to extirpate these pitiable nations from the face of the earth," referring to the two ways Europeans used to dominate the periphery. "One is by unjust, cruel, bloody, and tyrannical wars"—that is, the Europeans assassinated the inhabitants of the periphery. "The other way is that after they have assassinated all those, such as adult males, who can yearn for freedom—usually they do not leave any survivors of war except children and women—they then oppress survivors with the most violent, horrible, and hateful slavery." They assassinated the Amerindians; if they left any alive, they debased them, oppressing them with servitude. They spared women, to live in concubinage (sexual domination) and children, to be educated in European culture (pedagogical domination). And thus in the name of the "new god" (gold, silver, money, pounds sterling, or the dollar) there have been immolated to the god of nascent mercantilism, the god of economic imperialism, and the contemporary imperialism of the multinational corporations, millions more human beings of the periphery than those the Aztecs immolated to their god Huitzilopochtli—to the horror of civilized, religious-minded Europeans!

1.2.1.2 The philosophy that knows how to ponder this reality, the de facto world reality, not from the perspective of the center of political, economic, or military power but from beyond the frontiers of that world, from the periphery—this philosophy will not be ideological. Its reality is the whole earth; for it the "wretched of the earth" (who are not nonbeing) are also real.

1.2.2 Colonial Mercantile Philosophy

1.2.2.1 I call colonial philosophy that which was exported to Latin America, Africa, and Asia beginning with the sixteenth century (the universities of Mexico and Lima were founded in 1552 with the same academic ranking as those of Alcalá and Salamanca), and especially the spirit of pure imitation or repetition in the periphery of the philosophy prevailing in the imperialist center.

1.2.2.2 Latin American colonial philosophy was cultivated in the Hispanic periphery. Spain, like no other metropolitan power (through the influence of the Renaissance and the Iberian "Golden Age"), founded in its American colonies more than thirty centers of higher studies that granted licentiates and doctorates in philosophy (the majority with a view to ecclesiastical studies). The most famous faculties of philosophy were those of Mexico and Lima. Their professors published their works in Louvain, Leipzig, Venice, and other prestigious publishing centers of Europe, as in the case of the *Logica mexicana* by Antonio Rubio (1548-1615), which was used as a textbook in the University of Alcalá (one of its ten editions was the 1605 edition of Cologne). The Peruvian Juan Espinoza Medrano (1632-1688) published in Cuzco his famous *Cursus philosophicus* in 1688. The faculties in Bogotá, Guatemala City, Quito, Santiago de Chile, Córdoba del Tucumán, and others, can also be named. Nevertheless, all this was, although partly creative, a reflection of the neoscholasticism of Spain.

In the eighteenth century, the Baroque Jesuit educational program, with its *reducciones*—settlements of Amerindians converted to Christianity (the most famous were in Paraguay)—made important advances in philosophy, physics, mathematics, and politics. However, it never went beyond imitation, and it was doubly ideological: repeating in the periphery (and concealing the domination suffered there) an ideological process initiated in Europe.

1.2.2.3 The colonial mercantile stage in the Portuguese and first English colonies did not envision the foundation of philosophical centers in the periphery. Colonial elites were formed in Coimbra and London. This was the beginning of a cultural domination that would be perfected later on.

1.2.3 Colonial Mercantile Emancipation

1.2.3.1 Two centuries ago, in 1776 to be exact, the process of emancipation from colonial mercantilism began. In New England a group of valiant colonists arose against the British homeland and began a war of national emancipation. This process will continue in Luso-Hispanic America from 1810 to 1898—from the emancipation of Argentina and Peru to that of Mexico, and thence to the Caribbean. Puerto Rico, from being a Spanish colony, becomes an *estado libre asociado* (a "free associated state," a contradiction in terms) of the United States, which a half-century before had annexed Texas, New Mexico, and California, lopping them off from Mexico.

From Washington to Hidalgo, Bolívar and San Martín ignited the thought of emancipation, which did not become an explicit philosophy. Bentham sights it at the end of the eighteenth century, and Hegel describes it in his *Philosophy of Right* in 1821: "England understood that emancipating the colonies was more useful than keeping them dependent." The English empire had learned that it cost less to withdraw its bureaucracy and armies from its colonies. The emancipator heroes did not fathom the full impact of their deeds. The liberation of which the philosophy of liberation speaks was still an unsuspected future horizon. From them, nevertheless, present-day philosophers can imbibe a deep yearning for freedom.

1.2.4 Imperialist Recolonization

1.2.4.1 As soon as the first crisis of the industrial revolution could be overcome in England and France, principally around 1850—that is, when sufficient accumulation of capital was in place—the imperialist center began a second colonial age (in the second half of the nineteenth century). Now the Arab world, black Africa, India, Southeast Asia, and China are to undergo the impetuous onslaught of what will quickly become monopolistic economic imperialism.

1.2.4.2 Colonial elites were now systematically trained in the imperialist center. Oxford, Cambridge, and Paris were transformed into theaters of "reeducation," of brainwashing, until well into the twentieth century. The colonial oligarchies were brown, black, or yellow, and they aped the philosophy they had learned abroad. True puppets, they repeated in the periphery what their eminent professors of the great metropolitan universities had propounded. In Cairo, Dakkar, Saigon, and Peking—as in Buenos Aires and Lima—they taught their pupils the *ego cogito* in which they themselves remained constituted as an idea or thought, entities at the disposal of the "will to power," impotent, dominated wills, castrated teachers who castrated their pupils.

1.2.4.3 These colonized philosophers had forgotten their past. The Arab world did not return to its own splendid philosophy dating back to the ninth century. India was ashamed of its sages and so was China, though both nations had produced treasures of thought for more than three millennia. The past did not withstand the attack of modern imperialist metropolitan thinking, at least in its most progressive, modernizing, and developmentalist forms.

1.2.4.4 Modern European philosophers ponder the reality that confronts them; they interpret the periphery from the center. But the colonial philosophers of the periphery gaze at a vision foreign to them, one that is not their own. From the center they see themselves as nonbeing, nothingness; and they teach their pupils, who are something (although illiterate in the alphabets imposed on them), that really they are nothing, that they are like nothings walking through history. When they have finished their studies they, like their colonial teachers, disappear from the map—geopolitically and philosophically, they do not exist. This pathetic ideology given the name of philosophy is the one still taught in the majority of philosophy schools of the periphery by the majority of its professors.

1.2.5 Neocolonial Imperialist Emancipation

1.2.5.1 With the coming of World War II a new world power emerged. The United States took the lead in reapportioning the world at Yalta (1945). The colonies of the British empire and what remained of French and other European colonies were redistributed. The heroes of neocolonial emancipation worked in an ambiguous political sphere. Mahatma Gandhi in India, Abdel Nasser in Egypt, and Patrice Lumumba in the Congo dream of emancipation but are not aware that their nations will pass from the hands of England, France, or Belgium into the hands of the United States.

As in the first stage of colonization (1.2.2), philosophy has rich material to apply itself to. Freedom is a distant utopia, not a foreseeable prospect. Nevertheless, a substantive, explicit philosophy of national anticolonial emancipation has never been elaborated. There have been only manifestos, pamphlets, and political works (which implicitly include a philosophy but are not philosophy in the strict sense). The thinking reflected in them was the most polished of peripheral thinking in the modern world. Its thinkers situated themselves in an appropriate hermeneutical space, in the correct perspective. But it was not yet philosophy, even though the work of Frantz Fanon was already a beginning.

1.2.5.2 The new imperialism is the fruit of the third industrial revolution. (If the first was mechanistic and the second monopolistic, the third is the international effort of the transnationals, which structure their neocolonies from within.)

The transnationals do not occupy territories with armies or create bureaucracies. They are owners, directly or indirectly, of the key enterprises—production of raw materials, process industries, and services—of the periphery. Furthermore, the new imperialism exercises political control over its neocolonies and their armies. One utterly new feature is that the empire pursues a policy of cultivating desires, needs (4.3.3). This empowers it, through mass media advertising, to dominate peripheral peoples and their own national oligarchies. An ideological imperialism (4.2.7 and 5.7) is also at work here.

1.2.5.3 Progressivist philosophy of the center, when simply repeated in the periphery, becomes an obscurantist ideology. I am not thinking only of phenomenology or existentialism, or of functionalism or critical theory, of science that becomes scientism, but also of a Marxism that does not redefine its principles from the viewpoint of dependency (5.9.1.2-5). Ontology and nonradical criticism (such as that which thinks science cannot be ideology, because of its presuppositions or its real but unacknowledged goal) are thus the last ideological underpinnings of imperialist ideology (3.3.6).

1.2.6 Philosophy of Liberation

1.2.6.1   What is at stake is neocolonial liberation from the last and most advanced degree of imperialism, North American imperialism, the imperialism that weighs down part of Asia and almost all of Africa and Latin America. Only China and Vietnam in Asia, Cuba and Nicaragua in Latin America, and Mozambique, Angola, and Ethiopia in Africa have a certain modicum of freedom, certainly much more than other peripheral nations. Clearly they must know how to use the geopolitical division established in Yalta, must know how to rely on the politico-military power that controls the sphere outside the "partitioned" world, within whose frontiers they have achieved relative freedom. Thus China relies on the United States to safeguard its freedom from the nearby USSR, and Cuba relies on Russia to safeguard its freedom from the nearby United States. Far be it from me to trivialize the content of their politico-economic models. I want only to point out a geopolitical factor that peripheral nations can never forget or they will be lost. The cat can make a mistake; it is only toying with its prey. But the mouse cannot make a mistake; it will be its death. If the mouse lives, it is because it is smarter than the cat.

1.2.6.2   Against the classic ontology of the center, from Hegel to Marcuse—to name the most brilliant from Europe and North America—a philosophy of liberation is rising from the periphery, from the oppressed, from the shadow that the light of Being has not been able to illumine. Our thought sets out from non-Being, nothingness, otherness, exteriority, the mystery of non-sense. It is, then, a "barbarian" philosophy.

1.2.6.3   Philosophy of liberation tries to formulate a metaphysics (2.4.9.2)—not an ontology (2.4.9.1)—demanded by revolutionary praxis (3.1.7–8) and technologico-design poiesis (4.3) against the background of peripheral social formations. To do this it is necessary to deprive Being of its alleged eternal and divine foundation; to negate fetishist religion in order to expose ontology as the ideology of ideologies; to unmask functionalisms—whether structuralist, logico-scientific, or mathematical (claiming that reason cannot criticize the whole dialectically, they affirm it the more they analytically criticize or operationalize its parts); and to delineate the sense of liberation praxis. Post-Hegelian critics of the European left have explained it to some extent. Only the praxis of oppressed peoples of the periphery, of the woman violated by masculine ideology, of the subjugated child, can fully reveal it to us (5.9).

Bibliography

Abbagnano, Nicola. *Diccionario de filosofía.* Translated by Alfredo N. Galleti. 2d ed. in Spanish. Mexico City: Fondo de Cultura Económica, 1966.

Abellán, José Luis. *Filosofía española en América, 1936–66.* Madrid: Guadarrama, 1967.

———. "Leopoldo Zea: hilo filosófico entre España y México." *Anthropos* 89 (1988): 48–51.

Abril, Xavier, et al. *Mariátegui y la literatura.* Lima: Empresa Editora Amauta, 1980.

Actas: Primer Congreso de Filosofía y Filosofía de la Educación convocado por la Facultad de Filosofía, Letras, y Ciencias de la Educación de la Universidad Central. Quito: Cultura Ecuatoriana, 1954.

Actas: Segundo Congreso Extraordinario Interamericano de Filosofía. San José: Nacional, 1962.

Alcoff Martín, Linda. "Habits of Hostility: On Seeing Race." *Philosophy Today* 44 (2000): 30–40.

———. "Mestizo Identity." In *American Mixed Race.* Edited by Naomi Zack. Lanham, MD: Rowman and Littlefield, 1995.

———, and Eduardo Mendicta, eds. *Thinking from the Underside of History.* New York: Rowman and Littlefield, 2000.

Alvarez de Miranda, Angel. *Perfil cultural de Hispanoamérica.* Madrid: Cultura Hispánica, 1950.

Antología del pensamiento social y político de América Latina. Introduction by Leopoldo Zea. Selection and notes by Abelardo Villegas. Washington, DC: Unión Panamericana, 1984.

Anzaldúa, Gloria. *Borderlands/La Frontera.* San Franciso: Spinsters/Aunt Lunt, 1987.

Arciniegas, Germán. *Latin America: A Cultural History.* Translated by Joan MacLean. New York: Alfred A. Knopf, 1967.

Ardao, Arturo. "Assimilation and Transformation of Positivism in Latin America." *Journal of the History of Ideas* 24 (1963): 515–22.

Ardiles, Osvaldo. "Líneas básicas para un proyecto de filosofar latinoamericano." *Revista de Filosofía Latinoamericana* 1 (1975): 5–15.

Ardiles, Osvaldok Hugo Assmann, et al. *Hacia una filosofía de la liberación lati-noamericana.* Buenos Aires: Editorial Bonum, 1973.

——. *Filosofía de lengua española.* Montevideo: Editorial Alfa, 1963.

Arenal, Electa. "Sor Juana Inés de la Cruz: Reclaiming the Mother Tongue." *Letras Femininas* 10 (1985): 63–75.

Armstrong, A. M. "Contemporary Latin American Philosophy." *Philosophical Quarterly* 3 (1953): 167–74.

Berndston, Arthur. "Latin American Philosophy." In *The Encyclopedia of Philosophy,* edited by Paul Edwards, 4:396–400. New York: Macmillan, 1967.

Berndtson, C. Arthur E. *Readings in Latin-American Philosophy.* Columbia: University of Missouri, 1949.

Betancourt, Raúl Fornet. "La axiologia alemana y sus influencias en la metafísica espiritualista de Antonio Caso." *Revista de Filosofía* 21 (1988): 92–100.

——. "La filosofía de José Vasconcelos: exposición y valoración." *Revista de Filosofía* 14 (1986): 27–81.

——. "La problemática de los valores en la tradición filosófica latinoamericana del Siglo XX." *Revista Agustiniana* 36 (1995): 571–96.

Bethell, Leslie, ed. *Spanish America after Independence c. 1820–c. 1870.* Cambridge: Cambridge University Press, 1987.

Beuchot, Mauricio. *The History of Philosophy in Colonial Mexico.* Translated by Elizabeth Millán. Foreword by Jorge J. E. Gracia. Washington, DC: Catholic University of America Press, 1998.

Biagini, Hugo E. "Contemporary Argentinian Philosophy." In *Philosophy and Literature in Latin America.* Edited by J. E. Gracia and Mireya Camurati. Albany: State University of New York Press, 1989.

——. *Filosofía americana e identidad: el conflictivo caso argentino.* Buenos Aires: Editorial Universitaria, 1989.

Bibliografía filosófica del siglo XX: catálogo de la Exposición Bibliográfica Internacional de la Filosofía del Siglo XX. Buenos Aires: Peuser, 1952.

Brightman, Edgard S. "Personalism in Latin America." *Personalist* 24 (1943): 147–62.

Brüning, Walther. "La antropología filosófica actual en Iberoamérica." *Revista de la Universidad Nacional de Córdoba* 40 (1953): 935–65.

Caldera, Rafael Tomás. *Nuevo mundo y mentalidad colonial.* Caracas: El Centauro, 2000.

Cannabrava, Euryalo. "Present Tendencies in Latin American Philosophy." *Journal of Philosophy* 46 (1949): 113–19.

Carrillo Narvaez, Alfredo. *La trayectoria del pensamiento filosófico en Latinoamérica.* Quito: Casa de la Cultura Ecuatoriana, 1959.

Casas, Bartolomé de Las. *In Defense of the Indians.* Translated by Stafford Poole. Foreword by Martin L. Marty. DeKalb: Northern Illinois University Press, 1992.

Caso, Antonio. *El problema de México y la ideología nacional.* Mexico City: Libro-Mex, 1955.

Castro-Gómez, Santiago. *Crítica de la razón latinoamerica.* Barcelona: Puvill, 1997.

Caturla Brú, Victoria de. *¿Cuáles son los grandes temas de la filosofía latinoamericana?* Mexico City: Novaro-México, 1959.

Cerutti-Guldberg, Horacio. "Actual Situation and Perspectives of Latin American Philosophy for Liberation." *Philosophical Forum* 20 (1988–89): 43–61.

Chavarría, Jesús. *José Carlos Mariátegui and the Rise of Modern Peru, 1890–1930.* Albuqueque: University of New Mexico Press, 1979.

Clissold, Stephen. *Latin America: A Cultural Outline.* New York: Harper and Row, 1966.

Conversaciones filosóficas interamericanas (homenaje de centenario al Apóstol José Martí). Havana: Comisión Nacional del Centenario de Martí, 1955.

Crawford, William Rex. *A Century of Latin-American Thought.* Cambridge, MA: Harvard University, 1944; 2d rev. ed., 1961; 3d ed., New York: Praeger, 1966.

Criscenti, Joseph T., ed. *Sarmiento and His Argentina.* Boulder, CO: Lynne Rienner Publishers, 1993.

Cursos y Conferencias 48 (1956); issue dedicated to Latin American philosophy.

Dacal-Alonso, José. "La estética en Antonio Caso." *Revista de Filosofía* 13 (1985): 73–101.

———. "La Estética en Samuel Ramos." *Revista de Filosofía* 17 (1989): 9–27.

David, Guillermo. "Carlos Astrada: la larga marcha de la filosofía argentina." *Nombres* 9 (1999): 67–84.

Davis, Harold Eugene. *Latin American Social Thought.* Washington, DC: University Press of Washington, 1963.

———. *Latin American Thought: A Historical Introduction.* Baton Rouge: Louisiana State University Press, 1972; 2d ed., New York: Free Press, 1974.

———. "Social and Political Thought in Latin America." In *Twentieth Century Political Thought.* Edited by Joseph E. Roucek. New York: Philosophical Library, 1946.

———. *Social Science Trends in Latin America.* Washington, DC: American University Press, 1950.

Donoso, Antón. "Philosophy in Latin America: A Bibliographical Introduction to Works in English." *Philosophy Today* 17 (1973): 220–31.

Duran, Manuel, and William Kluback, eds. *Reason in Exile: Essays on Catalan Philosophers.* New York: Peter Lang, 1994.

Dussel, Enrique D. *América Latina: dependencia y liberación.* Buenos Aires: Fernando García Cambeiro, 1973.

———. *Caminos de liberación latinoamericana.* Buenos Aires: Latinoamérica Libros, 1973.

———. "The Ethics of Liberation as Opposed to the Ethics of Discourse." *Revista de Filosofía* 21 (1995): 93–114.

———. *Philosophy of Liberation.* Translated by Aquilina Martínez and Christine Morkovsky. New York: Orbis Books, 1985.

Echevarría, José. *La enseñanza de la filosofía en la universidad hispanoamericana.* Washington, DC: Unión Panamericana, 1965.

Fernández Retamar, Roberto. *Calibán and Other Essays.* Translated by Edward Baker. Minneapolis: University of Minnesota Press, 1980.

———. "Our America and the West." *Social Text* 15 (1986): 1–25.

Ferrater Mora, José. *Diccionario de filosofía.* Mexico City: Atlante, 1941; several subsequent enlarged editions.

La filosofía en América. Vol. 1, *Actas del IX Congreso Interamericano de Filosofía.* Caracas: Sociedad Venezolana de Filosofía, 1979.

Filosofía y Letras 38 (1950); articles on Latin American philosophy by Ferrater Mora, Frondizi, Zea, and others.

"First InterAmerican Conference of Philosophy, Papers and Discussions." *Philosophy and Phenomenological Research* 4 (1943–44): 127–235.

Fornet-Betancourt, Raúl. *Problemas actuales de la filosofía en Hispanoamérica.* Buenos Aires: Ediciones FEPAI, 1985.

Frank, Waldo. *América Hispana: A Portrait and a Prospect.* New York and London: Scribner's, 1931.

Frankl, Victor E. *Espíritu y camino de Hispanoamerica: la cultura hispanoamericana y la filosofía europea.* Bogota: Biblioteca de Autores Colombianos, 1953.

Fránquiz, José A. "The Concept of Freedom in Latin American Philosophical Thought." *Proceedings of the Fourteenth International Congress of Philosophy,* 1:193–200. Vienna: Herder, 1968.

Freire, Paulo. *Pedagogy of the Oppressed.* Translated by Myra Bergmann Ramos. New York: Seabury Press, 1970.

Frondizi, Risieri. *Fuentes de la filosofía latinoamericana.* Serie de Bibliografías Básicas 4. Washington, DC: Unión Panamericana, 1967.

———. *Los "fundadores" en la filosofía de América Latina.* Serie de Bibliografías Básicas 7. Washington, DC: Unión Panamericana, 1970.

———. "Is There an Ibero-American Philosophy?" *Philosophy and Phenomenological Research* 9 (1948–49): 345–55.

———. "On the Unity of the Philosophies of the Two Americas." *Review of Metaphysics* 4 (1951): 617–22. Translated from "Tipos de unidad y diferencia entre el filosofar en Latinoamérica y en Norteamérica." *Filosofía y Letras* 19 (1950): 373–77.

———. "A Selective Guide to the Material Published in 1939 on Latin American Philosophy." *Handbook of Latin American Studies* 5 (1939): 418–27.

———. "Tendencies in Contemporary Latin American Philosophy." In *Inter-American Intellectual Interchange,* 35–48. Austin: Institute of Latin American Studies of the University of Texas, 1943.

———. *La universidad en un mundo de tensiones: misión de las universidades en América Latina.* Buenos Aires: Editorial Paidós, 1971.

Frondizi, Risieri, and Jorge J. E. Gracia, eds. *El hombre y las valores en la filosofía latinoamericana, del siglo XX.* Mexico City: Fondo de Cultura Económica, 1975, 1980.

Gaos, José. *Antología del pensamiento de lengua española en la edad contemporánea.* Mexico City: Séneca, 1945.

———. *En torno a la filosofía mexicana.* Introduction by Leopoldo Zea. Mexico City: Alianza, 1980.

———. *Pensamiento de lengua española.* Mexico City: Stylo, 1945.

———. *El pensamiento hispanoamericano.* Mexico City: El Colegio de México, 1944.

García Astrada, Arturo. *América y las ideologías.* Buenos Aires: Universidad Nacional, 1971.

García Máynez, Eduardo. *The Philosophical-Juridical Problem of the Validity of Law in Latin American Legal Philosophy.* Cambridge, Mass.: Harvard University Press, 1948.

Gómez Martínez, J. L. *Leopoldo Zea*. Madrid: Ediciones del Orto, 1997.
———. "Pensamiento hispanoamericano: una aproximación bibliográfica." *Cuadernos Salmantinos de Filosofía* 8 (1981): 287–400.
González García, José M. "Pensar en español: tratado o ensayo." *Revista de Occidente*, special issue on *Pensar en Español*, 233 (2000): 21–36.
Gracia, Jorge J. E. "Antropología positivista en América Latina." *Cuadernos Americanos* 33 (1974): 93–106.
———. "Ethnic Labels and Philosophy: The Case of Latin-American Philosophy." *Philosophy Today* 43 (1999): 42–49.
———. *Filosofía hispánica: concepto, origen y foco historiográfico*. Pamplona: Universidad de Navarra, 1998.
———. "Globalization, Philosophy, and Latin America." In *Latin American Perspectives on Globalization*, edited by Mario Sáenz, 123–31. Lanham: Rowman and Littlefield, 2002.
———. "Hispanic/Latino Culture in the U.S.: Foreigners in Our Own Land." In *Kulturen zwischen Tradition und Innovation*, edited by Raúl Fornet-Betancourt, 94–112. Frankfurt: IKO, 2001.
———. *Hispanic/Latino Identity: A Philosophical Perspective*. Oxford: Blackwell, 2000.
———. "Hispanics, Philosophy, and the Curriculum." *Teaching Philosophy* 23 (1999): 241–48.
———. "Historia de la filosofía y filosofía latinoamericana." *Devenires* / (2000): 3–28.
———. "The Impact of Philosophical Analysis in Latin America." *Philosophical Forum* 20 (1989): 129–40.
———. "Importance of the History of Ideas in Latin America." *Journal of the History of Ideas* 36 (1975): 177–84.
———. "Latin American Philosophy Today." *Philosophical Forum* 20 (1989): 4–32.
———. "Panorama actual de la filosofía en América Latina." In *Actas: la filosofía hoy en Alemania en América Latina*. Cordoba: Instituto Goethe, 1985.
———. "Philosophical Analysis in Latin America." *History of Philosophy Quarterly* 1 (1984): 111–22.
———, ed. *Risieri Frondizi. Ensayos filosóficos*. Mexico City: Fondo de Cultura Económica, 1986.
———, and Mireya Camurati, eds. *Philosophy and Literature in Latin America: A Critical Assessment of the Current Situation*. Albany: State University of New York Press, 1989.
———, and Iván Jaksić, eds. *Filosofía e identidad cultural en América Latina*. Caracas: Monte Avila Editores, 1983.
———. "The Problem of Philosophical Identity in Latin America." *Review of Inter-American Bibliography* 34 (1984): 53–71.
———, Eduardo Rabossi, Enrique Villanueva, and Marcelo Dascal, eds. *El análisis filosófico en America Latina*. Mexico City: Fondo de Cultura. Económica, 1985.
———. *Philosophical Analysis in Latin America*. Dordrecht: Reidel, 1984.
Guadarrama, Pablo. *Valoraciones sobre el pensamiento filosófico cubano y latinoamericano*. Havana: Editora Política, 1985.

————, and Edel Tussel Oropeza. *El pensamiento filosófico de Enrique José Varona*. Havana: Editorial Ciencias Sociales, 1986.

Haddox, John H. *Antonio Caso: Philosopher of Mexico*. Austin: University of Texas Press, 1971.

————. *Vasconcelos of Mexico: Philosopher and Prophet*. Austin: University of Texas Press, 1967.

Hale, Charles A. *The Transformation of Liberalism in Late Nineteenth-Century Mexico*. Princeton, NJ: Princeton University Press, 1989.

Halperin Donghi, Tulio, et al., eds. *Sarmiento: Author of a Nation*. Berkeley: University of California Press, 1994.

Handbook of Latin American Studies. Washington, DC: Hispanic Foundation, 1936–; since 1939 a separate section on Latin American philosophy has been added. Prepared by R. Frondizi, A. Sánchez Reulet, and more recently by Carlos Torchia Estrada.

Hanke, Lewis. *Aristotle and the American Indians: A Study in Race Prejudice in the Modern World*. Chicago: Henry Regnery Company, 1959.

————. *Contemporary Latin America. A Short History*. Princeton, NJ: D. Van Nostrand, 1968.

————. "More Heat and Some Light on the Spanish Struggle for Justice in the Conquest for America." *Hispanic American Historical Review* 44, no. 3 (1964).

Hershey, John. "Recent Latin-American Philosophy." *Philosophy and Phenomenological Research* 13 (1952–53): 128–31.

Hierro, Graciela. *Ética y feminismo*. Mexico City: UNAM, 1985.

Höllhuber, Ivo. *Geschichte der Philosophie im spanischen Kulturbereich*. Munich: E. Reinhardt Verlag, 1967.

Hoyos Vásquez, Guillermo. "Compromiso vs. dependencia: desafíos de la filosofía latinoamericana." *Revista de Occidente*, special issue on *Pensar en Español*, 233 (2000): 21–36.

Index to Latin American Periodical Literature (1929–60). 8 vols. Washington, DC: Unión Panamericana, 1962.

Indice general de publicaciones periódicas latinoamericanas; humanidades y ciencias sociales. Metuchen, NJ: Scarecrow, 1961–.

Insúa Rodríguez, Ramón. *Historia de la filosofía en Hispanoamérica*. Guayaquil: Universidad de Guayaquil, 1945; 2d ed., 1949.

Inter-American Intellectual Interchange. Austin: University of Texas, 1943.

Jacobini, H. B. *A Study of the Philosophy of International Law as Seen in Works of Latin American Writers*. The Hague: Martinus Nijhoff, 1954.

Jaime, Héctor. "Facundo: el intelectual y la idea de nación en Latinoamérica." *Apuntes Filosóficos* 6 (1994): 27–38.

Jaksić, Iván. *Academic Rebels in Chile: The Role of Philosophy in Higher Education and Politics*. Albany: State University of New York Press, 1988.

————. *Andrés Bello: Scholarship and Nation-Building in Nineteenth-Century Latin America*. Cambridge: Cambridge University Press, 2001.

————. "The Sources of Latin American Philosophy." *Philosophical Forum* 20 (1989): 141–57.

————, ed. *Selected Writings of Andrés Bello*. Oxford: Oxford University Press, 1997.

Jornadas Universitarias de Humanidades. Vol. 2. Mendoza: Universidad Nacional de Cuyo, 1964.

Jorrin, Miguel, and John D. Martz. *Latin American Political Thought and Ideology.* Chapel Hill: University of North Carolina Press, 1970.

Katra, William H., ed. *Domingo F. Sarmiento: Public Writer (Between 1839–1852).* Tempe: University of Arizona Press, 1981.

Kempff Mercado, Manfredo. *Historia de la filosofía en Latinoamérica.* Santiago: Zig Zag, 1958.

Kilgore, William J. "The Development of Positivism in Latin America." *Revista Interamericana de Bibliografía* 19 (1969): 133–45.

Kunz, Josef L. *Latin American Philosophy of Law in the Twentieth Century.* New York: Inter-American Law Institute, 1950.

Larroyo, Francisco. *La filosofía americana: su razón y su sinrazón de ser.* Mexico City: Universidad Nacional Autónoma de México, 1958.

———. *Tipos históricos de filosofar en América.* Mexico City: Universidad Nacional Autónoma de México, 1959.

———, and Edmundo Escobar. *Historia de las doctrinas filosóficas en Latinoamérica.* Mexico City: Porrúa, 1968.

Lasalle, Edmundo. *Philosophic Thought in Latin America: A Partial Bibliography.* Washington, DC: Pan American Union, 1941.

Latin American Legal Philosophy. Cambridge, MA: Harvard University, 1948; contains translations of the following: L. Recaséns Siches, *Vida humana, sociedad y derecho,* 7–341; Carlos Cossio, *Fenomenología de la decisión,* 345–400; J. Llambías de Azevedo, *Eidética y aporética del derecho,* 403–58; E. García Máynez, *El problema filosóficojurídico de la validez del derecho,* 461–512; E. García Máynez, *La libertad como derecho y como poder,* 515–47.

Liebman, Seymour B. *Exploring the Latin American Mind.* Chicago: Nelson-Hall, 1976.

Lipp, Solomon. *Leopoldo Zea. From 'Mexicanidad' to a Philosophy of History.* Waterloo: Wilfrid Laurier University Press, 1980.

———. *Three Argentine Thinkers.* New York: Philosophical Library, 1969.

———. *Three Chilean Thinkers.* Waterloo: Wilfrid Laurier University Press, 1975.

Liss, Sheldon B., and Peggy K. Liss, eds. *Man, State and Society in Latin American History.* New York: Praeger Publishers, 1972.

Mariátegui, José Carlos. *The Heroic and Creative Meaning of Socialism: Selected Essays.* Translated by Michael Pearlman. Amherst, NY: Humanity Books, 1996.

———. *Seven Interpretative Essays on Peruvian Reality.* Translated by Marjory Urquidi. Introduction by Jorge Basadre. Austin: University of Texas Press, 1971.

Martí, José. *Our America: Writings on Latin America and the Struggle for Cuban Independence.* Edited by Philip S. Foner. Translated by Elinor Randall et al. New York: Monthly Review Press, 1977.

Martí, Oscar. "Is There a Latin American Philosophy?" *Metaphilosophy* 14 (1983): 46–52.

Mate, Reyes. "La lengua del esclavo." In *Revista de Occidente,* special issue on *Pensar en Español,* 233 (2000): 83–104.

Mateos García, Angeles. "La filosofía jurídica de Miguel Reale: una visión integral del derecho." *Paideia* 21 (2000): 185–201.

Mayz Vallenilla, Ernesto. *Latinoamérica en la encrucijada de la técnica.* Caracas: Universidad Simón Bolívar, 1976.

———. *El problema de América.* Caracas: Universidad Central, 1959; 2d ed., 1969.

Medina, Vicente. "The Possibility of an Indigenous Philosophy: A Latin American Perspective." *American Philosophical Quarterly* 29 (1992): 373–80.

Mendieta, Eduardo. "Is There Latin American Philosophy?" *Philosophy Today* 43 (1999): 50–61.

———, ed. *Latin American Philosophy: Currents, Issues, Debates.* Bloomington: Indiana University Press, 2003.

Merrim, Stephanie, ed. *Feminist Perspectives on Sor Juana Inés de la Cruz.* Detroit: Wayne State University Press, 1991.

Miliani, Domingo. "Utopian Socialism, Transitional Thread from Romanticism to Positivism in Latin America." *Journal of the History of Ideas* 24 (1963): 523–38.

Miró Quesada, Francisco. *Despertar y proyecto del filosofar latinoamericano.* Mexico City: Fondo de Cultura Económica, 1974.

———. "The Impact of Metaphysics on Latin American Ideology." *Journal of the History of Ideas* 29 (1963): 539–52.

———. "Lógica, significado y ontología: comentarios críticos." *Análisis Filosófico* 13 (1993):1–20.

———. "Objetivismo y subjetivismo en la filosofía de los valores." *Diánoia* 40 (1994): 85–108.

———. *El problema de la filosofía latinoamericana.* Mexico City: Fondo de Cultura Económica, 1976.

———, and Marcelo Dascal, eds. *Historicism and Universalism in Philosophy, in Cultural Relativism, and Philosophy.* Leiden: Brill, 1991.

Muguerza, Javier. "La razón y sus patrias." *Revista de Occidente,* special issue on *Pensar en Español,* 233 (2000): 7–20.

Nicol, Eduardo. *El problema de la filosofía hispánica.* Madrid: Editorial Tecnos, 1961.

Nuccetelli, Susana. *Latin American Thought: Philosophical Problems and Arguments.* Boulder, CO: Westview Press, 2002.

———, and Gary Seay, eds. *Latin American Philosophy: An Introduction with Readings.* Upper Saddle River, NJ: Prentice Hall, 2004.

Patino, Joel Rodríguez. "José Vasconcelos y el sentido de la historia." *Revista de Filosofía* 16 (1988): 99–117.

———. "El sentido del universo en José Vasconcelos." *Revista de Filosofía* 1991: 9–16.

Paz, Octavio. *The Labyrinth of Solitude.* Translated by Lysander Kemp. Grove Press, 1985.

———. *Sor Juana; or, the Traps of Faith.* Translated by Margaret Sayers Peden. Cambridge, MA: Harvard University Press, Belknap Press, 1985.

Pereda, Carlos. "Luces y sombras de la escritura filosófica en español." *Revista de Occidente,* special issue on *Pensar en Español,* 233 (2000): 54–70.

Pérez Marchand, Monelisa. "A Critical Study of Some Currents of Contemporary

Philosophical Thought in Latin America." Master's thesis, Johns Hopkins University, 1940.

Primer symposium iberoamericano de filosofía. Edited by Ernesto Cinchilla Aguilar, Vincente Díaz Samayoa, and Virgilio Rodríguez Beteta. Guatemala: Editorial del Ministerio de Educación Pública, 1961.

Ramos, Samuel. *Profile of Man and Culture in Mexico.* Translated by Peter G. Earle. Austin: University of Texas Press, 1962.

Reale, Miguel. "Axiological Invariants." *Journal of Value Inquiry* 29 (1995): 65–75.

———. "Situación actual de la teoría tridimensional del derecho." *Anales de la Cátedra Francisco Suárez* 25 (1985): 203–24.

Recaséns Siches, Luis. "Juridical Axiology in Ibero-America." *Natural Law Forum* 3, no. 1 (1958): 35–169.

———. *Latin American Legal Philosophy.* Translated by Gordon Ireland et al. Cambridge, MA: Harvard University Press, 1948.

Redmond, Walter B. *Bibliography of the Philosophy in the Iberian Colonies of America.* The Hague: Nijhoff, 1972.

Revista Portuguesa de Filosofía 17 (1961); issue dedicated to Latin American philosophy.

Ripoll, Carlos. *Conciencia intelectual de América: antología del ensayo hispanoamericano.* New York: Eliseo Torres, 1974.

Rippy, Merrill. "Theory of History: Twelve Mexicans." *Americas* 17 (1960–61): 223–39.

Robles, Laureano. *Filosofía iberoamericana en la época del Encuentro.* Madrid: Editorial Trotta, 1992.

Rodó, José Enrique. *Ariel.* Translated by Margaret Sayers Peden. Foreword by James W. Symington. Prologue by Carlos Fuentes. Austin: University of Texas Press, 1988.

Roig, Arturo Andrés. "Bolívar y la filosofía de la historia." *Verbo* (Madrid) 25, nos. 255–56 (1987): 525–60.

———. "¿Cómo orientarnos en nuestro pensamiento? La filosofía latinoamericana y su problema de hoy." *Revista Historia de las Ideas* 10 (1989): 189–206.

———. "La conducta humana y la naturaleza." *Cuadernos de Ética* 19–20 (1995): 117–31.

———. "Etica y liberación: José Martí y el 'hombre natural.'" *Homenaje a José Martí a los 100 años de Nuestra América y Versos Sencillos.* La Plata: Primer Coloquio de Estudios Latinoamericans: Facultad de Humanidades y Ciencias de la Educación de la Universidad de La Plata, 1994: 31–38.

———. *Filosofía, universidad y filósofos de América Latina.* Mexico City: Universidad Nacional Autónoma de México, 1981.

———. "Los ideales bolivarianos y la propuesta de una universidad latinoamericana continental." In *Fuentes de la cultura latinoamerica,* edited by Leopoldo Zea, 67–80. Mexico City: Fondo de Cultura Económica, 1993.

———. "Nuestra América frente al panamericanismo y el hispanismo: la lectura de Leopoldo Zea." In *América Latina. Historia y destino. Homenaje a Leopodo Zea,* edited by Horacio Cerutti-Guldberg, 279–84. Mexico City: UNAM, 1992.

———. *Sobre el tratamiento de filosofar e ideologías dentro de una historia del pensamiento latinoamericano.* Santa Fe: Centro de Divulgación "Colegio Mayor Santa Fe," 1973.

———. *Teoría y crítica del pensamiento latinoamericano.* Mexico City: Fondo de Cultura Económica, 1981.

Romero, Francisco. *Sobre la filosofía en América.* Buenos Aires: Raigal, 1952.

———. "Tendencias contemporáneas en el pensamiento hispanoamericano." *Philosophy and Phenomenological Research* 4 (1943): 127–34.

Romero Baro, José María. "The Epistemology of the Uruguayan Philosopher Carlos Vaz Ferreira." *Dialogue and Humanism* 2 (1992): 79–86.

Rowland, Christopher, ed. *The Cambridge Companion to Liberation Theology.* Cambridge: Cambridge University Press, 1999.

Sabat-Rivers, Georgina. "Biografías: Sor Juana vista por Dorothy Schons y Octavio Paz." *Revista Iberoamericana* 51 (1995): 927–37.

Sáenz, Mario. *The Identity of Liberation in Latin American Thought.* New York: Lexington Books, 1999.

———, ed. *Latin American Perspectives on Globalization: Ethics, Politics, and Alternative Visions.* Lanham, MD: Rowman and Littlefield, 2002.

Salazar Bondy, Augusto. *¿Existe una filosofía de nuestra América?* Mexico City: Siglo XX, 1968.

Sambarino, Mario. *Identidad, tradición, autenticidad: tres problemas de América Latina.* Caracas: Centro de Estudios Latinoamericanos Rómulo Gallegos, 1980.

Sánchez Reulet, Aníbal, ed. *Contemporary Latin American Philosophy: A Selection.* Albuquerque: University of New Mexico Press, 1954. Translated by W. R. Trask from *La filosofía latinoamericana contemporánea.* Washington, DC: Pan American Union, 1949.

Santos Escudero, Ceferino. "Bibliografía hispánica de filosofía." *Pensamiento* 58 (2002): 273–346.

Sarti, Sergio. *Panorama della filosofía ispanoamericana contemporanea.* Milan: Cisalpino-Golliardica, 1976.

Sasso, Javier. *La filosofía latinoamericana y las construcciones de su historia.* Caracas: Monte Ávila, 1998.

Schutte, Ofelia. "Continental Philosophy and Postcolonial Subjects." *Philosophy Today* 44 (2000): 8–17.

———. *Cultural Identity and Social Liberation in Latin American Thought.* Albany: State University of New York Press, 1993.

———. "The Master-Slave Dialectic in Latin America: The Social Criticism of Zea, Freire, and Roig." *Owl of Minerva* (1990): 5–18.

———. "Nietzsche, Mariátegui, and Socialism: A Case of 'Nietzschean Marxism' in Peru?" *Social Theory and Practice* 14 (1988): 71–85.

———. "Origins and Tendencies of the Philosophy of Liberation in Latin American Thought: A Critique of Dussel's Ethics." *Philosophical Forum* 22 (1991): 270–95.

———. "Philosophy and Feminism in Latin America: Perspectives on Gender Identity and Culture." *Philosophical Forum* 20 (1989): 62–84.

———. "Toward an Understanding of Latin American Philosophy: Reflections on the Formation of a Cultural Identity." *Philosophy Today* 31 (1987): 21–34.

Schwartzmann, Félix. *El sentimiento de lo humano en América.* 2 vols. Santiago de Chile: Editorial Universitaria, 1950.

Second Inter-American Congress of Philosophy (December 1947, Columbia University), in *Philosophy and Phenomenological Research* 9 (1949): 345–626. Most papers are in English. There are essays by Vasconcelos, Fatone, Romero, Zea, Frondizi, and others.

Serrano Caldera, Alejandro. *Filosofía y crisis: en torno a la posibilidad de la filosofía latinoamericana.* Mexico City: UNAM, 1987.

Seventh Inter-American Congress of Philosophy. Quebec: Université Laval, 1967.

Soehlke Heer, Peter. *El nuevo mundo en la visión de Montaigne o los albores del anticolonialismo.* Caracas: Instituto de Altos Estudios de América Latina, 1993.

Soler, Ricaurte. *Estudios sobre la historia de las ideas en América.* Panamá: Imprenta Nacional, 1961.

Stabb, Martin S. *In Quest of Identity: Patterns in the Spanish-American Essay of Ideas, 1860–1960.* Chapel Hill: University of North Carolina Press, 1967.

Symposium Iberamericano de Filosofía. Vol. 1. Guatemala: Ministerio de Educación Pública, 1961.

Thiebaut, Carlos. "Una mirada cosmopolita a la filosofía hispanoamericana." In *Revista de Occidente,* special issue on *Pensar en Español,* 233 (2000): 37–53.

Valle, Rafael Heliodoro. *Historia de las ideas contemporáneas en Centroamérica.* Mexico City: Fondo de Cultura Económica, 1960.

Vargas, Manuel. "Lessons from the Philosophy of Race in Mexico." *Philosophy Today* 44 (2000): 18–29.

Villegas, Abelardo. *Antología del pensamiento social y político de América Latina.* Washington, DC: Unión Panamericana, 1964.

———. *Panorama de la filosofía iberoamericana actual.* Buenos Aires: EUDEBA, 1963.

Villoro, Luis. "¿Pensar en español?" In *Revista de Occidente,* special issue on *Pensar en Español,* 233 (2000): 105–12.

Wagley, Charles. *The Latin American Tradition: Essays on the Unity and Diversity of Latin American Culture.* New York: Columbia University Press, 1968.

Wagner de Reyna, Alberto. *La filosofía en Iberoamérica.* Lima: Sta. María, 1949.

Williams, Edward J. *Latin American Political Thought: A Developmental Perspective.* Tucson: University of Arizona Press, 1974.

Zea, Leopoldo. *América como conciencia.* Mexico City: Cuademos Americanos, 1953.

———. *América en la historia.* Madrid: Revista de Occidente, 1957, 1970.

———. *Antología de la filosofía americana contemporánea.* Mexico City: Costa Amic, 1968.

———. "Contemporary Latin American Philosophy." In *Philosophy in the Mid-Century,* edited by R. Klibansky, 4:218–23. Firenze: La Nuova Italia, 1959.

———. *Descubrimiento e identidad latinoamericana.* Mexico City: UNAM, 1990.

———. *Discurso desde la marginación y la barbarie.* Barcelona: Anthropos, 1988.

———. *Esquema para una historia de las ideas en Iberoamérica.* Mexico City: Universidad Nacional Autónoma de México, 1956.

———. *La filosofía americana como filosofía sin más.* Mexico City: Siglo XXI, 1969.

———. *Filosofía y cultura latinoamericanas.* Caracas: Centro de Estudios Latinoamericanos Rómulo Gallegos, 1976.

———. "History of Ideas in Latin America: Recent Works." *Journal of the History of Ideas* 20 (1959): 596–600.

———. "Identity: A Latin American Philosophical Problem." *Philosophical Forum* 20 (1989): 33–42.

———. "The Interpretation of the Ibero-American and North American Cultures." *Philosophy and Phenomenological Research* 9 (1948–49): 538–44.

———. *Latin America and the World*. Norman: University of Oklahoma Press, 1969.

———. *The Latin American Mind*. Norman: University of Oklahoma, 1963. Translated by J. H. Abbot and L. Dunham from *Dos etapas del pensamiento en Hispanoamérica: del romanticismo al positivismo*. Mexico City: Colegio de México, 1949.

———. *Latinoamérica: Tercer Mundo*. Mexico City: Extermporáneos, 1977.

———. *El pensamiento latinoamericano*. Barcelona: Ariel, 1976.

———. *Positivism in Mexico*. Austin: University of Texas Press, 1974.

———. *El positivismo en México: nacimiento, apogeo y decadencia*. Mexico City: Fondo de Cultura Económica, 1968.

———. *The Role of the Americas in History*. Savage, MD: Rowman & Littlefield, 1992.

Zirion, Antonio. "Phenomenology in Mexico: A Historical Profile." *Continental Philosophy Review* 33 (2000): 75–92.